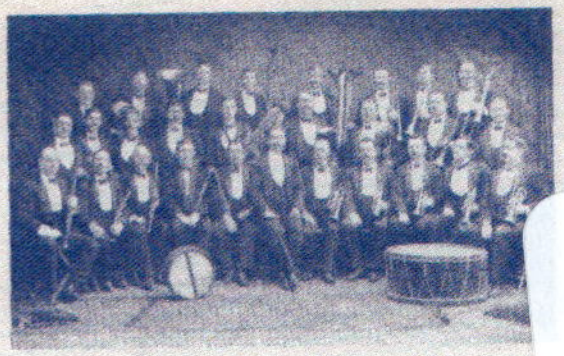

music and sound for anything

# *like the eye,*

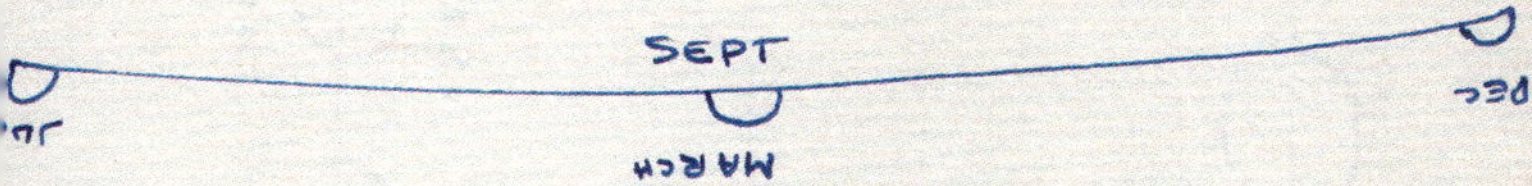


# the ear

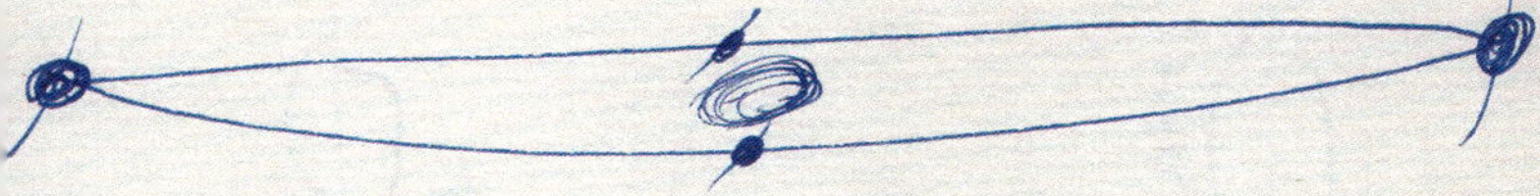

# doesn’t blink

The Archive of
Charlie Morrow

The Egyptian Book of the Dead: The Papyrus of Ani Egyptian Text Transliteration and Translation 1860 by E.A. Wallis Budge 3381

The Philosophy of Insanity, by a late inmate of the Glasgow Royal Asylum for Lunatics at Gartnavel. 1860 Spittal & Alison, Scotland publication. Book from collection of Drs. Laura and Lloyd Morrow, psychiatrists 4935

Historic Traces on Upper Manhattan 1895 Large map of Manhattan with early settlements and Historic Places by Morris William Ehrlich, father of Laura Ehrlich Morrow MD, CM's mother 2556

The Hours of Catherine of Cleves 1895 Four copies of 1955 publication, John Plummer, George Braziller NY 1955 2650

A Portrait of the Artist as a Young Man, James Joyce 1910 Compass Books 4917

Radio News Cover 1916 Cover of Radio News from April 1927. 3238

"The Interpretation of the Fire-Festivals" and "The Fire Festivals of Europe" 1916 the Golden Bough: A Study in Magic and Religion - Ch 63, 64 by James George Frazer published 2013. 3463

Historic Traces on Upper Manhattan by Morris William Ehrlich (2) 1927 Historical map of upper Manhattan with Indian place names. Town of Nieuw (Harlem) including modern Harlem and Washington Heights. 1910. 2831

Indian Legends of American Scenes by Marion E. Gridley 1927 M.A. Donohue & Company 5044

A Portrait of the Artist as a Young Man, James Joyce 1933 Compass Books 4917

Radio News Cover 1935 Cover of Radio News from April 1927 3238

114 Songs by Charles E. Ives 1935 Published book. 4111

From the Steeples to the Mountains 1939 Charles Ives Composition Music book For Bells or two pianos, trumpet and trombone. Published by Peer Int. 2633

Luomala, Katharine. Oceanic, American Indian, and African myths of snaring the sun. Vol. 168. Bernice P. Bishop Museum, 1940, pages 6-45 1939. 3461

Drinking Meditation 1942 On drinking a liquid for the first time in your life, observe the liquid enter your lips, inhabit your mouth, flow through the throat and beyond as the digestive tract and body chemistry are activated. Observe as it is processed and eventually leaves the body as sweat and urine. 1387

Vermont Harmony Shape notes 1940 Song book of Vermont Harmony and other sheets 1952

Crying Meditation 1942 While crying with eyes shut, notice the flashes of color through the eyelids. Follow willessly the spontaneous recollection of color seen before, perhaps while a fetus. This was the first clue to my journey to recall life before birth, my fetus life in my mother. 1388

The Shell: Five Hundred Million Years of Inspired Design 1942 By Hugh and Marguerite Stix Photographs by H. Landshoff Signed to CM, 1969. 3333

Sari Dienes Poems 1942 Original List, Sorted by Date by Jay Walbert for published book 5293

Sezuan, Bertolt Brecht play presented first in Zurich in 1943 1946 Sezuan is an International collaboration of Four Norwegian theater groups. This is an art piece B&W program guide 5655

The Shell: Five Hundred Million Years of Inspired Design 1947 (as above) 1969. 3333

Vesalius: The illustrations from his works, J.B. Saunders & Charles D.O. Malley 1947 world 5009

The Art of the Far East: Landscapes, Flowers, Animals 1950 16 Plates in Color from the Work of Old Chinese and Japanese Masters Iris Books, Oxford University Press, NY/Toronto, 1947. 3330

Chinese Ivory Sculpture 1950 by Warren E. Cox 3331

Style and Idea, Arnold Schoenberg 1950 Philosophical Library NY 5078

2 Treble Voice Ballads 1952 sealed envelope containing score 1691

The Human use of Human Beings. Cybernetics and Society, Norbert Wiener 1953 Doubleday Anchor Books 4936

The Face of the Arctic. Richard Harrington 1954 Schuman 5005

Music of the Pacific N.W. Coast 1955. 755

Jungle Soliloquy for Flute & Conga Drum 1955 Score in sealed envelope 1692

The Art of Fugue by Johann Sebastian Bach 1955 (1956). 3245

The Hours of Catherine of Cleves, Plummer 1955 intro and comments by John Plummer published by George Braziller, NY, Printed in Netherlands 1955. This copy bought by Laura Morrow MD and kept in the family home, 197 Passaic Avenue, Passaic, NJ, complete original - cut into two parts then rejoined as one volume - is in the Morgan Library 4078

CM Boy Scout Photo 1955 In Master Graphics 4284

Interruption Music (unknown to the conductor) 1956 Unknown to the conductor, the orchestra has met and planned this surprise, to be preformed while playing any work of music. At a pre-arranged minute, the musicians stop to belch, cough, and scratch. This concept can be used in other media as well as musical performance - for example, as an action by a football team in normal competetive play, or by the traders on a stock market floor. 2033

K2LIS Radio Call Card 1956 CMs' Amateur Radio card. from 197 Passaic Ave. Passaic N.J. 3765

Rhapsody on a Starry Night 2-1957 score w/notes in sealed envelope 1693

Prelude and Fugue for Piano 1957 Original score 1694

Incidental Music for 4 reeds, 2 cellos & Bass 1957 Original score in sealed envelope 1695

Biphonicos for Piano 1957 Original score in sealed envelope 1696

Wandering for Piano 1957 Original score in sealed envelope 1697

Symphonic Band 1957 Original score w/parts in envelope 1698

Sketch for Band 1957 Original score and parts for full concert band 1699

Concerto for Trumpet & Orchestra 1957 Original score 1701

Trio for Clarinet, Trumpet, & Horn 1957 Original score and notes 1713

Very Slow Gabrieli for Double Brass & Ghosts 1957 A slow motion performance of the Gabrieli 1597 composition "Sonata Plan e Forte" Sacrae Symphoniae #1, stretching it to more than five times its normal length. Performers' physical gestures are slowed as well. The 1957 composition is expanded through the addition of a Ghost (pulsed drone) Ensemble, and by pauses added to the music by CM to allow the Ghost Ensemble to be heard by the audience and performers in the performance space. The ghosts are a processional brass ensemble in four voices which slowly walks around outside of the performance space in hallways, stairwells and even out of doors. The doors, and if effective the windows, of the performance space are opened for this performance and not before so as to preserve the surprise acoustic effect. The pulsed drone is performed by the processional Ghost brass as long tones envelopes pulsed by breath accents in a steady beat. 1714

Psychic Music for Concert Band (no audible music) 1957 The musicians perform any work of music without making a sound; miming the performance. They create the music internally - mentally, emotionally - and psychically project it. A large conducted ensemble can soundlessly pretend to play their instruments, or alternatively, perform without any physical movement at all. While Psychic Music is devised for concert band, it applies to any performance: orchestra, opera, theatrical plays, tv news, etc. 2044

Air Music for Concert Band 1957 The musicians perform any work of music, playing their instruments with only breath and instrument mechanism sounds. For example, this gives a whisper and click version of a Sousa march. We hear the music minus its conventional surface. Non-wind players, such as violinists, simulate a wind sound with Air Music Mozart Symphony sounds like a soft rhythmic wind. Air Music of Wagner's Ring would be quite a blow. Air Music is devised for wind ensembles but applies to any ensemble. Since the normal sound surface of the source work is removed, normal instrumentation of source work can be reduced or expanded. While the initial motivation for Air Music was to create a sound transformation, Air Music also opens up possibilities for wide variety of performance attitude and interpretation from deadpan classical concert demeanor to - ahem - humor? 2055

Mushroom Ceremony of the Mazatec Indians of Mexico 1957 Notes from the Album on Folkways No.FR8975R. Gordon Wasson at Huautia de Jimenez 2608

Selected Poems of Ezra Pound 1957 signed to CM, A New Directions paperbook 4950

Civilization and its Discontents, Sigmund Freud 1957 The Hogarth Press and the Institute of Psycho-analysis 5003

The Bells, Manuscript and performance notes. 1957 setting of Edgar Allen Poe Poem 5230

CM Concepts List 1957 thru 1987 Concepts 5296

Schoenberg/Kandinsky Paper 1957 Rough Draft of CM paper on sound 5543

Concerto for Trumpet & Orchestra 1958 Original score 1701

Pedal-Tone study for Piano 1958 Original score in sealed envelope 1702

Brass Music Fanfares I, II, III 0 1958 Music for solo Bb Trumpet. Original score in sealed envelope. 1703

Piano Suite #1 1958 Original score in sealed envelope 1704

Duo for two Clarinets 1958 Original score 1705

Piece for Chamber Orchestra Percussion & Celeste 1958. 1706

Concerto for Piano & Large Orchestra 1958 Original score 1707

Tales of Angels, Spirits and Demons/Martin Buber 1958 Large Box #1 and #2, Hawkswell Press. Jerome Rothenberg and David Antin, translators 1919

Certificates and Commencement Announcements from Early Career 1958 Certificates of achievement, and other honors from CM's early career (1950s) 3135

Showbills/Programs from Early Career 1958 Showbills from Early Career: Summer camps and High School c. 1958. 3136

Compositions and Misc. Memorboralia from Early Career 1958 c. 1957. 3137

Workbook of Early Career 1958 Compositions in notebook from early career c. 1950s. 3159

Anatomy for the Artist 1958 by Jeno Barcsay Spring Books 3332

Very Slow Gabrieli for Double Brass & Ghosts 1958 One copy of Score And Two Copies of Gabrieli Sonata Pian'E Forte with added Drone & Interruptions to hear it. 3668

The Way of Zen, Alan Watts 1958 classic book on Zen 4059

The Goodly Heritage, Avraham Yaari 1958 Life of the Jewish Community from 17th to 20th Century 4244

Selections from Journals 4/56 thru 7/58 1958. 4312

Poeme- Partition A, Bernard Heidsieck 1958 Electre 1992 Signed to

CM 4731

The Spirit of Zen, Alan Watts 1958 Grove Press NY 4920

Concerto for Piano & Large Orchestra 1959 Original score 1707

Short Suite for small Orchestra 1959 original score in sealed envelope 1708

Eli Eli -Brasses, Percussion & Solo Trumpet 1959 Original score in sealed envelope 1709

Sonata for Clarinet & Piano 1959 Original score in sealed envelope 1710

Orchestra of Columbia University 1959 CM's graphite draft drawing on white paper. Partially destroyed in spring flood of 2000, Barton, VT 2045

Charles Ives 85th Birthday Festival Concert program 1959 Presented by Norwalk Symphony Society sent to CM by Joe Boldt with a letter that he had put the program together. 2745

Beat Zen, Square Zen, and Zen, Alan W. Watts 1959 City Lights Books 4240

History of Music, Marc Pincherle 1959 Illustrated History of Music 4860

Charles Ives 85th Birthday Festival Concert Program 1959 At Norwalk Connecticut Symphony signed ? 5250

ELLA - sound poetry 1960 CM's layered solo recording. Multitrack recording made at the CM residence,197 Passaic Avenue, Passaic NJ on a Tandberg 1/4 track recorder. Later transferred to half track 1/4 inch tape at CM's first studio, 365 West End Avenue, NY 1153

Sonata for Clarinet & Piano 1960 Original score in sealed envelope 1710

Second Piano Suite 1960 Original score in sealed envelope 1712

Twas Brillig 1960 Original score and notes. Manuscript 1715

Sonnet for Susan after a poem by John Keats 1960 Original score and notes 1716

The First Born Presents Festival Series 1960 Cafe Espresso Corner of 111 St. and Amsterdam Ave. March 7. 2537

American Symphonic Composers of a Hundred Years Ago 1960 Early Hand drawn Poster for Columbia University presentation artwork rough by CM 3772

Asymmetries 1-260, Jackson Mac Low 1960. 4035

Circles, Luciano Berio 1960 For female voice, Harp, two Percussion players. From EE Cummings poems1933-1954. 4237

White Sun Black Sun, Jerome Rothenberg 1960 Hawk Well Press 50 Broadway NY 4777

Twas Brillig 1960 Barnard Junior Class presents an original musical March 9 Minor Latham Theatre Music Chairman CM '61. 5438

REALLY 1961 This is a rubber stamp. It was created by CM when he was employed as a copy editor at the American Institute of Physics, NY, preparing scientific papers for publication in scientific journals. 1358

Mobile for Shakespeare Roman Haubenstock-Ramati 1961 musical score for sonnets 53 and 54 for voice and six players. 1511

Sonnet for Susan after a poem by John Keats 1961 Original score and notes 1716

Piece for Brass 1961 Tim Leigh piece. Handwritten pencil manuscript. 1963

Carlo Pittore File 1961 Several pieces of his work of multiples and cut outs,very creative stuff from Maine. Also an article in the Maine times about him and Bern Porter also from Maine. Also in this file an unopened cassette tape of poetry by Carlo, sent to CM. 3628

D 2 +D 3 Z Poemes Partitions, Bernard Heidsieck 1961 Lowe and Brydone. London Bernard Heidsieck 4730

Old Newland, Theodor Herzl 1961 Haifa Publishing Co. 5004

An English Song Book edited by Noah Greenberg 1961 Doubleday & company 5023

Franny and Zooey, J.D. Salinger 1961 Bantam Books 5085

Author: Please Destroy 1962 This is a rubber stamp. It was created when CM was employed as a copy editor at the American Institute of Physics, NY, preparing scientific papers for publication in scientific journals. 1369

Toccata 1962 During a performance, the musicians, actors, dancers, poets etc performing enter the audience and touch the audience a piacere. 1380

Dance Music for the Blind 1962 Dancers have sound makers, such as bells, attached to their bodies. The location of these sound makers is correlated to the choreography. The dancers transmit physical gestures via sound to the audience, which includes blind persons and sighted persons blindfolded or in complete darkness. 1535

Peter Pindar Stearns Trio Variations (1965) 1962 Original music from P.P. Stearns. Commissioned by CM for New music for trumpet and ensemble. Carnegie Hall May 22, 1963. 1891

CM Photo 1962 Young CM striped shirt by ME. 2876

National Music Camp alumni directory 1962 national music camp 5031

An Early Catalog and description of Compositions 1962 Cover letter of CM career of compositions from 1962 thru 1984. 5057

CM Stage Works List 1962. 5289

Sonata da Chiesa for Flute, Harpsichord, and Bassoon 1963 A virtuoso expressionistic work in four movements. Two years in the making, this work combines expressionistic, conceptual, and dramatic concerns. 1424

The Student Composers of Mannes College 1963 CM's caligraphy on orion skin. Partially destroyed in spring flood of 2000, Barton, VT 2041

The Pocket Theatre Presents "Vexations" by Erik Satie 9-3-1963 1963 CM attended this 18 hour event in which Satie's "Vexations" was repeated seamlessly by the team of pianists including John Cage, Philip Corner, John Cale. The concert was reviewd by The NY Times, wherein the CM was described: "one desperate whit cried ENCORE." 2042

Vexations by Erik Satie 1963 The Pocket Theatre Presents.Performed Monday, September 9. 3098

A Vision of Paris 1963 A Vision of Paris The Photographs of Eugene Atget and the Words of Marcel Proust by Arthur D. Trottenberg Macmillon Publishing, Co. 1963 3324

Filmwise 3&4, Gregory Markopolis 1963 Limited Edition Signed. 4to. side-stapled. 68pp. + 2pp. illustrations. Cover by Jean Cocteau, its layout by Richard D. Tuttle. A superb double issue devoted to the experimental filmmaker Markopoulos, signed and numbered by him (no. 252 of an unspecified #) 4140

Poems from the Floating World Vol. 4, Rothenberg 1963 Hawks Well Press Poems and stories from 22 poets of the day. 4156

Paterson, William Carlos Williams 1963. 4257

Clapping Piece, Yasunao Tone 1963 A B&W graphic piece with a second sheet of instructions. A music concept piece 4587

Blowin in the Wind, Sheet music 1963 Bob Dylan 1962 copyright 4663

Hark the Pterodactyl, Artemis Smith 1963 printed by Vague Press 4747

Between 1960-1963, Jerome Rothenberg 1963 Fulcrum Press London 4781

Phonetics, Bertil Malmberg 1963 Dover Publications 4947

Posada, Jose Guadalupe 1963 instituto Nacional de Bellas Artes/ México 5140

Tone Roads concerts - New School 1964 Through Philip Corner, I was asked to play trumpet in the Tone Roads Concerts at the New School. They were organized by composers Philip Corner, Malcolm Goldstein and Jim Tenney. Many say this series was the beginning of Downtown Music. It is named for the Ives work with the same title. 1411

Sonata da Chiesa for Flute, Harpsichord, and Bassoon 1964 A virtuoso expressionistic work in four movements. Two years in the making, this work combines expressionistic, conceptual, and dramatic concerns. 1424

Second Annual NY festival of the avant Garde 1964 CM assisted Charlotte Moorman in the organizing of this event which brought him in contact with many artists important to his work and activities He lent his reel to reel tape recorder which was stolen. 1441

Especially When the October Wind 1964 Original Score based on poem by Dylan Thomas. 1630

Prologue to Canterbury Tales 1964 Original pencil ScoreSetting of the opening lines of the Canterbury Tales by Geoffrey Chausser 1631

String Quartet #1 5-20-64 1964 Original score/Skins and other copies 1717

Sonata Da Chiesa 1964 Original Score and parts 1718

Four Pieces for Orchestra 1964 Original Score and notes 1719

Seven Incomplete Songs 1964 An Envelope w/ 7 song sheets, ideas, pencil notes 3 synergist samples 1966, Prelude and Canzon for Harmonium 1966Scherzo I 1967, Song of the Mystic animals' Notes for Bulgarian type vocal, Notes for Tape Collage 1970, Notes for unfinshed Cello theater piece, Music for Band day 1854

Miniature Sonata for Trombone and Piano 1964 Original score 1908

Cantata Music for Brass 1964 Original pencil score and Notes 1912

Program: Second Annual NY Festival of the Avant Garde 1964 CM assisted Charlotte Moorman in the organizing of this event which brought him in contact with many artists important to his work and activities He lent his reel to reel tape recorder which was stolen. 2043

And Thou Shalt Love. (Deut. 6:5-10; Nos. 15:40) 1964 Original Score and notes Expressionist liturgical song presenting a reaction that God might have upon seeing the state of the world, relative to having issued the Ten Commandments. Actor Edward G. Robinson introduced CM in the premier of this Union-of-American-Hebrew-Congregations First prize selection. 2066

Deuteronomy 6:5-10 Numbers 15:40 1964 Small copy and Original Skins 2634

New Directions in Music (20) 1964 Town Hall Sept 28 New works by CM and Gary Friedman Played by York String Quartet, Contemporary Music Workshop 2947

Program from 1964 ensemble concert 1964 Program from 1964 ensemble concert CM on trumpet Featuring Allen Ginsberg as poet Second annual NY festival of the avant-garde 3097

New Directions in Music 1964 Town Hall and Norman J. Seaman present New Directions in Music Featuring New Works by CM and Gary Friedman Town Hall Monday September 28, 1964. 3101

Andy Warhol & Gerard Malanga Post Card for Show 1964 19 copier machine images w/holograph or Typed poems {Poem Visuals) Backworks Gallery 3492

Black Panther party 1964 5th Ave. Vietnam Peace Parade Committee Protest Meeting poster. Feb 18th at Hunter College Special Filmed interview with Bobby Seale from Prison. Speakers: Don Cox, Rennie Davis, Juan Gonzalez, Gerald Lefcourt, Cleveland Robinson 3624

The Story of the Jew (2) 1964 A one volume piece of Jewish History published by Behrman House Inc. NY 4170

A Test of Poetry, Louis Zukofsky 1964. 4256

The Central Eskimo, Franz Boas 1964 signed to CM, Bison Book

4916

Henry Miller on Writing, Henry Miller 1964 A New Directions paperback original 4966

Christian Wolff for 1, 2 or 3 people 1964 Edition Peters no. 6822 C F Peters Corporation 5148

Christian Wolff, Trio 1 1964 Edition Peters, C F Peters Corporation 5149

Old Catalogs, including Commercials 1964 Important Dates and lists of Compositions and Commercial works from the 60's. 5182

I Cannot Give you a Tear, Applezweig/CM The Tide Rises 1964 Music, Two songs pencil 5307 Music Alaska Indian side 1&2 1965 Copy of recordTC: 3:00:00:00 O=-18db 29.97NOF Video Ref 48 kHz 823

Flowers - A Graduation Event 1965 Accept your diploma on stage and casually knock over the a floral display onto the first row of audience. This work takes it name from its accidental premiere in my graduation from Mannes School of Music, NY. Options: It may be performed at an event with the correct ingredients, such as funeral, a flower show. 1385

Rock Music 1965 Two or more people - each with a small rock in had - tap on a large rock, signaling to each other or playing rhythms, etc. They put their ear to the big rock when not playing. OPTIONS any large thing can be tapped on this way, an auto, the walls of a corridor, a pond. 1393

Flower Music 1965 While walking in a daze to the dais to receive your diploma, knock over flowers onto the graduates and/or faculty. Deny that you even knew it had happened. 1546

Prelude 1965. 1607

Sonata for Violin Unaccompanied 1965. 1614

Horse Songs 1965 Jerome Rothenberg's total translation of Navajo Horse Songs from Frank Mitchell's Blessingway, translated by David McCallester- thin discs in Alcheringa Magazine of Ethnopoetics, UBU web 1680

Two Parodies and a Farce 1965 Original pencil Score 1720

Season Song Cycle 1965 Original pencil Score 1721

Two Alleluias 1965 Original Score Expressionistic, two-part vocal music. Added organ part in pencil manuscript for first movement. 1723

Music of Kutchin Alaska Indians, Folkways Record side 1&2 1965 Copy of record TC: 3:00:00:00 O=-18db 29.97NOF Video Ref 48 kHz 823

This is the Garden (Text by e.e. cummings) 1965 Original Score poem 1724

Pars Artis/Eight Lunes 1965 Original Score 1725

Sonata for Violin Unaccompanied 1965 Original Score and Notes 1726

Violin Concerto 1965 Original Score 1727

Violin Concerto #1 1965 Original Score, Unfinished expressionistic work with only 2 movements complete 1728

A little warm up for You and Me 1965 Original score for presentation piece 1850

Rock of Ages 1965 Pencil sheets 1856

Hurry up Sundown 1965 Original song, pencil sheets Also in Box 7. 1892

Love's on Trial 1965 Song sheet 1893

Stefan Wolpe Scores 1965 Musical Score 1957

Philip Corner: Metal Mediations 1965 One page 2035

Contemporary Music at Twilight -17-1965 1965 Photo flyer and program for Town Hall performance by CM, Goodman, Reeve and Tucker. 2046

What's New for Trumpet & Ensemble 5-22-1965 1965 CM, trumpets & Edward Murray, piano/conductor Carnegie Recital Hall COMPOSERS: Noel G. DaCosta - Spaces (65), Charles Whittenberg - Polyphony (65) - later re-dedicated to Gerard Swartz, WIlliam Sydeman-The Affections, Durant Robertson- Velocity II(65), Meyer Kupferman Infinities Fourteen (65), Ursula Mamlok - For Seven 1 (63) II (65), Peter Pindar Stearns-Trio-Variations (65), Philip Corner - Strata Produced by Norman Seaman 2052

And Thou Shalt Love. (Deut. 6:5-10; Nos. 15:40) 1965 (see above) 2066

Pars Artis, Eight Lunes (Text by Robert Kelly) 1965 Minimal, expressionistic vocal music 2077

Jaj, De Szepen Muzsikalnak, Budapest 1965 Commercial music booklet from Budapest 2447

A concert of 20th Century American music 1965 Held at the New School for Social Research James Tenney Conductor 2567

Sing unto the Lord a New Song Program (2) 1965 Program, CM wins Composer award from American Conference of Cantors 2625

Rit--- A Tempo 1965 Original skins and a small copy 2635

WNYC 29th Annual American Music festival 1965 A postcard announcement for Contemporary music at Twilight, about (15) 2694

New Directions in Music poster 1965 An 81/2 x 11" paper flyer for Town Hall Concert Norman J. Seaman presents free Form Improvisation ensemble. New Works by CM and Gary Friedman played by York String Quartet. James Lee directs Brass Quartet. 2699

New music for trumpet & ensemble 5-22-1965 1965 CM, trumpets & Edward Murray, piano/conductor Carnegie Recital Hall COMPOSERS: Noel G. DaCosta - Spaces (65), Charles WHittenberg - Polyphony (65) - later re-dedicated to Gerard Swartz, WIlliam Sydeman-The Affections, Durant Robertson- Velocity II(65), Meyer Kupferman Infinities Fourteen (65), Ursula Mamlok - For Seven 1 (63) II (65), Peter Pindar Stearns-Trio-Variations (65), Philip Corner - Strata Produced by Norman Seaman 2726

Assorted Press from Early Career 1965 Assorted Press from Early Career c. 1965. 3138

Writings, Readings, and College Notes from Early Career 1965 Writings, Readings, Compositions, and College Notes from Early Career. 1965. 3139

15 short poems by Jerome Rothenberg 1965 Typewritten pages 3559

Avant Garde Music Festival Inc. Stationary (Letterheads) and envelopes. 1965 About 100 envelopes and 10 letterheads 3640

Avant Garde Music Festival 1965 Initial budget estimates and info on the First Avant Garde Music Festival 3673

Strata, Second Layers, Philip Corner 1965 A multi layered performance to be taped and tracks added as the piece progresses. With Philip Corner 3873

All the collected short Poems, Louis Zukofsky 1965. 4066

Four Suits, Alison Knowles, Tomas Schmit, Benjamin Patterson, Philip Corner 1965 Something Else Press 4080

Art Productions, Bern Porter 1965 Signed 4139

Imago 13 1965 A magazine which specializes in the long poem. This issue dedicated to Jack Kerouac of Mass. edited by George Williams, University of Montreal 4149

Avant Garde Music Festival Stationery 1965 3 Full boxes of Stationary on top shelf 4162

Dangling Conversation Arrangement for Simon & Garfunkel 1965. 4386

By Alison Knowles 1965 A Great Bear Pamphlet, Contains several short pieces(make a soup) etc. 4734

Mostly Blue, Robert Lax 1965 Journeyman Press NY 4879

Red Circle Blue Square, Robert Lax 1965 Journeyman Press, NY 4880

A Primer of Happenings Time and Space, Al Hansen 1965 Something Else Press NY. Claes Oldenburg, William meyer, Higgins Knowles, Mac Low, Brecht, Waring, Kaprow, Vostell, Vautier, Whitney, Eisenhauer, Schneemann, Tenney, Peter Moore Photos. Tarlow, Carmines, Levy, Watts, Jord Vaxling, Heidi vonBorn 4888

Voz sin pasaporte Voice without a Passport, Jacobo Glantz 1965. 4919

Bird of Passage, Sophie C. Trent 1965 signed, William Frederick 4983

Masterpieces in The Museum of Primitive Art, 1965. 5082

Avant Garde Music Festival Stationary 1965 3 Boxes Top Shelf Library 5242

A Healing Piece, Rough Draft 1965. 5271

CM Film Scores List 1965. 5287

CM Review from Town Hall Concert 1965 Passaic, NY Times, NY Herald 5464

A Call to Disarm Flyer 1965 Media Task Force Open MeetingNatl. Protest Judson Church April 15. 5586

Composition: A New You 1965 Handwritten Composition "A New

You."Unknown Title/Year 3171

Twinkle, Twinkle 1966 1 cd taken from cassette 1 cassette (master) 885

Twinkle, Twinkle - String Quartet 1966 1 cassette (master) 1229

Addiss & Crofut EASTERN FERRIS WHEEL 1966 Columbia Records 8746, Ed Murray, keyboards, John Bergamo percusion, 1360

Please Don't Pinch Cinzano Ashtrays jingle 1966 1448

Twinkle, Twinkle - String Quartet 1966 Short, conceptual variations on the traditional melody "Twinkle Twinkle" in a mixture of late classical/ early romantic styles. Score and parts 1711

Twinkle 1966 Short, conceptual variations on the traditional melody "Twinkle Twinkle" in a mixture of late classical/early romantic styles. 1711

Winter Music 1966 Original Score 1729

Virgin, Full of Grace 1966 Original Score 1730

Sightings (text by Jerome Rothenberg) 1966 Original Score, Expressionistic vocal work 1731

My Soul is Longing for Peace 1966 Original Score 1732

Hor Che I Cel/et la terra elvento tace #2 1966 Original Score filed w/ LeCha Dodi #3 and When David Heard #4/Puisque Je Voy 1734

Praise to the Lord 1966 Original Score 1735

Prelude to Friday Evening Service 1966 Original Score Expressionistic Jewish Sabboth music 1736

Fantasy for Repeated Notes 1966 Original Score 1737

Tunes For Eve 1966 Original Score Simple expressionistic piano music 1738

Old Fashioned Fantasy for Piano 1966 Original Score 1739

Sonata For Piano (to Vincent Sardi) 1966 Original ScoreExpressionistic piano music. Original Skins 1740

Two Part Invention 1966 Original Score 1741

Sonata for Cello 1966 Original Score 1742

Unaccompanied Flute Piece 1966 Original Score 1743

Three Droll Songs (Text by Artemis Smith) 1966. 1745

The Language They Speak 1966 Original Score Emotional tonal score depicting the lives of deaf children in the 60s information age. 1746

Spring is like a Perhaps Hand 1966 Original Score 1747

Cello Concerto/Sun Poem/Earth Poem 4-15-1966 Original Score 1748

A little Vocalise for Antonia 1966 Original Score 1749

Cheryl's Dream 1966 Original Score 1750

Concerto for Bassoon, Piano & Small Orchestra 1966. 1751

Processional 1966 Original Score and notes Expressionistic wedding procession music 1752

Dance Piece for Nancy 1966 Original Score 1753

An Apology 1966 Original Score Expressionistic piano solo 1754

Sonata da Camera 1966. 1757

Trio for Flute, Viola & Harp 1966 Original Score commissioned as a companion piece to Debussy trio 1758

Mi-Chamochah 1966 Original Score 1759

A Bouquet of Flowers 1966 Written notes for a sound performance on four separate pages to be synchronized. Canby non musicians 1958

Puisque Je Voy 1966 Expressionistic vocal music 2089

Hor che i ciel et la terra e i vento tace (Text by Petrarcus) 1966 Expressionistic vocal work 2100

L' Cha do dee (Traditional) 1966 Expressionistic vocal work 2111

When David Heard 1966 Expressionistic vocal music 2122

Winter Music- Night (I)- Day (II) 1966 Expressionistic music with pop influences 2133

My Soul is Longing for Your Peace 1966 Expressionistic chamber work 2144

Two-Part Invention 1966 Simple expressionistic piano music 2155

Virgin, Full of Grace 1966 Expressionistic liturgical music 2166

Unaccompanied Flute piece (To Thomas Nyfenger) 1966 Expressionistic solo flute work 2177

A Little Viola Tune 1966 Expressionistic viola solo 2188

Fantasie on Repeated Notes 1966 Conceptual expressionistic work for large brass with acoustic games, based on echoes across the performance space 2200

String Quartet II 1966 This work is more modal than Quartet I Two more copies in copier form 2211

Praise to the Lord 1966 Expressionistic vocal work. 2222

Sonata for Unaccompanied Cello 1966 Expressionistic cello music 2233

Old Fashioned Fantasie for Piano (on the Monical Troche) to Light Fingers 1966 Expressionistic piano work based on an iso rhythm 2244

Sound design for Simon and Garfunkel's Parsley, Sage, Rosemary, and Thyme album. 1966 "Head charts" and sweetening instrument selection 2255

What's New for Solo Trumpet - trumpet recital 1966 Commissioned and recent works for trumpet 2460

Summer Institute For the creative and performing Arts in Judaism 1966 Program. CM performs Piano Fantasie 2522

Deuteronomy 6:5-10 Numbers 15:40 1966 Small copy and Original Skins 2634

WNYC 29th Annual American Music festival 1966 A postcard annocement for Contemporary music at Twilight, about (15) 2694

Postcard "Listen" by Max Neuhaus 1966 Published in 1979 and Given to CM in 1982 Signed 3613

Black Panther Party File 1966 Five pieces of Party Memorabilia.

Information sheets about the Panther 21.What has happened to the party nationally. A Poster for a Black Festival with Music and Speakers. An article What We Believe. A large Graphic Piece. Power to the People. A booklet Strangers to justice. Also a Name and number of a Panther project organizer. 3614

Music Today newsletter American Music Center 1966 View from the Bottom of the Heap, Article By CM 3748

Avant Garde Music Festival Papers 1966 Statement of purpose, budgets, financials etc. 9 copies A folder of notes, legal forms, charter, income tax etc. 4015

The Under-wood Jeffrey Kindley 1966. 4071

Something Vol. 2 #1 Cover By Andy Warhol 1966 A Vietnam assemblage. Rothenberg, Ginsberg, Tenny, Corner and others. 4073

Aboriginal Myths and Legends, Ronald Robinson 1966. 4144

NFMC letter of Congratulations for " Sonata da Chiesa" 1966 From Ms. Robert Fisher 4294

A letter to CM from John Cage 1966 Letter requesting CM to contribute some works to a book project and exhibition. 4314

David Bedford, Music for Albion Moonlight 1966 Universal edition of poems by Kenneth Patchen for soprano and six instruments. Music and directions by David Bedford 4516

New Music Ensemble Program Sheet. 1966 Program for Marshall Field House, Tues. May 11. William Sydeman, Charles Whittenberg, Ursula Mamlok, Durant Robertson, Meyer Kupferman, CM and group (Edward Murray, Sue Alden, James Corwin, Virgil Blackwell, Dorthy Kaplan, Lucille Hymovitz, Styra Avins, Gary Berlind, Patrick Dama, Joseph Gurt.) 4527

Congratulations from Young Composers Contest 1966 CM wins Class 1 first Award for "Sonata da Chiesa", Letter from Mr. Robert Fisher 4680

Chance Imagery, George Brecht 1966 Great Bear Pamphlet 4718

Incomplete Requiem for W.C. Fields, Al Hansen 1966 A Great Bear Pamphlet 4726

Manifestos 1966 Great Bear Pamphlet 4728

Some Thing HANOI, 1966 A collection of poems from many of our friends from the New Wilderness. Book is in bad condition. Cover by Andy Warhol 4751

The Twin Plays, Port-au-Prince & Adams County Illinois Jackson Mac Low 1966 A Great Bear Pamphlet 4761

Das schriftbild der neuen musik, Erhard Karkoschka 1966 Hermann Moeck Verlag. celle 4987

Language Box Box Language, Bici Hendricks 1966 Black Thumb Press 5020

CM Film Scores List 1966. 5288

Original Score Box #'s 1966. 5294

Resource Opera, Music by CM 1966 Skins and Copies 5418

NY Festival of Contemporary Music First planning document and Budgets 1966 Page 1 is fading away 5637

Addiss & Crofut EASTERN FERRIS WHEEL 1967 Columbia Records 8746, Ed Murray, keyboards, John Bergamo percusion, 1360

Trilium - tv spot score 1967. 1445

Twinkle 1967. 1520

A Little Brigati Music 1967 A rock opera examining the ritual of stardom. Scored for singer and stage band with pre recorded soundtrack including sound effects, interviews with rockstar Dave Brigati and his mother, and the "voice of the poet" (Jerome Rothenberg) 1644

And as I Sat 1967 Original Score (pencil) Text F. Scott Fitzgerald "The Great Gatsby" 1760

Season in Sea 1967 Original Score 1761

Menuchah 1967 Original Score Expressionistic liturgical song in Hebrew. 1762

Charrad Beloved 1967 Original Score by Jerome Rothenberg. Expressionistic chamber music. 1763

Havdalah Service 1967 Original Score Expressionistic liturgical work for the transition from sabboth time to daily time. 1764

Organ Sonata 1967 Original Score 1765

Organ Music for Sabbath Eve 1967. 1766

Marilyn Monroe Collage 1967 Original Score (pencil)A violin, viola, and cello score provides musical continuity between bites from films and recordings of Monroe and fragments of Monroe's voice from a television interview. Two versions are available: one fully produced, the other in which thrThis piece is part "idea" music, part film score, part expressionism. It is concerned with the star as victim, and performance as confession. 1768

Twinkle 1967 Original Score, variations on twinkle, twinkle. 1769

Naomi & Ruth 1967 Original Score with production notes and ScriptExpressionistic liturgical opera. An orchestra of guitars is placed behind the audience, while several chamber groups perform on stage and aside the audience. Two bass narrators echo each other from either side of the stage. The six-pointed Star of David is inscribed by sound signals from these locations. 1770

Bareysheet- Reduction of Part 1 1967 Original Score Skins/ReductionsExpressionistic music for synagogue, based on the opening sentence in the Old Testament ("In the beginning..."). In Hebrew. 1771

String Quartet #3 1967 Original Score/Skins Sound-oriented, relatively nondramatic exploration of daily life. In performance a string quartet (two violins, viola, cello) play CM's fully notated 60ish music. The accompanying environmental sound track is composed of ambient sounds gatherelectronic elements were produed on Buchla modules at

Morton Subotnick's NY University sound studio with the help of Michael Chaikovsky. 1772

For Cantor & Three Voices 1967 Original Score 1773

Chamber Symphonies 1&2 1967 Original Score Skins and pencil notes 1774

Das Murraistuck 1967 Original Score 1775

Excursions from Largo Op 3 No. 3 1967 Original Score Skin Conceptual expressionistic music. Based on a shift from slow to fast. 1776

Dream Sequence 1967 Original Score Conceptual expressionistic chamber work in two movements. First movement points to "idea" music, second to film score. 1777

Willow Mist 1967 Original Score 1785

Willowmist 1967 Original song sheet 1830

Turn on 1967 Original song sheet 1832

The Color of my Mind 1967 Original song sheet 1834

Stewart's Music 1967 Pencil song sheet 1835

Farmer Brown 1967 Original song sheet 1836

Hey People 1967 Original Song sheet 1841

I Can Love Again 1967 Original song sheet 1842

Light a Match 1967 Original Music Song sheet 1843

Schemes 1967 Original Song Sheet 1846

Planetarium Event 1967 Sounds and verbal notes for performance 1851

Rock of Ages 1967 Pencil sheets 1856

Prince Matchabelli Spot 1967 Original pencil score for TV commercial, Storyboard and cues 1860

Alex Stokowski 1967 Michael Lessac song from Columbia record arranged by CM 1970

Chamber Symphony #1 1967 Incomplete expressionistic chamber music 2266

Chamber Symphony # 2 1967 Incomplete expressionistic chamber music 2277

Organ Sonata, Prelude (to McNeil Robinson) 1967 Virtuoso unfinished organ work 2288

Organ Music for Sabbath Eve 1967 Expressionistic liturgical work 2299

Sh'ma 1967. 2311

Near the Wall/Near the wall/Peace piece 1967 Original Scores and notations. Moody, expressionistic music to accompany a political dance work protesting the Vietnam War. 2322

Season in Sea (Text by Wm. Williams) 1967 Expressionistic chamber music. 2333

Cheetah 1967 Conceptual vocal picture of cheetah scream. 2344

Das Murraistuck 1967 Expressionistic piano music. 2355

Elijah program (10) Mystery play by Martin Buber 1967 program for Little Theatre, Purchase, NY 2783

American Judaism Winter 65/66 (5) Reform Jewish Congregation of Merrick (6) 1967 Also Misc. Press 2818

Festival Time (3) 1967 A Theater for Peace, A salute to the United Nations program at the Brooklyn Museum. CM does music for Near the Wall of Lion Shadows, for Kathleen Coine and William Shorr. 2835

String Quartet III by CM 1967 Two covers from Other Media NY, Stockholm 2923

The Imperial Collection of Audubon Animals 1967 The Imperial Collection of Audubon Animals The Imperial Quadrupeds of North America Original Text by John James Audubon, F.R.S. and the Rev. John Bachman, D.D. Edited with new text by Victor H. Cahalane Forward by Fairfield Osborn Illustrated by John James Audubon and John Woodhouse Audubon Hammond Incorporated, Maplewood, New Jersey 3329

Anthology of Concrete Poetry, Edited by Emmett Williams 1967 Something Else Press, NY 4086

Popular Entertainment #1, Philip Corner 1967 A Great Bear Pamphlet 4155

Popular Entertainments by Philip Corner 1967 A Small printed Pamphlet of Great Bear Press 4234

Musica da Camera, Robert Moevs 1967 A musical score, Published by Rutgers State University 4238

Barry A. Bloomfield Letter 1967 Letter about CM concerts 4290

National Federation of Music Clubs 1967 Letter to CM about music to be performed at Convention 4291

National Federation of Temple Youth Letter 1967 Commission to compose a musical piece centering around the Book of Ruth 4292

LACH Camp Institute Letter 1967 Thank You Letter for participating 4293

CIRCUS 1967 A musical event by CM. A different and dark piece, in four continuous sections. 4359

Diary, Cage 1967 How to improve the World (You will only make matters worse, Continued Part 3 John Cage 4714

A Filliou Sampler (2) 1967 Something Else Press 4722

The Cursive Scandinavian Slave, Bengt Klintberg 1967 Something Else Press 4723

Popular Entertainments, Philip Corner 1967 A Great Bear Pamphlet 4736

Sweethearts, Emmett Williams 1967 Something Else Press - text changes page by page 4862

The Mechanical Bride: Folklore of Industrial Man, Marshall McLuhan 1967 Beacon Press 5002

Music Cultures of the Pacific, the Near East, and Asia by William P.

Malm 1967 Tokai University Press 5022

The Music of the Jews, Aron Marko Rothmuller 1967 A.S. Barnes and company Inc, 5097

Ms. Kay Gifted Reader, Advisor 1967 A flyer handout from Ms. Kay. A nice piece of NY reality of the day. 5232

CM Sound Art List 1967 5290

Circus, Complete Transcript 1967 Performance piece by CM. 1967-1970 Synopsis, Games and Acts 5398

A Program of Chamber Music Poster Flyers (15) at Library & Museum of the Performing Arts Lincoln Center 1967 Trio for Flute, Harp & Viola CM, Fantasy and Dancing Music 5520

A Concerto for Bandoneon and Orchestra with Solo Harmonica and Virginals 1968 A work for the traditional South American bandoneon (super concertina) in a post-expressionistic sound-oriented style. 3

Groovin'/Do you feel it -- A Fantasie 1968 Original pencil Score and Stage notes,One bound copy. The Rascals and the orchestra with additional drums and electric upright bass move through a medly of their songs. The orchestra plays textures and counter musics as The Rascals sing “Groovin” and “Do You Feel It”. The Rascals become more and more puppetlike until they become a broken record. 14

40 North, 67 West 1968 Moody, sound oriented, post-expressionistic film score. Instrumentation includes acoustic instruments, rhythm section with electric bass and electric guitar, underwater bells and electronic effects, especially repeating delay. Film and score relate to life of fish and fishermen in the North Atlantic. 25

He is There -- Charles Ives arranged by CM 1968 An arrangement of Ives by CM. Harpsichord and calliope, tuba and piccolo, string quartet and drums make this CM/Ives work a music of fast color changes. For Addiss & Crofut Columbia Records album, John Hammond, producer. 36

Erev Shabbat Service 1968 Expressionistic Jewish liturgical work in English. 47

Dialogue for a Woman and Trumpet (Text by Robert Somerfield) 1968 An old-fashioned melodrama in which one of the two characters is a trumpet player who never speaks, only expresses himself through trumpet music. The score is coloristic and jazzy. 58

Look Around (Collaboration with The Rascals) 1968 A recorded effects sequence. CM’s track is primarily a sound collage of marching feet, various weapons, Adolf Hitler taking the solo at the bridge, and a baby crying at the end. 69

Ray of Hope -- Arrangement for The Rascals 1968 This project grew out of “Groovin/Do You feel It” and uses the same techniques of rock band/orchestral arrangement with musical asides. The CM track goes on after the tune ends. This is coarse, coloristic noise music with 2 contra bassoons, full brass, and nasty amplified violin played by Paul Zukovsky.

Zoo Music 1968 Four cassette machines carrying visitors go the zoo. They walk in a fluctuating square formation. The four tapes are played back in formation and in sync. They can be heard on fixed loudspeakers or handheld ones. Recordists: Alison Knowles, Philip Corner, Gabriel Weiss, CM. Central Park Zoo NY 102

4 Tracks in Raw Pulses 1968 Four tracks generated from single-pulse sources, pulsing in different relationships to each other. This is a very loud piece. The piece takes advantage of super bass effects created by custom-built, extra-large woofers. Requires five audio channels for play-back. 114

Christmas 1968 instrumental 138

4 Tracks in Raw Pulses 1968 Four tracks generated from single-pulse sources, pulsing in different relationships to each other. This is a very loud piece. The piece takes advantage of super bass effects created by Jack Weisberg's custom-built, extra-large cor and derived super bass. Unrecorded are other versions which use handbuilt oscillators to stream continuous sine, triangle and square waves which createdfields. Within the envelope were rhythms of beats from detuning unisons, and rhythms from oscilator driven sound gates. 1097

Tea Music 1968 Two women, a pianist and a violinist, rehearse and have tea. They are assaulted by a sound track which propounds the sexist rules of society, and then by a sexy airplane stewardess, who explains what to do in an emergency. Premier at Washington Square Church, NY Performed at SUNY New Paltz by Edna Golandsky, piano and Linda Cummiskey, violin 1112

Michael Lessac SLEEP FASTER WE NEED THE PILLOW 1968 CM (Arranger), CM (Conductor), Bobby Donaldson (Drums), John Hammond, Sr. (Producer), Eric Weissberg (Guitar), Tony Glover (Harmonica), Howard Collins (Guitar), Jeff Levine (Bass), Paul Motian (Drums), Russ Payne (Engineer), Stan Tonkel (Engineer), Michael Lessac (Vocals), John Castronova (Organ, Piano, Celeste) 1361

CM Town Hall Concert 1968 Through concert promoter Norman Seaman, I had a free of charge night for a concert at Town Hall. Inspired by my collaborations with The Rascals, I wrote a rock tableau with libretto by Jerome Rothenberg, A Little Brigati Music. And created Sound Piece for rock amplified piano, performed by my wife Edna Golandsky. 1412

Birth of the War God (Aztec) (12)+ Copies 1968 Multiple copies in 8 1/2 x 11" size. 1488

Silent Meditation 1968. 1632

Old Dance Suite 1968. 1634

Arturstuck 1968 Original Score with Stage setup 1791

The Fly and the Donkey 1968 Original Score and Cues 1803

Steve 1968 Original song sheet 1837

Chalk Talk 1968 Original song sheet 1838

Ginger Ale 1968 Original Song Sheet 1840

Love went straight to my head 1968 Original Song sheet 1845

I can see Flowers 1968 Original Song Sheet 1848

Unfinished song(lyricist forgotten) 1968. 1852

S'Vivon 1968 Pencil Score 1858

Coffee Bean 1968 Original pencil music for coffee bean 1862

Music for Karate 1968 Various pieces of original music in envelope 1863

A Boys Best Friend/Christmas 1968 Original pencil notes and finished songs for both titles. 1886

Loves on Trial 1968 Song sheet 1893

Ray of Hope 1968 Original skins, 1895

Three Hundred Love 1968 Original son sheet 1896

September Rain/Why Can't I Cry 1968 Original song sheets 1897

Yesterday's Rules 1968 Original Song sheet 1898

Every Day a Sunday 1968 Original Pencil Songsheet 1899

Ice Dreams 1968 Original song sheet 1901

Kids 1968 Original Song Sheet 1902

Judi 1968 Original Song Sheet 1903

Firefly, April Rainbow, Billy, Givin up on Love, It hurts to be In love 1968 Song Sheets 1904

Balloon Farm Tunes, Question of Temperature 1968 CM arranger credit on hit song. Song sheets for nine songs, http://en.wikipedia.org/wiki/The_Balloon_Farm 1905

Some/Thing # 4/5 1968 New poetry collection, edited by Jerome Rothenberg and David Antin 1939

Soliram, Azulao, JimmySong, Alisan for Eastern Ferris Wheel 1968 An envelope with several compositions by Addiss and Crofut, along with recording notes and contacts with John Hammond, Sr, Columbia Records from sessions. 1950

64 Fanfares for Four Antiphonal Trumpets 1968 Music by Tom Johnson 1951

Erica Appiezweig Compositions 1968 A notebook with several handwritten song sheets of pop type tunes. 1953

Futz and What Came After, Rochelle Owens 1968 Copier pages from a book in a paper binder 2024

Sonata II 1968 Original Score (pencil) and notes Expressionistic sound-oriented solo work. 2366

Sound Piece for Electric Piano Original & Skins 1968 Very loud virtuoso sound piece mixing post-expressionism with noise. The piano sound is captured by microphone and contact microphone and amplified through a Fender twin reverb guitar or bass amp with foot pedal effects: wa-wa, tremolo, reverb, fuzz. Feedback is used throughout at different sound levels. 2377

Twenty Beats for Annie 1968 Short conceptual sound piece. 2388

Four for The Rascals 1968 Original pencil Score This humorous work takes advantage of implications and sound images of the Latin folkloric bandoneon in the hands of a virtuoso. It evokes U.S. 60s rock artists The Rascals. 2399

Bandoneon and Clarinet Duet, In Memorium to Che Guevara. 1968 This memoriam takes advantage of implications and sound images of the Latin folkloric bandoneon in the hands of a virtuoso. 2410

Town Hall & Norman Seaman Present Concert 1968 Town Hall Jan. 19 1968 Works By Philip Corner, George Flynn, Linda Francis, Malcolm Goldstein, Carol Marcy, Antonio Miranda, Gregory Reeve. CM plays trumpet in the Red Gongs 2525

Robert Mumper & CM 1968 Premier Recital in Paris Dec. 10 Poster & program 2526

20th WNYC Festival of American Music Program (9) 1968 Program CM Sonata No.2 OP.8 For violin. Unaccompanied Parade and performance 2624

Four Mondays at Corpus Christi Church, Western Wind (5) 1968 "The Birth of the War God" performed by Western Wind Monday Oct, 30th translation by Jerome Rothenberg 2809

Birth of the War God color photo. 1968 This art became the CD cover artwork. 2810

View from the Bottom of the Heap, Original typed five pages 1968 First Draft with corrections and second draft mimeo copy. Polemic essay for July/August 1966 issue (Vol. 8 No. 6) of Music Today, the newsletter of the American Music Center. Republished on line 2015. 3934

Tom Phillips Trailer, edition Hansjorg Mayer 1968 Signed for CM 4041

Artego How could you be so Naive O.D. Wells 1968 4051

Ida Gertrude Stein 1968 Vintage Books 4064

Caterpillar 5 1968 A book from a small publisher Clayton Eshlman NY, From a series of 10 Poetry news and reviews 4176

Four Quartets, T.S. Eliot 1968 published book 4258

Letter from Robert Mumper 1968 Letter to CM about Violin sonata, very impressed by CM work. 4295

Balloon Farm 1968 Mike Appel Balloon Farm session scores in Box 7. 4495

Genesis Song, CM music, 1968 Poem Translated by Jerome Rothenberg University of California Press 2 Copies 4634

Simon & Garfunkel Greatest Hits, Song Book 1968 Music Sales Limited, London Great early photos cover 4666

Triangle Event (The Doppler Mirage, Jack Weisberg 1968 Notes on Event, Planning, sketches and ideas. Weisberg Brochure on sound Company. 4682

Sightings, Further Sightings, Jerome Rothenberg 1968 Black Sparrow Press, L.A. CA. 4784

The Music Workshop, Zygmunt Krauze 1968 Flyer for Music Workshop Concert 4811

Dieter Rot, Emmett Williams (2) 1968 HJ Mayer, Stuttgart 4863

Ferdinand Louis Zukofsky 1968 the Chaucer Press 4939

Vergiss Mein Nicht, CM, Bach 1968. 5176

Birth of the War God, Aztec (15) 1968 Copies Located on Black Shelf One Copy Box 77. 5266

American Symphony Orchestra, Leopold Stokowski , music DirectorJoseph Eger, conducting. 1968 World Premiere Groovin/"Do You Feel It" by CM Garden State Arts Center July 11th Commissioned by Mr. Eger 5489

New American Filmmakers Series at the Whitney Museum of Art Poster 1968 - 7 Unusual Programs of independent made Films Includes Eat the Document NY Premier of Moonwalk One. CM score not mentioned 5511

New Years Eve Piece (to Toru Takemitsu) 1969 Expressionistic, sound-oriented music for acoustic orchestra. 91

Ga Guerre - a short film by William Fertig w/CM score 1969 Lament for the violence of cock fighting. Made as a protest against violence, especially the Vietnam War. The music is intense and coloristic. 125

Impulse 90 1969 Acoustic instruments in a post-expressionistic sound-oriented score. 136

Sh'ma Yisrael 1969 Conceptual, sound-oriented setting of traditional Jewish liturgy. 147

Satan in Goray (Text by Jerome Rothenberg) Sound poem w/CM studio tooling. 1969 A multitrack recording by CM with Rothenberg's 1968 voice on home tape recorder with its built-in effects. This is one of the first pieces made in the CMA studio, 365 West End Avenue, NY, and is a sound- and performance-oriented work. 158

Symphony with Two Clowns 1969 A conceptual work in which the performance is taken over by two clowns/mimes who "turn weapons" on the audience and orchestra. The horn section in a transparent protected booth saves the day, when their sound pours out of a revolving ceiling array of loudspeakers. 169

Piano Concerto (incomplete) 1969 Post-expressionistic, sound-oriented dramatic composition. 180

Wall of Sound 1969 This is a very loud continuous sound piece. The output of 2 oscillators fixed at a natural major 3rd is continuously varied by equalization and effects via a mixing board. Requires a high powered sound system with super woofers, the physical aspect of the sound is essential. 191

Four Soundhead Shows 1969 Four one-hour shows created for children's radio at WBAI FM NY. They are a structured, multilayered sound profile of the times, with performances by many artists including poet Jerome Rothenberg and Don Cox, the Grand Fieldmarshal of the Black Panthers. 247

Soundscapes for Knoll Furniture Show at the Louvre 1969 Sound collages for installation as three period environments for Knoll furniture. The the most interesting period was the 20's, which mixed fragments of Josephine Baker singing and the sounds of toy trains. 513

Morningstar Chant 1969 transfer from 2 track master 707

Drum Chant 1969 transfer from 2 track master needs a new mix 708

Breath Chant 1969 transfer from 2 track master, 1970 ? 709

Moonwalk One 1969 This NASA documentary on the Apollo 11 mission was a huge task. Much more music was written and recorded than was used. The various elements included: the title tune, "Goodbye Mother Earth;" country blues band; bassoon with stopwatch; and pure noise such as a rocket takeoff and biomedical sounds. The biomedical sequence, which was scored humorously with explosions and sound effects, was censored by NASA. Sound music on baroque pipe organ is mixed with telemetry throughout. 779

Personal Chants 1969 Personal Chants is composed, chanted and self-recorded by CM at his home studio. These four chants were the beginning of CM's exploration of a personal music in which the voice leads the music, the mind and the body forward. They opened up a rich period of work including breath-healing ceremonies, and A Healing Piece created for the Wooster Group which used the drum chant as the spine for a group-healing journey. These works are spatial and intended to be played loudly over two widely separated speakers. 983

AIM Film Score 1969 Commissioned for film by Martha? about NY 4 artists: Osorio, Rosenquist, Each artist is rejected in a single movement. Home made sound processing is used. 1096

Subway actions (GLCA performance workshop) 1969 Scored actions for guerilla performance in the NY subways - including silent game of catch on platforms and in the cars, singing continuous sound on the platforms while trains pass noisily eclipsing the vocal sound then revealing it. Workshop participants were Great Lakes College Association arts program in New York. 1383

O Vos Omnes, reconstruction 1969 Slow performance of Victoria's O Vos Omnes on trumpet by cm, pitch shift by tape speed. 1414

Hella 1969 A multitrack recording by CM with his own voice on Tandberg home tape recorder with its built-in effects. One of the first pieces made in the CMA studio, 365 West End Avenue, NY, this is a voice with head/hand motion improvised exploration of the word "hella". 1502

Aerospace, International Paper 18 Flutes 1969 - 60 and 30 second TV commercials 1521

Breath Canon 1969 Original song sheet and notes. 1615

ATM Film Score 1969. 1668

Casual 1969 Original Music 1781

My First 1969 Original Music 1782

A Dream within a Dream 1969 Original music 1783

Born to Love Alone 1969 Original Music 1784

Sh'ma Yisrael 1969 Original Song (Vocal Solo) 1797

A Dream Within a Dream 1969. 1798

Bells for Michael 1969 Original pencil score A vigorous sound-oriented work using the ringing effects of the piano.

In the years that Edna Golandsky and I were together, I wrote her several large works for piano including Sound Piece, Bells for Michael, and Recomposition Les A'dieux. 1799

AIM Original Score and cue notes. Educational film covering the work of five artists from East Hampton, NY. Music relating to the visual art of five artists working in East Hampton, NY A sound-oriented piece using processed and unprocessed female voice and percussion. Osorio, Rosenthal. 1801

Music for Marti Buber's play Elijah 1969 Original Skins, Mailer and Programs Premier at Marymount College of the Sacred Heart 11 copies of printed program with Original Score by CM for performance February 3 - 6. 1802

Goddard Music #1 (not used) 1969 Original composition 1847

Snackups 1969 Original Score for Snackups commercial 1861

Dark Shadows 1969 Original pencil score for 30 & 60 sec. spots 1864

Puma Crisis 1969 Handwritten original score with cues 1882

Rite Diet 1969 Original handwritten score and notes. 1883

Sweet Dreams - John Avildsen feature film 1969 Score/song sheets for five songs Conceptual sound-oriented music includes: Paul Zukofsky performing multitrack violin collage, mulitrack CHOIR I & II (Dante-Rothenberg), MULTI-PIANO COLLAGE, BREATH PRELUDES I & II. Title Song: OK Bill. [needs clarification] 1906

One a Day-Rider/One a Day-Little girl 1969 Onion Skins for TV score for One a Day Commercial 2 voices without words, 2 bass flutes, marimba, 2 guitars, bass, timbali, sand blocks 1909

The Bells of St. Martin 1969 An antiphonal brass prelude to the Vanilla Fudge song. Released on Atlantic Records album Adrain Barber, producer 1955

Knoll Furniture Show at the Louvre 1969 CM created three sound environments for three periods of Knoll furniture 20's 40's and 60's. 2505

Woodstock Tapes edited at CM Studio 1969 Stan Goldberg and Wavy Gravy edit woodstock tapes for Earth Peoples Park benefit album. Allen Ginsberg and The Living Theater record at CMs Studio. 2506

Aerospace, Skins 1969 multiple flutes 2636

Hermeneutics: Dick Higgins 1969 Interpretation Theory in Schleiermacher, Dilthey, Heidegger and Gadamer. 2672

Recipe for Sounding Jerome Rothenberg's Beadle's Testimony (3) and original 1969 Sound Poem instructions. 2718

WBAI Free Music Store Presents Poster (2) 1969 Washington Square Methodist Church 133 W. 4th St. 3 Came back by Alexander Reik, Action Music by Tom Johnson, Tea Music by CM, NoN Stop By Boguslaw Schaeffer and Clarinetist Aurelian Popa. 2752

Sally Gross, Spencer Holst Poster, Baudelaire 1969 A concert of dance to a reading of Baudelaire prose poems (in Translation) Michelson-Bagley Gallery 306 W.81st St. 2975

Copyrights and original CM scores 1969 Copyright information for CM Music and Lyrics. Scores: "No Road," "Heavy," "Sh'ma Yisrael." 3357

Four Young Lady Poets, Carol Berge, Barbara Moraff, Rochelle Owens, Diane Wakoski 1969. 4065

Griot, A journal of Native Consciousness Abrams 1969 VOL 1 #1. 4241

Technicians of the Sacred, Edited by Jerome Rothenberg 1969. 4255

Breath Chant Plus 1969. 4426

Kenneth Gaburo, Lingua II: 1969 Produced by Lingua Press. A large Format book of word art. 4483

Town Hall Concert Programs 1969 Norman Seaman presents, Marilyn Monroe Collage, Sound Piece for rock amplified piano, A little Brigati Music. Edna Golandsky, David Brigati, Arthur Weisberg, CM 4512

Proposal for a Recital 1969 A letter giving choices of scores for a Recital which could include Bells For Michael, Animal Clackers, Reconstruction: Beethoven Farewell Sonata, Requiem for the Victims of Kent State, and Soundpiece for Amplified Piano. 4543

A Ray of Hope 45rpm 1969 Cavaliere- Brigati Horn arrangement by CM 4544

Technicians of the Sacred, Rothenberg 1969 Anchor Books Doubleday & Co. Soft cover book with Cover Missing. 4762

NOTATIONS, John Cage 1969 Something Else Press, Collection of Music Manuscripts from Various composers 4810

Dieresis, Bern Porter: Rockland 1969 #73 of 100 Signed to CM 4884

Caterpillar 8/9 1969 Clayton Eshleman 4942

Introduction for Parapsychology 1969 Parapsychology Foundation INC 4946

Nine Chains to the Moon, R. Buckminster Fuller 1969 Southern Illinois University Press 4967

Anarchism and other essays, Emma Goldman 1969 Dover 4970

The Lore of the Chinese Lute 1969 the Voyagers Press 5030

Towards a Poor Theatre, Jerzy Grotowski 1969 Simon and Schuster

5098

The Effect of Sound Playback on the Toadfish, James Fish 1969 From the Behavior of Marine Animals, Vol. 2 5486

Poland Magazine 1969 History and Art Stories, Photos. 5562

Haitian or Jamaican Art on Canvas 1969 2553

Dark Dreams 1970 Long moody sound pieces on head charts. A fusion of rock, jazz, and new music. [the term "sound-pieces" needs clarification] 202

Heads, Tails 1970 Sound-oriented music with acoustic instrumentation. 213

Telephone Music (Commissioned by AT&T) 1970 Very loud sound work mixed in stereo, designed for tri amp playback with super woofers. The physical qualities of the sound are fundamental, using phone sounds in a nasty, raw way. 225

The Juggler 1970 Animated film score. 236

Patience 1970 Quiet very slowly changing sound-oriented work, existing only as a stereo mix on audio tape. 258

Whales of the Indians 1970 A sound collage with poets Jerome Rothenberg and George Quasha reading their own and found materials, processed whale sounds, and self-recorded Seneca Native American music from the Salamanca, NY. 269

Brass Quintet 1970. 280

Blue Music for Woodwind Quintet 1970 Sound-oriented post-expressionistic music with a blue mood. 291

Green Music for Woodwinds 1970 Sound-oriented music with acoustic instrumentation. 302

Blood 1970 Sound play in which dreams and ambition are portrayed through a live action pianist. The piece employs film images of that performer, body function amplification on the performer, computer, and a statue filled with blood. 313

The Unknown Man 1970. 324

Instant Music 1970. 336

A Special Organ Piece for Patrick 1970 Sound- and spatially-oriented music with four layers of organ for playback in stereo or quad. 347

Triangulation Pieces Mars & Moon, Dessert Flatbeds 1970 In these outdoor events, music is performed live with amplification on a flatbed truck. The music is instantly transmitted to two other sound sources, also on trucks. The three sources move out from a common starting point in triangular formation on: 1)Sea Coast; 2) Desert; 3) Mountains. Three fast noisy vehicles start the event by zooming out in the three directions. 358

Clearasil full mix 1970 "too long", HL 376

w/o bells 1970 "too long", no leader 377

w/o vocals 1970 "too long", no leader 378

w/o vocals & bells 1970 "too long", TL 379

High Rope 1970. 714

Here is New Jersey 1970 This score was written twice with the original chamber orchestra version being the most innovative. Due to budget, the piece was rescored for string quartet with keyboards and percussion. The original score --"Q2"-- is an independent work, in which interrupted fragments of 18th-century music collide with sound-oriented music. 890

Late 60s 1970 Master (for now) CD 1 of 2 audio CDs from cassette: 8 Tracks 901

Late 60's 1970 2 audio CDs 975

Soundhead Series: Bad Vibes 1970 B289 71/2280309 61052 1451. 1124

The Soundhead Show #1 master 1970 7.5 ips 1170

Moon Mars Doppler Shift 1970 Planetary radar is modulated with sound and music, bounced off the surface of a rotating Moon, Mars, etc, captured on return to Earth, transformed by the journey. 1371

Shortest Way to Heaven (no center image) 1970 Hyper-loud sound collage of rocket sounds and childrens' voice. It is a two speaker mix done so that no center image forms, metaphorical of parallel worlds that never meet due to technicalities. 1446

Short Soundhead Shows: Anatomy of a Soul Tune (Tony May); Bad Vibes (Marshall Efron) 1970 Two five-minute pilots for radio: "Anatomy" describes the technical side of a recording studio production of a song. It was intended to be followed by a series of techie shows. "Bad Vibes" is a radio comedy on the politics of daily life, and was also intended as the first in the series. 1557

Jitanjafora 1970 A score by Lloring Barber 1571

Sonia 1970 studio sound track/montage 1643

Here In New Jersey 1970 score for documentary 1664

Bach Reconstruction for Trumpet, Trombone, Vibes 1970. 1700

Requiem for the Victims of Kent State 1970 Built entirely on cadences, the first section empties into a sound treatment of chorale "O Haupt Voll Blut und Wunden," with the last note sounding like a gunshot. 1722

Sixty-Six Songs 66 for a Blackfoot Bundle 1970 Initiation ceremony with props based on the English translation of Black Foot Native American text and instructions by Jerome Rothenberg. The piece includes body painting and slapstick humor. "Bundle" refers to the medicine bundle, the traditional medicine person's collection of medine power objects. The Commissioned by conductor Arthur Weisberg for amplified ensemble: Frederic Rzewshi, organ + piano; Alan Blustein, clarinets; Raymond Des Roches, percussion, Garrett List, trombone; Frederick Sherry, Cello; Phyllis Bryn - Julson, soprano; Janet Steele (?) alto, Eliot Levine, baritone voice 1755

Heavy 1970 Original Score 1779

Baroque Music 1970 Original pencil score 1786

Happy Birthday 1970 Original music 1804

Network 1970 Scene Discriptions and cues /and notesMixture of homemade electronic music and sound processing, and sound- oriented rhythm and acoustic music. 1805

Green Music 1970 Original Score 1806

Instant Music 1970 Original notes for performance 1807

Blood 1970 Original script for performance piece 1808

Kyrie for Boys Choir 1970 Original pencil Score Simple melodic setting of liturgy in Greek. 1809

Earth Poem 1970 Original score for Earth poem/Sun Poem 1810

A Special organ piece for Patrick 1970 Original Score 1812

Blue Music 1970 Original skins 1813

American Express Heads/Tails 1970 Original Score and cues 1814

Dark Dreams 1970 Original Score and handwritten cues and notes 1815

Two Shubert Reconstructions Piano & Violin 1970. 1816

Requiem for Victims of Kent State 1970 Original pencil Score and notes 1817

Bach Reconstruction for Trumpet, Trombone and Vibes
1970 Original Score 1818

Bach Reconstruction for Flute & Guitar 1970 Original pencil Score 1819

Bach Reconstruction for Piano & Oboe 1970 Original score 1820

Bach Reconstruction for Piano, Cello, Clarinet 1970 Original score, skins, notes 1821

Each Day 1970 Original song sheet 1839

Canon Finger Music 1970 Original Score 1849

Douby Dough 1970 Original handwritten sheet. Words and music by Frank Corre 1874

Earth Poem 1970 Original Song sheet 1876

Disposable Environment 1970 Original Score for International Paper spotalso contains music for Aerospace 1879

How Can I ask the Morning, Dec. 1, 1970 Original song sheet. Also Heavy song sheet 1884

Marco Beach Hotel 1970 Original song sheet 1885

American Airlines Demo 1970 Handwritten pencil music 1887

No Road 1970 Original skins and copy 1888

Please Tell Love for Me 1970 Song on Jerry Rothenberg Poem 1894

Four Orchestral Pieces Jan. 1 1970 Twenty Five Pages and Original skins 1907

Bach Reconstruction for Piano and Oboe 1970 Another in this series of radical, homoacoustic translations. 1922

Bach Reconstruction for Flute and Guitar 1970 A reconstruction work in which only the pitches of the source music were retained; new durations and locations for every pitch were composed. [more explanation of "reconstruction"] 1933

Beethoven Reconstruction "Opus 81a Les Adieux" 1970 Music sheets (copies) Original pencil score. A vigorous sound-oriented work using the ringing effects of the piano. In the years that Edna Golandsky and I were together, I wrote her several large works for piano including Sound Piece, Bells for Michael, and Recomposition Les A'dieux. 1944

Eclat Partition 1970 An eight minute piece for small orchestra with notes in booklet form. 1962

Please don't let me make you Cry 1970 A song sheet by Frank Levy 1969

SOUNDHEAD & Collected Drawings 1970 Copies of Drawings by Ulrich Tasche from Germany and from NY. CM met Tasche. Tasche drew CM as"SOUNDHEAD" - original drawings are in CM collection here. 2004

Whip Cream 1970 Instrumental jazz love song. 2040

S Press Catalogues and Lists 1970 S Press has two unleased audio cassette publications of CM works. They are not listed here. Nicolas Einhorn and Michael Koehler, Munich Germany 2049

Moonwalk One 1970 Aug 16, 1984MLV#R05820. 2187

The Music of CM (13) 1970 Town Hall & Norman Seaman present Sat April, 26. 2474

Postcard Portfolio of Christian Vogt 1970 A photo portfolio sent to CM 2648

Allegheny College CM concert 1970. 2875

GGK Advertising Dine-A-Gram Ad Piece 1970 GGK was one of the first agencies that CM worked for producing jingles and sound pieces. 2899

The Western Wind Vocal Ensemble presents "Music in the World" 1970 The Western Wind Vocal Ensemble presents "Music in the World" Featuring the "Canticle for Brother Sun" by CM 3008

Information on Grants from the Foundation Center 1970 Prepared by the Librarians at the Foundation Center 3174

Directions for Body Movements 1970 Directions for Body Movements 3395

Dick Higgins A BOOK 1970 Original typewritten manuscript, w/ notes on type spec and format, also two pages of corrected proof. 3475

Reconstructions Folder, Bach, Schubert, Beethoven. 1970 Other Media, Bach Schubert, Beethoven Reconstructions 3655

66 Songs for a Blackfoot Bundle (2) Copies from Other Media 1970 In an English working by Jerome Rothenberg, Music by CM 3669

Late Afternoon Chant 1970. 3676

Evening Star Chant 1970. 3677

Drum Chant 1970. 3678

CM Personal Chants. BEAR CASSETTE 1970 CM's first release. Recorded in 365 West End Avenue Studio. Released as New Wilderness Audiographics 7706A b permission. 3679

Radio Art, Four Soundhead shows 1970 Other Media, Stockholm 3749

The Subway A workbook Project for GLCA 1970 Notes and procedures for event planning. Developed by CM as a guidebook for social events. 3860

CM Artist 1970 A promotional piece in Draft form with notes. 3872

Leonard St. Poetry Gallery Moves to Ohio Performance Space 1970 Poetry By Armand schwerner, Michael Andre, Alan Davies, Ray Di Palma, Mary Jane Leach, Linda Parker, Susan Howe, Eileen Myles, Richard Bandanza. Funded By NY State Council on the Arts. 3880

Business Cards for CM (3) 1970 Changing Business cards over the years (3) 3948

Selected Operas and Plays of Gertrude Stein 1970 Edited and with an introduction by John Malcolm Brinnin 4037

Die Fabelhafte Getraume Von Taifun Willi, Dick Higgins 1970 Art by Bern Porter, Signed to CM 4069

National Anthems of the United Nations and their Allies, Boston Music co. Boston MA. 1970 4143

Cinema/Sound Music library Catalog 1970 Second Edition, no date 4161

Requiem for the Victims of Kent State, CM 1970 A nice clean copy of the original Score. 4200

Dick Higgins A Book 1970 Original typewritten manuscript, w/notes on type spec and format, also two pages of corrected proof. 4269

Signal Life 1970 Communicating on Synthesizing Non Memory. 4339

SiMi's Song 1970 Original Song Sht. 4357

Avant Garde Festival Flyer 1970. 4369

Philip Corner for 5 amplified drawing 1970 This piece has not yet been figured out. It is believed to be a Philip Corner piece. 4378

Notes for a Rothenberg Poem Setting 1970. 4383

Earth Day Parade 1970 Software Hotel 4437

Gematria 1970 Rothenberg Poem with rhythm notes from CM a number Poem. 4496

Counting Twos Threes & Fives Pulsing 1970 Two pieces by CM 4616

Die Fabelhafte Geraume Von Taifun Willi, Higgins 1970 Pub. Abyss Foundation, Richard C. Higgins Illustration, Signed Bern Porter 4709

Happening & Fluxus 1970. 4710

Hermann Hesse Poems selected and translated by James Wright 1970 The Noonday Press 4909

Swallow the Lake, Clarence Major 1970 signed to CM, Wesleyan University Press 4926

In one side & out the other 1970 The Ferry Press 4948

Selected Cantos, Ezra Pound 1970 A New Directions book 5006

Aug. 4th screening of Sweet Dreams & Ga Guerre 1970 notes -John Avildsen feature film and William Fertig short film 5115

Crazy Dog Events, Jerome Rothenberg 1970 Crow Indian, A free poem from The Alternative Press 5154

CIRCUS, an outline 1970 A musical event by CM 5156

66 Songs For a Blackfoot Bundle, Rothenberg 1970 Composed for theater by Jerome Rothenberg with Music by CM. This is a working script for a show, with props and sequence of events. Written for Arthur Weisberg and the Theater of Sound. Further notes by CM 5233

Alcheringa, Ethnopoetics Fall 1970 Volume1 #1 editors, Rothenberg, Tedlock First Magazine of Tribal poetries 5247

Terry Blaine Press Kit 1970 Bio, Photos, Invitations to other shows. Danny's Skylight Room, Adelaides Soho Supper Club with Mark Shane 5249

Secret Book of Moses On The Great Name (2) 1970 Mimio Copies 5253

CM Projects List 1970 Four Pages of Projects Listed 5292

Signal Life, Communicating on Unsynthesizing Non Memory Level 1970 Looks Like a CM Concept 5338

CMA Sales piece EARLY Resume and Clients 1970 Also Recorded Material and Concerts listed 5339

New Music in Education, Daniel Goode 1970 A paper critical of the Music Education we inherited from Europe. 5342

Frederick Marantz Piano Recital Flyer for NWF Presented by CM and Sonia Marantz 1970 CM Plays at Intermission Requiem for the Victims of Kent State 5348

Moonwalk One 1970 Follow-up with Sean Mccann on Producing an Album on Recital records. Sonicraft transfers Original invitation to Screening at the Museum of Modern Art NY from Dr. Laura Morrow 5514

Publishers and Broadcasters of Spoken word and Art Audio A list of: 1970 Personal contacts list 5616

S Press edition publishes poetry on tapes 1970 West Germany background info and catalog list 5625

Woodcut B&W print 1970. 2554

Light Music for Piano and Jazz Band 1971 Original Score notes and Skins Sound-oriented mix of new music and jazz colors. 369

Fourth Chant (two versions) 1971 Intense, personal chant recording by CM 380

Please Tell Love for Me (Text by Jerome Rothenberg) 1971 Imagistic Rothenberg poem "Tell Love for Me" is sung/spoken by CM to his coloristic rock score performed by Jerry Friedman, electric guitar; Pat Rebillot, Hammond organ; Andy Muson, electric bass; Alan Schwartzberg, drums

To See Opportunities Others Miss 1971 Intense collage of sound, intended to translate the experience of very loud sound to lower volume levels. 402

Piano Ditty 1971 Sound-oriented short work. 413

Lamentation 1971 Sound-oriented, notated vocal chant based on Fox Native American text in English translation. 424

Sacha Kolin -- Continuous Testimony 1971 Sascha was asked to speak extemporaneously for the length of the tape, 30 minutes. This unbroken dialogue became the sound track for a film about her studio. There is film which CM never had a copy of. 435

Poland 1931 (Text by Jerome Rothenberg) 1971 Original Score, Notes and Cues. Sound collage and multitrack texts written and performed by Jerome Rothenberg: (1) Poland Collage (layers include Dutch Schultz' last words read by Rothenberg, Scott Joplin piano rags from Nonesuch recording, Bob Dylan singing his song fragment "I Pity the Poor Immigrant,: fragments from Ruth Rubin's archive of Yiddish songs sung by old persons, slowed down Jewish wedding march); (2) The Beadle's Testimony (all of the syllables of the poem were sorted into lists and counted, read by Rothenberg, and hand-spliced to "mechanize" the delivery); (3) The Rabbi's Testimony (voice and bass clar in voice rhythm); (4) The Steward's Testimony (layers of tape delay). 447

Circus 1971 A multimedia stadium event showing life rituals as theater. Eventually the audience is stampeded out into a cleansing, gentle second event. The piece uses complex high and low technology transformations and very loud sound. [clarify] Work contains three songs, How can I ask the Morning? Ballon Man Fat Lady 458

Synchronous Breathing and Healing 1971 Using a single leader, a group can through attentiveness learn to follow and breath in unison. This procedure can be used as the center of healing ritual. The score outlines sound and ritual recipes for individuals and groups to explore CHECK TO SEE IF SAME AS OMP-10009 469

Noyes & Laybourne: Guerilla - music 1971. 1138

Paper World. International Paper 1971 60 and 30 second tv commercials 1362

Seven Miniatures by Tom Phillips 1971 11/100 signed art piece. 1541

Air Music 1971 Through-composed work with colors and rhythms of air blown through whatever musical instrument (including cupped hands) is specified. Or instruments in a groups setting. Could be an orchestra, a band. 1611

Piano Trio Works 1971. 1675

Violin works 1971. 1676

Fiddle Chant 1971 Original handwritten Score Composed by transcribing CM's chanting voice. 1733

Vas You Dere, CM? 1971 Original Score, Pencil notes. Light hearted sound and spatial music. 1744

Flute and Guitar Piece 1971 Original Score with pencil ideas and stage notes. A music play including large ear props; an allegory of social and familial deafness. 1756

Breath Chant 1971 An intense breath chant, four-track quartet, working with mannered echos and affirmations. The piece is sound-oriented, and originally intended for very loud amplification. Now it is not so restricted. 1767

Spirit Voices 1971 Notes and Original ideas for performanceShamanic opera based on concepts from Siberian shamanism. The piece represents a spiritual journey: preparation, air journey, water journey, subterranean journey, return. The shaman is bound and released, generates the sounds and gestures that are amplified through the prerecorded soundtrack of chorus, brass, and flutes. This loud and violent work mixes the primitivist and technological. 1792

A Tuba Recital 1971 Original notes and Score Praises, Incantations, Games, Adventures and Chants 1793

Beethoven Op 81a Les Adieux reconstruction 1971 Original Score. In the few years that Edna and were together, I wrote her several large works for piano including Sound Piece, Bells for Michael, and Recomposition Les A'dieux. 1794

Sonata Pian'e Forte 1971 Original Score and Notes 1795

CMs Morning Music 1971. 1796

Bach Reconstruction for Piano, Cello, Clarinet 1971 Using all Bach's notes, changing their lengths and positions in time. 1844

Animal Crackers or Aminal Clackerz 1971 Original handwritten Score Sound-oriented piano work which requires pianist to vocalize. 1866

Two Schubert Reconstructions for Piano and Violin 1971 composed variations on Schubert's song, Wanderers Nachtlied. In 2019, this setting is incorporated in Serenade II 1966

Licorice Music 1971 The piano is prepared with bells and the pianist also uses a Seneca Native American rattle. The clarinet part is transcribed from chant. Commissioned by American composer, clarinetist Meyer Kupferman 1977

Three Personal Chants: Morningstar, Late Afternoon, Drum 1971 Morningstar Chant: lead and answer with headphone; leak feedback reverb Late Afternoon Chant: lead with five tape delays. Drum chant: lead + 3 delay bass drum with solo chant. [clarify] 2310

Net of Sun Net of Moon 1971 Pawnee Hand Game Visions for Paul Blackburn. A Rothenberg signed poster 2484

Stage Works 1971 Flute & Guitar Piece 2642

Music and Sound for Anything (6) CM Associates 1971 Early CMA promotional piece design ideas. 2761

Humanistic Perspectives in Contemporary Art 1971 Writings of Eric Andersen, Conceptual art projects etc. 2926

The Circle of Dance from Lisa Aronson 1971 A small folio of circular graphics, sent to CM 2932

"Original Sacred Harp: Standard Melodies." 1971 "Original Sacred Harp: Standard Melodies." Edition.The best collection of sacred songs, hymns, odes, and anthems ever offered the singing public for general use. Published by the Sacred Harp Publishing Company, Inc. Cullman, Alabama. 3262

CMA Prospectus for 1971 & 72 1971 An informal outline of all projects for the two companies. CM Assoc. and Soundhead 3718

Stanzas for Iris Lezak, Jackson Mac Low 1971 Something Else Press, Barton, VT 4081

The Tablets I-XV, Armand Schwerner 1971. 4129

The Tablets I-XX!V, sounds of the River Naranjana, Armand Schwerner 1971. 4131

Other Media original letterheads and Mechanical 1971 Dick Lopez, art director 4209

I've Left, Bern Porter (3) 1971 Three copies Of I've Left by Bern Porter 2 Hardcovers Signed for CM one soft cover not signed. Published by Dog Ear Press 4220

Pablo Picasso Poems, Walton Press 1971. 4243

A Healing PIece by CM with special love for Jerome Rothenberg 1971 List of Groups doing pieces at Performance. Complete performance order in seven parts. This appears to be the original piece for the performance group. 4499

Beethoven Op.81 a Les Adieux Music: CM 1971 Pub by Other Media NY, Stockholm 4500

Tea Music Poster, C CM, Kent Wood, Marilyn Dubow, Edna Golandsky 1971 WBAI Music Store Presents Sound Pieces at Washington Square Church. also Tom Johnson Richard Bull, Boguslaw Schaeffer, Zygmunt Krauze, Alexander Reik and other voices. 4556

Edna Golandsky Piano Recital Program (2) 1971 Library & Museum of the Performing Arts, Lincoln Center NY Thursday September 23. 4641

The Progressive Rock Market 1971 Two Booklets on the Demographics of the Progressive Rock Market Info from key radio stations around the USA about the growth of the market and influence on the public. 4658

Imagine sheet Music, John Lennon 1971 Sony Music Publishing 4664

A Book of Testimony, Jerome Rothenberg 1971 Tree Books 4786

The Mental Traveler, William Blake 1971 Drawings by Emil Antonucci 4813

The Tablets I-XV, Armand Schwerner 1971 Signed CMs Copy 4831

Sound Head Show, Materials 1971 Notes and Ideas for Sound Head show 4838

The Latitude of Henry Miller, John G. Moore 1971 Walton Press For Charles 1980 Illustration by Bern Porter 19446/6/66 4864

Moving, Bernadette Mayer 1971 Angel Hair 4933

Formalized Music, Iannis Xenakis 1971 Indiana University Press 4953

A Moment by Robert Lax 1971 A small poetry booklet by Journeyman Press NY 5060

The Death of the Proscenium stage, Dan Isaac 1971 The Antioch review 5108

A workbook for Creating Art projects by CM 1971 CM transformation Series Papers Subway Workshop 5195

Edna Golandsky Pianist 1971 Program from State University College performance. Feb. 27. CMs "Bells for Michael (69) performed. Flyer was in the flood and has water Damage. There are two. 5234

Underground Newspaper, Copier Not sure of Title 1971 Anne Bean, Kipper Kids, Paul Burwell, John McKeon 5400

Sunny Maranz Passport Photos 1971. 5454

Full Circle 1971 Presented by The Theater of Sound by William Sydeman 66 songs for a Blackfoot Bundle, By CM. To go with Jerome Rothenbergs performance. Sequence of Events List 5582

CM's NY Transformation Series 1971 Three Workshops 1. The Subway, 2 Platform Chanting. 3.12-4-1971, Transformation series 5609

Bullet 1971 Sound art installation - super slow moving audio bullet crosses a space so listeners can walk around it. 5680

A Healing Piece 1972 A non-verbal ritual for actors, with or without audience, commissioned by and in the repertory of The Performance Group: Wilhem Defoe, Spalding Gray, Elizabeth LeCompte. 33 Wooster Street (SoHo), The Performance Garage, New York City, Renamed The Wooster Group. The piece grew out of workshops exploring CM's techniques and the company's drills. Some audience found themselves left out, raising questions about how best to 480

The Birth of the War God 1972 Dramatic setting of Aztec text as translated to English by Jerome Rothenberg via Spanish translations from 16th Century. A complex vocal work created in the sound studio by CM recording his own multitrack recorded chants, then transcribing them for the Western Wind Vocal Ensemble. The work mixes a variety of chanting styles. It reflects the horror 491

Chanting Music 1972 Studio recordings of chanting voice. 502

Cokboy (Text by Jerome Rothenberg) 1972 A live radio play in which Cokboy, a fusion of the Baal Shem Tov and Trickster, appears in the Old West. The setting is sound-oriented, for audiotape, two actors, sound effects, and piccolo. 524

Apsis 1972 Audience is bound in a web by chanting weavers. The web is woven in loops, each of which is connected to one central point. Each audience member is encouraged to join the chanting as they are tied in. 535

Ascent to Mount Carmel -- St. John of the Cross (Text by Jerome Rothenberg) “on a dark night” 1972 Original pencil score and Notes. Setting of the ecstatic text by San Juan della Cruz (St. John of the Cross) translated to English by Jerome Rothenberg. Using melody in verses, this setting fuses personal and composed chant, as it sets St. John’s inner journey “on a dark night”. 546

Gesture Song: Greeting Music 1972 This chant is based on greeting gestures. At first, a chant is associated with each gesture. Then the sound is dropped and the music hopefully continues in the mins of listeners via gestures only. This is CM’s first gesture music since “Psychic Music.” 558

Apsis 1972 (see above)1088

Meditation on a Persian Theme 1972 Original score and performance notes. Variations on “Dota Yori,” Persian “chant” folk song. Instrumentation includes voice, chamber orchestra, and Persian instruments, and was commissioned by Nassrin Farrokh, a Persian singer. The setting is conceptual, an additive treatment of the chant. 1113

Life before Birth 1972 In chanting workshops, I met people who talked about remembering life before birth, the sensory memories of their time as a fetus in their mother. These pre-birthers stimulated me to make my own journey into the sensory past, experience by experience. Crying with eyes shut triggered the images of color seen before birth. I then recalled the tremendous storm of the birth itself and my first smells in air after being in amniotic fluid, the doctor and nurses in the birthing room of Beth Israel Hospital, Newark NJ on the 9th of February 1942. The remembered smell of the sweaty male obstetrician completed the recollection. 1389

Sun Chant 1972 The phrases of the chant are called by the leader and echoed by the group. This melody became the theme music of the annual New Wilderness Solstice celebrations. It was sung by CM to open SUNDAY - a celebration of solar energy. A version of the Sun Chant was recorded on tape as a live stereo mix at Record Plant Studios, NY Studio B, CM leading the RPS staff singing. It was used as a sounder for the International Radio Solstice broadcast from RPS in ?1978.1402

Greeting Piece 1972 Improvisation scheme Chanting and gesturing, forehead with high voice, mouth with mid range, chest with bass note. di dee dee dee di dee in tthree octives oo o oo, oo oo ho ho ho h ho ho after establishing the pattern, leave the voice out, so that the listeners continue to hear the no longer sung voice 1434

Sixty-Six 66 Songs for a Blackfoot Bundle 1972 This second setting of “66 Songs” is entirely in personal chant form. It is more visceral than the previous setting. Original Skins, 4 Copies of Other media 8 1/2 x 11. 1558

Ray Kelly in front of Fire paintings for CM's Spirit Voices Spring Equinox 1987 at No Se No Gallery, Rivington & Forsythe St. NYC. Also, 4 slides of Fire Paintings by Joan Waltemath 131 Bowery NYC 1570

Organize for Nuclear Disarmament Poster 1972 Volunteers Needed Poster for June 12 rally in NYC 1577

Circular Symphony 1972 A circular standing and seating formation is the context for a series of systematic compositions based on position, sequence, geometry, and transaction. [based on transaction? 1585

Grandma Music 1972 Expressionistic, vocally-influenced chamber work. 1600

Five Different Music 1972. 1665

The Birth of the Wargod 1972 Aztec: a chant piece for six voices, unaccompanied. Summer. English version of text, Jerome Rothenberg. Commissioned by The Western Wind vocal ensemble, NYC. 1673

Trumpet Concerto -- "The Military" 1972 12 pages. This work was written for "An Evening with the Two CMs, Ives and CM," at Alice Tully Hall, Lincoln Center, NYC. The music is coloristic and political. The trumpeter in the piece is unable to overcome emotion and complete playing Taps, the traditional military bugle call for the end of the day and for the end of life. An offstage trumpet player must be brought in to conclude play it. 1778

Granma Music 1972 Original pencil Score, Skins 1823

Air Music 1972 Original Pencil Score 1824

Birth of the War God (Aztec) 1972 Original pencil Score 47 pgs. Script for performance 1825

Licorice Music 1972 Original pencil Score w/notes 21 pgs. 1826

Cokboy 1972 Original Score, Poem and notes 1827

Two of a Kind 1972 Original song sheet 1831

Charles Ives: Variations on America arrangement for symphonic band 1972 Original Scores, Skins copies and variuos pieces of cut music w/5 smaller copier copies. Ives wrote this work for organ. In arranging it for symphonic band, the idea was to recreate the organ colors, translating them into related band colors. Painist, Fred Marantz helped a great deal with the translation of Ive's original organ colors into a wind ensemble arrangement. 1859

Chapel 1972 Original Score, notes and Cues 1870

Spirit Voices 1972 Hour long event - ideally at night outdoors - with surround sound playback of sound track plus amplification of chanting voice and saw player. Pots of fire. - Processional - Preparation for Shamans Journey - binding self- Air Journey- Water Journey- Subterranean Journey- Return to Earth with kitten. Sound track was produced by CM in CM studio, 365 West End Avenue, NYC Concept drawing 2021

Morning Music 1972 Chant-like chamber music for four parts without specific instrumentation. 2088

A Healing Piece, Prefatory Note 1972 CM's Prefatory Note 2469

Sound Graphics Designs 1972 Rough Design ideas for Sound graphics logo. Includes Voice prints of two styles and original art of sound waves. 2698

New directions in music Poster 1972 An 8 1/2 x 11" paper flyer for Town Hall Concert Norman J. Seaman presents free Form Improvisation ensemble. New Works by CM and Gary Friedman played by York String Quartet. James Lee directs Brass Quartet. 2699

A Night of Vision Chanting 1972 Experimental Intermedia Foundation Presents CM: A Night of Vision Chanting January 24th 224 Center at Grand 3056

Sounds Out of Silent Spaces: A performance ritual 1972 Poster: Sounds Out of Silent Spaces: A performance ritual at the Experimental Intermedia Foundation, Philip Corner and Julie Winter. 3471

Arts for Life 1972 A Festival for nuclear Disarmament June 5 at Damrosch Park at Lincoln Center 3481

The Blessing Way A Celebration 1972 with Jerome Rothenberg, CM, Carol Weber, The Western Windand Shira & Stephen Flam. A George Cochran Production. 3729

People's Victory Orchestra and Chorus 1972 Part of a Happening or Concept piece write down your thoughts and send them Anonymously. 3845

Woman rite score by Beth Anderson, words by Ana Perez 1972. 3963

8 Claps 1972 Original pencil Sheet Music for performing this piece. Leader & Group 4006

Mac Low 36th Light Poem in memoriam Buster Keaton 1972 4:50 m -6:18 Sat. Jan. 1972 Signed for CM with Best Wishes, Jackson Highgate 6/3/75 4033

A Book about Love & War & Death Dick Higgins 1972 1972 Something Else Press Barton, VT 4048

The Fall of America Poems of these States 1965-1971 Allen Ginsberg 1972 signed 4061

1 walked out of 2 and forgot it, Toby MacLennan 1972 Something Else Press, Barton 4072

Found Poems, Bern Porter 1972 Something Else Press, Millerton NY 4082

Program Notes by Tom Johnson 1972 To be read while Hearing "An Hour For Piano" 4235

Schaefer Beer Song 1972 Song Sheet and some notes 4358

Wild in the Street Horn Parts 1972 Scores for Horns Garland Jeffreys, Record Plant recording 4385

ETTA 1972. 4440

Sounds from Silent Spaces Poster 1972 At The Kitchen with Metal Meditations Philip Corner. Can also be found in Master Graphics, Carolee

Schneemann art 4493

Western Wind Impartial Vibrations Poster 1972 Birth of the War God by CM 4564

Village Voice entertainment section 1972 A good cross section of working musicians and venues of the times. 4675

Village Voice review of CM Spirit Voices 1972. 4676

The Foxfire Book, Eliot Wigginton 1972 Anchor Books 4945

Shamanism: Archaic Techniques of Ecstasy, Mircea Eliade 1972 Princeton/Bollingen 4971

Recital Options for performance pieces. Blood, Keyboard Music, Tuba Recital 1972. 5228

The EAR INN is Open 1972 Flyer, Now Serving Lunch and Dinner at the Landmark James Brown House of 1817. Menu with Prices. Menu Design by Jean Dupuy and Olga Adorno 5238

Chanting Music 1972 Studio recordings of chanting voice 5265

The Sprit Voices at The Space, Poster CM 1972 Performers are James A. Lee, Rhys Chatham, Gordon Mumma, Stephan Johns, Larry Fishkin, Janet Steele, Ann Garvey, Laura Greenberg, Dan Epstein. 5515

Blessingway -- A celebration with Jerome Rothenberg and the Western Wind 1973 A ritual performance which began the New Wilderness events and the New Wilderness project, although the name New Wilderness came months later. 569

Sunrise Event -- Solstice Event I 1973 We asked the city to print a poster inviting the citizens of NYC to sing from their roofs to welcome summer at dawn or to celebrate by making music in Central Park with Carol Weber and me. We went onto the Great Lawn with a friend and his small child. We sang and danced. The media -- unexpectedly, as we had not sent a press release -- was waiting when we arrived, advised by the city. We were a big news item, and since then I have used the media as a part of my events. 580

Wadi 1973 Collaborative music composed and performed with Carol Weber in the CM studio in NYC. The piece is chant with sound effects and processing, and was composed for the Ze'eva Cohen Dance Company. It portrays the environments of women in Middle East, and uses very loud binaural sound with 2 widely-spaced channels. 591

America (Time/Life TV series) 1973 13 half-hour sound tracks with original soundwork, new recordings of traditional music, and a theme for string quartet: "America Lament." This "Lament" is incorporated in the later work:"4 Rose Stations". 602

The One of No Way (Text by Armand Schwerner) 1973 A chant work with strong atmosphere, built around the poet's voice, invoking antiquity. 613

Four Multimedia Shows for Heublein Products 1973 Big, coloristic, sound-oriented conceptual jazz charts. John Doswell Productions 624

Breath Language Studies with Farmers and Farm Animals 1973 Synchronous breathing was attempted with farm animals in an effort to project oneself into the animal. The results varied with the expressiveness of individual animals. 635

New Wilderness Preservation Band pieces: bells and laughing, barking, whispering, muttering, declaration of Independence, live jam with ethnographic tapes, voices, calling music, laughing music, continuous singing, pure counting music, live and multi-track bugles 1973 Bells and (laughing, barking, whispering, muttering, bugles...) Declaration of Independence Mash, Live jam with ethnographic tapes, Voices, Calling music, Laughing music, Continuous singing (on inhale and exhale), Pure counting music, Number Language, Live and multitrack bugles [needs clarification] 646

Say Grace - a cheer 1973 At the beginning of a meal, when it is time to "Say Grace" The leader says to a group "Give me a G - they all reply G, Give me an R, all reply R, GIve me an A, all say A, Give me a C - they say C, Give me an E, E. What do you have? All say GRACE. Short piece for voices: leader and group of one or more. good for a family meal or festive. Written down after being performed for 30 years! 1179

The Number 6 1973 Wild in the Streets - Garland Jeffreys - CM arrangement 1335

SOHO NEWS Living Music column 1973 Reviews 1399

An Evening with the Two CMs - Ives and CM 1973 concert program, poster, sound recordings. The NY Imperial Pickup Night Guard Military Band, Henry Schuman, bandmaster struck up the music on January 23, at 8 PM in Alice Tully Hall. This anti war protest was presented in Lincoln Center. The forces included a large wind band of top freelancers and the pianist Zita Carno, playing the Requiem for the Victims of Kent State. The Packer sisters of Rye twirled their batons in white costumes and then dr This splendid concert was produced by George Cochran, and designed and programmed by yours truly. I enjoyed the theater and good response, but it was one of my last concert hall concerts in this period of my life. I espoused MUSIC OUTSIDE THE CONCERT HALL, preferring to work in the ambience of public spaces and on the airwaves. I found the blank canvas of the quiet concert hall too blank. I also began to hear site specifically, and to pr The ceremonial perspective of the chanting became pronounced in all my work and writings. Every work was contextualized in location and time. I wrote about these ideas in my journals and in essays like Voice in the Wilderness and in the long term evolving manuscript and lecture. 1410

Charles Ives - Intercollegiate March - arrangement for symphonic band CM 1973 This symphonic band arrangement was created for the "Two CMs, Ives and CM" concert. It is a very beefed-up version of the original arrangement by Becker. 1433

The Permanent Song of My Upstairs Neighbor 1973 A solo performance in which the vocalist repeatedly chants the short nonverbal musical phrase which I had heard through the ceiling from the autistic child living in the apartment above. The vocalist slowly walks in one direction until bouncing off another wall, etc until the song is done. 1447

Wild in the Streets - Garland Jeffreys - CM arrangement 1973 2:58 www.youtube.com/watch?v=3RzBZsOeqOQ My name is incorrectly given on the credits as Charlie Brown 1453

Anthology of N. American Indian & Eskimo Music 1973 Photocopy of notes from Folkways Records compiled and edited by Michael I. Asch from the University of Alberta. Folkways Record Album #FE 4541 19783 1522

Two Songs about a Dead Person Jerome Rothenberg 1973 Concept art piece given to CM. 1544 MME. Shekinah, Jewish Soul Healer and Adviser 1566

CM, Chanter, Collagist, Composer 1973 Poster for promoting projects 1685

America Lament 1973 Original score, skins and performance notes. 1871

Violin Concerto for Cantor and Violin 1973 Original handwritten score. 1872

Charles Ives - General Wm. Booth Enters Heaven arrangement for symphonic band 1973 This symphonic band arrangement was created for the "Two CMs, Ives and CM" concert. It is a very beefed-up version of the original arrangement by Becker. 1989

Sunchant 1973 Original notes for sunchant performance. 2475

Garden of my Father's House, Poster/Program 1973 A concert of new music for Clarinet by Meyer Kupferman. 2477

A Vocabulary for Sharon (Belle) Mattlin 1973 A graphic piece by Jackson Mac Low 2498

"BlessingWay" a Celebration, Poster (3) 1973 Jerome Rothenberg, CM, Carol Weber, The Western Wind & Shira & Stepen Flam. 2560

New Wilderness Letter Poetry Supplement Vol. 1 # 3-43 copies all are stained from flood. 1973 A four page supplement of a variety of poetry. 2724

Postcard from Valentina 1973 asking CM to be their valentine 2997

Sounds out of Silent Spaces, flyer 1973 meditations with Music (and Dance, events, design) Every Last sunday of the month at Experimental Intermedia Found. Loft 537 Bway 5th Floor 3501

Thumbprint Art by Miralda 1973 Barcellona 3649

Sunrise Event 1973 2 Copies of Sunrise Event, Solstice Celebration No. 1 with Summer Solstice Event 1976 & Signals and Calls for Mass Brass and on Roof. Also Bicentennial Drum & Bugle Coast To Coast Taps. 3666

Carolee Schneemann Kinetic Theater Poster 1973 Subtle Gardening or Cooking with Apes a signed poster Fylkingen, Ostgotagaten Sept. 2. 3696

Native Americans in the Arts Presents Coon Cons Coyote and Sly Old Bag at AICH 10E. 38th St. NYC 1973 An 8 1/2 X 11 Poster for Two American Indian Comedy Plays 3732

Phill Niblock and CM an Intermedia Celebration 1973 slides, text, video, performance, audio at the Experimental Intermedia Foundation 224 Centre St. at Grand 3808

Alison Knowles Letter To CM 1973 Alison talks about her Bean Project 3868

A Living Man, Sten Hanson 1973 Poem (1971) Printed in Sweden 4068

Open Poetry, Simon & Schuster NY 1973 Emmett Williams, Ronald Gross, George Quasha 4079

Alice in Wonderland edited by Doon Arbus Photos by Richard Avadon 1973 The Forming of a Company and the Making of a Play. No Info as pages are out of order, book was detached from Spine 4236

Leonard Crow Dog Master Photos, Story, Newspaper, letters, CM's "breathing in and out" for Crow Dog and Wallace Black Elk. AIM Spritual Leader Poster and Court case report. 1973. 4267

Summer Garden 1973 Museum of Modern Art, Pages of Lineup of Talent, Program and Garden Drawing 4285

CMA Ad (2) 1973 An early CMA ad for Trade Magazinecan also be found in Master Graphics 4492

Invoice from Village Voice for Rothenberg Concert w/ New Wilderness Band 1973 Tues. Nov. 27 Village Voice Rate Card, Bill and AD. 4514

Garden of my Father's House Poster 1973 Meyer Kupferman, Clarinetist and Composer Concert Poster featuring new works by CM and others at Carnegie Recital Hall. 4563

Alice Tully Hall Lincoln Center for the Performing Arts An evening with Two CMs 1973 George Cochran Presents Program of Musical Selections CM 4630

The Ladder to The Moon, Dick Higgins 1973 Barton, VT Unpublished Editions. Cover has water damage 4719

Breaking Open, Muriel Rukeyser 1973 Random House NY 4766

Sacha Kolin 1973 Catalog from Show at Everson Museum of Art, Syracuse NY 4804

D2 +D3Z Poemes Partitions, Bernard Heidsieck 1973 Limited Edition #315 Includes two records 4832

Salt seller, Marcel Duchamp 1973 signed to CM, Oxford 4961

A Composition Notebook of CM Notes 1973 It looks like a contacts list of Agencies and contacts of the day. 5075

The Journal of Psychiatry and Law 1973 Federal Legal Publications

INC 5092

Espahor ledet ko uluner! 1973 signed by Guy de Cointet 5100

Two Issues of Vanguard, Vancouver Art Gallery 1973 Article on Sound & Sound Sculpture 5260

CM, An Evening of Chanting Music. 1973 Paste up for a Promo Piece with Quote by John Rockwell, The NY Times. Second Quote by Jerome Rothenberg. 5272

Village Voice Review of CM's Blessingway and Birth of the War God 1973. 5337

An Evening of Chanting Music CM Composer, Collagist, Chanter 1973 Intro By John Rockwell, NY Times. Paragraph By Jerome Rothenberg. 5542

George Cochran letter to Laura CM 1973 With NY Times clipping about Two CMs 5570

Cards: Scientific Descriptions of Nature 1973 A Composition 5607

Job 1974 Meditative liturgical work. Slides of images drawn from the 21 etchings of William Blake's "Job" are projected onto a massive stretch screen in a church before, during and after the musical performance. Multi-slide projector presentation designed and edited by John Doswell. The organist teaches the organ to breath. The percussionist orbits (processes) the aisles around the pews 21 times striking 21 metal instruments and one large orchestral bass drum each orbit. The score describes 21 actions for a parading percussionist playing hand held and fixed location instruments while moving through the church. Premier, 1975, Washington Square Church, New York City. Bruce Ditmas, Percussion; Paul Abels, Organ. Documentary photos by Maureen Morgan 1

Brother John Variations 1974 12 pages. Original Score and notes, skins. Simple and easy-to-rehearse idea variations, some using a rhythm section. For vocals and orchestra. Based on French folk melody, "Frere Jacques." 657

Leucheux Calendar -- A Collaboration with dancer Frances Alenikoff (Text by Richard Grossinger) 1974 Simple conceptual settings using free associations to the names of the moons or months of the Canadian Subarctic Leucheaux natives. The piece is for dance. 669

New Wilderness Fish Cross-Species Event for Fish 1974 Working with underwater loudspeakers, members of the New Wilderness Band performed for fish in music and fish language from the yacht Unicorn, on the morning of Aug. 9, l973. The media coverage was broad. The previous night, President Richard Nixon had resigned. At noon, Ford would take the oath of office. Later, CM was sited in Congress and in Albany for misusing public funds. A few hundred dollars had been granted (by CAPS) for the poster. 680

New Wilderness Riff Off -- Open Jam in Central Park 1974 The public was invited to come to Central Park to jam with us. Unfortunately the invitation did not work. We had a nice jam by ourselves and with the media, who called it the "jam that did not jell." 691

Violin Concerto with Cantor 1974 This chant transcribed work connects two existing works, each written around the story of a baby. The Kaddish was performed by request at the funeral of a friend's child by request, stretching the role of ritual artist into real life, real death. The birth text sound "Baruch," a number blessing, was composed on the birth of the healthy baby of that name, to violinist Yuval Waldman and his wife Kathy. 702

Fish and Frog Languages 1974 Using the transactions decoded by animal communication scientists and our own ears, we perform in the language of frogs and toadfish. First we work in the the frog and fish sounds, then we translate into number language and into music. [first person plural okay?] 713

Kaddish in Tibetan Style 1974 Original notes and Musical score. The solo vocalist, playing a hand-held gong, slowly sings the Jewish mourner's prayer in Aramaic, a syllable for each full breath. New chant by CM. [clarify] 724

Ho Ho -- Healing Chant 1974 Holding on to the father shirt or to someone holding it somewhere down the chain, we chant the "ho ho chant". It is a litany with improv. segments between the returns. [clarify] 735

Jew's Harp Imitation Chant 1974 The solo chanter either performs alone or leads a group in participation. The chant is the vocalization of the Jew's harp sound, using overtones, lip, and tongue movements. 746

The Number 6 1974 A counting piece, a music of pure numers in space. This work is based on speaking the numbers one through six inot microphone one through six. Each micropone has its own amplifier and its own loudspeaker. The speakers are Number patters and performance by CM. Mastered by Hugues de la Plaza. Produced by CM Associates, Inc. 1027

Kaddish: a setting in Tibetan style 1974 the solo vocalist, playing a hand-held gong, slowly sings the traditional Jewish mourner's prayer in Aramaic, a syllable for each full breath, in new chant melody by CM. The Kaddish memorial prayer for the dead is prayer for the living. for armand schwerner. written on the passing of Armand's father. CM s caligraphic score in color representing the voiceThe original score is on paper. CM copied it onto parchment. NOTE: REDUNDANT CATALOGUE ENTRIES HAVE BEEN DELETED 1089

Traveller's Meditation 1974 Eyes shut, open and shut them rapidly like a camera shutter to capture a brief image. Eyes shut, watch the image dissolve in your inner vision. Repeat at will. This meditation explores the human as a machine and can be performed while travelling on a moving vehicle. 1386

Dali 1974 A piece by Richard P. Hayman 1506

Music of the Kutchin Indians of Alaska 1974 Photocopy of notes from Folkways Ethnic Library Album # FE4070 recorded and edited by Craig Mishler. 1523

Kaddish: a setting in Tibetan style 1974 Setting of the traditional Aramaic text for Jewish memorial prayer for the deadfor Armand Schwerner. 1674

Book of Numbers 1974 Compositions using numbers only. It explores number logic as music and audible number relationships, including translated language of fish and field frogs. Though speech-based, the patterns translate easily into other sounds. 1689

Cloud Song (Text by Robert Duncan) 1974 Song SheetSimple unaccompanied systematic setting. 1789

New Wilderness Event for Fish 8-9-1974 1974 Budget notes, Performance notes, Original poster Art, and reviews. Front pg. Variety review Performance from boat through underwater speakers, listern for fish via underwater microphones 1913

Esther K. Comes to America 1974 Jerome Rothenberg's book. Unicorn Press 1930

Ebb Tide, (a musical horspiel) Dick Higgins 1974 A Higgins manuscript written at Silver Hill, New Canaan Connecticut. 2026

Alpha & Omega 9-01-1974 Post Card Poetry of Jerome Rothenberg Stone Press Weekly No. 9 G.P. Skratz, Ed. 2030

The Number 6 1974 (as above) 2064

New Wilderness, Cross Species Concert 1974 CM and the New Wilderness Preservation Band Aug. 9th on Little Neck Bay 2453

L'Amfiparnaso Poster 1974 A Madrigal Comedy with Puppets and Pasta at the Theatre 428 Lafayette St. 2515

Music of the Kutchin Indians of Alaska 1974 Notes from Verve Folkways Library Album No. FE 4070. 2518

An evening with Two CM Flyer and press release 1974 Alice Tully Hall at Lincoln Center 2571

Ebb Tide by Dick Higgins 1974 a play to be heard and be heard twice. Two Copies 2669

Silver Hill 1974 City with All the Angels 2677

Music for Twenty Musicians by Dick Higgins 1974 Dick Higgins Barrytown NY 2678

City with All the Angels by Dick Higgins 1974 A Radio Play 2679

The Two Statues 1974 A musical piece by Marco & Sylvia Rosale for CM and Sunny on their Wedding Day. Hand painted Sheet Music. 2802

Musical Mysteries of Liturgical Chant by Jonathan Cott 1974 Newspaper article mentioning CM and other composers reformulating Chanting. NY Times 1 Oct.13. Two Copies 2817

Favorite (Old man Beavers Blessing Song) 1974 A Graphic piece by

Jerome Rothenberg. A design that looks like a Cigar label. 2944

Touch. Smell Bite or Lick by Frances Alenikoff 1974 Drawings by Frances Alenikoff Signed to CM. 2992

Marriage Certificate and Wedding Plans 1974 to Sonin Mararty 3081

Audiographics Brochure 1974 Brochure of first Audiographics series New Wilderness Order Form for Cassettes Explanation of Audiograph Series 3123

An Evening With Two CMs 1974 An Evening With Two CMsIves and CM Alice Trully Hall The Lincoln Center 3211

Wolfgang Amadeus Mozart: Later Symphonies 1974 Full Orchestral Score of Symphonies 35-41 Dover Publications, Inc. NY 3321

Music for Various Pods and Spores 1974. 3467

Samizdat (self published) A poster for an installation of self published book art of Soviet artists. 1974 A poster for an installation of self published book art of Soviet artists. Rima and Valerie Gerlovin 3473

Sounds out of Silent Spaces 1974 First Sundays each month at Experimental Intermedia Foundation. 537 Bway 5th floor 3573

New Wilderness, Cross Species Concert Photos 1974 Contact Sheet and Negatives from Concert 8 x 10 glossy of CM w/gong on boat 3707

Life Not the same without CM 1974 A Homemade Postcard from Jerome Rothenberg to CM side two being a poem, sent from Salamanca NY 3728

Numbers by Richard Kostelanetz 1974 From World/Summer 1974 An article on numbers as concepts and ideas 3833

Music of the Mind and the World, Tony Conrad 1974 A flyer describing the recorded music 4024

Flyer George Cochran Artists Concerts (2) 1974 CM The composer and the Media also Very special attractions CM Chanting Concert. 4025

Kari Bacon Events Press Kit 1974 Karin Bacon was a producer of large scale special events. CM also was an International producer of Large scale events. 4032

City With All the Angles, Dick Higgins 1974 A radio Play with photographic illustrations by Bern Porter Unpublished editions, Glover VT. 4053

The Innerworld of the Outerworld of the Innerworld, Peter Handke 1974 Signed 1987. 4054

The Urban Review Vol. 7 #2 1974 April 4252

A performance piece by Ilhan Mimaroglu from Idols of Perversity 1974 A graphic statement overlayed on his score that was probably used in EAR magazine. 4317

Blessing Way Poster & Press CM Jerome Rothenberg, Carol Webber The Western Wind and Shira & Stephen Flam 1974 A Concert at Washington Square ChurchCM performs Birth of the War God with Western Wind and BlessingWayConcert promoter George Cochran 4561

An Evening with two CMs Poster 1974 Alice Tully Hall at Lincoln Center review by Alan Hughes 4562

Washington Square Church Christmas Concert Graphic Flyer 1974 Eyes shut, open and shut them rapidly like a camera shutter to capture a brief image. Eyes shut, watch the image dissolve in your inner vision. Repeat at will. This meditation explores the human as a machine and can be performed while travelling on a moving vehicle. 4584

Orgone V for flute and trombone, John Beaulieu 1974 A B&W graphic musical piece 4586

Turned on to Composing Newspaper 1974 Article from Bridgeport Sunday Post CM with students from central high 4597

City with All The Angels, Dick Higgins 1974 a Radio Play with Photographic Illustrations by Bern Porter Unpublished Editions Signed by Both to CM 4737

Womens Work 1974 A Group effort published by The Print Center NY short pieces by 16 Woman artists, Knowles, Forti, Dienes, Oliveros, Lockwood, Wood, Winter, Weber, Anderson, Lucier, Forbes, Summers, Greenberg, VanGunden, Apple. 4742

Sparrow 24, The Cards by Jerome Rothenberg (2) 1974 Black Sparrow Press 4778

Exact Change, Henry James Korn 1974 Book of Short Fiction, Published by Assembling Press, Brooklyn NY 4793

Clairvoyant Journal, Hanna Weiner 1974 Angel Hair Books 4799

Ebb Tide, Dick Higgins 1974 A Play to be heard Twice Rough Copy 4 Pages w/cover sheet One full Manuscript Silver Hill, New Canaan Connecticut Nov. 15. 4814

Dr. Sadhus Muffins, Steve McCaffery 1974 Signed to CM 4904

TSNX C24VA7ME 1974 Sure CO Venice CA 4907

Bacchae sonnets, Armand Schwerner 1974 The Cummington Press 4976

La Poesie Lettriste, Jean-Paul Curtay 1974 signed to CM, Seghers 4979

The Music of Africa, J.H. Kwabena Nketia 1974 W.W. Norton & Company 4980

Poland/1931, Jerome Rothenberg 1974 signed to CM, A New Directions book 5027

The Myth of the Eternal Return, Mircea Eliade 1974 Princeton, Bollingen 5043

Imaginary Music, Tom Johnson 1974 Two-eighteen Press 5050

Directory and Minutes of Annual Sacred Harp Singings 1974 The Sacred Harp Publishing Co. 5088

City Lights Anthology, Thelonious Monk 1974 City Lights Books, 5099

The American Dance Asylum presents- More Dogs and People

Dancing 1974 flyer - Bill T. Jones and Arne Zane 5117

Interlude, Hugh Davies 1974 music notes 5135

New Wilderness Fact Sheet 1974 With Partial 1974/1975 season events. Concert of Keyboard Music by CM Edna Golandsky Keyboard Artist 5229

1974 Ideas and Layout for the Game. Other side is Turn of the Decade Ideas CM ideas 5506

Ear Inn is Open Menu Flyer 1974 Proprietors RIP Hayman and Nina Lundborg. Menu Design by Jean Dupuy and Olga Adorno. 5632

History of Washington Square Church Architecture, Paul Abels 1974 A single Copier sheet 5643

Bass, Bledsoe, CM Finances 1974 Letters and papers - CM settings of Bass poems read by Bledsoe 5649

Ascending Music 1975 Original score and notes. Solo bass trombone - echoed systematically by spatially dispersed trombones, horns and tubas - plays a systematically accumulating line moving gradually from lower to upper registers. This ascent spills out into a high-register. 2

Premier Concerto. Nightingale 1975. 472

Couperin: Nightingale 1975 Dry 473

Premier Concerto. Allemonde 1975. 474

Couperin: Allemande 1975 Dry 475

Premier Concerto.Sarabande 1975. 476

Couperin: Sarabande 1975 Premier Concert 477

Premier Concerto. Gigue 1975. 478

Couperin: Gigue 1975 Premier Concert 479

Premier Concerto. Prelude 1975. 481

B Minor Mass opening 1975 take 1 - use take 2 ID 7. 482

B Minor Mass opening 1975 good take 483

B Minor Mass aria 1975. 484

Clerambault 1975. 485

D scale 1975. 486

minor scales pt 1 1975. 487

minor scales pt 2 1975. 488

The Number 6 @ Phill Niblock 1975. 645

CM New Music Sampler: Khurbn: Peroration for a Lost Town 1975 Reading and Poetry by Jerome Rothenberg (excerpt) 697

Exploration of the Eagle Voice 1975 Setting an even breath rhythm, the soloist, with each phrase, comes closer and closer to an eagle voice. At maximum, the eagle possesses the soloist. Then the eagle voice vanishes little by little, phrase by phrase, until the soloist is breathing calmly to his or herself. 757

Summer Solstice Event 1975 Sun chant and circle dance by astronomers and astrologers at the precise moment of the summer solstice. 768

Chanting in Six Voices 1975 Solo chanter in six different voices, each being a different vocal character. These voices are performed on six different microphones. Each mike is hooked up to one of six channels of amplification, each with its own monitor. This is an exploration of musical dialogue between different characters of the self. 780

Ho Ho on My Father's Shirt 1975 The solo chanter, holding his father's shirt, explains that everyone is requested to connect with this object. The chanter and the shirt are touched by those around, who are touched by those around them, and so on. The song is made up of several ground figures all using "ho Ho" as lyrics. The soloist leads each line into the participation, then solos. 791

Fire Poem (Text by Jerome Rothenberg) 1975 This 9th-century Jewish text from Spain, by Yannai, describes the vision of the burning bush. This setting of Rothenberg's English translation features a lead voice, transcribed from CM's orally composed chant, with four instrumental or vocal echoes. The work was commissioned by baritone Elliot Levine for recital w/soprano, alto, tenor and bass sackbuts. 802

The Number 6 @ Phill Niblock 1975. 963

Hymn Transformations 1975 Sacred harp hymns are varied through numbered transformations, adding repetitions, echoes, etc. The alterations serve as examples of how to transform traditional music by processes which are "easy enough to do by ear." 1001

Who Knows (nose) 1975 The performer says WHO, then points to his or another person's nose. Short piece for voice and gestures, written down after being performed a few times. for Simone Forti 1178

Beethoven Symphony V1 Recomposition Distribution 1975 Conducted by radio or video, an entire orchestra is distributed, singly and in groups, in a park or public garden where the public can stroll through. The first step is to design the seating plan and the communication system. The orchestra should arrive for the performance and depart afterward in its own time to the park or garden, one by one or in groups. OPTIONS, other well known works can be presented in this format. AN EQUALLY INTERESTING ACCESSIBLE SITE CAN BE CHOSEN such as a large library, the main street of a city, a highway, an unused airport runway or terminal, use your imagination. 1384

4 Simone 1975. 1390

Drawing Letters in the Air 1975 One large letter at a time, inscribed the letters of a name in the air so that another person or audience can read them. This is used in Four Rose and other cm works. First was deon at the Ear Inn Thanksgiving Feast. 1394

A Few Drawings 1975 A book by Guy De Cointet signed to CM 1493

Job at Washington Square Church (Press) (10) Also Job Photos 1975 Reprinted from Music/The AGO-RCCO Magazine June 1976 Premier, 1975, Washington Square Church, NYC. Bruce Ditmas, Percussion; Paul Abels, Organ. Documentary photos by Maureen Morgan 1526

Ghost Dance of the Red Nations 1975 L.I.U. Brooklyn Center NY. Spring Weekend Conference March 20 thru April 4th 1542

Beneath The Turtles Shell 1975 A Cure in one continuous strand of events. With Antonio Zepeda, Barbara Benary, CM, Cica, Greg Borst, Porras and Jeff Maron. 1563

A Number Blessing 1975 In this conceptual work, a number is assigned to each letter sound of the Hebrew word for blessed, "Baruch," with the "ch" treated as one. Reducing the text systematically, the poem is stated in each verbal form and then translated to a number. Ends up with 11111, the unity. 1582

Ear Inn Thanksgiving Art Feast 1975 Artists gathered for a performance feast in the soon-to-open Ear Inn. Its owner, composer RIP Hayman, opened the space to the community of artists, many of whom were regulars at New Wilderness events. Each artist provided food and performance or celebration objects/environs. The NWF was a sponsor. 1602

Six fingered Guitar Man 1975 Early pencil composition 1829

Fire Poem (Text by Jerome Rothenberg) 1975 Original Score and production notes 1868

The Song of Deborah 1975 Original Scoresetting of English translation of song from the old testiment 1873

Smell the Roses - arranged CM for TV spot 1975 Music Sheets for IBM use of Mac Davis/Doc Severinsen Tune. 1875

Incredible Bread Machine 1975 Original Score for Scene 6. 1877

Audiographics Cover Art 1975 Master art for Audiographics Sampler Cassette 2020

Song of Deborah 1975 Epic song chant setting for one unaccompanied voice. The text is an English translation of a feminist Biblical text about three women: Deborah the Judge, whose advice leads to Sisra's defeat, Yael the Queen, who kills the fleeing Sisra, and Sisra's mother who waits for her dead son to return. 12th century BC. 2022

Fifth Avenue Pigeons 1975 Original skins and stage production notes. A systematic work in which two clarinets echo each other, also performing are 2 dancers. 2199

New wilderness Explorations of Indian sound and oral poetry 1975 A presentation by CM, Jerome Rothenberg and Avery Jimmerson April 25, at Harder Hall, Alfred University 2450

Jerome Rothenberg, Poland, POSTER 1975 J.R. reading from POLAND 1931 & A Senaca Journal, accompanied by New Kabbalah Blues Bandwith Philip Corner, Carol Weber, CM & Friends. St. Marks Church. 2559

Central Park artists proof, 1975 Woodcut Artwork signed by Ray Guit given to CM 2562

Why Be Good Poster 1975 A performance by Mary Nell Hawk with the Bowery Bum-ettes. Part of the St. Mark's Poetry Project. 2653

Dick Higgins Manuscript Envelope mail from Barrytown, NY 1975 Shipping Envelopes from Dick. 2708

Placing (a study in Location) by CM 1975 Dedicated to Tom Johnson Notes on Breath, Chanting. Rhythm, Sound. 2719

New -Old explorations of sound and oral poetry poster (5) 1975 A New Wilderness Event with Jerome Rothenberg and the New Wilderness Preservation Band at the Washington Square Church. Host: Rev, Paul Abels 2749

Love song for Yu by Llorenc Barber 1975 Musical artwork with explanation from Madrid 2869

20th New Wilderness Event at Washington Sq. church (1) 1975 Featuring guest artist Anne Waldman, Poet joined by CM and friends. 2894

New Wilderness The Grand Reunion flyer 1975 An evening with Jerome Rothenberg and Armand Schwerner with The New Wilderness Preservation band featuring Carole Weber and CM and friends 2895

Placing a study in Location by CM (2) 1975 Dedicated to Tom Johnson an important part of my location. 2 copies 2959

Child of Tree, Percussion solo 1975 Copyright 1975 by Henmar Press NY. Notes for performance. 2971

EthnoPoetics 1975 An international Symposium of Poets and Scholars April 9-12 at University of Wisconsin, Milwaukee.On the Evening Performances program is Jerome Rothenberg 2985

The Interior and Exterior in Zen Buddhism by Toshihiko Izutsu 1975 Sent to CM by Anne Colonomos 3004

New Wilderness Preservation Band Performance 1975 Poster for New Wilderness Event Spencer Holst: Storytellings including "Homage and Imitaton of Jackson MacLow" NewWilderness Preservation Band: Bruce Ditmas, Joan La Barbara, CM, Harvey Schwartz, Carol Weber 3032

Cisco House 1975 Real Estate Pamphlet from the Sale of Higgins' House 3083

The Relationship of Jewish Music to the Harvard Dictionary of Music (1st Ed) 1975 By CM Articles on: Folksong, primitive music, exotic music, oriental music, arabian music, Georgian music, scale, mode, church modes, melody types, rythm for Dr. Joanna Spector 3091

The Grand Reunion 1975 The New Wilderness Foundation and Washington Square Church Present The 21st New Wilderness Event "The Grand Reunion" 3214

The Brook 1975 Poster for the Brook a performance space at 40-42 West 17th St. NYC. Sponsored by The New Wilderness Foundation. 3472

On Obtaining Nixon and Agnew Speeches 1975 Letters to NBC from Carolyn Oberst production assistant to CM. 3594

New Wilderness Event #19 Contemporary N. American Indian Chanting 1975 Greg Borst, Indo American Composer and performer with a group piece composed by CM 3698

New Wilderness # 20 poster 1975 Guest Artist Anne Waldman, poet joined by CM and Friends 3699

A Fish, Frog, Violin & Hymn Counting Concert, poster and Flyer program (2) 1975 The 17th New Wilderness Event at Washington Square Church Multiple posters in Box 65. 3705

B&W glossy 8x10 photo of Spencer Holst and Tui St. George Tucker 1975 3714

New Wilderness Events Poster Jerome Rothenberg & NW Preservation Band 1975 Tuesday Nov. 27 at Washington Square Church Poems Chants for voice & rattle NW band is Bruce Ditmas, Joan La Barbara, CM, Harvie Schwarz, Carol Weber. 3721

CM's Chanting Book Notes and Research 1975 Notes, Letters and Research papers for a book on Chanting. Publishers comments and some wonderful illustrations by Mary Nell Hawk. 3792

John Guth at Eric's 88th st and Second Ave. 1975 special guest Jack Dryden on String Bass 3809

Compose by Numbers (15) 1975 An article by Tom Johnson about CM's The Number Six. Johnson says "CM's Number Six is the most extreme musical statement I have heard all season" 3832

Avery Jimerson, Seneca singer postcard flyers (10) 1975 Postcard Flyers, A New Wilderness Event at the Washington Square Church 3869

10 Leonard St. Poetry Reading Series Poster 1975 Move to Ohio Performance Space 64 Wooster St. Oct. Nov. Alan Davies, Ray Di Palma, Mary Jane Leach Nov. Linda Parker, Susan Howe, Eileen Myles, Richard Bandanza, Michael Andre, Armand Schwerner 3920

4 Ray A Conceptual piece 1975 A mailing by Ray Johnson to be completed or added to and sent back. This is CM's response. 3923

RIFF-OFF New Wilderness Preservation Band at Central Park Great Lawn, 1975 A Jam with CM, Carol Weber, Philip Corner, Julie Winter, G. Richardson Cook, Paul Abels. Bring your own instruments. Sponsored by NYC Parks, Recreation & Cultural Affairs. 3944

Water Harp Concert at Castle Clinton Battery Park NY, Ray Kelly 1975 Ray Kelly's water Harp, 1 photo with two technical drawings of the Harp. 3961

Marilyn Wood and the Celebration Group Celebration in City Places 1975 Nice printed cover with a single sheet printed program 3966

My Life As a Game 1975 CM designs a board Game based on Themes and Times in his life. A draft of a concept. 3990

Celebrate Community Solidarity at Washington Square Church 1975 A performance by and sponsored by The Performers. NWF artists original mechanical pasteup included. 4026

Word, Hannah Weiner 1975 A Journal of Hannah Weiner Edition of 300, this is 294. 4151

@Phill Niblock. Performance of all pages of the piece but the last 1975 The Adult Life Of Toulouse Lautrec Signed 4153

Horse d'Oeuvres, Four Horsemen 1975 A small book by the four Horsemen published by PaperJacks, Ontario. Rafael Barreto, Paul Dutton, Steve McCaffery, bp Nichol. 4173

The Complete works of Constance DeJong 1975 Three of four books 4253

Accor, a composition for sentient instruments by Larry Miller. Sent to Jean Dupuy & Ear Magazine 1975 Photos of the Remote Music Machine 4299

Scores by David Dunn, Music Language and Environment 1975 A large work of musical notations, art, and a composition for solo piano and electronic sounds. 4484

Anne Hammel Pooh Kaye Solo Work Poster 1975 May 8, 9th 122 First Ave at 9th. 4566

Nathaniel Tarn Notes towards A Program Center Institute Department of Comparitive Aesthetics 1975 Letter to CM 1977

Postcard 1978. 4619

New Wilderness Fair Poster 1975 Sullivan County Main Campus Community College 4626

The Number Six, CM 1975 For Solo Chanter and Six Microphones Premier at the Loft of Phill Niblock NY 4640

Proceedings of the National Academy of the Avant Garde, Henry James Korn 1975 Assembling Press, Brooklyn NY 4720

Travesties, Tom Stoppard 1975 Grove Press, A Play 4767

Between Two Points, Geoffrey Hendricks 1975 Dreams and Journal from Meditative Rituals at Byrkjefiellet, Norway Hendricks Chronology of the American Artist 4840

Carnal Refreshment, James Camp 1975 Burning Deck, Providence 4874

Three Tenors, One Vehicle. James Camp, X.J. Kennedy, Keith Waldrop 1975 Signed to CM 4875

The Garden of Effort, Keith Waldrop 1975 signed to CM. Burning Deck 4924

Small is beautiful, E.F. Schumacher 1975 Harper Colophon Books 5040

Artist access recording studio, pamphlet 1975 flyer and equipment list 5137

Number Pieces, CM 1975. 5155

The Number Six, CM 1975. 5226

Personal Chants, CM 1975 Cassette Tape Cover, Might be the Last one 5243

Dali, Rip Hayman (14) 1975. 5301

University of Colorado, Fiske Planetarium Letter to CM 1975 Letter from Gerrit L. Verschuur Director about theme for a show. 5505

Poets and Writers, Inc. Benefit at The Kitchen. Poster 1975. 5507

Schoenberg/Kandinsky Paper 1975 Rough Draft of CM paper on sound 5543

Moray Show Art & Music 1975 Large woodcut color poster. 2544

Chanting Workshop 1976 A two-day workshop exploring breath, chanting, listening, and concepts of the body as a bell.CHANTING Recipes & Commentaries By CM (4 Copies) 813

Summer Solstice Event: Signals and Calls for Mass Brass on Roof 1976 This event on the rooftop of the Clocktower Gallery in NYC at sundown was made up of a series of conceptual signalling and geometric formation pieces. Included were Circular Symphony, dots - single dots, pulse series dots, and a signal arrangement of military bugle call taps. [clarify dots, etc.] 824

Panda Chant 1976 This is a memorial piece for a well-loved house cat. The chanter rocks between two microphones, purring, etc [A Meredith Monk piece with this title 1984]. 835

An Hour of Changes 1976 This piece explores the characters within the self. Each performer improvises in a character for a prescribed time, then moves instantly to their next character for the same amount of time, and so on for the hour of changes. The characters hear each other and may work off each other. A time-keeper may be used, or synchronized watches. 846

Bicentennial Drum & Bugle: Coast-to-Coast "Taps" 1976 For the United States Bicentennial, drummers and buglers follow the sundown in a coast-to-coast arrangement of the military bugle call "Taps." The musicians are placed half-mile apart. Missing links are okay. Start "Taps" at the east coast and go west at earshot intervals. T 1224

OcOrc at Holy Redeemer Church NYC 1976 The long reverberation and dark strange atmosphere of this east village church and its friars attracted Mary Nell Hawk, who arranged for OcOrc to have the place a jam and a recording. 1427

New-Old explorations of sound & oral poetry 24.23a. 23. (9) 1976 Armand Schwerner, Poet and Musicians at Washington Square Church 1478

There are different kinds of writing- 111876(10) 1976 A one hour long Duet for reader and solo bass recorder Spencer Holst & Tui St. George Tucker Washington Sq. Church 1479

Poems Songs & Transformations(16) 1976 Jerome Rothenberg Poet & CM, Composer at the Washington Square Church. Feb. 1st 1483

New Wilderness Events April 1976 (10) 1976 An Events flyer from NWF and Meet the Composer Inc. 1485

Environ Music Festival Flyer (5) 1976 A music festival at 476 Broadway & Grand, 11th floor. with David Murry, Philip Wilson, Kalaprusha Ahrah Difda, Stanley Crouch, Kahn Jamal, Sunny Murray, Hamiet Bluiett, and other guest artists. 1504

Bike In 1976 Poster for Bike in sponsered by Transportation Alternatives on June 6th in NYC also small handbill with route and meeting points. 1561

A Healing Piece Brochure 1976 Printed Piece with text by Michael Rumaker A non-verbal ritual for actors, with or without audience, commissioned by and in the repertory of The Performance Group, NYC. The piece grew out of workshops exploring CM. 1567

Canticle for Brother Sun 1976 Original notes and score, 44 pages. Celebratory setting of St. Francis of Assissi's text, translated from Italian to English by Jerome Rothenberg. Music by CM. Antiphonal music for 6 voices in 2 separated groups of 3. 1652

Chanting Book 1976 Complete manuscript for Book "Chanting" with early notes and papers. Included are a poster for Breath River Route a performance by Malcolm Goldstein & Alison Knowles and a Special Editions Catalog from July, 1985. A self instruction guide to chanting -- functional ritual singing -- with many original chants. 1865

New Wilderness Events Poster 3-0-1976 Poster for March events 1935

Canticle for Brother Sun 1976 3 More copies Original notes and score. Celebratory setting of St. Francis of Assissi's text, translated from Italian to English by Jerome Rothenberg. 1943

Wave Music I: 40 Cellos at Sunset with Gulls 1976 102 pages. 40 cellos in a semicircle, one virtuoso soloist in front. Six celli in the ensemble are virtuosi and echo the soloist, seven are good section players, 26 are student-level or better. This piece is ideally performed at sunset out-of-doors, with seagulls, 1978

Alphabets of Arleen Schloss 1976 A concept book piece #5 Copyright 1976 by ASK LTD. 2025

C Pooh Kaye NWF 1976. 2240

White Columns at 325 Spring St. Poster 1976 A series of presentations Callard, Clifford, Douglas, Gordon, Kelley, Komoski, Miller, Roddy, Shane, Smith. 2465

Philip Corner Artwork 1976 an 11x17" calligraphy piece, to CM 2467

Avery Jimerson Seneca Singer Postcard 1976 A New Wilderness Event at Washington Square Church About 300. 2534

New Wilderness Newsletter Environ Presentation (3) 1976 July and August performance listings 2696

American Variations on Jewish themes, Flyer (6) 1976 Yuval Waldman violin 2734

Book of Job Photos 1976 12-8 x 10 glossy photos of the performance. Original envelope from Maureen Morgan Ardsley NY to CM. 2793

Metapoetries Poster (2) 1976 A concept poster by Dick Higgins 2800

New Wilderness June 1976 Events flyer Includes Summer Solstice

76, June 1st Tom Johnson, 2nd Philip Corner, 3rd Phill Niblock, 4th CM. A bicycle event with R.I.P. Hayman and CM. and Jackson Mac Low June 16th at Washington Square Church 2850

New Wilderness events April 1976 (2) Newsletter of upcoming events. 2853

A Fish, Frog, Violin and Hymn Counting Concert Poster 1976 New Wilderness Events #17 at Washington Square Church, Mostly the music of CM. 2910

Spencer Holst and Tui St. George Tucker Poster (1) 1976 Poster for There are different kinds of writing. A one hour long duet for reader and solo Bass recorder. A NWF event. 2914

Philip Corner A group of sound writings 1976 Silence, Elementals, Sounds out of silent spaces, Dec+sion. signed 2963

Chanting 1976 Chanting Recipes and Commentaries by CM A New Wilderness Audiograph Composition 3140

What-If, Could-Be: A historical fable of the future, by Richard Saul Wurman, illus. R.O. Blechman 1976 Wurnan, Richard Saul, Blechman, R.O., "What-If, Could-Be: A historical fable of the future." American Institution of Architects. 3302

Maria Del Mar Bonet, "Cancons De Festa" 1976 Maria Del Mar Bonet, "Cancons De Festa", Cançons de Festa is really a record dedicated exclusively to traditional Mallorcan songs, this time fundamentally ballads, gloses (poetic verse) and cançons de picat (improvised verse). 3367

Schedule of Workshops and Performances in NYC for U.N. Special Session on Disarmament 1976 Scan in Graphic scans on Drobo 3380

Sixty-Note Fanfares, Tom Johnson 1976 for four antiphonal trumpets 3499

Leonard Crow Dog Poster 1976 A large autographed poster of Crow Dog by Davis. 3647

Ascending Music 1976 Two copies of Music Other Media NY & Stockholm 3667

Crow Dog and Black Elk (a Poem) May 1976 6 copies from New Wilderness Bezoar Box 535 Gloucester, MA 01930

1976 A printed piece in three panels folded 3680

New Wilderness #22 poster Poems & Song Transformations Jerome Rothenberg and CM 1976 Washington Square Church 3700

New Wilderness Poster #21 Jerome Rothenberg and Armand Schwerner 1976 and the NW preservation Band featuring Carole Weber and CM 3701

New Wilderness AudioGraphics Catalog 1976 An Early Rough Draft of the First Catalog 3733

Calling OM Philip Corner 1976 A letter to CM from Phil about live horn sound performance 3736

Philip Corner Files & Sounds out of Silent Spaces (CM) poster in graphic 3759

1976 A folder of Philip Corner pieces, press, letters, photos and mis-memorabilia. Elementals, Sounds out of silent spaces, The Brook. 3759

Signals And Calls For Mass Brass & Sunchant (4 signed copies) 1976 A New Wilderness Event Celebrating the Summer Solstice. At the Clocktower 108 Leonard St. NYC 3782

Exploring a New Wilderness by Tom Johnson 1976 An article from the Village Voice 3978

Summer Solstice postcard WBAI-FM 1976 Postcard is different than the ones in Box 14 Multiples. A scan exsists in Mastergraphics 3992

Synergy & Music 1976 A paper by CM about informal and spontaneous music, energy fields between musicians 4009

CM Sacred music composer. 1976 A short paragraph of thoughts on sound. NYC 4014

Bill Jubobe, Bob Cobbing 1976. 4063

ONE, Philip Corner 1976 Signed copy Includes two pages of Chants from CM. 4137

Chanting Book 1976 Recipes & Commentaries by CM Design by Mary Nell Hawk A New Wilderness Publication. Best copy has been scanned. Find in Master Graphics 4223

The New Wilderness Foundation Inc. (16) 1976 Original Letterheads, Programs, Advisors, Directors etc. 4224

A Decade and Then Some, Allen Deloach 1976 Contemporary Literature Signed by Allen and White Buffalo 4247

EAR original Letterhead 325 Spring St. Rm. 208 NY 1976. 4328

73 Ways to Celebrate the Arts Downtown Poster 1976 Lower Manhattan Cultural Council poster showing 73 non- profits that bring Arts to Lower Manhattan 4363

Mayday Medley Flyer 1976 Laurie Temple Presents an evening of variety 4364

Music Festival Flyer, Environ, 1976 Saturday July 31, a Festival with Hamiet Bluiett & F.T.I.C. free form Telepathic inspirational choir and other performers 4412

Horse Song 13 Horse Song 12 Four track Master Recording CM enginer 1976 Notes from the session on Voices, positions, balance etc. Second Page is About Multi Track recording 4525

Ocarina Orchestra Flyer and B&W photos 1976 B&W 8x10 photos of some members, also some copier Ocarina styles along with New Wilderness Oc Orch addresses and phone list. Photos by Lisa Kahane. 4578

Three Tablets Armand Schwerner 1976 Book is signed to CM has some water damage. 4621

Real Art Ways, Hartford CT Poster Flyer, 1976 Mardi Gras benefit for RAW A batch of music and two films By Phill Niblock 4628

Exploring New Wilderness by Tom Johnson 1976 Five Copies of story from The Village Voice November 8. 4632

New Wilderness Events NewsLetter for April,1976. 4651

Homage to Leona Bleiweiss #1-5 Jackson Mac Low 1976 Copyright 1976 by Jackson Mac Low Xereox copies of 1-5 with handwritten notes for a second performer. 4657

Higgins postcard, Cognitive Questions 1976. 4670

Wanted Poster Drummers & Buglers Solstice Event 1976 Early June Concerts at CM Studios, Tom Johnson, Phill Niblock, Philip Corner. 4679

More, Alison Knowles 1976 Unpublished Editions 4725

Legends & Fishnets, Dick Higgins 1976 Unpublished Editions Signed to CM 4729

Miscarriage in Vermont, Lois Unger Freefield 1976 Small booklet by Land Press, West Glover Vt. 4744

Classic Plays, Dick Higgins 1976 Unpublished Editions , NY and Barton VT signed for CM Book is in rough Shape 4749

Big Idea 4, 1976 Lucier, Corner, Higgins, CM, Knowles, Hendricks, Mac Low and others 4846

Five Traditions of Art History, an essay, Dick Higgins 1976 A poster Barton VT Dec. 30. 1975. 4856

Collected Early Poems of Ezra Pound 1976 A New Directions book 4972

Big Deal 4 1976 Big Deal 4992

The Book of Takes. Paul Zelevansky 1976 Z Artscorp Inc. Books 4995

Rhetoric and Philosophy in Conflict, Samuel IJsseling 1976 Martinus Nijhoff/The Hague 5089

The Painted Bride Quarterly, Oliveros 1976 Pauline Oliveros article on Sonic Meditation 5187

A Paper by Studio 224 About Breath for Musicians 1976. 5261

Homage To Leona Bleiweiss #1 Quadrumanous 1976 Jackson Mac Low 5273

Chanting Recipes & Commentaries 1976 Collected Thoughts and writings on Chanting Design by Mary Nell Hawk 5297

Spencer Holst Stories A NY Times Book Review 1976 Camel through a Needles eye 5459

Soundings Press Catalog Peter Garland 1976 Santa Fe, NM 5468

Letter of Recomondation from Philip Corner Associate Professor of Music At Rutgers 1976 Mills College 5532

International Mail Art exhibition poster 76-80 Five Years research project 1976 Don Emery, Michael Mollet, LA Dada 5560

Ear Magazine East, Flyer 1976. 5612

Desert Plants, Walter Zimmermann 1976 Paperback. Interviews with 23 American Composers including CM 5689

HANNAH WEINER 1977 Recording of poetry performance at St.

Mark's Church, NYC, 2 Nov. 35 Minutes dialogue from 1/4" tape on a 7" roll. 816

New Wilderness Audiographics 1977 CM and Ondina Fiore produced poets, musicians, visual and performance artists, actors, in the original series of 24 tapes. 16 additional Audiographics cassettes were produced between 1980 and 1987. 857

Sky Song Chant 1977 The singer with hand-held beater and hand held gong watches the sky, using the sky as his score and conductor. A tempo for steady even beats of the beater is chosen watching the speed of the wind, giving the beat of the hand-held gong. The melody is given by the color of the light and time of day. Every time a bird or birds appear, a second melody instantly begins. The bird melody is shaped as the birds' line of flight, tracking the trajectory in pitch wiggles, speed, and intensity. When the birds are out of the visual field of the chanter, melody one resumes. In Morrow's usual version, there's an accent or downbeat on the first of 6 note groups. 868

Vision Chant (Dream song) 1977 The vision singer (with or without hand gong) works with at least one witness, a silent observer. The vision singer closes eyes, and drops instantly into the dream world of the nonsleeping, watching the visual images in the head. The chant begins perhaps just before. This chant has been the basis of CM's work since he found it. Doing it on the radio has brought many strong responses. Groups have learned to vision sing. [perhaps we should clarify or leave description to another format]. 879

Mermaid Ocarina Song 1977 A systematic melodic formula, using the single hole black clay flute in mermaid form. Every line is built on a full breath -- deeply inhaled and totally exhaled. The tiny little tail of the breath gives detail to the form. 891

Conch chorus 1977 A two evening event created for the Northeast Kingdom of Vermont in the auditorium of Lyndonville State College. It mixed NYC experimental artists, Native American and North Indian performers, and local rock bands. 902

Planetary Radar and Telephone Lines 1977 Planetary radar -- modulated by a montage of realtime telephone call-ins -- bounces voices off the neighboring planets. Planetary rotation Doppler shifts theradar, and transforms the sound colors. Rebounded, demodulated, the radar is broadcast on Earth radio. Similar pieces can be done with modulated sonar and radar bounced through the sea, the Earth, or through other media. 913

40 Cellos 1977 Track 1 999

Dream Song postcard 1977 Small edition post card designed by Dick Higgins published by Other Media 1092

Hannah Weiner - Seeing Words - Rehearsal 1977 St. Marks Church: rehearsal Nov. 2.1168

Excerpts SVR - 1 1977 1256

Phill Niblock Interview 1977 1259

J. D. - Solo and with Carmen Kolodzey 1977 All Dressed Up, etc. Live performance, Experimental Intermedia. 1264

Ode to Gravity: CM and New Wilderness Audiographics 1977 1376

OcOrc at Bread & Puppet Circus 1977 60 black clay mexican fish ocarinas were handed out to players who sat in the audience in Glover Vermont, B&P amphitheater. 1426

A Benefit for the Crow Dog Defense Poster(35) Original Paste up on back of CGM-10465 1977 Two Ceremonials Lenard Crow Dog & CM Washington Square Church May 19. 1481

Leonard Crow Dog Story(7) 1977 History of Wounded Knee and Crow Dog incarceration. 1482

Post Valentines Day OCK-IN 1977 Ocarina Orchestra at Millenium 66e. 4th St. A free Concert 1539

Disco-Roller Skating Soiree 1977 Invitation to event to Benefit the Institute for Art and Urban Resources Inc. at the Empire Rollerdrome, Brooklyn 1568

Distributed Symphonies 1977 Perform any symphony of choice with the musicians and chorus if any distributed in a location or multiple locations. The conductor is wirelessly delivered to each performer. This may be a park, a neighborhood or disparate locations on Earth or in the Universe(s) known and unknown. 1581

OcOrc New Wilderness Ocarina Orchestra 1977 The ocarina orchestra was formed as a social and musical project. Musically it is an orchestra of like instruments akin to circular symphonies and heard pieces of the Wave Music series. Like the herd pieces, OcOrc is also an outgrowth. 1586

Pieces for Ocarina 1977 A group of conceptual melodic formulae using Mexican traditional clay flutes in various forms. Every line is built on a full breath - deeply inhaled and totally exhaled. The tiny little tail of the breath gives detail to the form. [Do we want to repeat this metaphor verbatim?] 1595

Healing. A Gathering of Healers 2/26/1977 Book created for performance. 8.5" x 11" book bound with 2 metal rings at top. Book compiled by Mary Nell Hawk with help from Cathy Shull(c) by individual contributors A publication of the New Wilderness Foundation Inc. 365 West End Avenue, NYC 1681

Hannah Weiner: Readings from Clairvoyant Journals 1977 live recording -St. Marks Church, NYC rehearsal for reading.Hannah Weiner, Sharon Matlin, (psychologist) was transfered to CD by Steve Smolian. Opening was used by (?) poetry magazine 2002. Recorded and produced by CM 1690

Nine Songs from musical show A Different Song 1977 An envelope with nine individual song sheets. Wedding, One Day Learn to Love Me, A Different Song, When I am the Boss, Going Home, Lullabye, Mother in Law, D'Malley is my name, So Vot could be Wrong. 1853

My Blue Book 1977 A conceptual book. 1869

G E Diamond Slotter 1977 Original Music for GE Spot 1880

Don't Cry Child 1977 Original song sheets for Going Home, Wedding, Lullabye, Mother in Law, D'Malley is me name, So Vat could be wrong?, A different song, When I am the Boss. 1890

A Year of Daily Variations of Bugle Calls and Other Music 1977 Concept for the West Point Wildcats. Every day is numbered (aren't they all?) using the Winter Solstice as Day 1. Each day number is translated into 16th notes grouped in fives -- to be counted on the fingers. This pattern of fives is the ground rhythm, played on drums. Every note of each bugle call played on that day is set in proportion to that rhythm. 1911

A Gathering of Healers/Mary Nell Hawk 2-26-1977 Five workshops with Art and Healing 1920

The Topology of the Will 1977 A paper on Breathing and sound 1925

Score in C 1977 Score by Lawrence Kucharz #10 1960

New Wilderness events Flyer 1977 A general informational brochure on colored stock. Explaining Events, The People, Finances, and Goals. About 150 copies 1964

Wave Music: 40 Cellos. Posters 1977. 1967

Bacchae sonnets - author's manuscript copy Armand Schwerner 1977 - for Chšgyam Trungpa, Rinpoche 2034

Hannah Weiner: Readings from Clairvoyant Journals 1977 live recording -St. Marks Church, NYC rehearsal for reading.Hannah Weiner, Sharon Matlin, (psychologist) Was transfered to CD by Steve Smolian. Opening was used by ? poetry magazine 2002. Recorded and produced by CM 2104

Wave Music I Cover art 1977 Original photostats of Cello Player artwork used on Other media Publishing NY & Stockholm 2476

New Old Science Flyer, Invitation (100+) 1977 Investigating common ground between astrology, physics, theology & music. A New Wilderness event with Paul Abels, Philip Corner, Dick Dobrin, Armand Schwerner & Julie Winter at Washington Square Church. 2558

Keynote Magazine Cover Portrait Photos (3)11x14" 1977 CM ocarina and conch photo originals. (3) 2575

Stone Arch Bridge momento 1977 No. 19 of 100 Mary Nell Hawk 9 E. 3rd St. NY, Delaware NY June 24. 2592

Hit Singles 1977 A collection of poems from eight artists Editors Vincent Katz and Paul Schneeman Open Window St. Marks Church 2606

The Snowflakes of Giordano Bruno by Dick Higgins and other small postcards from '77 and '78. A small three fold card of Higgins poems signed Christmas '77. 2681

Higgins Correspondence to CM 1977 Various notes and letters to CM from Dick Higgins. 2682

Higgins Letter to CM 1977 Letter from Dick to CM from Italy 2712

Cisco House Brochures (6) 1977 A brochure of the old farm dick Higgins bought and remodeled in Barton VT. The brochure was produced in an attempt to sell the property. 2713

Dick Higgins Correspondence 1977 Various Messages and notes from Dick to CM 2715

Stone Arch Bridge Momento (2) with original flyer (1) 1977 Paper for thoughts and Sounds, Envelope for things and Stones, Wax paper for leafs and Herbs Delaware NY June. Mary Nell Hawk 11/100 and 16/100. 2722

New Wilderness Press releases 1977 Press from Tom Johnson and NWF 2727

Benefit Concert for Ear magazine Poster (6) 1977 Tuesday March 1 at Washington Square Church. Large lineup of performers. $3.00. 2730

Simca Heled Poster (8) 1977 Generic poster for promotional needs. 2733

New Old Agriculture Invitation (2) Also two post card reminders 1977 New Wilderness Thanksgiving performance feast. Nov. 24 with readings 2738

A Gathering of Healers 1977 Five workshops, a participatory ritual, and dinner with artists who use healing A New Wilderness event. 2739

Sign me Up! (9) 1977 Subscription form for New Wilderness Letter 2740

Music for forty Cellos, poetry and Dance. 1977 Original paste up artwork. Presented by New Wilderness Foundation and Wave Hill. Supported by NYSCA and Natl. Endowment for the Arts. 2746

Spirit Voices Artwork 1977 Hour of Changes 2755

StoryWeaving 1977 New Wilderness Events NY Woman space Theater Workshop and New Wilderness preservation Band Thursday Jan. 16 Washington Square Church. Host: Rev Paul Abels 2756

Holst Flyer 1977 A reading of poetry and Stories by Mary-Ella Holst and Spenser Holst Dec. 19 at the Bragr Times Bookstore NYC 2784

Benefit Concert for Ear Magazine (10) 1977 Tues. March, 1 Washington Square Church $3.00 2788

Cross Rhythms Concert 1977 Two evenings of original music and dancing at the Alexander Twilight Theater, Lyndon State College. Richard Hayman, New Leaf Band, Bala Krishna, Greg Borst, CM, Ten Mile Shuffle Band. 2851

Birth Celebration for New Wilderness Audiographics 1 Large and 3 small Posters 1977 Performances by artists on brand new cassette series. Corner, Holst, Lockwood, Mac Low, Schechnes, Schwerner, Weiner at Washington Square Church. 2852

Green Mountain Post #5 1977 Hippie Magazine from NY with office in Montague MA. Poems by Spencer Holst. 2856

Quod Tibi Magis Delectabilis by Lloreng Barber 1977 Manuscript by Lloreng Barber 2868

Kontext Sound 1977 A compilation of sound poetry Edition of 1000 Copies Chronology of Sound poetry thru Modern. Discography. Sten Hanson interview 2874

Bellsquiet, Phil Corner 1977 Manuscript for performance of Bellsquiet. 2897

Emmett Williams's Ear (L'Orecchio di Emmett Williams) 1977 Dick Higgins piece for four antiphonal trumpets 2903

CM & Chief Harry Watt Photo 1977 8x10 photo by Howard Sherman 2906

Healing, a booklet by Mary Nell Hawk 1977 # 89 of 200 handmade book of Healing thru the ages. 2911

Wave Music at Wave Hill 1977 Programs, Letters, Research, Posters, Artwork, Botanical Garden Brochures, Contract. 2916

Ear Magazine flyer with original photostat artwork. 1977 John Cage signature at top, Original artwork by Ariana Cot 2957

Beneath the Turtles Shell - poster, event at Washington Square Church 1977 A cure in one strand of events. Traditional Yaqui Indian Deer Dance music ritual 2977

Riff-off 1977 Poster: New Wilderness Preservation Band invitation to a Riff-Off at the Central Park Great Lawn on 81st Street CM, Carole Weber, Julie Winter, G. Richardson Cook, Philip Corner, Paul Abels 3031

Wave Music 1977 Other Media, NY and Stockholm Wave Music with CM 3057

Solstice Changes for Bells, Godfried Willem Raes 1977 Solstice Changes for Bells (piece IV) Full Score 3 players and one conductor/technician Roland's Round 3087

Insert for CM's Audiographics Tape 1977 Insert for CM's Audiographic Tape: A Variety of Chants, The New Wilderness Foundation Featuring: Panda, Healing, Counting to 9 in 3 Locations, Sun Chant, Chant with Watches, Mass Chant on Ho Ho 3165

Bound Mary Nell Hawk writings: "Healing" 1977 Mary Nell Hawk Writings"Healing" 3311

Poster/Schedule for Summer Solstice 1977 Schedule for Summer Solstice: New Wilderness Celebration Radio 3374

Ghost Dance 1977 New Wilderness Grant Information with card to CM Fiona David and Marilyn '77. 3375

Christmas card from Dick Higgins 1977. 3484

Nine Postcards from Dick Higgins 1977. 3486

Four Fanfares for the month of June, Dick Higgins 1977 Four Fanfares, I- Canon, II-Stars, III-Tarantara, IV- Hymn for Trumpet 2 in Bb. 3498

Sing Cuckoo, Fanfare for Summer, Tui St-George Tucker(4) copies. 1977. 3500

Philip Corner-AG7701 Breath Chants 1977 Audiographics Cassette Insert 3510

Philip Corner-AG7701B Metal Meditations 1977 Audiographics Cassette Insert 3511

Leonard & Mary Crow Dog AG-7702A Peyote Songs 1977 Audiographics Cassette Insert 3512

Leonard & Mary Crow Dog AG7702AB Peyote Songs 1977 Audiographics Cassette Insert 3513

Spencer Holst AG7703A Reading From his stories 1977 Audiographics Cassette Insert 3514

Spencer Holst AG7703B1 The Institute for the Foul Ball Part 1 1977 Audiographics Cassette Insert 3515

Spencer Holst AG7703B2 Institute for the foul Ball Part 2 1977 Audiographics Cassette Insert 3516

Annea Lockwood AG7704A Tiger Balm 1977 Audiographics Cassette Insert 3518

Annea Lockwood AG7704B Malaman 1977 Audiographics Cassette Insert 3519

Jackson Mac Low AG7705A Poetry and Music 1977 Audiographics Cassette Insert 3520

Jackson Mac Low & Pauline Oliveros AG7705B Homage to Leona Part 1 1977 Audiographics Cassette Insert 3521

Jackson Mac Low & Pauline Oliveros AG7705B Homage to Leona Part 2 1977 Audiographics Cassette Insert 3522

CM AG7706A Personal Chants 1977 Audiographics Cassette Insert 3523

CM AG7706B Healing Chant and Others 1977 Audiographics Cassette Insert 3524

CM AG7706C Hour of Changes 1977 Audiographics Cassette Insert 3525

Jerome Rothenberg AG7707A Six Horse Songs for Four Voices 1977 Audiographics Cassette Insert 3526

Armand Schwerner AG7708A Readings 1977 Audiographics Cassette Insert 3527

Armand Schwerner AG7708B Sophocles Philoctetes, trans. A.S. 1977 Audiographics Cassette Insert 3528

Richard Schechner 7709A New Guinea Tapes 1 1977 Audiographics Cassette Insert 3529

Richard Schechner 7709B New Guinea Tapes 2 1977 Audiographics Cassette Insert 3530

Richard Schechner 7709C New Guinea Tapes 3 1977 Audiographics Cassette Insert 3531

Hanna Weiner AG7710 Readings from the Clairvoyant Journals 1977 Audiographics Cassette Insert 3532

Sampler Cassette AG7711 Excerpts from Series 1977 Audiographics Cassette Insert 3533

Alison Knowles AG7712A Natural Assemblages and the True Crow 1977 Audiographics Cassette Insert 3534

Talking Band AG7914A Kalevala:an epic of Finland 1977 Audiographics Cassette Insert 3535

R.I.P. Hayman AG8115A Dreamsound, India Transformed 1977 Audiographics Cassette Insert 3536

R.I.P. Hayman AG8115AB Hearsayseeing 1977 Audiographics Cassette Insert 3537

Jonathan Albert AG8116A Love Songs 2: The Shuman Dreams 1977 Audiographics Cassette Insert 3538

Donna Henes AG8120A Roll'Em on Honey 1977 Audiographics Cassette Insert 3539

Tom Johnson AG8122A Secret Songs 1977 Audiographics Cassette Insert 3540

Patty Mucha AG8124A Cross Fire 1977 Audiographics Cassette Insert 3541

Ocarina Orchestra AG8126A It must have been the candle 1977 Audiographics Cassette Insert 3542

Bread & Puppet Theater AG8129A Music from Joan of Arc, Goya and their plays 1977 Audiographics Cassette Insert 3543

Bern Porter AG7913A Found Sound 1977 Audiographics Cassette Insert 3545

Alkion Knowles AG8112A 1977 Audiographics Cassette Insert 3546

Anne Tardos AG8137A Gatherings 1977 Audiographics Cassette Insert 3547

Alene Schloss AG 8128A How she sees it By Her 1977 Audiographics Cassette Insert 3548

Bernard Heidsieck AG8233 Le Carrefour de la Chaussée d" Antin 1977 Audiographics Cassette Insert 3549

Barbara Benary AG 8442A Gamelan Son of lion 1977 Audiographics Cassette Insert 3550

Dick Higgins AG8140A Sound Poems 1977 Audiographics Cassette Insert 3551

R.I.P. Hayman On The Way 1977 Audiographics Cassette Insert 3552

R.I.P. Hayman Sounding the I Ching 1977 Audiographics Cassette Insert 3553

New Wilderness Letter #1 1977 Vol. ! #1 CM & Rothenberg, Eshleman, Cohen, Lenowitz. 3554

Gem Duck 1977 An Opera in 5 Greys and 6 acts by Alison Knowles. With Phil Corner, Malcom Goldstein, Daniel Goude, Jackson Mac Low,

Amparo Rossello. At the Experimental Media Foundation 224 Center St. 3569

Vision Singer and Witness Artwork 1977 A positive and Negative blow up from the original postcard by CM. 3648

New Wilderness Letter Story 1977 Origins and development of New Wilderness Letter 3709

Wave Music Review by Rochelle Ratner (50) 1977 From the SoHo News June 23, 1977. About 50 copies 3725

Phill Niblock Music and Film Poster 1977 Film from Portugal and Brasil, Music: Arthur Stidfole, Barbra Held Produced by Experimental Intermedia Foundation at St. Marks Church in The Bowery 3753

Leonard Crow dog visit to CM 4-2-77 1977 Thoughts on the way to a Vision Telling The vision 3919

Solstice Satellite Illus. (3) 1977 Illustration of Radio broadcasts from space from Westar 4, uploads and downloads for solstice event. 3937

Andor Orland Poster 1969- 1977 1977 A Science-Art Multimedia Lecture Presentation. 3969

Taltet, The Tent Project 1977 Sweden's touring tent group of performing Artists travel to 30 towns and present their show about Save our Jobs 3970

Ear Magazine Subscription Ad (2) 1977 John Cage Endorsement at top of Ear Magazine subscription ad. 3974

New Wilderness on Transfigured Night Postcard 1977 Five Live Concerts on WKCR-FM 1-2 AM Brooke Wentz Host Mon. CM and Mary Jane Leach Note. Passing. Note other presentations by Arleen Schloss, R.I.P. Hayman 4021

The Choice, Rose Drachler 1977 Signed To CM in honor of a sudden andreal friendship 4038

Mind Breaths Poems 1972-1977 Allen Ginsberg 1977 City Light Books 4042

Cross Country 8/9 1977 a magazine of Canadian-US Poetry 4070

The work, the Joy, the triumph of the will, Armand Schwerner 1977 Postcard message signed 4128

Wystawa Poster, Laboratorium Sztuki Galeria El 1977 Sztuka, Motorcycle Art 4184

Antivalues art magazine Poster 1977 Polish poster from Uni Art 4186

New Wilderness Letter origins Page 1+2 1977. 4205

"Towards an Allusive Referential" from A Dialectic of Centuries by Dick Higgins 1977 An Original Manuscript with corrections 4213

New Literary History 1977 A Journal of Theory and Interpretation of Print Vol 8 1976-77. 4242

Sea of Celli, Press (20) 1977 Wave Music for forty Celli 4279

New Wilderness Letter Vol.1 #1 1977 Editor Jerome Rothenberg

4304

Lesbian Couples Flyer 1977 A workshop on closeness and intimacy by Bernice Goodman 4330

Horse Film Cues and music 1977 Music for Kentucky Horse Park entrance film 4382

Nighthawk! Warren Burt soft cover book 1977 Part 1: 40 theo-Rhetical Musical Statements. A happening type performance 4482

Song of Bubbles Poster and Music by Julia Lebentritt 1977 Back of Poster is Julia's Excerpts from Lecture On Time a Multimedia Gig. A sound artist 4559

Jackson Mac Low Photo 8x8 Glossy for Catalog, Photo by Toby Olson 1977. 4574

Night Shift w/Rip Torn presented by the Labor Theater, Poster 1977 Play by Martin Goldsmith Directed by C.R. Portz 4575

13th Annual NY Avant Garde Festival Poster 1977 Held at the World Trade Center 19th of June. Large list of Participants on Oversized color Poster 4594

Theater for the New CIty Moving Poster Talking Band 1977 Winter Schedule Talking Band Spiderwoman Workshop 4620

Real Art Ways Space flyer, Hartford CT 1977 John Cage Autograph on Flyer. Back has Empty Words by John Cage Graphic of John Cage and in the RAW Gallery the John Cage Scores Collection. 4627

Real Art Ways Gala Opening Weekend Newspaper insert Hartford CT 1977 Philip Glass/Solo Music. Program Notes Laurie Anderson, Phil Corner 4629

New Rituals and Ceremonies in the Environment, SEMINAR poster 1977 Director Marilyn Wood also with Annea Lockwood at Ghost Ranch Santa Fe, New Mexico 4639

Lee Bridges, Introducing the Author 1977 Available for Recitals 4650

Letter to Ondina from Jim Theobald 1977 Graphic letter about two pieces for EAR magazine 4673

Letters from Phil Dadson about CM events 1977 Phil Dadson c/o Fine Arts School University of Auckland Auckland New Zealand 4695

The Epitaphs, Higgins 1977 Made in Italy Richard C. Higgins 4711

Gem Duck, Alison Knowles 1977 Pari & Dispari - Signed to CM. Alison Knowles 4712

Casablanca Carousel, Marina La Palma 1977. 4746

Society of the Spectacle, Guy Debond 1977 Published by Black and Red, Detroit 4764

Cage's Train, John Cage, Nino Monastra 1977 Audio Tape and book Signed To CM 4800

Six Fillous, Steve McCaffery, Dick Higgins, B.P. Nichol, George Brecht, Dieter Roth, Robert Filliou 1977 B.P. Nichol's translation of Robert Fillious 14 Chansons et 1. 4803

Life on his wife's casting couch, Dick Higgins Postcard (9) 1977 West Glover, VT Milwaukee 4853

Phantom Pod, Cardarelli, Hollo, Malone 1977 Phantom House, Pod Books Signed to CM, Kirby Malone 4872

Londonettes & Underground Reading, Tony Green gee 1977 Signed to CM 4882

Kontexts, winter 76/77 1977 publications 5013

The Microcosm, Nathaniel Tarn 1977 Membrane Press, signed 5101

Coaccident poetry music performance 1977 program flyer 5132

A selection of 'sounds heard", Hugh Davies 1977 poems 5134

Wave Music Program (Cellos) 1977 Fri. June 10th at Wave Hill, Bronx, NY 5142

Doug Dobins Photo Glif, Hornby Is. BC 1977. 5163

Homage to Jackson Mac Low on my 35th Birthday, CM. 1977 A series of 7 basic forms of number and word repetitions. 5164

Graphic Art Piece Invitation, Timothy Samara 1977 A Creative Invitation to an Open House, Autumn Harvest House Warming. 5165

Gematria 27, Jerome Rothenberg, Harris Lenowitz 1977 Combinations of Numbers and Letters to produce a code like system. A concept piece from Rothenberg. A small box with cards inside. Membrane Press 5172

Songs of Healing and Entrance, Rochelle Ratner 1977 Printed for Friends, Christmas. A small booklet of thoughts and poems. 5173

Variety Theater: An Anthology of Sound Poetry, Ruppenthal & Wendt 1977 Audiozine Publication copy C. Amirkhanian, Steve McCaffery 5202

New Series of Poetry Readings at Bragr Times 1977 A Poster NOTICE, Schwerner, CM, Holst, NWF Friends 5316

Rolands Round - Godfried Willem Raes 1977 transposed score for the Ghent Carillon. Radio Solstice 5321

New Wilderness Holiday Get Together Invitation 1977 CM's 365 West End Ave. Apt. 8C. 5332

The First New Wilderness Audiographics Catalog (2) 1977. 5349

Reindeer Werk, Dirk Larsen, London 1977 An Art piece Card Catalogue Limited Edition of 100. 5387

Decadance Advance Postcard 1977 Judith Scott Theater Presents at the American Theater Lab, Jan. 27-30. 5389

All City Marching Band Performance Schedule 1977. 5429

Waves, R.I.P. Hayman score for Ensemble 1977. 5470

Sterling Info and Letters 1977 William Manning, Craftsbury Common VT Letter about scholarships 5504

Limited edition Calendar by Dan Murray 1977 The Calendar of Poems, In memory of my son Jimmy. Woodcut type artwork on Cover 5533

Action/Dialog/Action/Music 1977 Other Media CM Needs Backing 5561

Music from RUTGERS program 1977 Phil Corner, Noel DA Costa, Michael Smolanoff and others at Carnegie Recital Hall 5578

From Scratch, A letter from New Zealand Phil Dadson 1977. 5580

Scippio Henderson 1977 Letter stating his interest in working with Solstice project. 5581

Benihana -mus. only 1978. 90

If you ever meet a Dinosaur, Camilla During Dadson 1978 1. Wrinkly Fingers 2. In the Band 3. Autumn Leaves 4. In my Garden 5. Clap,Clap 6. You'll never Guess 7. Insect Dance 8. Who's That? 9. Flying 10. Rosie 11.Get Out 12. We can hear you 13. Let's make noises 14. My Place 15. Can you eat your T 632

Requiem for George Maciunas 1978 Water sprinklers of all sorts are set out on a large lawn. They perform the requiem in a long symphony of changes. 924

Night sky chant 1978 The singer with handheld gong watches the sky, using the sky as his score and conductor. A tempo is chosen watching the speed of the wind, giving the tempo of the handheld gong beat. The melody, which is derived by formula, is sung at this tempo and unfolds its parts. The mood of the melody is given by the color of the light and the time of night. Every time a breeze or wind comes up, a second melody instantly begins. This melody is shaped by the breeze, tracking it in pitch wiggles, speed and intensity. When the breeze is gone, the chanter resumes the first melody. 935

Turtle Ocarina Songs 1978 A melodic formula systematically using the four-hole brown clay flute in turtle form. Every line is built on a full breath -- deeply inhaled and totally exhaled. The tiny little tail of the breath gives detail to the form. 946

New Wilderness Country Fair Stone Arch Sullivan County, Program (1) 1978 100 New Wilderness and local upstate NY artists collaborated in a designed event at Loch Sheldrake, NY. Visually prominent throughout the day was a maze by Gray MacArthur with a gauze-curtained sculpture by Donna Byars at its center, and balloon sculptures by Maude Boltz. At the end, a concert band -- playing works of Hayman, Mac Low, Zummo, and Morrow -- disappeared into a corn field with little lights blinking like fireflies. 957

Two Different Kinds of Whistling 1978 The whistler -- accompanied on hand gong -- alternates between an exhaled whistling and an inhaled whistling. The participants gradually take over from the whistler. 968

Sunday: Skysong for Solar Energy 1978 "Sunday" -- an event for solar energy organized by CAN, led by Mrs. Robert Redford -- April at the United Nations north patio, NYC. CM, Leonard Crowdog, Carman Moore, Robert Redford, et. al., with TV and radio news coverage worldwide. CM [what's CAN?] 979

At First Vespers 1978 This work is for Christmas Eve at midnight in the Cathedral. One soprano is near the altar, the other at the opposite end of the room (in the premier, with the choir, organ, and orchestra). Each soprano has a crotale bell. All echoing music clearly comes from the two ends of the sacred space, except for crotales struck in unison. 990

A Voice in the Wilderness: Seance vs. Vision Music 1978 Essay by CM. Included in the book, Sound Poetry: A Catalogue. For the Eleventh International Sound Poetry Festival, Toronto, Canada, October 14 to 21. Edited by Steve Mcaffery & BP Nichol Underwhich Editions Press, Toronto 1196

New Music Chants and Whistles & Gesture pieces 1978 Held at the Bath Dance Works, Bath Maine Monday October 5th A Free Concert 1490

Sound Poetry - a Catalogue 1978 For the 11th International sound poetry Festival in Toronto Canada. 1497

Emergency 1978 Many vehicles with sirens travel -- perhaps long distances -- with their sirens on and arrive at a common place at the same time. There they perform together. They fall silent. Later they depart, simultaneously, and their sirens turn on systematically. 1513

Georg de Cristel conceptual piece 1978 Speaking short poetic patterns for meditation onto tape, which is then sonagraphed and photocopied then make copies of copies diminishing the original blackness. 1525

Summer Solstice Posters '78 Thru '87 1978 from New Wilderness Foundation. 1560

Wave Music II: Solo Parades 1978 Each musician leaves his/her house and begins to play. Each continue playing all the way to the performance site, meeting other musicians along the way. The arrivals are staggered. When all have arrived, the final section is played. 1569

A Calendar: The Year of The Messiah 1978 A setting of this calendar poem (translated from the ancient Hebrew) for Jews'-harp playing chanter. The piece is very emotionally intense, strophic song, sometimes performed with hand drums.Performed with Glen Velez, hand drum, at 12th International Sound Poetry Festival 1980, Washington Square Church NYC 1583

The Train to the Plane 1978. 1636

Mazola Collection 1978 A group of pieces from CM's work in advertising music. The collection includes "Ma-z oo-la" and "Corn Goo-oodness." 1645

2 Recipes: Hymn Transformations A Year of Daily Variations for Bugle Calls and Other Music 1978 6 pages. Collection. Based on the hymn "Meditation by Elisha West." Concept for the West Point Wildcats. Every day is numbered (aren't they all?) using the Winter Solstice as Day 1. Each day number is translated into 16th notes grouped in fives -- to be counted on the fingers. This pattern of fives is the ground rhythm, played on drums. Every note of each bugle call played on that day is set in

proportion to that rhythm. 1660

Impulse 90 1978 Handwritten music, skins 1881

Eighth Notes & Variations for Regina Beck 1978. 1910

Color Matrix 5-23-1978 1978 A performance piece by Peter Zummo 1954

Four fanfares for the Month of June 1978 Notes and performance cue cards for a sound piece by Dick Higgins or Jim Theobald. Also contains Sing Cuckoo (fanfare for Summer by Tui St. George Tucker, and Summer Alleluia. 1959

Wave Music II: 100 Musicians with Lights 1978 A spiral of 100 musicians stands ready under the moon as a Native American singer sings his song. The sounds move outward through the spiral in canon form, to become a multicural dance rhythm. The heraldic, systematic melody sounds in the  horns and gradually becomes marching dance music. Five expanding rings of 20 musicians each turn their little body lights on, and move out playing and blinking. [multicural?] 2011

Other Media Master Cover Art 1978. 2019

A Noted Vocabulary for Eve Rosenthal 1978 A musical Graphic Art piece by Jackson Mac Low 2490

American Horse Oglala Sioux 1978 A silkscreen poster by Kat Brennan 2492

Snug Harbor Cultural Center 1978 Contemporary Music and Poetry presented by Armand Schwerner. CM performs Dream Songs, Whistling and Gesture Music 2529

Benefit Concert for Ear Magazine 8.5 x 11" Poster 1978 With Beth Anderson, Michael Cooper, Nina Canal, Rip Hayman, CM and a large list of Artists. At 425 Broome St. 2535

Storefront A to Z festival 26 day performance event 1978 Poster and set up info for Concerts every night from Sept.18 Thru Oct. 13th. Concerts at 51 Prince St. Storefront for Art and Architecture. Horzontal Vertical Band performs final night. 2538

Five Concerts of Improvised Musicat AIMI Studio 686 Lexington Ave. Poster 1978 Sat 19th CM and Lesley Dalaba and Derek Bailey. 8 Posters 8.5 x11" 2539

Annual Avant Garde Festival 2nd Cambridge River Festival 20 May 1978

1978 Large Color poster 2545

Computer Portraits of CM #25805, 25806 1978 Early computer art dot Matrix prints 2574

Sensations of the retina #200 1978 A seven page Graphic work by Bob Cobbing. Two Copies #15 in the intermediate series of Gronk. An edition of 200 copies 2577

7, 5x7 Photos from Mary Ellen Morrow 1978 Performance and casual photos By Mary Ellen Morrow 2580

Cabrillo Music Festival 1978 Concert Program Booklet 2611

Crow Dog The Silent Singer (2) by Richard Erdoes 1978 Photocopy of an article in Sing Out w/photos, also a copy of benefit poster 2619

Rare NY Visit Bern Porter Poster art by Charles Stanley (2) 1978 Bern Porter Poetry reading Jan. 11-15:11th with CM and Rip Hayman ,14th with CM 2654

Postmodern Performances: Some Criteria and Common Points By Dick Higgins 1978 Original Manuscript West Glover VT. July 16 salvaged from CM house flooding. Some damage to page one. 2706

Beneath the Turtles Shell Poster (2) 1978 A healing Presentation by Antonio Zepeda, Barbara Benary, CM, Cica, Greg Borst Porras, Jeff Maron. 2736

Jazz Composer Showcase Poster (4) 1978 Sponsored by New Wilderness Foundation and The Human Arts Association Presented by La Mama Etc. 2762

NY Mosaics (3) 1978 1900-1933 A brochure about the early Italian Craftsmen and architects. Mary Nell Hawk 2764

Food for the Soup kitchens 5 1978 Oct. 4th CM performance 2771

New Wilderness fair in Sullivan County program (15) Loch Sheldrake, NY July 1st 1978. 2779

11th International Sound poetry Festival Catalog Toronto Canada Oct.14 to 21. 1978

1978 edited by Steve McCaffery and bp Nichol Published by Underwhich Editions, Toronto 2792

Summer Solstice Music and Light 1978 Original poster concept Art for June 21, 1978 Produced by New Wilderness Foundation 2795

CM Color Photographs (2) 1978 Two Different sides of CM. Color enlargements for display or print. C-Prints A long haired CM shot for Jagermeifter, and the formal wear concert type promo. 2808

Heart of the Earth Survival School 1978 A yearbook from a progressive American Indian School. Drawings, Photos, Poems. Included is the brochure for the We Will Remember Survival Group. This is a Wounded Knee remembrance dedicated to Hilda Red Bear 1973. 2839

Higgins Girls in Vermont 1978 Photo of Jesse and Hannah Higgins in Barton Vt. Photo by T. J. Walbert 2892

A New Series of Poetry Readings 1978 Readings at the Bragr Times 165 Duane St. at Hudson NYC. Partly funded by a grant from The Cosmic Pig. Holst, CM, Schwerner. 2898

Jazz composer Showcase 1978 La Mama ETC presents The Human arts Association & New Wilderness Foundation 2907

New Wilderness Events 12 & 13 Poster 1978 NW preservation Band, James Camp Poet, Spencer Holst, small Visions. 2912

Summergarden 1978 Fanfare celebration at Museum of Modern Art NY. Summergarden Notes, Program and memoribila, Horn in F by Jim

Theobald, Sing Cuckoo by Tui St. George Tucker. Score for Fanfare for the month of June by Dick Higgins. Ascending Music by CM. 2915

Selected pages by Michael Gibbs 1978 A manuscript signed to CM. Limited edition of 300, this is copy 109. Art text and concept text pieces. Published in Amsterdam 2965

Music/Language Performance 1978 Poster for Freely invented Music/Language Armand Schwermer, Butch Morris, CM, Mercer St. NYC. 3030

Snug Harbor Cultural Center Three July Programs 1978 Snug Harbor Cultural Center Three July Programs Contemporary Music and Poetry Featuring New Wilderness Wind and CM Performing Dream Songs 3201

Summer Solstice Music and Light 1978 Celebration in Central Park 3205

Artwords and Bookworks 1978 An International exhibition of recent artists' books and ephemera Co-curated by Juth A Hoffberg and Joan Hugo Artist's Space, NYC Herron School of Art, Indianapolis, New Orleans Contemporary Art Center 3215

"Sound:Space" by Bernhard Leitner 1978 NY University Press, NY. Signed to CM; not by the author. 3259

A Notated Vocabulary for Eve Rosenthal by Jackson Mac Low 1978 Performance Instructions Copyright 1978 NY 3343

Original Collage Poster 1978 Original Collaged Poster Reads: "That's the real turn-on" "Zoun Zounds," "Cheap Thrill" 3344

Manuscripts and Correspondence with Dick Higgins 1978 Chapters authored by Higgins about the Parceling of Higgins' land. Scheduling for Higgins' projects 3358

Correspondence with Dick Higgins about writings 1978. 3373

Performance Instructions for A Notated Vocabulary for Eve Rosenthal 1978 by Jackson Mac Low 3391

Banner Workshop Notes/Banner-making directions 1978. 3400

Dick Higgins Bio/Bibliography 1978 Draft 5.78 Final type spec and design was by Jay Walbert at Creative Image studio, Newport VT. Soft cover edition was printed by Derby Port Press, Derby Vt. Mezzotint B&W cover shot of Higgins. 3474

Snowflake on turning forty by Dick Higgins 1978 Postcard of Higgins work exhibited at the Cooper Hewitt Museum, the Smithsonian Institutions National Museum of Design Fall. Sent to CM with message of major lectures at NYU. 3485

Spencer Holst & Tui St. George Tucker AG7703C There are different kinds of writings 1978 Audiographics Cassette Insert 3517

Dawn of the Solar age Musical Score 1978 A musical piece by Carman Moore 3558

Sounds of the sacred Mountains Music and Myth of the Tibet 1978 At the Museum of Natural History. Huston Smith, Ernest McClain, Lobsang Lhalungpa, Lama Norlha, Dhondup Namgyal 3577

The Six Perfections (We have only four) By Alison Knowles 1978 Postcard for a show on April 21, 8 PM. Silkscreens on Cloth Music by Philip Corner, Alison Knowles, and Malcolm Goldstein. Samaya Foundation 46 Warren St. NY 3591

Yoko Ono Postcard from Jean Brown to CM 1978 Ono postcard published by Edition Staeck:69 Heidelberg 1 Postiach 471 Original graphic serie 4: munchennr. 8 Yoko Ono offset 1971 A HOLE TO SEE THE SKY THROUGH '71 Also copy of NY Post article Charlotte Mormans presentation of Yoko's CUT Letter written on the back by Bob Carroll to CM 3592

CM, Glen Velez, Bruce Itmas Photo 1978 8x10 Glossy CM on Horn Glen w/Drum A Bruce mixing board 3602

CM, Glen Velez, Photo 1978 8x10 Glossy shot CM, Glen w/hand Drum 3604

Fiscal History Ear Magazine 78 & 79 1978 Expense Book. Description of the Project under Rip Hayman and a copy of an ad & catalog to that date. 3642

Clutching The TRE MOK by Lawrence Upton 1978 A word art piece on brown paper 3683

Jerome Rothenberg Folder 1978 Contains, A Poetry Broadside from Cream City Review signed to CM. Three Postcards from Jerry To CM, Invitation to a reading and reception for the publication of Jerome's book A Big Jewish Book: An Article by Mary Stoffier Santiago Shamanic Connections. Notes and copies of pages from A Big Jewish Book. A small invite to a reading at Ed Venture Readings NY. BEZOAR publication of poems. Gloucester MA. A Postcard from STONE PRESS WEEKLY 1974 Alpha & Omega from Rothenberg's Seneca Journal...These items were salvaged from the flood at 1961 Roaring Brook Rd. 3731

Unpublished Editions Dick Higgins Memo 1978 A message from Dick to Philip, CM & Alison about Chuck Caramello Center for 20th Century Studies Univ. of Wisconsin at Milwaukee. An interesting note about his fascination with the new Arts. 3739

Symphony In Clay for Ocarina Orchestra 1978 A last minute Symphony by Phil Corner written on a note pad on the way to the Train Station for CM. 3775

Letter and Score to CM from Tom Johnson in Paris 1978. 3795

Letter from Tom Johnson 1978 Tom is explaining his number system which he and Philip Corner had developed. He then expounds upon that idea and creates another system. 3827

Sound Poetry a Catalogue 1978 Catalog for the Eleventh International Sound Poetry Festival in Toronto Canada. Oct 14 thru 21. Edited by Steve McCaffery and bp Nichol. Entries for CM, Higgins, Heidsieck, Hanson, and others. 3847

Note from Tui St. George Tucker to CM, also Christmas card from

Tui 1978 Tui reports on the playing of his piece Tadkow on WBAI-FM. She mentions the New Wilderness Foundation. 3848

Cercando Un Estel by Llorenc Barber 1978 A beautiful Manuscript 3865

Intermedia Performance: #443 Theory and Practice, Loire Dec. 28 1978 Moderator Dick Higgins, NY University. Dick Higgins, Philip Corner, Allison Knowles, CM Respondent: Charles Caramello, Center for Twentieth Century Studies, University of Wisconsin, Milwaukee 3915

Blue Lotus Word Cloud, Norcris Tollomeem 1978 Very nice artwork of a concept of the Word Cloud by Norcris Tollomeem 3924

Winter solstice poem by Burt Porter 1978 Seasons Greetings from Burt 3925

Chanting, Dancing, Counting, Healing and Fiddling 1978 New Wilderness in Milwaukee The Center for Twentieth Century Studies & School of Fine Arts Present: Bells and Chanting, Number Counting, Fish & Frog Language, A Healing Ritual Fiddle concerto on Jewish Cantilation & more. Under the direction of CM 3926

Ear Magazine letterhead, New Wilderness Foundation (2) 1978 Two original Ear Letterheads 3931

New Wilderness Ocarina Orchestra Concert Poster 1978 A concert poster By Cynthia Eardley for Tuesday June 5th in connection with The Independent Artists Sculpture Show on Wards Island, NY 3976

Letter to CM from Jane (Jerry Walkingbird) 1978 A funny letter to CM. 3996

Vision Chanting Trance. Dance & Trance 'n Dance 1978 Dream Singing Dream Song, Mindscreen, Worldscreen 4010

New Wilderness Fair in Sullivan County 1978 Booklet from Sullivan County Community College from Julia Jacobs. Page 10 has info on the New Wilderness Fair with CM. 4011

Handbook Silence 2, edited by Susan Mernit & Rochelle Ratner 1978 poetry 4040

Craft Dinner, bp Nichol 1978 Photo of Jesse and Hannah Higgins in Barton Vt. around 1978. Photo by T. J. Walbert 4046

Angel Simone Forti 1978. 4047

LE Jardin Japonais Pierre Garnier 1978 Signed 4049

LE Jardin Japonais Tome 2 Pierre Garnier 1978. 4050

In England Now That Spring Steve McCaffery & bp Nichol 1978. 4052

The selected Poetry of Vicente Huidobro, 1978. 4055

A, Louis Zukofsky 1978. 4060

Open Letter third series #9 Fall 1978 A Canadian Quarterly, McCaffery, Wah and others. 4067

Works OEUVRES, Sten Hanson 1978 Other Media, NY 4083

St. Francis Preaches to the Birds 1978 Bread & Puppet small booklet of woodcuts Published by Janus Press, Newark Vermont 4171

The Last Supper Flyer (3) 1978 Program for a presentation by Animal Magnetism Group. Midnight and 1:30 With P.N. Drennan as interactive Christ, other players, Music by CM. 4199

New Wilderness Facts Pages 1+2 1978 A general overview of New Wilderness methods 4204

Ritual Drama & Poetry Workshop Flyer 1978 Workshop led By Stanley Diamond for the New Wilderness Foundation 4229

Jazz Rock Fusion, Julie Coryell & Laura Friedman 1978. 4254

Human Arts Festival, New Wilderness Papers 1978 Informational letter, Funding Material, Artists List Graphic Poster 4268

Solstice 88, Notes, Permits 1978 Press, Letters, Park Rules, Phone #s etc. 4271

Summer Solstice 78 Budgets, Papers, Press 1978. 4272

When the Brass Goes Marching In, Press (3) 1978. 4277

Ululating Chants, Press (11) 1978 Night of Vision Chanting 4278

Buffalo North American Indian Culture Center Inc. 1978 Proposal written with the help of CM 4296

Arleen Schloss ITSA Poem 1978 Part of a 10 minute poem performed at the Robert Freidus Gallery April 1978. 4301

Beth Laurin Sculptural Pieces 1978 Four Printed pieces from a show 4306

Greg Borst, Within the Circle (3) 1978 Talking with Greg Borst about native American Music Photocopies of a Sing Out article 4307

Native American Press Material and Richard Erdoes 1978 Grant Proposal as artist and photographer. Nine copies of Chief Seattle's Message. Two Copies of Seneca Indians give him Culture Shock by Peter Zummo 4320

A letter from Gabor Toth 1978 From Ear art file. He would like to know if Ear would like to publish two of his Stamps. 4327

Sullivan County Community College Work Folder 1978 Material from Sullivan County Project 4333

Art & Music Benefit Concert 1978 Flyer and Performance 4379

Settings of Rothenberg's Event Music III 1978 Score 4381

CM Parade, Johnson 60 note fanfares, Moore: Fanfare slo, Tucker: Summer is, Niblock: E Fanfare, Higgins: Fanfare, Corner: Calling Om, CM: Ascending Music 1978. 4384

Greg Borst Family Photos 1978 Performance Photos of Borst Native Indian Music from Audio Graphics file 4391

Poster miniatures of CM event posters, were used in a show 1978. 4396

Theater for the New City 1978 List 4478

NY Mosaics 1900 -1933 Brochure (2) 1978 Mosaic Documentation project project director Mary Nell Hawk. 4522

New Rituals and Ceremonies in the environment, a seminar (POSTER) 1978 A sixteen day seminar in northern New Mexico. 4568

Nikhil Banerjee, sitar evening Ragas Poster 1978 Marc Gold Concert at MacMillan Auditorium Columbia University 4610

Human Arts Association & New Wilderness present Jazz Composer Showcase Flyer 1978 James Newton Quartet, Famoudou Don Moye Solo percussion Don Pullen Quintet Olu Dara okra orch. Kalaparusha Maurice Mcintire Quartet, produced by Amos Ryce 4660

Poetry on Tape file 1978 Audio Graphics and other poetry collections on tape, with listings of new releases.

Audio Arts, Art services brochure with John Cage, Philip Glass,Talking Band, and others 4674

Epickall Quest of the Brothers Dichtung and other outrages, Dick Higgins 1978 Printed Editions, NY also has an advance ad flyer for the book. Water Damage 4732

Novalis Hymns To the Night, Translated by Dick Higgins 1978 some water damage Treacle Press 4733

Primera Entrega, Jacobo Cortines 1978 Signed to CM 4765

ON Turtle's Back, Dennis Maloney 1978 Signed to CM White Pine Press Buffalo NY A Biogeographic Anthology of NY State Poetry 4770

A Seneca Journal, Jerome Rothenberg 1978. 4782

Ebb Tide, Dick Higgins noted Copy 1978 A play to be heard twice. Silver Hill New Canaan Connecticut Nov. 15 1974. 4791

KINESIS, Vol.1 #1 1978 A News Journal of Nonverbal Communications 4825

Eighth Assembling 1978 A Collection of Otherwise Unpublishable Manuscripts compiled by Richard Kostelanetz 4848

Eighth Assembling, Kostelanetz, Korn 1978 A Collection of Otherwise Nonpublishable Manuscripts Doria, Frank, 4852

Jerzy Grotowski Bibliography 1978 Teatr Laboratorium Also two copies of Holiday and A brochure from the Kosciuszko Foundation 4855

Movings etc. for Outside, Heloise Gold 1978 Self Published piece Signed to CM 4866

Deciphering America, Michael Gibbs 1978 a traveling Collection, Peter Frank, Richard Hayman, Dick Higgins, Alison Knowles, Jackson Mac Low, Steve McCaffery, Opak Nations, B.P. Nichol, Jerome Rothenberg, Carolee Schneemann, and others. 4878

Doc Oxide and other reflections, Tony Green Gee 1978 Signed To CM 4881

World & Classes-On Having Words, Chris Mann 1978. 4894

Unmailed, Vernita Nemec 1978. 4898

Craft dinner, bp Nichol 1978 Aya Press 4923

The Musicians, the Instruments, Peter Riley 1978 The Many Press 4930

Var ungdoms hjalter, Jan Olsheden Stellan Olsson 1978 signed to CM, printer Industria Grafica SA 5025

The Drama review 1978 NY University/School of the Arts 5037

Musik 68-78 1978 A small booklet of Underground Art and Photography by several artists. Published in Germany 5061

Agreement, Peter Seaton 1978 Asylum's Press NY 5080

Flyer for Works in Science and Art by Stefan Eins 1978 signed by painter, gallerist, ex-Catholic monk Stefan Eins 5121

Door window dryer box 5 shaggy dog operas: program by Tom Johnson 1978 program for play 5124

On Singing, Phil James 1978 Spring NYC. The Long Song for CM 5174

Jagermeister Color Ad 1978 CM poses for photo used in Ear Magazine 5239

All Stars Booklet 1978 Maude Boltz hand made art. Gift to CM 5257

A Noted Vocabulary for Eve Rosenthal (3) Jackson Mac Low 1978. 5302

Flyer for Works in Science and Art by Stefan Eins 1978 A single Sheet 5315

Jim Theobald Piece for Bb Trumpet, Horn in F, Trombone 1978. 5329

Theatre For the New City Lovely Rita Promo 1978 Back side of mailer is Coming for 78/79 Season. Includes Talking Band, Bread & Puppet, a musical by Rosalyn Drexler and others. 5347

Tom Johnson Representative Works 1968-1978 April 20, 1978 Hunt Union Ballroom State University College Oneonta NY 5353

Shigeko Kubota, Video Gallery Show Flyer 1978 Japan House Gallery, 333E. 47th St. NY 5392

Celebrate St. Mark's in the Bowery Flyer 1978 Several Events Puppet Parade, Storytelling, Music and Dance by The Silkscreen Project 5394

Tommy Mew 1978 Conceptual Artist Director of Fluxus West Package of promo pieces and letter to RIP at Ear Magazine 5395

OP a Music news Paper from NY 1978 Interesting articles of the times, NY Clubs and Bands from 70's. 5396

Michael Sahl Recording announcement of Cassette Release. 1978 Mary Rowell violin, Michael Sahl piano and others 5452

Western Wind Concert Flyer 15th Anniversary Program 1978. 5461

Jessica Goodyear Resume 1978 Unique Layout and Design for a Resume. Very NY City period piece 5474

How to Play Fanfare in Six Parts, Jim Theobald Sing Cuckoo, Tui St. George Tucker Fanfair for Summer, Fanfair for the Month of June, Higgins Dawn of the Solar Age, C. Moore 1978 Notes by Philip Corner 5484

Dancescope Vol. 13/no.1 Simone Forti also Garden and Crawling articles 1978 5487

Child's Artwork, To CM from Carl 1978 Crayon on Paper, CM's Large

Sun, Flowers and CM's Living Room. 5537

Art artist & The Media, Planstudio 1978 Siepmann Nr 16 5577

Postcard artwork from Bruce McClelland The Dracula Poems 1978 Sent to New Wilderness 5603

Creative Time Inc. New band 1978 Creative Time presents Art On The Beach August, 22nd 6:30 PM 5654

American Indian Artists TOPI /HOPID 1978 Inspired By Jerome Rothenberg became a group Topi - HOPID/ 3804

Handmade Greeting Card "Thanks CM" from Vincent, Candy, Marilyn 1978 Very nice color cartoon artwork of three kissing CM. 3840

Resting Upon Emptiness 1979 The very poetic titles of movements from an old Chinese lute suite are spoken by the band members in English one phrase at a time. The band echos each spoken line by playing an original unison melody that fits the words of the movement titles as unsung lyrics. 557

Earum Magnus (Bern Porter) 1979 Film of Bern Porter's ear listening to CM chant. Also involved were Dick Higgins, Charles Stanley, and Scott B. [Scott who?] 1002

4 Rose and 16 Performers with 4 Chords Binding 4 of Them 1979 16 performers are tethered, four to each of four roses. They play and move. This composition is dedicated to poet Rose Drachler, echoing back to "Apsis". 1013

OcOrc Attack of Empire State Building. 1979 The OcOrc announced via the press that it would attack and occupy the Empire State Building. OcOrc marched, playing, up the street to the Empire State Building, through its halls and up the elevators. OcOrc put flags at the four cor OcOrc - short for New Wilderness Ocarina Orchestra 1024

Jacksonville: Toot'n Blink 1979 This was the first version of Toot'n Blink, a composition for boat horns and light conducted by command. This performance fell apart in development, and never happened. Chicago sponsored of the premier in 1982. 1035

Barcelona Event 1979 1. Toronto: Four fires lighted in sequence with singing and dancing on shore. A fifth fire answers from an island. 2. Maine: Two fires are lighted on neighboring sea jetties. Around each fire is half of the group of performers that has been working together on a ritual sequence. At a synchronized starting signal both groups begin. Both sites are recorded. The recordings later are played in sync. 1046

Transcanada Sunrise 1979 Skysong sung in Nova Scotia -- following the movement of the sun --is repeated east to west across Canada at hour delays on the Canadian Broadcasting Corporation national radio network. 1057

Surveillance 1979 Standing behind a large glass window or door, observe the rhythm of passersby. Even if your window were a peephole in a thick stone wall some people will know you are there. The waves between seer and seen form this piece. Try double doors with small space in between to compare the piercing. 1068

Motion Music 1979 While swimming, jogging, walking steadily, or possible operating a vehicle, focus on the earth rolling your own motion with it. 1079

Neighbornote Study with 1) + and - notation2) . (dot) notation 1979 This conceptual game uses pluses and minuses to indicate upper and lower neighbor notes. Patterns of pluses and minuses then generate pieces that move systematically around fixed pitch areas. This generalized piece can work with a wide variety of instrumentation. [what about dots, as in 2)?] 1090

OcOrc at Glyptoteket Copenhagen 1979 Poul Borum,1425

Djurgarden event - stockholm 1979. 1431

Sky Song WBAI 1979 poster by Geoff Hendricks 1432

Group Chant 1979 Group vocal exploration of the word "soft." The piece is notated graphically. 1491

Report from the Front Beth Anderson 1979 Guerrilla criticism concerned with The Kitchen's New Music NY Festival. Music Critics assoc. conference of 1979. A review of CM's presentation. Pg.3 w/note to CM. 1516

Letter from Alison Knowles 1979 Please send an item to the House of Dust, to be included in a museum installation. 1518

House of Dust 1979 A letter to CM to send an object to be included in the exhibit at the Oakland museum. 1573

Grand Conch Chorus 1979 The Grand Conch Chorus grew out of the Ocarina Orchestra. It is an improvisational and composition-playing group effective in outdoor events and concerts. The Conch Chorus has been associated with peace events ever since more than 50 members marched with Bread and Puppet Circus at the head of the New York Disarmament Parade in 1982 that drew over 1,000,000 spectators. 1587

Entrance Music 1979 The soloist plays a horn from outside the concert space, through a wall or closed door. The approach starts as far from the space as is audible to people inside and continues to the door. The opening of the door and entrance into the concert is the second part. Moving through the audience and whispering through the horn in many ears is the third part. Arrival at center stage and bowing is the end. 1590

New Wind Band 1979 This artists' wind band, varying from 10 to 30 members, played together for three years. Many of its members wrote for it as did guest composers and conceptualizers. It was performance-oriented and geared to celebrations. Its finest moment was at Solstice '82 in the Band Shell at Lincoln Center, NYC. The music, often conceptual, ranged from the improvised to the rigid, from the new to the ethnic and old. 1601

Piano Works 1979. 1666

Goodbye Mother Earth 1979 Original Score and staging notes 1788

New Wilderness Letter Vol. 1 #3 and 4 1979. 1921

Sky Song Posters, Postcards (Vision Singer) Flyers (C. M. Whats new for Trumpet 60's) 1979 About 500 postcards from Vision singer & Witness 500+ posters from Sky song 300 Flyers from Trumpet 1931

Wave Music III: 60 Clarinets. 6-21-1979 Posters, Flyers. 1979 500+ posters from wave music 60 Clarinets 40 Flyers from same 1932

CM Documents 1970-1979 Flyers 300+. 1934

Love Songs II, The Shuman Dreams 1979 A number sound system based on articulation Original Manuscript by Jonathan J. Albert 1956

Eric Andersen Scores 1979 Gift from Andersen to CM 1972

Wave Music III: 60 Clarinets and a Boat 1979 Ten contrabass clarinetists sit in a circle on the seawall of Battery Park, NYC, playing the lowest and slowest augmentation of the theme in a ten part canon. Ten Eb clarinets, ten Bb clarinets, ten A clarinets, ten bassett horns, four alto clarinets, ten bass clarinets form their own groups. They join the contras, already playing, one group of ten at a time. As arranged, after the last note of the clarinet orchestra ended, the fireboat docked nearby sounded its horn. 2000

Mysteries of the Rose (for CM) 1979 Dick Higgins script for a Film 2028

Ludwig Schwarz - death announcement 1979 Schwartz was an extraordinary builder of jewharps in the Austrian tradition: bent metal with metal tongues in different sizes. The harps and Schwarz were introduced to CM by Georg Buchler? an Austrian musician. 2050

Love among the Mutants 1979 by Merrill Acoghieri & Joe Tripician 6 June 2235

Akwesasne Notes 1979 Winter issue. Published by State University of NY at Buffalo. 2446

Hvedekorn #3 1979 Arts Magazine 2483

Beth Anderson & Michael Sahl Poster 1979 Music from Codes & Puzzles and from the heart 2511

Beth Anderson & Michael Sahl 1979 Concert poster for Music & Codes and puzzles from the Heart at the Kitchen Ctr. 2517

Summer Celebration Wave Music III 1979 Press release, Poster and original poster mechanical for Battery Park June 21. Wave Music III 60 Clarinets. Produced by New Wilderness foundation and Lower Manhattan Cultural Council. Added 3-12-13 about 60 yellow posters. 2568

Three Stains, Coffee time serenade 1979 Conceptual art piece by CM 2576

Like the Indians Sing by Jans Brincker 1979 Ceremonial musician and event maker CM. A review of performance in Copenhagen. Also review of Voices from the depth of Consciousness by Jan Jacoby 2604

The Common Thread of Life 1979 An art event celebrating the sprit of the United Nations Oct. 24 By Andor Grand 2607

Let the Sun Shine In Sheet Music 1979 Song from the musical Hair Words by James Rado and Gerome Ragni Music by Galt MacDermot 2645

Voices of the Eye By Nina Yankowitz 1979 A book of Paint Readings and scanning. 2647

Station Hill Catalog of books 1979 Dick Higgins Barrytown NY 2674

Music for Trumpets and Trees Dick Higgins 1979 Dedicated to CM, West Glover VT 11 8x10" photo art pieces 2675

Dick Higgins Music for Trumpets and Trees 1979 Another copy but in a printed Envelope and signed, 750 of 775. 2676

A Celebration of Morning by Dick Higgins 1979 An announcement from Printed Editions for forthcoming art book. Has some stains from the flood. 2716

The Phenomenology of Aural Appearances (30) by Rip Hayman 1979 Poster for a Concert at The Franklin Furnace Tues May 22, a very dark and soft event 2729

New Wilderness Dream Fest Poster (70) 1979 Performances, visuals, information, and all night goings on by artists that work with dreams. 2731

Ear Inn Performances Jan-Feb. (2) 1979 Ear Inn 326 Spring St. NY 2737

Dream Fest Invitation 20-1979 performances, visuals, a film by Stan Vanderbeek, sleepover, breakfast and more. Held at Edens Expressway 537 Broadway NY 2744

C See Sea Suite for Barbara Held by Rip Hayman 1979 Nov. 24 A slow and gentle flute piece 2754

200 RPM 1979 A musical Drama featuring some lesser sung heros and heroines of our American Bicentenial. At the Hudson Guild Theater NYC. Presented by The Labor Theater. 2768

Ocarina Orchestra at Whitney Museum Flyer 1979 A small copier flyer for Oc Orchestra Wed. Feb. 7th. 2799

Garden of Eden, Adam Purple Press 1979 Destruction of Garden of Eden in NYC. Press and articles 2823

CM/Glen Valez - Min Takana workshop 1979 686 Lexington Ave. Nov. 19th CM (chanting, ocarina, bugle, jew's harp) 2837

Readings & Performances at the Urban Jungle Poster (4) 1979 New Wilderness sponsored performance at Gallery Saireido 382 W. Broadway 2845

Musical Insects of the World Poster (1) 1979 a large poster by Chris Kluge. 2847

Dawn Song, Lullaby Linda Velez Chili 1979 Music for two songs Dawn Song and Lullaby also Linda Velez chili recipe 2872

6th Annual Symposium on Contemporary Music Poster (7). 1979 Guest Artist CM Composer and Chanter. Program copies and newspaper story. 2908

CM Documents gallery announcement for documents 1970-79 1979 installation-Ray Kelly June 14-28 at Buecker & Harpsichords 465 West Broadway NYC Opening June 13 5-8. 2966

The Goose 1979 Notes and Orchestra Cues Dick Higgins 3062

New Wilderness 1979 Press and Photographs on the New Wilderness Foundation 3067

Correspondence between CM and Billie Maciunas 1979 regarding Toronto Sound Poetry gathering, which Billie heard about through Dick Higgins. Use of Billie's farm for accomodations at the event discussed. 3096

Akwesasne No Es 1979 A Journal for Native and Natural Peoples Autumn 1979 Issue 3.104

The Prospect Mountain Sculpture Show 1979 program from an Homage to David Smith August 1 - October 15 An Exhibition Organized by Lake George Arts Project Inc. 52 Hendrick Street, Lake George, NY 3112

Ocarina Orchestra 1979 Clipping from Ear Magazine describing the Ocarina Orchestra 3134

People of the Totem: The Indians of the Pacific Northwest 1979 by Norman Bancroft-Hunt and Werner Forman University of Oklahoma Press, Norman and London 3317

Correspondence with Jackson Mac Low 1979 about payments 3359

Correspondence with Bern Porter about Found Sounds 1979. 3360

Maine Event Flyer 1979 Flyer for October 6-12. 3556

Artwork By Demo NYC 1979 Five pieces of art signed Demo NYC. Black ink on Copier paper. 3557

Plugg 140 W. 24th St. 1979 Fri. July 18th with Lytle/Cartwright, Flono, George Meteslsey ensemble, Mary Jane Leach and this Guy in the magazine, Produced by Tod Jorgensen. 3571

Concertos Folder, Violin Concerto with Cantor, The Goose Concerto 1979 Other Media 3656

Number Music Folder, Fish & Frog Languages, The Number six, Book of Numbers 1979 Other Media 3657

Piano Works Folder: Piano Ditty, Prelude, Bells For Michael, Requiem For the Victims of Kent State, Twenty Beats for Annie, Animal Clackers, Sonata for Piano, An Apology 1979 Other Media 3658

Stage Works, Flute & Guitar Piece, Spirit Voices, Job, 1979 Other Media 3659

Five Different Music, Grandma Music, Air Music, Licorice Music, Morning Music, Light Music. 1979 Other Music 3660

Message from Dick Higgins 1979 Message about closing on Vermont property. 3671

6th Annual Symposium on Contemporary Music Poster 1979 Guest

Artist CM Composer And Chanter. Symposium Director Thomas Read. A program at the UVM Recital Hall Feb. 21st. With a sunrise chant by CM on Feb. 20th. 3687

Min Tanaka solo Dance Poster w/Derek Bailey guitar 1979 Nov. 14-16 Washington Sq. Church 3697

For ROSE - Flower Performance, CM 1979 A performance piece by CM in which participants are the stems and flowers. Two pieces salvaged for the flood at Roaring Brook. 3746

Public Arts Free Speech Catalog Flyer 1979 Performance festival May 15-19 at 75 Warren St. NYC CM performs on May 17th. JPG in Graphics 3757

Ear Magazine scraps and pieces. 1979 Includes a picture of the Conch Band by Mary Nell Hawk and diagrams of strange musical instruments 3787

Morning Trumpet Song for CM 1979 November with Love. Phil Jams Instructions on the back page, to be played facing the sun etc. 3789

Music gallery poster CM, Michael Snow, Steve McCaffery, in Concert 1979. 3800

City Ditties (songs) by Regina Beck 1979 at Eric's 2nd Ave. & 88th St. 3814

Carolee Schneemann HomeRun Muse (2) 1979 Postcard announcement for text and slides show at Franklin Furnace 3841

CM, Michael Snow, Steve McCaffery Concert 1979 Concert at Music Gallery Dec. 14th. A great poster printed on top of a California dept of Corrections Lethal Gas Chamber- Execution Record form 3879

What I did at 75 Warren St. 1979 Performance notes with illustrations from CM 3935

Festival of Disappearing Arts, Poster 1979 Merzaum Collective and Washington Project for the Arts Present. The Baltimore- Washington International Festival. Hannah Weiner's Clairvoyant Journal and Jackson Mac Low's verbal musical pieces. From NY. 3967

Printed Editions Fall/ Winter Catalog 78/79 1979 Members, John Cage, Philip Corner, Geoffrey Hendricks, Dick Higgins, Alison Knowles, Jackson Mac Low, Pauline Oliveros 3973

Wave Music 60 Clarinets 1979 Was to be performed on top of the World Trade Ctr. but permission could not be obtained so it was performed by the sea wall. 4007

International festival of Mail art, Audio art, Copy art, Video Art, Artists Books. 1979 A flyer from Brazil asking for submissions for an International catalog. 4022

The Street Book, Henry Moscow 1979 An encyclopedia of Manhattan street names and their origins 4114

Grupo Texto Poetico, 1979 Mercedes Calpe, Bertomeu Ferrando, David Perez, Rose Sanz 4146

Making Mud, Merle Steir 1979 A Booklet, forth in a series, Signed to CM 4195

Storefront for Art and Architecture, Program for October 1979 A black and white flyer for Performances including CM, Simone Forti, Phill Niblock, Arleen Schloss, and others. 4198

Maine Poetry Festival Book 1979 Most of the Best of the Maine Poets, Bar Harbor ME. Printed by Marcel Nuss at Regal Printing, Ellsworth Me. 4222

Writers Guild of America Registration Envelopes 1979. 4264

Maine Event 1979 Posters, Newspaper, Chanting CM Press 4274

Wave Music III 1979 Notes, Letters, Musicians list, Schedules etc. 4275

Wave Music Art from Marilyn Steinman 1979 For CM 4281

New Wilderness Foundation 1979 Summer Activities Press Release 4286

Summer Garden 1979 Letter to CM from Earl Hatleberg, project Director for Summergarden. 4366

Marathon Event 1979 Folder 4456

New Wilderness Letter Cover Photo #11 1979 B&W Photo of Letters Flying off the Page 4549

Happy Birthday on a paper Bag 1979 From Jackson Mac Low 4662

See Vermont, Patty Oldenburg 1979, Poets Cooperative, Burlington, VT. Printed at Troll Press St. Johnsbury VT. Signed To CM 4713

More, Alison Knowles (2) second edition 1979 Printed Editions 4724

Tales of the Edge and Other Changes, Jackson Williams Barnett 1979 Signed copy 4735

Vermont Haiku, Larry Freifield 1979 Published by Land Press, West Glover VT. 4748

Dick Higgins A Bio/Bibliography 1979 Threadneedle Editions, West Glover Vermont. Design and layout Jay Walbert, Creative Image Studio, Newport VT. Photo by Eugene Williams 4760

B R MTZ V H, Jerome Rothenberg 1979 Perishable Press Signed Copy 4785

Svend Nielsen, Nar visen Far Brod 1979. 4815

CAGE, Nino Monastra 1979 Audio book w/Cassette Tape Lots of photos 4821

Congo Poeme Pygmee, Pierre Garnier 1979. 4833

Blason Du Corps Feminin, Pierre Garnier 1979. 4834

Rythmes Et Silence, Pierre Garnier 1979. 4835

A Critical (ninth) Assembling (Precisely: 6789) 1979 Albert, Cage, Corner, Doria, Filliou,Frank, Heidsieck, Higgins, CM, Porter, Rothenberg, Schwerner, Weiner, and others 4850

Raven Issue #1 (2) Scott Lawrance Healing Issue 1979 Edition of 500 Ganges B.C. CM 3 poems Copywrite Other Media 4865

Right Hemisphere Left Ear, Paul Dutton 1979 Coach House Press, Toronto 4885

White Rushes, Phil Demise 1979 Signed Poem. Booklet NotBook Editions 4891

Names in the Cosmic Ocean, Ernest Robson 1979 A satire of cosmic nonsense with phonetic music 4892

The Book of Numbers, Paul Dutton 1979 Porcupine's Quill 4908

Danish literature, Poul Borum 1979 signed to CM, Det Danske Selskab 4913

Whos listening out there, David Antin 1979 Sun & Moon Press 4929

The Poet's Encyclopedia, Michael Andre 1979 Unmuzzled Ox foundation 4938

Connaissez-vous? Le Spatialisme 1979 signed to CM, Editions Andre Silvaire 4940

Var Forsiktig Med Den Dar Yxan, Eugene 1979 Embryo 4955

Lost Paper One, Higgins 1979 A mini portfolio of FLUXUS and related artists published by Station Hill Press Barrytown NY Limited edition of 1000 Dick Higgins 5069

Saloons of the Old West, Richard Erdoes 1979 Alfred A. Knopf Inc, signed to CM 5096

Manifested, Phil Demise 1979 Ogeogenschein Press 5103

The business of Being an artist, 1979 application 5118

Zbs foundation announces the 1979 air season 5119

Snow and the study of Trees, Larry Freifeld (4) 1979 Drawings by Don Sunseri The Land Press West Glover, Vt. A small booklet of poems by Freifeld. 5159

And/Or Notes Dec. 1979 December Calendar of Events from this Seattle Arts Newsletter 5189

Cooper Square Festival Folder 1979 Festival photos and paperwork. Catalog Show Introduction Nice Group of papers 5235

Ear Magazine Volume 5#2 Cover Artwork By Jaron Lanier 1979 Manhattan as a Clarinet by Jaron Lanier 5240

Criminal Code Reform Acts of 1979/1980 and Anti Draft Poster 1979 Guerrilla Action Group 488 Greenwich Street NY 10013. 5254

Yoshi Wada with Richard Hayman Show promo cards. 1979 Galvanized Voice in two parts, Samaya Foundation 46 Warren St. Yoshimasa Wada with Richard Hayman and Jmani Smith improvised Singing in unison 3 Male Voices. Art on Cards by Yosi Wada 5256

Living Music, Torrington, CT 06798 1979 Flyer for Winter Consort Road Sheet No. 10A gathering at Baja. Summer performances and Workshops in New England and West Early Civil Rights group, Common Ground 5274

A Calendar: The Year of the Messiah 1979 Photocopies of this piece, could be Rothenberg 5284

Performances The EAR Inn Jan. & Feb. Poster 1979 Bern Porter, Phill Niblock 5317

Michael Byron Composers Forum Flyer 1979 Pieces Anthology Series Contains many New Wilderness Peoples works 5330

Armand Schwerner Writings 1979 Signed to CM 5351

First NY Art Parade 1979 Line-up for Marchers 5352

Vermont Institute of Community Involvement Catalog 1979. 5439

Sound, Buddhas, Treatise on Music, 1979 Sakya Pandita (1220), Tsong kha pa, The Way of Pure Sound, Thomas Mann, D.T. Suzuki, Star Spangled Banner 5476

Invitation to a Concert in Denmark, CM Performs 5480

Mail Art Piece by Madam X Unlimited. National Bad Guy Day Letter graphic 1979 Mailed from San Diego CA to Ear Magazine NWF 5518

Twins, Button-Bean 1979 Original art by Alison Knowles Two pieces Water Damage but Restorable With Mats. #11 of 25 signed to CM #8 Artists Proof 5544

Banana Dupuy 1979 Jean Dupuy 5558

International Mail Art exhibition poster 1979 Dan Emery, Julie kous? 5559

Voda Film Premieres, Andy Voda Poster for Chants Chance 1979 Parts based on Alison Knowles poem House of Dust Sept. 28th at Anthology Film Archives NYC 5597

Ear Magazine welcomes the participans in NEW MUSIC NY Festival of Composers, Flyer 1979 Computer graphic copier paper. 5635

Mazola jingle 1980. 83

Vintner's -RH Remix 1980. 84

Nickelodeon 1980. 89

Conch Music for Art On The Beach 100 Blows, 100 Cymbal Crashes: Blows and Strides Downhill Through Audience 1980 The conch player and the percussionists start in a long line at the tip of the hill. They perform 100 blows which includes systematic steps forward, down the hill, and onto the sand. Maneuvers follow a comic concert, and a line of fires glow as the sun goes down. 113

Test Tones 1980 test tones 551

United Way 1980 different approaches 552

United Way 1980 different approaches 553

United Way 1980 different approaches 554

United Way 1980 march (sound designey) final version 555

CM & Bert Porter 1980. 606

CM & Bert Porter 1980. 607

Blueberry Morning 1980. 633

The Goose (for Dick Higgins) 1980 Breath sounds from the chorus and the Uillean (Irish lap) pipes are the groundwork for this piece. The chorus clacks rhythms with wooden sticks. The pipe part is partially improvised. The piece is somewhat theatrical in that the pipes ar The Goose was written for a concert at University of Vermont, Burlington, VT. 668

ARTS FOR CHANGE 1980 1. urban 2. soft sarah dash-vocals robert camp-bass Bersein/CM-hock 745

Wave Music IV: Drums and Bugles 1980 Reveille June 11, 1980. Retreat June 20, 1980. The piece is based on "A Year of Daily Variations for Bugle Calls and Other Music." (1978) 1101

Principles for Playing Chorals and Other Music Using the Sky as Conductor. 1980 Use the sky as a source of information with which to conduct music: the wind, clouds and birds imply tempo and phrasing; light, color, intensity, and weather imply mood. 1114

Realisations for the New Wind Band. 1980 "Ihr Gestirn, Ihr Holen Lufte" "New Britain Sacred Harp p.45" [confirm my quotes and more] 1125

NPR 1980. 1126

Far Out at Sea 1980 Seven More Copies This choral opera is based on the H.C. Anderson's classic, "The Little Mermaid."Danish poet Poul Borum's wrote the libretto and lyrics, in English, on commission by the Danish vocal ensemble, Ars Nova. The end of the original story was changed by Borum from "She'll suffer in purgatory less if you children act good," to Wittgenstein's "Eternity belongs to those who live in the pr Sound processing and sampling are used to create the aging of the characters' voices over time, an under water sequence, and an atmosphere of obsessiveness. The world premier at Nikolajkirk, Copenhagen was recorded and broadcast by Danish Radio. It included solo dance choreographed and performanced by Nanna Nillson 1143

Far Out at Sea part 2 1980 Seven More Copies (as above) 1144

Blink Jam 1980 in the late 1970s and early 1980s the Experimental Intermedia Foundation held a series of exciting concerts of avant-garde and electro-acoustic music at Phill Niblock's loft in the SoHo district of NYC. These concerts were were then packaged into a series of hour-long radio programs entitled "Concerts by Composers" and distributed to interested radio stations around the United States. This ninth program in the series features music by Larry Kucharz, Charlie Morrow, & Takehisa Kosugi. Larry Kucharz is perhaps best known for his ambient electronic music, however he has also worked extensively with sound poetry and sparse, acoustic compositions that are often formed around a single chord. In this program Kucharz introduces an excerpt from his text-sound composition "Renwick Street", as well as one of his wind quintets. Charlie Morrow is an intermedia artist who is perhaps best known for his sound installations. In this program we hear two excerpts from one of Morrow's Memory Events, held in March 1980 at the Experimental Intermedia Foundation. The first, "The Year of the Messiah" entails Morrow reading from an 8th Century text with musical accompaniment provided by the

Ocarina Orchestra. This is followed by a excerpt of an improvisational "Blink Jam", in which the entire audience chants while focusing on the afterimage one sees when blinking for a prolonged period of time. 1374

Twelfth International Sound Poetry Festival - organizer 1980. 1438

12th International Sound Poetry Festival Letterhead 1980 14 days of events at The Kitchen, Washington Square Methodist Church NWF. Letterhead 1476

Politics and Music 1980 Essay on Politics & Music 1484

Bicycles to Dreamland (5) 1980 Presented by New Wilderness Foundation, Fusion Arts, Experimental intermedia Foundation. Supported by Meet the Composer. A Dream Event 1508

The Poetry Project 1980 Dec. Illustration courtesy of Doug Taylor. A reading event at St. Marks church NYC. Poster Design by Vicki Hudspith. 1527

12th International Sound Poetry Festival Poster (100+) 1980 April 11- 21 at The Kitchen 484 Broome St. NYC and Washington Square Church 1534

Prune Flat & Light Touch Flyer 1980 A presentation of two works by Robert Whitman. Prune Flat from 1965 & Light Touch from 1976. Dia Art Foundation NY 1562

The Horizontal - Vertical Band 1980 An improvisational duo of hand percussion, horns, ocarinas, Jew's harps, and chanting voice. Part of the concept was a sound system with front and back speakers. Each performer has two mikes to allow body panning. One set of mikes pans front and back, the other left and right. 1588

Altered States 1980 CM recorded a version of his "Pieces for Ocarina" for use in the shamanic scenes in Mexico. John Corigliano is the composer of all of the soundtrack music except for this episode, recorded at his request. 1594

The Barcelona Event: A Day For Gaudi 1980 This event is inspired by Catalonian archetect Antoni Gaudi and the park he designed. And it is also inspired by a project never undertaken: his design for eight lights to be erected along the Mediterranean sea wall lining part of the city. At dawn a procession led by the uniformed horseback Police Buglers begins in the Placa de Catalunya and wends its way through the streets of the city, gathering people as it goes, until it reaches the hill and Gaudi's Parc Guell. Here all day long a variety of performers take advantage of Gaudi's vision -the space he created -- to express their own. There will be music and dancing; the traditional Cobla brass band and the traditional Sardana dance, both expressions of the city's long history of commitment to artistic and political independence. Radio and TV build audience and generate excitement for the light spectacle. Searchlights erected along the sea wall promenade where Gaudi first imagined his own lights, and at dusk these are illuminated -- visible throughout bar. 1609

Seven Pieces for Solo Ocarinas 1980 5 pages. Short ocarina works. Licensed by Warner Borthers for use in feature film "Altered States" 1635

Evening Star 1980. 1637

Keeping On cues 1980 music for darmatic feature film written and directed by Barbara, Cabin Creek Films, NYC 1639

Concertos 1980 The registration of several concertos 1662

New Wilderness Letter 9 1980. 1683

Don't Pollute my Mind 1980 Original Music words and Music by C. Terence Coveny 1790

A Poem for The Shekinah on the Feast or the Sabbath 1980 Poem with musical notes. 1929

Ear Magazine (box 2) Healing Book 1980 June /July 1980 (41) issues April/May 1980 (16) issues April/May 1981 (7) issues June/July/Aug 1981 (1) issue A Gathering of healers book. These are the salvaged ones with some flood damage and staining. (12) copies 1940

Film Scores 1980 An Envelope containing a collection of CM's film Scores. 1942

DATA DD1 4BS 1980 A small conceptual booklet and script about War. IRA, Sadat 2031

Other Media Covers 1980 Misc. covers from other media scores 2039

Paz Muro - diverse graphics 1980 Paz Muro, Jorge Manrique, 17, Madrid 6, Spainmet CM in Madrid through Pepi Muro, ? her son. CM was performing though auspices Barbara Held, Llorenc Barber. 2053

Pelican Dance; Bugle Tune 1980 1 sound disc; 45 rpm, stereo. 7 in. + program notes. CM and Glen Velez; Horizontal Vertical Band. Music, performance, recording: CM Music, performance: Glen Velez. 2097

Jerome Rothenberg: Vienna Blood 1980 A poetry reading by Jerome Rothenberg. No date. 2112

MTA 'Train to the Plane' 1980 MTA-351 :30 'Why didn't I' 2220

Fred Alan Prod rl Keeping on pt2 1980 First Draft Keeping on pt2. 2243

Fred Alan Prod rl Keeping on pt1 1980 First Draft Keeping on pt2. 2245

Hole in Space umatic video 1980 B&W audio tr 1&2 In 1980, artists Kit Galloway and Sherrie Rabinowitz (K&S) created a "Hole in Space" by linking bigger-than-life displays in NY and LA with a satellite. 2337

CMA show reel (old) 1980. 2352

CMA demo reel version #1 1980. 2353

Arch Ensemble , for experimental music 1980 Poster program for Dec. thru May listing six performers each month. 2463

New Wilderness Guest Book 1980 The guest book for NWF, with names, addresses, doodles, etc. 2479

Festival of International Experimental Music 1980 Illustration of medieval underground musical machine 2486

Horizontal Vertical Band Art 1980 Original photo and artwork for the Horizontal vertical Band 45 rpm record. 2494

Enigme 1980 An original artwork by Henri Chopin, a signed gift to CM 2497

The Bent Head of Flowers 1980 Art Poster w/poem by Elaine Randell. Judith Walker Posters No. 4. 2499

Une idee en L'air Performances 1980 Poster of Performances and Exhibitions in NYC 2500

Original CMA business card design art 1980 Small photostat of Standing musicians with business copy underneath. 2510

For Simone, Postcard 1980 About 30, All Parts of the Body Can do Each Others job 2530

Avant Garde Festival of NY Poster 1980 A large poster, Great graphics of Passenger ships. Festival held at Passenger Ship terminal at 55 St. 2548

The Goose, Concerto for Uilleann Pipes, Orchestra, Chorus 1980 For Dick Higgins & Ted Levin 2563

11, 8x10 photos by Mary Ellen Morrow 1980 Performance photos 2581

Found Musical Essays 1980 1. On the New polyphony for Dick Higgins 2. On Musical texture for Phill 3. On teaching composition For Charles Dodge 4. On the secrets of playing the Jews Harp for CM. Signed Sten Hanson NY, Canal St. West End Ave. Nov. 1980. 2588

Music of CM & The Western Wind 1980 Concert on June 25 at Concert Hall of the Abraham Goodman House Color mailer with program on back. 2596

Valentine and Birthday card CM 38 1980 from Alison Knowles 2603

Fencott and Cobbing in NY 1980 A paper book By Fencott and Cobbing. Fencott an experimental poet, and Cobbing a sound poet. 2651

Bob Cobbing 1980 A paper book of graphic Copier art 2652

Ensems '80 3 Posters 1980 two acts of alternative music: Philip Corner, Alison Knowles, actum, Barbara Held, Taller de Musica mundana, Eduardo Polonio, CM, Javier Maderuelo, Emiliano del Cerro, Suso Saiz, Antoni Caimari, Rodriguez Pico i a coma, Jean Passini. 2655

Great Wind Event Poster (3) 1980 Riverside Park Boat Basin with Rip Hayman, New Wind Band, New Wilderness Ocarina Orchestra. Sari Dienes. 2658

Snug Harbor Cultural Center Poster (3) Three July Programs 1980 Produced by Armand Schwerner 2659

Inauguration Event Poster 1980 A large Handmade Poster for Hail to The Chief, All Hail Discordia. Poster Program. 2660

Stop Cobbing & Fencott in Baltimore 1980 A Paper copier book from Cobbing 2661

Village Voice Centerfold Solstice Reviews (30) 1980 Reviews from the Voice and an Asian paper. 2663

Dick Higgins 8x10' Glossy 1980 photo of Dick Higgins from Barrytown NY 2670

Dick Higgins Art 1980 Color key overlays of spatial arrows. 2680

The Politics of Music by CM 1980 with Translation of theme Saskia Sassen Koob 2683

Piano Album by Dick Higgins 1980 A collection of short piano pieces. Printed Editions, NY. Water stained front cover 2711

Encontre de compositors I (22) sa pobla 1980 A B&W 8.5 x11" paper poster about 22. 2728

Artwork of Maude Boltz 7 color prints 1980 Photocopies of her artwork and photos of past events or festivals. 2742

Great Wind Event 1980 Music from NWF Wind Band played at the Great Wind Event. Text is from The Art of the Lute. Music by CM. 2747

Synaesthetics June poetry readings 1980 Thur. nights 8 PM at 10 Leonard St. Sat at 2 PM. 2751

The Western Wind presents The Music of CM (5) 1980 The concert hall at the Abraham Goodman House 2778

The Light Opera Program Western Wind (4) 1980 CM and the Western Wind. A ritual healing with Tools and Weapons. 2781

Recital De Música Personal (19) 1980 El Taller de Alejandría, Barcelona 2789

Spirit Voices Art 1980 Original Artwork for Spirit Voices 2794

Spider Woman Theater 1980 poster for Theater group performance 2804

CM and Associates Band Poster 1980 Original screened photo and first print for mechanical. Art and design by Alison Knowles. 2806

Leading Edge music Series posters (9) 1980 Department of Music, Texas Tech University 1980 & 81 Music series, Ron Pellegrino, Director. CM, composer, vocalist, ritual artist March 11, 1981. 2814

Great Wind Event, Original mechanical for Poster 1980 Ruined in the Flood at the Archive in Barton. 2820

Penny Kemp and CM Niagara-Erie Writers present at people art/bio 1980. 2836

15th Annual Avant Garde Festival of NY poster (1) 1980 Large festive poster of ships by Jim McWilliams for event at passenger ships terminal at 55th St. 2878

Art Goldstein Studio Photographer NYC 1980 A Page of stamps as a creative door opener promotion. 2887

Anti War Parade NYC 1980 Possibly 1980's America's entry in Iraq. Parade Itinerary and production notes of CM. 2896

UVM Symposium on Contemporary Music 1980 Music of CM 2909

Mechanisms Of Defence 1980 50 Covers from Paul Borum 2919

The Second Coming Poster Fusion Arts Hiro Art 1980 112 First Ave. Hiro Arts Cafe by Downtown Magazine 2950

John Cage Catalog from Edition Peters 1980 List of Cage works 2962

12th Annual Int. Sound Poetry Festival Original poster. 1980 Fri. April 11th The Kitchen 484 Broome St. NYC 2964

Round Sound 1980 CM, Sten Hanson collaborative sound poem 2967

Summer Solstice Poster 1980 June 20th, at Riverside Park organized by CM 2989

Benzene Magazine 1980 Autumn Dick Higgins' poems appear 3006

Sound Images Sten Hanson and CM 1980 Other Media Drawings by Sten Hanson and Peter Schumann. Composition by CM 3016

Poetry of Rose Drachler 1980. 3034

Edizioni Francesco Conz Leinwande/Tele/Works on Cloth 1980 Biography, interviews, and art of Francesco Conz. Dick Higgins mentioned in biographical notes. 3050

Anagram Picture Song by Jean Dupuy 1980. 3094

Jeannette Murray Recent Paintings 1980 November 18-December 24th At Gallery Consalvo LTD. Five Faneuil Hall Market Place Boston Massachusetts Second insert: You are invited to the NY farewell to the new work November 14th 141 Wooster Street 3095

Photograph of Dick Higgins 1980. 3099

Jan Tyson and Kevin Power 1980 Poem and print in bifold, bound card 3103

The Light Opera 1980 A Ritual of Healing with Tools and Weapons La MaMa and the Western Wind Vocal Ensemble Presents The Light Opera concieved and composed by CM 3109

Books from Maine 1980 Books from Maine Poetry, Novels, Manifestos, Artists' Books, Practical Manuals, Portfolios, and Postcards Distributed by The Maine Writers and Publisher's Alliance 3120

The Enigma of Buster Keaton 1980 by Janet Hamill 3175

Presentation of Natural Assemblages and the True Crow 1980 Printed Editions Presents by Alison Knowles 3206

Granvocio 1980 Essay on homemade instruments, the avant-garde, and Granvocio 3294

Kenny Rogers Greatest Hits 1980 Music and Lyrics Edited by Milton Heu Cherry Lane Music, Co., 3325

The Rolling Stone Illustrated History of Rock and Roll 1980 A New Edition of the Best and Most Complete History Brought Up-to-Date and Expanded Edited by Jim Miller A Random House/Rolling Stone Press Book 3326

Magazine Article about CM's career, "Weird Time CM," by Jon Kalish 1980. 3370

Card-advertisement for New Wilderness Listening Room 1980 Card-sized advertisement: "Listen! 3379

Correspondence with CM and Unikun, Emil Kristof about "Laborem Exercens" 1980 concerning CM's role 3413

The Non-Profit Alligator 1980 New Wilderness Art Work 3420

Biography and Music of Greta Monarch 1980. 3435

New Wilderness Events/Copier Graphics/NWF Masks and Art 1980. 3451

"Cope" by Paul Borum 1980 given to CM 3457

Horizontal/Vertical Band Recorded live at Quadrasonic Sound, NYC. June 27th, 1980. 3466

Birthday Card to CM from Alison Knowles in Italy 1980. 3483

Ken Hiratsuka Art 1980 Four pages of Ken's Art on Yellow lined pad. 3497

CM looks back at Expressionist Music 1980 A three page paper with an opening statement by Armand Schwerner 3504

Concretismo '80 1980 A set of limited edition B&W postcard photos from six artists. These were from Angel Cosmosto CM 3586

Really Love NY Alison Knowles and Philip Corner 1980 A promotional flyer for 3596

When John Lennon was slain 1980 A sound poem of what Yoko Ono said... o no o no..... 3599

A Coal Mine Production Poster 1980 Art by Tod Jorgensen for June 4th performance. Film. Poetry, Dance Party. Producer is Arleen Schloss. 3606

The Arch Ensemble for Experimental Music Poster 1980 Poster, Invitation and Tickets sent to CM from Berkley CA. The Arch Ensemble Tom Buckner, Musical director. 3610

Simone Forti Poster 1980 At the Performing Garage. Simone Forti performs Jackdaw Songs, with others assisted by Dance Theater Workshop. 3611

First Catalog of The Concrete Poetry Archive 1980 Catalogue #1 Oxford, England 3612

New Music America brochures (2) 1980 Held at the Walker Art Center, Minneapolis MN Sound instalations by various artists. Environmental music by CM, Charleemagne Palestine, Richard Lehrman, Christopher Janney. 3627

Vlastos and Friends Flyer 1980 An exhibition at the Nicolaysen art museum in Casper Wyoming 3636

Sonatas Folder, Fiddle Chant, Sonata for Violin Unaccompanied, Sonata II, 1980 Other Media 3653

New Music Calendars Vol. 1 #6 and #7 1980 A publication of Composers Forum with ads from major artists and orchestras. 3682

Vocal Music of Charie CM Program from The Abraham Goodman House Concert by The Western Wind 1980 June 25, Also color flyer for concert 3694

Anagram Picture Song by Jean Dupuy 1980 A folio of original poems for the sound text issue of EAR Magazine. Also an installation at Lincoln Ctr. for the Arts Dec. 5 with performers Jon Ericson, Tony Kuiak, Mary Thomas 3720

CM & Tom Buckner & Big Black Tumbas 1980 An Early poster for a performance at 337 E. 8th St. 3723

Air March Haydn Jean Dupuy 1980 An art piece By Jean Dupuy, May 7, signed bon voyage, Richard 3745

Sometimes I Wonder 1980 A CM Doodle on a Cocktail Napkin. And there are some Times in every Time. 3777

Annual Avant Garde Festival of NY 1980 An informational sheet about the history of the event and the ideas for this years festival. Sent to CM from Charlotte Moorman with note, Will you be with us? 3793

CM Horn & Harp 1980 Onsdag d. 16 Kl 13:00 In Denmark 3811

Center for Celebration Brochures (10) 1980 Founding Members of the Board of directors, Karin Bacon, Donna Henes, Ralph Lee, CM, Cathrine Milinaire, Antoni miralda, Marilyn Wood. 3824

KUGLA Art Poster 1980 Radnja Slika Zeinimuro, The Action of Pictures Design by Dubravka Sikic for Presentation at Galerija -Zagreb. 3836

4 Simone A White Pine Press Art postcard by CM 1980 Also a Postcard by Mikhail Horowitz, Stopping by Indian Point on a Snowy Evening. A note on the back about CMs Post Card from Dennis 3838

Postcard from Dick Higgins to CM 1980 Dick says he went swimming with a topless mermaid at the public Beach 3854

Christina Yuin Recent Photographs at the Kitchen Gallery 1980 September 9-27 1980 Artists Reception Sept. 13 1-6 PM 3857

Carl VO Kids/Tech Blue Sky CD 1980 3888

CMA Special Reel for WRG 1980 3891

CMA Video Sample Beta SP 1980 3892

Original manuscript for Ear International issue Review of 2nd Alternative Music Festival 1980 Second annual Alternative music Festival NY/ Valencia Knowles 3914

Min Tanaka Solo Dance duo with Derek Bailey Guitar Poster 1980 Poster for different venues CM on Nov. 19th with Glen Velez. other workshops listed. 3921

The Plainfield Festival Poster "Cruelist Month" by Margo Lee Sherman 1980 Sat, August 23 at the Community Center. 3922

Fire on the Water Program 1980 Jacques Marchais Center of Tibetan Art, The first week of Summer, a program of Tibetan Music, Firewater rite, Midsummer buffet, Ocarina Orchestra 3932

Envelopes, A Letter from: 1980 Laurie Anderson, David Byrne, David Harrington, Meredith Monk, Pauline Oliveros, The Residents, Henry Threadgill, John Zorn. Probably an Ear magazine promo. 3949

Olatunji Center for African Culture Brochure 1980 Babatunde Olatunji Bio and program notes for his Dance troupe. Also, an 8x10 glossy photo of Babatunde 3951

The Communists Band 1980 3 8x10 B&W photos and original handwritten lyrics. Marxist Mona Lisa, Blonds, Cats in Heat, Camouflage. 3979

Communications Spritual Analysis Speech, an evolved Social...1980 Notes on projection of self image. Body image 4013

Drive on Body Weather Laboratory 1980 Body Weather as a state of mind. A single sheet flyer. Atmospheric pressure may be a good visual metaphor, but body weather does not exist without our will and awareness. 4019

Richard Alpert, Time Expands to fill the Mold 1980 A postcard for a performance at LA Mamelle Inc. San Francisco Drawing by Richard Alpert 4020

Dali, RIP Hayman (2) 1980 A work written at the request of Salvador Dali. This appears to be a cover letter. The piece may be seperate, however the conductor using a toothpick as a baton may be the total concept. 4027

The rise of alternative music in Sweden (2) 1980 A small magazine format piece explaining the political power of music in a small country. From revolt to adaptation. Start up Networking and associated small labels, and independent means of production. 4029

The Apple of his Eye, Lois Unger Freifeld 1980 Signed to CM, Typeset at the Chronicle, Barton, VT 4062

42 Merzgedichte, Jackson Mac Low 1980 signed by Jackson and Anne Tardos in Memoriam Kurt Schwitters 4088

Embryo 12, Hermetic Back Poem, Sten Hanson 1980 Sten Hanson, Johan Donner, CM von Hausswolff, Rolf Borjlind-Carsten Regild 4097

Paper Air, Jackson Mac Low 1980 Vol. 2 #3 John Cage pg. 36 writes about Jackson. 4103

Gee-Whizzels, Bern Porter 1980 Maine Coast Printers, Rockland ME. Signed 4110

Music: A pictorial Archive of Woodcuts & Engravings 1980 841 Copyright Free Illustrations 4121

Text Sound Text, Edited by Richard Kostelanetz (2) 1980 William CM & Co. NY Text Sound Art & Sound Poetry Fluxus People, Audio Graphics people NEK 4134

Dan Erkkila, Paperwork Poster(25) 1980 at Cornelia Street Cafe 4148

Encontre De Compositors I Sa Pobla 1980 A program from a concert in Mallorca 4167

CM A Recipe for Sounding: Jerome Rothenbergs Beadles Testimony 1980 Notes On Soundings on the Back 4228

SingOut Vol 28 #6 1980 Folk Song Magazine 1980 4250

Composer Will Chant for Sunrise 1980 Burlington VT Free Press

Aug. 24 WRUV Broadcast 4270

New Music America Takes Over a Town, Press from Village Voice (10) 1980. 4276

Jean Dupuy "Food Stamp" 1980 Given to CM 4288

Parnassus Poetry in Review 1980 History and philosophy of Parnassus in Review with highlights of Volumes 1-9. Listed Board of Directors, Funding Sources. 4313

Wolf Rogolsky Information and resume. 1980 writer, wine maker, director of GGK Advertising, met CM in 1979 4316

Handwritten Mailing Labels List from EAR Magazine. 1980. 4318

Healing Arts Folder 1980 A combination of various articles on healing. 4332

Original photo artwork for Humazoo Graphic 1980 Original Artwork and 5 printed posters 4336

Slow Hands, a piece for Video, voice and Synthesizer 1980 by Abby Luby 4338

Performance & Workshop Promo Flyers 1980 A Performance fact sheet of types of shows or workshops which CM will produce, Also Other Media Flyers for the same purpose. 4350

Wave III folder and other Events. 1980 Planning and budget info as well as more event ideas and proposals Nanna's Machine Dance, Running on the Walking street. 10 Events for Media. Rates for further usage in USA and Canadian Markets, etc. 4353

Sweden Folder 1980 4356

Jean Dupuy, Banana Dupuy 1980 Banana art and other French Folk songs copies. Photo from Columbia University Lecture 1980. CM conducting 4372

12th International Sound Poetry Festival Letterhead 1980 14 days of events at The Kitchen, Washington Square Methodist Church NWF. Letterhead 4377

Waves Waving 1980 A number piece by CM on small paper. 4409

Dream Event 1980 Venezia 4436

Halloween Parade 1980 4446

Hidemi Project 1980 Location Info 4451

Sunday Show 1980 Folder 4474

That Dada Strain 1980 Folder 4477

Beth Anderson, Duo, Solo and a Trio Poster 1980 42 Merzgedichte, Jackson Mac Low 4504

AudioGraphics Promo Photos 1980 Group shots of Cassettes for promotional use 4507

Burt Porter Bio and Poetry 1980 Burts Poetry 4515

New Music America Festival, Catalog of Performers 1980 Held in Minneapolis/St. Paul, Sun June 1st. Presented by Minneapolis Star and Walker Art Center. David Byrne, Phllip Glass, Alvin Curran, Lester Browne,

Laurie Anderson, Charles Amirkhanian 4521

Muslim Soup, by Tina Oldknow 1980 Original Manuscript by Tina Oldknow for New Wilderness Letter 11. 4545

New Wilderness Great Wind Event 1980 Sat Oct. 4 1980 sponsored by the Kitchen Center. Event at Riverside Park Hayman & CM Solos and Duets Flyer, Press Graphics, Fact sheet, Drawings Types of Kites. Plans for TV opportunities. Six Paper Airplanes Toy. 4550

Danspace presents, Free Lance Dance w/Steve Paxton. Lisa Nelson, Nancy Stark Smith, Danny Lepkoff, Christina Svane. Contact Improvisation Concerts 1980 At Third St. Middle School 4576

Ocarina Folder Press, Flyers, Museum Mile Birthday (5)performances, Solstice, Summergarden Crystal Score by Rip Hayman 1980 Whistle #5 Peter Robinson contact Sheet. 4579

Sari Dienes Drawing by CM, Sari Dienes Caracature by Jose Gregorio 1980 Small 4x5" drawings Of Sari 4600

Post card Gallery openings (5) CM, Warhol, Basquiat, Keogh, Mann, Rifka and Ancient NY Mosaics, Rimma & Valery Gerlovin at Emily Harvey 1980 4605

Will the Sun Come Back Illustrated Booklet by Mary G 1980 A beautiful hand illustrated booklet by Mary G 4606

Fanfare for CM's Birthday by Inge and Ivar 1980 To be played on his new piano, from your Danish friends 4614

Downbeat Magazine CM story and Picture 1980 June 4615

It's at MOMA, Arleen Schloss 1980 A five page printout of announcement FRIDAY13 A special evening of Performance Art, Video and Music sponsored by Junior Council of the Museum of Modern Art. Photo of Arleen by Chris Von Hohenburg. 4642

CM at UCSD 1980 Concerto for musician and video projection. Recently presented in NY, a collaboration with Nam June Paik. Includes on video Laurie Anderson, Peter Gabriel and Urban Sax. Special guest UC professor George Lewis. 4648

Europe 1980, CMA 1980 Carol Tuynman & CM. Concert For Magnetton band, First Music Festival with Catalunya and Valencia Barcelona Milano, Spoleto, Spello, Firenze other Lists of Activities, programs 4669

Chant for Peace, Donna Henes Poster 1980 Backside describes the first Women's Pentagon Action events 4672

Music and writings of Malcolm Goldstein 1980 From Wheelock Mountain several pieces of music, songs, stories from Malcolm from 1968 -1980. Photo and press. Niblock's Loft, Dana Reitz, Roulette concert series postcards 4681

Fall Festival of World Music Poster 1980 Benefit concert Fri Nov. 3rd Loeb Student Center NYU 4689

Letter from Charles Bernstein 1980 Letter contains photos of him. Letter states he will be a part of the Sound Poetry Festival. Letter is

Signed, 4705

The Labor Theater POWER poster 1980 Nat Horne Theater NYC 4708

Natural Assemblages and the True Crow, Alison Knowles 1980 Printed Editions, spine stain 4716

I Can Walk Through the World as Music, Philip Corner 1980 Philip Corner, Signed to CM 4717

4 Simone, CM (2) postcards 1980 White Pine Press 4741

Performance Poetry: Ellen Marcia Zweig Critical Approaches to Contemporary Intermedia. Signed to CM 4798

4 Simone, CM (40) 1980 All things can help each other 4854

Partition V, Bernard Heidsieck 1980 A book of poems and text and 6 Audio Plastic Records 33 rpm Signed to CM 4887

Starting off From Dead End, Michael Donohue 1980. 4899

Intrepid, Bill Williams & Flossie's special 1980 Editor: Allen Deloach 4941

The temple. Janet Hamill 1980 Telephone books 4996

Scenarios, Richard Kostelanetz 1980 Assembling Press 5008

Collective Consciousness, Jean Dupuy 1980 signed to CM, Performing Arts Journal publications 5017

Corpus Troporum IV, Gunilla Iversen 1980 signed to CM, Almqvist & Wiksell international 5032

The Arthur Cantor film collection 1980 Arthur Cantor INC 5107

Michael Cooper reading recent poetry & prose An indication of Green 1980 flyer 5129

The Face of Mannes, newsletter mentioning CM 1980 newsletter mentioning CM 5138

Music of the N. American Indian Catalog of music also a beautiful ink drawing of a Dancing Indian, signed by the artist 1980 Recordings and music of different tribes for sale by Canyon Records. 5146

Money for food Press 1980 A small catalog of Brian Buczaks and Geoffrey Hendricks smal handmade editions.With Alison Knowles, Dick Higgins, Avant GardeFestival, Something Else Press, In Grey She Ate, Memorial tribute to George Maciunas 5151

Sound Graphics, A folder of Good Listening Examples 1980 16 Examples of speaking and Chanting variations. 5161

Poul Borum, MacMoon Project 1980 Poul Borum, 37 Havnegade, D 1058, Copenhagen K, Denmark -1-154024. 5170

Swedish Book, Build Your Own Instrument 1980 By Ljudleks Lanken Great Graphics and Drawings, Instructions for building Homemade Instruments. 5192

Language 1980 Jackson Mac Low article in small publication with other writers and Artists 5193

Listening to Rothenberg, CM 1980 A two Page article by CM 5194

Mary Jane Leach, List of works collected of like instruments 4 or more. 1980 At Third Street Middle School 5214

Islands of the Moon, Steve McCaffery 1980 Book from the Students at Sir Alexander Mackenzie Senior Public School in Scarborough. Language Arts Project 5218

Sound Poetry Fest Signed Releases 1980. 5221

Texas Tech University Presents CM Flyer 1980 Sixth Guest in the Leading Edge Music Series. CM Demo "Dream Singing and other Chant Procedures." 5224

Ronald IN 'T Hout, Rotterdam, Holland 1980 Promo piece for Photographer with 5 Glossy Postcards. 5279

WHERE Postcard Promo for Jean Dupuy 1980 At Emily Harvey Gallery, no date. 5281

Doing A Project, CM Draft 1980 A Guidebook for Art Presentations, The Subway Workshops How to put together an Event. 5282

The Pig Song, Canadian Beer and Ale 1980. 5310

Dreamworks, New wilderness 1980 A New Wilderness project. Mechanicals, Pasteup of pages 5318

The Ink Tank Promo Piece 1980 Filmmakers Promotional piece, Creative Director R.O. Blechman, Ex Producer Brian O'Connell 5326

Program Notes, CM 1980 Program Notes for a Concert, CM, Higgins, Steve McCaffery, Armand Schwerner, Ted Levin Where, When ??? 5333

Work Schedule for Emile Leonard Show 1980 CM, Shalom. Scott 5336

American Indian Community House, Newsletter 1980 1978 Thru 1980 Meetings and Events calendar 5368

Letters, Plans and Programs for Spain. Also Bios and letters from Carol, CM, Glen, Review 1980 Madrid, Valencia, La Musica Ceremonial de CM Program Glen Velez Program 5386

Touchstone Center Flyer 1980 Festival in honor of The Earth and Sky 141 East 88th St. NY 5402

My Life as a Game 1980 Drawings and ideas for a Game of Life 5405

The Creation of a Dictionary of Native American Literature 1980 A Letter from Brian Swann. Do we need such a Dictionary, ? Format, Greenwood Press 5412

Letter to CM from Monika Bring 1980. 5423

CMA Stationary Sample 1980 365 West End Ave. 5437

Richard Meitin and CM Photos 1980 5x7 B&W photos 5442

12th International Sound Poetry festival, Review by Rochelle Ratner 1980 Held April 12-21 at the Kitchen. CM mentioned also Velez, Porter, Ocarina orchestra 5448

Dear Mr. Freilicher Poem by CM 1980 Reb' Nachman of Marmitzaah 5450

Music for Wilderness Lake by Murray Schafer Press Kit 1980 Outline of the Film and Bios 5453

List of International Festivals and Contacts 1980 5503

Letter w/Photos of Ken Hiratsuka and students carving rock art 1980. 5528

The Blended Life (working title CM Story) 1980 CM's Life Story 5606

12th Annual Sound Poetry Festival Letterhead 1980 Committee listed, Sponsored by New Wilderness Foundation 5644

Sound and Text Pieces, Peter Van Riper 1980 537 Bway NY 5651

Video Reel Credits List, CM Associates 1980. 5658

Barkcloth Painting 1980 Bird & Rabbit Barkcloth Painting 2551

Fragments of A Life Line 1980 Isolated Energy Passages in the Human Heart 7 pages of Auricle and Ventricle Contraction Graphics (each beat makes two sprial Loops) 2928

Developers 1980 Handwritten composition: unknown title/year Composition: "We are the developers" 3164

O.ARS Contributors List 1980 P.O. Box 814 Cambridge, MA 02139 A Listing of Contributors 3818

Possible CM performance piece written by a copyist. 1980 3 Acetate and colored pens score for performance. CM; Higgins music for trees? 3852

George's Delight for Wind Band 1981 Head chart melody with procedures for variations. 224

Birdsong for Windband 1981 Head chart melody with procedures for variations. 335

Principles for Playing Chorals and Other Music using Sky as Conductor 1981 Use the sky as a conductor: the wind, birds, and cloud movement imply tempo and phrase; the amount and color of light and weather, mood; and so on. 446

Emerald Island 1981 demo 550

Wave Music VII: 30 Harps 1981 live performance at St. John the Divine, NYC 699

Wave Music VII: 30 Harps 1981 live performance at St. John the Divine, NYC 986

Wave Music VII: 30 Harps 1981 live performance at St. John the Divine, NYC 996

Inauguration Event 1981 A group of close friends gathered at Washington Square Church, where we often perform, to react through work and discussion to the first inauguration of Ronald Reagan. 1136

Original version 1981 A musical distraction with announcer, orchestra, referee, judges, bucket boys, dancer, and two sound fighters. This event took place in Gleason's Gym and packed the place. CM won unexpectedly -- as there was to be no winner -- ear [full names for Hanson and Santes] See review by Tom Johnson in Village Voice and book compiling his reviews: THE VOICE OF NEW MUSIC (1991) An anthology of articles on the evolution of minimal music in NY in 1972-1982, which originally appeared in the Village Voice. Published by Apollohuis, in Eindhoven, Holland, but also available from the Two-Eighteen Press. Table of contents available soon. Poster - art directed by Sten Hanson 1147

Sound Images (with Sten Hanson) 1981 A collection of drawings by Hanson and CM, used to generate small sound performances by them. 1158

Death in Africa: An American Participation Lumumba Hammarskjold Sadat 1981 The leader chants the text. The group responds and develops it instrumentally. 1169

Warren Smith 1981. 1176

Gesture Music I, II, III 1981 Using gesture -- especially hand signals -- as music, with and without sound, solos and duos and group pieces are developed. 1180

Dawn music with stone sculptor and stone rubbings at St. John the Divine 1981. 1428

Spring Is 10-23-1981 Original song sheet - ? if Cummings text, likely 1969. 1444

Heavyweight Sound Fight Posters 1981 A musical distraction with announcer, orchestra, referee, judges, bucket boys, dancer, and two sound fighters. This event took place in Gleason's Gym and packed the place. CM won unexpectedly -- as there was to be no winner -- ear [full names for Hanson and Santes]  See review by Tom Johnson in Village Voice and book compiling his reviews: THE VOICE OF NEW MUSIC (1991)

An anthology of articles on the evolution of minimal music in NY in 1972-1982, which originally appeared in the Village Voice. Published by Apollohuis, in Eindhoven, Holland, but also available from the Two-Eighteen Press. Table of contents available soon. Poster - art directed by Sten Hanson 1538

Poetry Reading by Dawn McGuire & Mark Melnicove 1981 Tues Jan. 9th College of the Atlantic Bar Harbor ME. 1543

Art On The Beach (8) 1981 CM and the Ocarina Orchestra perform on Sunday July 12 1981 produced by Creative Time. 1551

Great Wind Event Slides (21) 1981 Great Wind Event Slides 1576

Equestrian Music I Cavalry Band 1981 Original Score and performance notes Systematic processional and horse dance music for Royal Cavalry Band, of Stockholm, Sweden. 1656

Direct Disc: May 6, 1981 direct disc/Horizontal Band. 1658

Spring Is 10-23-1981 Original song sheet - ? if Cummings text, likely 1969. 1659

Many Mansions 1981 Television film score 1661

Equestrian Music II 1981 Systematic processional and horse dance music for Royal Cavalry Band of Stockholm, Sweden. 1667

AT&T picturephone meeting service 1981 5 pages 1672

Tamborine Ambling for Glen Velez 1981 Four movement piece written for Glen Velez, Dec 15 Experimental Intermedia Foundation Concert. Copies on hand have concert program on backside. 1687

Keeping On - feature film score 1981 A coloristic and minimal blues score for film by Barbara Kopple. Features Major Holly on scat/bass, Peggy Blue, and Toots Thielsman, who whistles the theme song. 1855

Wave Music V: Conch Chorus and Bagpipe 1981 Day long event, solstice celebration, Lincoln Center Band Shell, 21 June Wave V: Grand Conch Chorus Solstice moment with spanish bagpipe noon of solstice day sunset, too. [reorganize this] 1867

Voice Dance 1981 A studio work for voice -- reminiscent of Major Holly scat/bass -- and metronome clicks 1878

Stockholm Snab 1981 A chain of performers spaced within earshot of each other echo the composition one after another from the outskirts to the center of town. 1889

Great Wind Event 10-4-1981 Notes, Posters Invitations, Photos and Permits for Riverside Park NY. event 1941

Summer Solstice Music 1981 event broadcast Valse, Gaillarde, Waves, C Minor March, Rhythmic figure for pitch stack, The Magic Cross, Wind symphony-Daniel Goode, CM, Riding on the wind, Blue Drone and Canon, Bird Songs, Overture, Earpiece, New Britain, Georges Joy, Hope, Canon for Summer Solstice, Asparagus, My private beach, Summer Alleluia, procedure, C/Moore 2023

Songs for Spring 1981 3 pages. Words and music to one song--CM; words to one song--Terry Blaind & Thomas DeSisto 2070

Nannas Machinedance 1981 music film by CCM 2195

MTA 'Train to the Plane' 1981 MTA-351 :30 'Why didn't I' 2252

Four Horsemen, Canadian sound poets 1981 First NY appearance of Steve McCaffery, B.P. Nichol, Paul Dutton, Raphael Baretto-Rivera. Friday Feb. 9th Sponsored by Canadian Consulate & New Wilderness Foundation. 2451

Zygmunt Krause Letter 1981 A large letter to CM from Warsaw, some damage. 2466

Conch Chorus 1981 Sundown Set 6:30 7-12-81 2473

Great Wind Event 10-9-82 Flyer (20) 1981 Program Flyer Artists Listed 2482

Mail Art 1981 An 8.5 x 11" envelope with many post me stickers and various artistic stamps and rubber stamps. Sent to CM 2491

Carnaval 81 Sevilla Poster 1981 A color poster from Carnaval Sevilla 2495

Keynote magazine 6-81 (15) & 7-81 (4) 1981 Issues of Keynote magazine CM is on the Cover. 2509

Airlie 3 Poster 1981 Third invitational seminar on the art of radio 2513

Tambourine Mumbling For Glen V 1981 Score Notes for Glen on tambourine 2520

T.B.K.T.T.C. Performance at Grommet gallery 1981 2524

Summer Solstice 1981 Poster 1981 About 60 Newsprint posters 2532

Heavyweight Sound Fight Poster (45) 1981 SoHo Baroque Opera Company presents 2550

Horizontal vertical Band at the ZONE 1981 Friday March 26, Springfield MA. 2569

Ten Ways Of Looking at a Bird 1981 Score for Violin & Harpsichord By Dick Higgins Printed Editions 2594

Encapsulation 1981 A piece for Cello, Metals, Voice and Video by Abby Luby 2599

Heavyweight Sound Fight Photo Art 11x14" contact sheet 1981 by Jean Dupuy 2618

Wind Band Invitation to Play Music Nite June 16 1981 Fifth Ave. & 102nd Programme Wind band and Special Guests. Wind Band Dance Jam 2630

Music Department Allegheny College Poster New Old Music Event organized by CM 1981 Original poster and a poster with production notes of musical pieces times. 2656

CM In Residence Poster Allegheny College 1981 Jan. 26-29 On Campus 2657

New Music Alliance Newsletters (3) 1981 New Music Alliance board is to provide advice to those who take on running the festival each year. 2700

Ten ways of looking at a Bird For Violin and Harpsichord by Dick Higgins 1981 Photographic and musical interpratations of Higgins photos of Roger Berard. Printed Editions, West Glover VT. 2707

Twenty six Mountians for viewing a sunset from by Dick Higgins (2) 1981 Printed Editions Dick's sound art. 2710

Envelope 1981 A subscription based mailing of various poets works which were delivered in an Envelope. #3 #4 #5 #6. David Abel, Haroldo de Campos, J.A. Lee, 2720

Ear Magazine Benefit (7) 1981 Small Poster for May 25 & 26 at 425 Broome St. 2723

Louis Moreau Gottschalk 1981 A biography of LMG prepared for Other Media Records 2790

Great Wind Event 10-4-1981 (3)A Poster and Childs artwork 2791

CM Associates Trade Ad 1981 Three copies of Trade Ad for CMA "It would be easier if we just showed you our reel." 2796

Alternative Museum presents CM and Glen Velez. Cross cultural

New music. Poster w/Press info. 1981 Fri. May 8 Alternative Museum 17 White St, NY 2803

Boxing Photo 8x10 glossy for heavyweight Sound fight. 1981 2826

Dreamworks Vol.2 #1 1981 Exploring Dreams and Film by Center for the Humanities UCLA published by Human Sciences Press 72 Fifth Ave. NY. This issue contains an ad for New Wilderness Letter Dream Issue. 2857

Experimental Intermedia Foundation (8) 1981 Program for a performance with conceptual art on back (4 Glen Tambourine) 2918

Dick Higgins Business Card Art & Texts 1981 Business card from Barrytown, NY 2933

Jean Dupuy Confession Under Luna 1981 A conceptual text piece for CM on 3 Pages 2935

The Dodecaphonic System: Macrotonics, Dick Higgins 1981 A Higgins Manuscript from Barrytown NY about a metric tonal system of 10 notes rather than 12. 2936

Letters from Dick Higgins to CM 1981 His letters and notes to CM about Vermont and properties. 2939

Keynote 1981 June 1981 Edtion of Keynote, a Magazine for the Musical Arts including the WNCN Program Guide CM is the cover story 3068

Wind Band 1981 Wind Band Tuesday June 16th 1981 Museum Mile Featuring CM performing Bird Songs, George's Joy 3124

Summer Alleluia 1981 Hymn for Solstice by Tui St. George Tucker written for full participation 3128

Heavyweight Sound Fight 1981 Small Poster. A musical distraction by Sten Hanson, CM, and Carles Santos 3132

Oyster Dream 1981 Live Sound Art: Amolified water spills, rock knocks, shell scrapings 3148

UCSD Presents CM 1981 Poster From The UCSD InterArts Consortium an the Center for Research in Computing and the Arts (CRCA) is pleased to present" Events Producer and Composer: CM with special guest: George Lewis 3153

Poster: New Writing Series 1981 UCSD Presents New Writing Series Featuring CM with Jerome Rothenberg. CM, an internationally known composer, performer, sound-poet, and event maker, will perform works of his own and shared compositions stemming from over two decades of collaboration with Rothenberg and other U.S. and European poets. 3154

Great Wind Event 1981 Riverside Park Sat Oct. 10 Music by CM New Wind Band, Grand Conch Chorus 3176

Actividades Culturales. Martes Universidad Complutense De Madrid 1981 Actividades Culturales. Martes Aula De Musica Undecimo crso de creacion musical A cargo del compositer CM A las 12,45 horas Facultad de Flosofia, Edificio A 3217

"For the Birds," by John Cage. 1981 Trans. Charles, Daniel. Marion

Boyars Inc, Salem, NH. Poetry by John Cage. 3261

Poster for William Hellermann New Music: City Games 1981 Poster for release of New Music: City Games Alternative Museum 3336

"Summer Alleluia" Hymn for Solstice by Tui St. George Tucker 1981 Full participation piece for Solstice 3425

Issue of Performance Art featuring a New Wilderness Audiographic Advertisement 1981 page 17 3430

Issue of the WXPN express featuring CM in a Program Guideand Issue of Stony Hills with picture of Carol Tuynman of New Wilderness 1981 3432

Alison Knowles On the Book Of Bean 1981 Proofs from New Wilderness Letter #11 The First Guided tour through The Book of Bean. Some copier graphics included. Proof pages with Mary Nell corrections. 3476

George Quasha, Auto Dialogue on the Transvironmental book. Reflections on The Book of Bean. 1981 second proofs for NWF newsletter. 3477

Heavyweight Sound Fight Flyer 1981 Black and white small flyer for soundfight. Photo of Sten Hanson, CM and Carles Santos 3482

Spirit Voices, small Poster 1981 Modern Ceremonial Composition Based on Siberian Shamanism at Antilles Field. Presented by the Voorhees Assembly Board 3490

CM AG 8130A COA Workshop 1981 Shurefire fires & chanting on Maine jetties. Audiographics Cassette Insert 3544

Bell Roll Performance by RIP Hayman Lumnai Gallery Tokyo 1981 Letter to CM from RIP from Tokyo Hilton and news article of his ship lost at sea. Letter in Chinese and Gallery announcement 3567

Kitchen 10 1981 Tenth Anniversary Celebration June 15- 71 Ten Years of new Dance, Music and Video Byrne, Glass, Monk, Anderson, Eno, Paik at Bond International Casino 3568

Jackdaw Songs Simone Forti with the Wooster Group at the Performing Garage 1981 Poster: March 30 thru April 15th 33 Wooster St. assisted by Dance Theater Workshop 3574

An Afternoon/Evening of Poetry & Music Performance 1981 Saturday June 28th withJohn Beaulieu, Charles Doria, Mitch Highfill, CM, David Abel, Jackson Mac Low, Mary Jane Leach, Franz Kamin at 10 Leonard St. Prospect Books. 3575

Bern Porter and Mark MelniCove ON TOUR 1981 The Eternal Poetry Festival 3576

Bread & Puppet Museum Opening 1981 Poster with another sheet of Summer Events 3578

Tunnel Hum Poster 1981 By Bonnie Barnett Sat June 13th 3PM Part of New Music America 3580

Geoff Hendricks Sky Show 1981 Presented at The Old Public School NY. People were invited to bring something about the Sky. Five Postcards of skies by Hendricks included. 3597

Illusion & Reality Postcard Show 1981 Flyer Postcard Call for Entries. April 22 thru May 5 that Otto Tron Gallery 101 UWRF River Falls WI 54022. 3607

Testing the Boundaries, Dick Higgins 1981 A sound art piece manuscript with accompanying map of Voyelia. To be performed for 4 minutes. 3641

Landscapes by Jack Ox (2) different in same folder 1981 Black and White ink drawings of mountainous landscapes. Approx. 15" x 36" 3646

Events Envelope 1981 Scores from Heavyweight Sound Fight, Toot & Blink Chicago, 2 of Each. Other Media. 3665

The Bean Garden, program by Alison Knowles 1981 A program/poster for the Knowles and Ecart Group 3689

Taller De Creacion Program (12) 1981 A Black and White program Musicas Ceremoniales por CM 3692

Taller De Creacion Program, Glen Velez (5) 1981 Programs 3693

New Wilderness Foundation History and mission Statement 1981 Contains History and Mission, Case Statement, Financial Statement, Progress against Budget Staff and Board of Directors, Advisory board Artistic and executive Directors Resumes. IRS 501(c) Determination Letter 3708

New Wilderness Foundation Audiographics Project Narrative Report July 1981 A report on the progress 3710

Bill Rabinovitch Illustrations from Boat Event 1981 Four Illustrations 8 1/2 x 10. 3722

Company Week Poster, Derek Bailey 1981 Derek Bailey draws together improvisors for a week of music making at the ICA in London. Poster lists artists and dates. CM May 20th. 3738

Maine Poets Festival 1981 Workshop Folder with pieces from Bern Porter, Cary Lawless, Mark Melnicove, Pittore. Schedule Of events, and phone list. Articles: Selling poetry in Maine, Giving a Poetry Reading 3805

Experimental Intermedia Foundation Dec. Schedule 1981 CM Gesture Music and Other Works 3812

A Program in Audio Production by C. CM 1981 A paper on the basics of using sound and sound equipment. A draft with corrections and ideas with other 3823

Peter Riley 1981 Seven Performance photos and Reviews from Company Week. 3829

CM Writings while traveling 1981 Notes written on SAS airlines stationary to himself and others 3842

University of Madrid Actividades Culturales Feb. 1981 Flyers (20). 3850

Franklin Furnace Celebrates its fifth Birthday with Benefit performance by Laurie Anderson. 1981 Schedule for April thru July in Newspaper format w/large photo of Anderson 3878

La Musica Ceremonial De CM 1981. 3881

Gesture Music, Original Typed score for type setting.1981 by CM, Other media records 365 West End Ave. 3882

Mary's Drawings of Ojai Vernal Equinox 1981 Three page handmade booklet with humorous drawings by Mary 3913

Crossovers Performances Poster 1981 178 Franklin St. (Tribeca) Lots of performers and a crossover exhibit with Cage, Corner, CM, Anderson, Niblock, Mull, Mac Low, Sommer, Van Riper, Vonnegut 3928

Music of the World Brochure 1981 A small brochure from this independent label 3962

Canon For the Summer Solstice by Jackson Mac Low 1981 Original Manuscript June 14th A scan exists in Master Graphics 3991

Concert by Barbra Held and Joseph Kubera NY Post Cage 1981 Playing works by Rip Hayman, Doris Hays, Peter Zammo, Dan Godde, Nils Vigeland and William Hawley at the University Complutense, Aula De Musica 4031

Soundings No. 11, Peter Garland 1981 Anthology 4117

Soundings No. 12, Peter Garland 1981 Anthology 4118

Wobbling, Bruce Andrews 1981 Roof Books, 300 Bowery NY 4125

PREFaces & Other Writings, Jerome Rothenberg 1981. 4130

Poetry Project at St. Mark's Church 1981 Huge List of performers, John Cage, Allen Ginsberg, Jackson Mac Low, CM, Hannah Weiner, Armand Schwerner, Carlo Pittore, Marc Nasdor Jan. 1&2 at Ukrainian National Home 140 2nd Ave. 4203

Jean Paul Curtay intro by John Cage. 1981 A short intro by John Cage and a list of Body Sound art Performances, shows and Lectures 4208

The Other Publishers Catalogue 1981 4 Pages of Printed Editions Books in this Catalog. Higgins, Corner, Mac Low, Knowles 4215

Art News Dec. 1981 Peter Frank Story art music 4263

Crystal by RIP Hayman 1981 A piece for percussion instruments. A pattern to be repeated by each part with instructions 4303

Media Space, Perth, Western Australia 1981 Five Pieces of Conceptual Art from Media Space Paul Thomas, Allan Vizents, Julian Goddard 4305

Media Space Perth, Western Australia 1981 Two Pieces, Photo Notes and photos by Paul Thomas 4324

What to do this weekend, Martha Carroll staff writer for the Herald News. 1981 In the Ring, Heavyweight Sound Fight at Gleason's Gym 4329

Balloon Piece 1981 Production notes and script. Funding and photos. Produced by Sten Hansen and CM. Goodyear Airship photos and press and Albuquerque Festival brochure 4346

Euro Avant Garde Art Talk 1981 At the Ear Inn talk by Nicholas

Zurbrugg 4365

Ear Inn Feb. 1981 Events Flyer Groundhog Day Coming out party for Audiographics series, surprise guests 4367

Spirit Voices Solo Chanter Cue sheet for CM performance 1981 Snakey Chant and Binding arms, Breathing and Voiceless roars, Back of throat chant, and Brass solo. No Date or other info. 4407

Museum Mile Poster, 4th Annual street Festival 1981 Poster R.O. Blechman 4558

Spirit Voices Folder 1981 Planning, Timeline and Performance notes several copies 4609

CM performs New Music at Bath Dance Works, Bath Maine Press Release 1981 A healing Ceremony Music is the Healing Code 4646

John Zorn's CROQUET Poster 1981 Call for Open rehearsals Soundscape 500 W. 57th St. 4671

Alvin Curran letters 1981 To CM, A revision of "My music history" a signed piece. From CM about upcoming events 4704

Heavyweight Sound Fight 1981 Sten Hanson, CM, Carles Santos Held at Bobby Gleasons Gym Envelope contains Photos, Negatives, Small Poster flyer, Budgets and petty cash. Meet the Composer Inc. More Contact sheets from Mac Mcbride. Program notes. 4773

M.u.(z.i.e.k.) 2, Zweitschrift 8 1981 CM Pg. 65-69 Sten Hanson Pg. 70-71 Bernard Heidsieck Pg. 17-24. 4820

Open Places, Eleanor M. Bender Editor 1981 A collection of writings from many people. Stephans College, Columbia Signed to CM 4861

Sugar Teat, Robin Kay Willoughby 1981 White Pine Press Signed to CM 4867

The Z-D Generation, Edward Sanders 1981 Station Hill Press, Barrytown NY Zola- Diderots Produced at Open Studio, Rhinebeck, NY 4870

Coherence, Don Wellman, editor 1981 O.ARS/1 Cambridge MA Rothenberg Pg.149. 4901

Study no. 41 for player piano, Conlon Nancarrow 1981 Soundings Press 4932

Aural literature criticism, Precisely 10 11 12, Richard Kostelanetz 1981. 4951

Gesture Poems, C.E. Thalenberg 1981 Mosaic Press 4954

Recyclings, 1959-1981, Kostelanetz 1981 Future Press 4959

The Roots of Ticasuk, Emily Ivanoff Brown 1981 Alaska 4965

Lasers and Holography, Winston E. Kock 1981 signed to CM, Dover 4985

Hudson (1-16), Harry Lewis 1981 The Print Center 5015

Symmetries, Tom Johnson (2) 1981 218 Press 5033

Text 12, Mark Karlins & Bruce McClelland 1981 National Endowments for the Arts 5083

"I just wanted someone to know", Bette Craig and Joyce Kornbluh

1981 Flyer for play, Equity Approved Showcase production 5114

Great wind event flyer, CM, Trish Burgess 1981 flyer for show 5131

Anne Tardos, Performances of Workings Derived From Video Show Promo Flyer for Fri. Sat. Feb 6 &7 1981. 5203

Challenge Boxing Flyer, Program 1981. 5204

Third invitational seminar on the art of radio 1981 A Score 5286

Spirit Voices Cue Sheet Graphs 1981 Also find Spirit Voices Color Photos in Photo Cabinet 5328

Rimini-Italia proposal 1981 Letter inviting CM to festival and CMs Ideas for a project C. Other Media 5385

Statement of Plans 1981 Two metronome composition by CM 5455

The Future of Music, R.I.P. Hayman 1981 Written for New Aspect Art News, Taipei Taiwan 5472

Challenge, A San Francisco Special Event 1981 Tony Labat vs. Tom Chapman, Angel Rodriguez vs. Louise Loo Top Champion Women Boxers. Needs Restoration 5550

Boxing Poster Kezar Pavilion 1981 Louise Loo vs. Angel Rodriguez and 5 other Matches 5551

Rigsby Angels, Artists Proof 1981 Signed to CM by David Rigsby 5557

Heavyweight Sound Fight Flyer and negatives by Mary Ellen CM.

1981 35mm Negatives of Promo Shot 3 Boxers 5572

Company Week, Derek Bailey, Poster Letters And Notes 1981 Flyer for May 23 at ICA in London 5587

Chuck Stein Xeroxed Designs 1981 5650

DATA DD1 4BS A handmade booklet with story and pictures 1981 This is a postal code in Scotland, which may be relevant. This could be Guy de Cointet 2600

Girl War Poster 1981. 3727

Interaction Concert Carnegie Recital Hall 1981 Photo Flyer of the Band Jan. 12 sponsored by Concert Artists Guild 3859

Jamaica Presentation 1982. 85

WINS Logos #1 1982 drop outs track is damaged 104

“Oil Heat’s a Dinosaur” no v/o 1982. 124

Jamaica Presentation 1982. 134

Jamaica Presentation 1982. 296

BP for bp 1982 CM adaptation/arrangement of bp nichol excerpt form “text on the opposite page”. CM’s voice on exhale and inhale. accompanied by bass flutes. published on disc. Musikworks, Toronto, Canada 1020

Poul’s Song, Conch Dance 1982 Recorded in Denmark, Tranglen Studios, Copenhagen 1122

Brilliant Silence Part One - mix 2.24.1982. 1134

Metropolis Copenhagen 1982. 1135

Metropolis Copenhagen 1982. 1137

Wave Music VI: Toot 'n' Blink Chicago New Music Chicago Festival and Broadcast 1982 This event was created for the annual New Music America Festival in Chicago. It is a public event and a radio/tv event, honoring John Cage. Boaters were rehearsed to use their boats in the piece, which took the form of a drama. The fast Night Boat Squadron, just over the horizon, sped to Chicago's mile long Navy Pier. 1191

On the Beam 1982 A struck, amplified steel beam generates a sound field which generates pitches and colors to be further develped on flute, zoomoozaphone (Harry Partch instrument), and vocal barking. Written for Dean Drumond and Stephanie Starin. 1202

International Radio Solstice '82 broadcast 1982 International radio broadcast, celebrating the first day of summer (and winter below the equator) with a satellite mix of live events in Sweden, the USA, New Zealand, Canada, Denmark, and Italy. 1213

The Light Opera western Wind 1982 The six singers of The Western Wind vocal Ensemble and six Bhuto dancers lead by Min Tanaka work under Tom O'Horgan's direction in darkness with various sources of light. They explore the dual nature of the tool/weapon. The work includes guns and a jack hammer trio on lar Premier: La Mama Theater, NYC, Exceptional Poster by Japanese designer. 1236

Winter Solstice '1982 event broadcast Live mix of December rites from Alaskan women; New Mexico Pueblo Indians; a Beijing reporter; Australian aboriginal musicians; a NY celebration by artist Donna Henes; and from Italy, bells, bagpipers, the Pope, and composer Alvin Curran. 1324

A Participatory Chantabout (50) 1982 FLYER, To invoke the Female Forces of the Universe present in all People. On the evening of the Winter Solstice 12-21. On the Beach at Battery Park Landfill. Donna Henes 1477

Grand Conch Chorus Poster (100+) 1982 Press photo press release and small posters from a copy machine of two performers from the Grand Conch Chorus (25) Lincoln Center Damrosch Park Broadcast by International Radio Satellite. June 21st Photo credit: Lisa Kahane. 1487

Latin Music Percussion & Melody Glen Velez 1982 Musical notes on different Latin styles and drum patterns. 1509

Ear Magazine Maritime Rites (3) 1982 Ear Magazine poster U ask for it!! 1549

T.B.K.T.T.C. Performance (13) 1982 CM, Santos, Dupuy, Halberet Schwerner, Velez, Tuynman, Harvey, Adorno, Xatrec, Unuagist at Grommet Gallery NY 1550

Time for Celebration 1982 3 pages. CM at his most MOR. Words and music 1589

Music in the Key of J original art mechanical for ads 1982 Two studio live cable TV broadcasts, directed by Edmund Chibeau with the OcOrc,

New Wind Band, Horizontal Vertical Band, English guitarist Derek Bailey, composer Richard Hayman, performance artist Alison Knowles, Canadian sound poet Steve McCaffrey 1599

Show of Arms (with RIP Hayman) FESTIVAL event 1982 An event for the military bands of the five armed services of the USA, designed for New Music America, Washington, D.C. Each band marches a separate route playing music specially composed or standard marches recomposed by Hayman and Morrow. These parade routes cross over each other. Whenever bands meet, they roll up their sleeves and wave, roll down the sleeves and move on. At DuPont Square, they all meet, roll up, wave, and play The Grand Finale. 1610

Dawn Song (Lullaby, Linda Velez Chili) 1982 Single sheet copier score 1613

Adsuite/U.P.S. Liftoff, Borden Raindancer, Carrier Living Room- Bedroom, Mercedes Resale 1982 Instrumental music. 1671

New Wilderness Letter 11 1982. 1682

Oriental Cooking Show 1982 Original script and sound notes 1780

Dick Higgins 1982 An original Higgins Musical work 1857

Light Music 1982 Music using light, flashing and moving. 1900

New Wilderness Letter #11 12-0-1982 Five boxes 1918

Postcard from Heaven 1982 Musical work by John Cage for 1 to 20 Harps. A printed manuscript. 1946

Variations on a Natural Theme for Orchestra by Dick Higgins 1982 A Musical performance work by Dick Higgins by Printed Editions NY. 1947

Sonata for Prepared Piano 1982 A musical performance piece printed by Printed Editions, Barrytown, NY 1948

Trinity 1982 A musical concept piece by Dick Higgins w/ Autograph for CM 1949

Solstice 1982 - 6-12 1982 event broadcast Notes and posters, permits and letters for solstice event 1968

International Radio Solstice (1) 6-21-1982 event broadcast Poster art ideas and mechanical pieces, Satellite transmission online charts. 2032

Toot & Blink - Master 1982 Time: 8 mins. 27 secs 2067

Carrier Furnaces 1982 Arctic/800UGCA-4030. 2229

Carrier 'Ice Age' 1982 3 spots 6/29/84 84v65179. 2232

Music in the key of J 1982 4 3 82. 2301

Music in the key of J B3 1982 4 3 82. 2302

Music in the key of J 1982. 2306

Ancient NY Mosaic/The Gerlovins 1982 music by CM stereo 2319

Music in the key of J 1982 Ocarina Orch. Glen Velez Apr. 2340

Music in the key of J 1982 vt #2 show March 25. 2341

Music in the key of J ISO 1982 tp #3/4.3.82. 2342

Jackson Mac Low Retrospective Concert 1982 A celebration of his 60th birthday. Poster has list of performers. Higgins, CM, Corner, Cage,

Knowles etc. 2456

Summer Solstice 1982 Flyer (100) Grand Conch Chorus, International Radio Satellite 2480

Bookworks 1982 Poster An International Conference of Artists, Writers and Independent Publishers 2521

Anti War III Poetry Performance Festival 1982 Coordinator, Nancy du Plessis At Middle Collegiate Church Hall to benefit War Resisters League 2527

Ear Inn Program for March,14 1982 CM performs Ascent of Mt. Carmel 2528

The Ear Inn Program 1982 Program Of Barbara Held, Gilbert High, and Kathleen Kernell. Performing CM's Reconstruction of Bach B minor sonata 1st Movement and La Rosa Enflorece Ven Querica, Ven Amada. 2540

Large B&W Ink painting By Carlo Pittore 1982 Signed artwork to CM 2-9-82. 2547

Solaire Ensemble - stations 4 Rose Drachler 1982 Concert announcement postcards for presentation at Bargemusic Ltd. World premiere of Stations for solaire ensemble. 2566

Live at 10 Leonard Flyer Posters (about 50) 1982 April 6, 1982 Premier of Synaesthetics, Derek Bailey, Steve McCaffery, Patricia Burgess, CM, Carol Tuynman, Glen Velez, performers. 2573

Hermetic Back Poem. Sten Hanson 1982 A photocopy of 7 pages. 2587

Clean & Safe Seventh Annual Big Apple Radio Awards 1982 CM Musical Director JFK Express Metro Transportation Authority 2593

Young Fluxus by Ken Friedman & Peter Frank w/Elizabeth Brown 1982 Signed Copy to CM, an Explanation of the Fluxus movement and its artists 2597

Rouge by Jean Claude Riedel Publications 1982 A magazine format art Gallery Piece. CM Sound fight on Pg. 40 and 41 Many other artists Represented with photos of their works. Two original Dupuy Pieces inside. 2598

Way Down North 1982 Very nice art piece, The spinal cord is the golden String that links the sky and the Earth. 2614

Summer Solstice 82 Program (15) Grand Conch Chorus, International Radio Satellite 1982 Handbill Program 2631

MC 7 Map Coordinates Birthplace of Civilization Atlas 1982 A collection of art works from visual artists and poets on matters political, social and economic. By David Cole & Paul Zolovansky 2662

Saint Columbia by Dick Higgins 1982 For Vocal quartet or chorus, string quartet or string orchestra. 2673

Notes for Dick Higgins Audiographics Tape 1982 and contract 2684

Russian Samizdat Art 1960-1982 Brochure Poster 1982 An Exhibit designed and curated by the Geriovins Russian Self publishing 2691

NY Correspondence School Dinner Invitation 1982 A Symposium; Every participant is invited to propose a toast, followed by discourse to determine its meaning. 2692

Two Choreographers Julie M. Finch and Linn Walker 1982 A5 x 7" postcard type mailer for the performance. Music by CM and flutist Barbara Held (6) copies 2693

Piano Sonata #2 by Dick Higgins Graphis #192 (2)copies 1982 Song published by Printed Editions 2704

Dick Higgins Bio/Bibliography 1982 An original typed manuscript which was later designed and typeset by Jay Walbert at Creative Image and printed by Derby Port Press in Vermont. 2705

More thoughts on Dragon OFF 1982 Letter from unpublished editions about board meeting 2714

Fylkingen (16) Artist lineup flyer 1982 NY Music in Stockholm 2725

A Requiem for the Avant Garde and a Call for Resurrection by CM 1982 polemic essay 2757

1982 International Radio Solstice original artwork for Event June 21. 2776

The Grand Harp Event 1982 Black Poster or invitation printed in gold ink (14). 2777

Vision in Disbelief 4, poster 1982 Austrailian Center for Photography Biennale of Sydney poster Design by Hilarie Mais 2787

1982 International Radio Solstice Original poster idea art 2797

Raw Magazine pub. by Real Art Ways a page of Horizontal vertical Band 1982 with Glen Velez and CM appearing March 27. 2849

Russian Samizdat (self published) Art Poster 1982 exhibition at Visual Studies Workshop Rochester NY

Result of Circumstances of Contemporary Russian Culture 2860

Post Me stamp series 1982 A sheet of postage stamps from Carlo Pittore. For CM the music maker among us. Happy Birthday Feb. 9. 2862

Musicworks magazine #19 Philip Corner Piece 1982 "Certain Distilling Processes" pg.18 5259

Pastiche Group Show, Grommet Gallery 1982 Vol. 1 #2 Newsletter Emily Harvey Publisher 2863

Counterpoint Renga scorebook #22 a paper by The Concerned Artists Demanding Abolition of Nuclear Arms 1982 Based upon Japanese collective poetry renga in which the participants keep multiplying. Sent to CM from Udo Kasemets 2925

Dick Higgins Variations on a Natural Theme & Sonata for a Prepared Piano 1982 A printed editions REVIEW CARD for each of the above titles. 2934

A Flux Essay for a few of my Flux Friends 1982 Higgins suggesting Flux projects for his friends including John Lennon, Yoko Ono and John

Cage. 2937

Counting Duets by Tom Johnson 1982 A counting score signed for CM, and all the things that count. Editions 75, 75 rue de la Roquette 75011 Paris. 2956

Etching from Wolf Rogosky 1982 1982 An etching by Maxwell a gift to CM from Wolf Rogosky. 2970

Bard of the Ring 1982 Schedule/Flyer for Bard of the Ring - Poetic Sparring 3092

Down Town 1982 Published by the Lower Manhattan Cultural Council Summer 1982 Vol. 5 No. 6 Arts Activties in lower Manhattan 3110

A Memorial Concert of the music of Cornelius Cardew 1982 for the Benefit of his Family Tuesday May 25 Symphony Space NY CM performs in "Paragraph Seven - the Great Learning" 3111

Dressing Our Wounds in Warm Clothes 1982 Flyer for Ward's Island Energy Trance Mission Photographs by Sarah Jenkins, Donna Henes by participation projects foundation at Women's Gay Alternative and The Universalist Church 3113

Anthony Braxton and Muhal Richard Abrams 1982 The Kitchen Presents composer's concerts at Symphony Space 3117

3rd Anniversary Public Sale and Dress Up 1982 The Participation Project Foundation Inc. Independance Day 3118

Alternatives 1982 Vol. II No. 3 Audio Independents Radio Newsletter May/June 1982 Featuring article on 1982 International Radio Solstice by CM and Carol E. Tuynman 3119

How to Eat a Lobster 1982 Maine Poets in NY Poster at World Headquarter's of Poe's Overland Expeditionary Troop 3121

New Wilderness Events and Audiographs/New Wilderness History and Statement of Purpose 1982 Brochure describing staffing, goals, and finances and NWF Typed 3122

Music from Inside a Snowdrift 1982 Museum Mile Festival Protest War and Nuclear Madness Fifth Ave and 90th St. Featuring Beltain, The New Wilderness Wind Band and friends 3177

Publication Announcement: The Book, Spiritual Instrument 1982 by Jerome Rothenberg and David Guess 3199

C.A.T. Gallery Publication 1982 Collective Art Technology Directors: Peter Sepp and Lisa Sellyeh Toronto, CA Publication of C.A.T. Gallery: drawings and prose 3283

Summer Solstice 1982 Radio Signals CM drawing of radio broadcast emanating to different stations. 3284

Celebration: A World of Art and Ritual 1982 Signed to CM Office of Folklife Programs and Renwick Gallery of the National Museum of American Art. Published by Smithsonian Institution Press, Washington, D.C. 3316

Inuit: The North in Transition 1982 by Ulli Steltzer The University of

Chicago Press 3318

Inua: Spirit World of the Bering Sea Eskimo 1982 by William W. Fitzhugh and Susan A. Kaplan Published for the National Museum of Natural History. The Smithsonian Institution Press, Washington, D.C. 3319

Yves Klein 1982 by Pierre Restany Ste Nlle des Editions du Chene, Paris 3323

Sonorità Prospettiche 1982 Cura di Franco Masotti, Roberto Masotti, Veniero Rizzardi, Roberto Taroni Commune Di Rimini 3328

"You Can't Hug with Nuclear Arms: Photos from June 12 and Related Disarmament Demonstrations" by Jennifer Warburg and Doug Lowe 1982 Foreward by Reverend William Sloane Coffin 3350

"Floating Worlds: A book of essays, images, and letters about how artists feel about having children," by Aviva Rahmani 1982. 3351

The Eyes Have It: an Arctic Year, a Sound Art Project 1982. 3368

Radio Script for the Second International Solstice Radio Broadcast 1982. 3372

Notes on Sun Chant 1982. 3396

Mailer from the Solar Lobby 1982 explaining the Solar Energy National Security and Employment Act October 3444

Earworks, An exhibition of musical scores and sound art, Cards (8) 1982 Small announcement cards for reception at Grommet Gallery 537 Broadway, NY 3502

New Wilderness Board Notes and Letters 1982 Higgins, Knowles, Underhill, CM, Gorewitz, Duesing, Bacon, Korn, Hayman, Schechner. info. 3555

ARTCOM Magazine 1982 Vol .5 #17 Other Media Full Page ad on Back Cover. Charlotte Moorman photo, Takes on Paik, Warhol's TV 3560

Pauline Oliveros postcard 1982 Independent Composer, Performances, Lectures, Workshops, Writings, Consultations.Mt. Temper NY Sent to CM about missed interview with Ramon 3581

Sari Dienes show postcard for A.I.R. Gallery 1982 Show at 63 Crosby St. NY. May 18th-June 54 Opening May 18th 3617

Donna Henes Flyer 1982 A black and white flyer with personal note to CM about the review of his book 3620

Benefit Concert for Volume B&W Poster 1982 Volume the international catalogue & directory of audio work in the arts.Concert with Laurie Anderson and Peter Gordon's Love of Life Orchestra. Held at Irving Plaza SUN May 11 at 9 PM 3621

Alison Knowles Biography 1982 Fluxus, Higgins, Happenings, Bean - manuscript 3622

Russian Samizdat Art 1982 Die Cut Folded Graphic piece, promo for art show In NY and Washington. Curated by the Gerlovins Russian Art from 1960 thru 1982. 3626

Maritime Rites Poster 1982 A series of environmental concerts for radio in stereo by Alvin Curran. 3633

Toot & Blink Production notes 1982 A performance for boats conducted by radio broadcast. Schedules and actions. 3645

Nuclear America Itinerary Map 1982 A piece produced by Womans SAC (Survive and Continue) Map of US nuclear sites and what is stored there. 3681

Art for the Earth Poster with John Cage, CM, Donna Hennes & others. 1982 A gathering of artists, designers, musicians and event makers at the NY International AYH Hostel 891 Amsterdam Ave. 3688

New Music America July 1982 Cage, Other Media Interview with John Cage by Peter Gena Pg. 6 Other Media full pg. ad Pg. 51 Kitchen touring ad Pg. 50 Audio Graphics and Pg. 48. 3702

New Wilderness Audiographics 80-81 Final Report 1982. 3711

New Wilderness Fact Sheet 1982 Letter to Fred. Lets Do It!!! 3712

Music from Inside a Snowdrift, Museum Mile festival, June 8th 1982 featuring Beltain and The New Wilderness Band Protest the War and Nuclear Madness June 12th at United Nations. 3724

Ionizations postcard KOPN 1982 KOPN 89.5 fm presents CM Live May 12 10 PM 3744

Real Art Ways RAW 7th Season Program 1982 A catalog of performances for the season, CM & Glen Velez perform on Saturday March 27(page 20) Horizontal Vertical Band 3747

Toot & Blink Chicago 1982 Other Media, Stockholm Environmental Work for Boats Conducted by Radio Announcer 3750

A Phantom Typewriter piece by Henri Chopin 1982 A 5x7 art piece 3760

Trevor Wishart Samples 1982 An introductory letter from Trevor with samples of his writing and illustrations. Sun Landscape, Beach Singularity, Tower of Babel, and others. 3780

Collective Farm, SAMIZDAT 1982 Brochure for the promotion of a book of the first three issues which were added to the collection of the Museum of Modern Art. 3783

Letter from Alison Knowles 1982 letter about her getting a radio date with Klaus Schoening of WDR Koln Radio 3813

Summer Solstice 1982 Flyers (3) B&W and Press release draft. 1982 Solstice 82 Flyers (2) Lincoln Ctr. & Damrosch Park Monday June 21. 3820

Bread & Puppet Poster for Volunteers 1982 Call for Volunteers for Summer Solstice Celebration in Central Park. Fri. June 12. 3831

Listen! new Wilderness Listening Room Business Card Hans Wewerka, Edition Modern address on back 1982 Hans Wewerka Edition Modern, Elisabeth Str, 38 8000 Munchen West Germany Tel. 089;373781 Z.K. IDYLL soundscape 3856

Ear Works at the Grommet Gallery Postcards (25) 1982 Many artists Listed for show sponsored by Ear Magazine at Grommet Gallery 537 Broadway 3867

Memorial Concert for Cornelius Cardew (1936-1981) Bio and Concert Program. 1982 Alvin Curran, Christian Wolf, Philip Corner, Annea Lockwood and others. 3955

Ear Magazine Vol. 7 #2 Peter Frank interviews CM 1982 Music Media or Media Music interview with CM. Peter Frank was the Art critic for The Soho News, while CM was the music critic, Tom Johnson was the music critic for the Village Voice. 4030

Themes and Variations, John Cage 1982. 4093

The Word and Beyond Cosmologists of the World 1982 Higgins, Morris, Smith, and Phelps published by the Smith NY 4165

Other Media Copyright List 1982 Copyright Records from 1954-1982. 4212

Live at 10 Leonard Presented by Synaesthetics Poster with extra artwork. 1982 April 6, 1982 Performance spot/A show with Steve McCaffery, Patricia Burgess, CM, Carol Tuynman, and Glen Velez 4217

Perception, Don Wellman 1982 O.ARS Toward a New Poetics 4248

Eugenia Balcells Sound Works Book 1982 Letter To CM, small photos for Ear Magazine 8x10 B&W Also: 2 B&W 8x10 TV Screen shots. 4289

Tunnel Hum II by Bonnie Barnett 1982 Artwork for Tunnel Hum 2 Promotion from the files of Ear Magazine also an 8x10 B&W still photo of tunnel Hum 4297

Bern Porter signed and Numbered Piece. 1982 printed by Maine Coast Printers 4302

Notes on Five easy pieces for guitar by Laurie Spiegel 1982 Four Pages of Musical notation for guitar. Probably submitted to EAR magazine. 4319

ARTHEA, gestation sonore Amazing instruments and sound art 1982 Three copies of a promotional brochure with great photos of creative instruments 4326

Solstice II Production notes 1982 A Folder of misc. production notes from the second Solstice event 4343

Toot & Blink Chicago 1982 Program notes and planning papers 4349

Ear Magazine Benefit Flyer 1982. 4368

Maritime Rites, Alvin Curran 1982 A series of environmental sound works which take place on or near various bodies of water. Copies of score, photos, maps 4393

Radio - NY Art Parade, Important Credits 1982 Notes on Credits for the Radio show Joan Labarbara host. The first NY Art Parade produced and directed by Henry Corn. 4411

Running on a Walking Street: Stroget Dash- Copenhagen 1982 A Small script idea for a music film by CM and Friends. 4415

Jewish Heritage Museum 1982 Folder 4455

Roskilde Sound Art Museum 1982 Radio 4462

Roskilde Viking Museum 1982 Radio 4463

Talking Horns 1982 Folder 4476

Dick Higgins. NWF 1982 Artist Access Studio time Sheet for Prudential Demo & Gas Pipeline 4497

Who, Where and Why by Theobold 1982 Percussion Part along with set up notes for the performance 4503

Biennial Adelaide Festival of Arts for 1982 Letters and Telex from Silver Harris to CM 4513

NY City Lullabies Flyer 1982 Julia Lebentritt project director A presentation of NY Folklore Society. A NWF project which she took on herself. That is why it is not an Audio Graphics tape. 4519

Retrospective Concert for Jackson Mac Low in celebration of his 60th Birthday Concert Program and Press by Tom Johnson 1982 Sept. 12 at Washington Square Methodist Church. Produced and coordinated by Anne Tardos and Charles Bernstein. A great lineup of NWF musicians. 4529

Friends of the Earth 1982. 208 West 13th Lookout Project. 4685

Mis. Press and NY Scene 1982 June New Wave Guide, Solstice Ads, Bands etc...KOPN Program Guide 4548

Earth Ambulance Nuclear America Itinerary 1982 Womans SAC (Strategic Air Command Caravan), Map 1982 A graphic piece by Helene Aylon, Rescued Earth. A map showing the Nuclear Weapons Facilities and Targets. A great Anti Nuc piece of Art! 4557

Photo of Flag art by Eleve Lerochereuil 1982. 4588

Miami Miralda Festival of the Arts #5 poster, newspaper 1982 Large Graphic spread and several pages 4590

Proverb for Two Violins, Alison Knowles 1982 Original art piece probably from Ear Magazine 4622

82' Airwaves Newsletter Solstice issue 1982 Article by Carol Tuynman and CM about solstice Berkeley CA 4623

KPFA Folio, Newspaper Solstice notice 1982 Janet Rose talks about New Wilderness Foundation pg. 22 Cover signed from Jerry Rothenberg with regards from Charles Amirkharian 4624

Sun Radiants & Shadow, Phyllis Yampolsky 1982 Illustrated papers of a ceremony for the Summer Solstice Festival in Central Park 1985 Includes map of the park and actions for Ceremony materials and persons. Nine Pages. 4643

Carman Moore and Ensemble Flyer 1982 In Concert at Judson Church with three new Works. 55 Washington Sq. South 4653

Susan Sugar and Wendy Woodson Recent Works, Program 1982 CM sky Song choreography & Performance other performers and musicians 4677

Shadow Project, Alan Gussow 1982 Amy Manso letter from her all night adventure 4683

Lookout Project Poster and meeting notes 1982 Spring Equinox Anti Nuke Festival, Alan Gussow Life Yard Project, Remi Barclay Bosseau, Eric Salzman, Wayne Pease 4684

The Arts as a Universal Language Meeting Notice 1982 Friends of the earth 208 West 13th Lookout Project. 4685

Reverence for Life Poster 1982 A letter from Remi, asking CM to come to a meeting and become involved. 4686

LifeYard Project statement 1982 The start of a national movement. Started in Santa Cruz headed by Nicki Marx California painter and sculptor. Alan Gussow painter and sculptor. 4687

CM notes from the Lookout Project, Committee List, 1982 Community Affirmation Statement 4688

Becoming a listener, An approach to the Aesthetics of Radio, by Don Druker Coordinator of Radio for The National Endowment for the Arts. 1982 Manuscript sent to CM, Signed D.D. was former film Critic for the Chicago Reader and former editor of Focus. 4690

Company Week Folder, Derek Bailey Originator 1982 Meeting notes and sketches, Ideas from CM. New Wilderness, Press and Poster 4691

Oral Complex, Bob Cobbing, Clive Fencott, John Whiting 1982 Audio Arts, London Guest artists to the studio 4696

Maritime Rites, Alvin Curran, Info for use in Ear Magazine. 1982 Environmental Sound Works Alvin Curran Roma, Italy 4697

The Biebers Horspiel, Rothenberg 1982 Draft 1/21 The Beaver's Radio drama New Wilderness Foundation produced by CM for WDR, Jerome Rothenberg poetry and reading 4698

Alison Knowles Letter 1982 To CM, about The House of Dust 4703

Totems, Stanley Diamond 1982. 4752

Steve Mccaffery, Peace Piece, Chinese Sonata 1982 Submissions from Steve for Ear Magazine 4802

Study No. 37 For Player Piano, Conlon Nancarrow 1982. 4829

Totems, Stanley Diamond 1982 Signed to CM 4896

Parallax, Alan Loney editor 1982 a Journal of Postmodern Literature and Art 4897

Heart in utter Confusion, Steve Kowit 1982 Published by Dog Ear Press, Hulls Cove ME 4902

Throne/Falcon EyE, Hugh Seidman 1982 Signed To CM, Vintage Books, Random House 4906

L=A=N=G=U=A=G=E. Bruce Andrews & Charles Bernstein 1982 104 Lyndhurst Ave, Toronto Canada 4915

Short, Charles Doria 1982 signed to CM, Assembling Press 4918

Chinese Folk Poetry, translated by Cecilia Liang 1982 Beyond Baroque Foundation 4937

The Difficulties, Charles Bernstein issue 1982 Viscerally Press 4974

Love Songs. Bruce Andrews 1982 Pod Books 4990

Sex, performance, and the 80's. The flue Double issue 1982 Franklin Furnace 4991

That man who ground moths into film 1982 signed to CM. Peter Licht 4997

Egz book of frogs, Franz Kamin, Kathy Bourbonnais 1982 Station Hill Press 5019

Sound and Sentiment 1982 birds, weeping, poetics, and song in Kaluli expression. University of Philadelphia Press 5079

Druids mark solstice euphoniously, John Rockwell and papers on solstice 1982 NY times article and papers on solstice 5123

1981-1982 CM's works in progress 1982. 5125

Body Sound Feast 1982 with Jean Paul Curtay French Avant Garde Poet, composser, performence artist Experimental Intermedia Foundation. 224 Centre St. NY 10013. 5141

The Book of Kells, Dover Publication 1982 Color plates for reproduction 5205

The Final Academy Magazine, William Burroughs 1982 Statements of a Kind Arts publication stories and Art. Statement on The Final Academy. Darby, Nuttall, Wilson, Giorno, Balch, Sommerville, Bockris, Savage, Mottram, Mason, Miles, Wilson, 5270

Carolee Schneemann, mailer 1982 Spring performances. Five postcards of "More Meat Than Joy" 1979 photo by Herbert Migdoll "Water/Light/Water Needle" 5276

CM's Music for Handmade Instruments 1982 A folder of instrument designs and Ideas. Some ideas by Skip LePlante Music for Statue of Liberty 1984. 5300

Letter to CM from Philip Dodson 1982. 5303

Little Man Music CM Words, Susan Halloran 1982. 5308

Donna Henes, 7th Annual Winter Solstice Celebration Press Release 1982 Battery Park, December 21, WNYC, Lower Manhattan Cultural Center Battery Park Map 5331

Poetry Readings at 10 Leonard Street. small Poster 1982 Zweig, McMahon, Collum, Masters, Selby, King, Watson. Music and Words w/ CM, and others 5372

Exit Art - postcard 1982 The Right of Culture to Change itself. Founded by Jeanette Ingberman and Paco Colo Funding for the Arts Postcard 5414

More on Monday Concerts 1982 Listings for Monday Concerts at the Church of Saint Thomas More Western Wind perform Jan, 25 1982 Music for a Sacred Space: Mass for 5 voices by William Byrd, Canticle for Brother Sun by CM 5458

List of Funded Events, for New Wilderness July 1982 - July 1983.

5462

Ad World's Music Man CM 1982 Review, HeftEells, Rich, Green Agency 5465

International Radio Solstice Program Planning New Wilderness, Program DACS 1982 Carol Tuynman, NPR, Brigitta Robinson, Distribution Schedule, Funding. 5478

CB Travel Letters 1982. 5517

Speak Up Speak Out Stickers by Bern Porter 1982 Stickers in a small envelope, appear to be stuck together 5535

Alison Knowles, Fishes of the Philippine Seas 1982 Artist Proof 1982 signed For CM 5556

The Second International Radio Solstice New Wilderness Foundation 1982 Tech Notes and script of the event and planning 5614

The Newband, Kleinert Gallery, Woodstock, NY Program 1982 Concert with CM's and Joan LaBarbara's compositions composed for the New Band. zoomoozophone 5630

A Year of Daily Variations for Bugle Calls and Other Music 1982 Folder of FANFARE, Formations Forming, Tooting off Buildings, group Responses, Lights and Horses. 5653

List of Artists showing their projects Rimini Italy 1982 CM listed 5660

February At the Knitting Factory, Poster 1982 47 E. Houston, NY 3968

Bread & Puppet theater music 1983 1 CD from damaged cassettes 906

CMA Demo Reel 1.18.83 1983 1141

Wave Music VII: 30 Harps - rough mix 8.1.83 1983 St. John the Divine - P258 1152

Ear Motet 1983 A vocal exploration "CM's voice" of the word "ear," processed using a Synclavier. 1225

Wave Music VII: 30 Harps 1983 Thirty harpists sit in a figure-8 formation, wearing headphones over which they hear a cue track and drums via local FM link. The music traces through its spatial organization the the motion of sound waves. This is followed by lively dance music in the form of an additive canon. 1247

Solstice '83 event broadcast 1983 June 21, 1983 Public event in NY at Riverside Park Rotunda. Live international radio broadcast included New Zealand, Bermuda and Denmark. Production Notes and Radio Transmission rates. 1313

WKCR CM Festival 12 hours 2.8.73 CM Festival 1983 12 hour broadcast captured on 10 inch x 1/4, cassettes live and rolling from 365 WEA studio 1354

Benefit Concert for Ear Magazine(4) B&W posters 1983 World Premiere of Ear for Ear by John Cage performed by Western Wind. To coinside with Ear Exhibition “Musical Scores and Sound Art” at the Grommet Gallery, NYC. A large list of artists and performers. 1536

Lake George Ice and Air Event 1983 Sculptor Bruno Laverdiere clay horns were sounded by CM and musicians across the frozen Lake George (NY) as church bells rang to each other from opposite shores, from sunset till darkness. 1592

New Wilderness Big Mix 1983 This is a multitrack collage/mix of samples all the New Wilderness Audiographics artists work. Designed by CM, this was assembled on 24 tracks and mixed to stereo at Record Plant Studios, NYC by Jay Messina. 1596

4 Rose Stations 1983 String quartet in memoriam Rose Drachler. A recording of Rose reading her poem “The Counting Made the Corners Right.” 1678

Variation on a Danish Hymn 1983 Conceptual variations on a old Danish hymn, in Danish. 1833

Something Else Newsletter 1983 Dick Higgins Something Else Press Newsletter Vol.3 #2 Oct. 2027

Tablet XXIV 2-4-1983 1983 Dick Higgins Tablet XXIV, and short note to CM. 2029

VCA Teletronix Opt. Demo rl 1983 Act III c.1983 Renaicance c. 1984 Luminare c. 1985 stereo audio 2196

Light Opera 1983 edited master 1983. 2303

Music in the key of J ISO 1983 edited master 1982. 2343

First NY Art Parade 1983 A newspaper format Advertisement and lineup for September 27, 1983 at 7 pm. Also parade notes, staging areas etc. 2441

Cubist Prints and Cubist Books 1983 An Exhibition poster, Prints from the Weiss Collection. Oct, 18 1983 2489

FYLKINGEN 1983 Ostgotagatan Poster for performances in 1983 2502

Ice & Air Show Poster 1983 Concert poster for Works of Ten contemporary Artists on frozen Lake George Feb. 19-21. 2549

Ice & Air Show Flyer (6) 1983 Concert Flyer in Color for Works of Ten contemporary Artists on frozen Lake George Feb. 19-21 1983. 2564

Music for the Movies Toru Takemitsu 1983 A promotional flyer for Screenings at Studio 8. 2595

Earworks Invitation About (20) Grommet Gallery 1983 An Exhibition of musical Scores and sound Art curated by Jean Dupuy 2632

Song for any voice(s) and instrument(s) by Dick Higgins 1983 Graphis 192b 1983. 2671

Big Mix Control Room Sheet 1983 Record Plant Studios Tues. Nov.8, 1983 CMA enginer Jay Messina & Steve Marcantonio, Audiographics mixes Mac Low, Crow Dog and all others. 2701

Benefit Concert for Ear Magazine Poster (18) 1983 Concert April

8,1983, Exhibit of EARWORKS Musical scores and sound art March 11 thru April 16. 2732

Tunnel Hum USA by Bonnie Barnett, Flyer (25) 1983 July 31, 1983 Simultaneous live events in San Francisco and NY, mixed live and uplinked by Satellite. Also an advance flyer explaining the concert event. 2735

Sunday Readings at Newfoundland poster (2) 1983 March 6 Grand opening THREE DUOS Hettie Jones and Khan Jamal, Harry Lewis and Butch Morris, Armand Schwerner and CM 2763

The Making of Americans 1983 tenth annual marathon reading of Gertrude Steins The Making of Americans. At the Paula Cooper Gallery 155 Wooster St. NYC 2769

The First NY Art Parade 1983 Tues Sept. 27, 1983 7 PM Madison Ave from 104 to 72 streets. Made possible by Natl. Endowment for the Arts. 2773

Summer Solstice '83 Poster 1983 Tuesday June 21 Riverside park with Live transmission to International Radio Solstice. A New Wilderness Celebration 2812

Four Fertile events by Donna Henes Poster 1983 A poster for four events by Donna Henes all located in NYC. Summer Solstice, Autumn Alter, Winter Solstice, Vernal Equinox. 83-'84 Graphic poster By Susan Turner 2813

China Transformed 1983 An Event By RIP Hayman featuring Barbara Benary, erhu, nanhu Sat Hon, dizi: David Simons, zhenn, Hsueh Tong and Dian Chen, dance. 2842

WKCR CM Festival 12 hours 2.8.73 CM Festival 1983 12 hour broadcast. captured on 10 inch x 1/4, cassettes, live and rolling from 365 WEA studio 2893

Ten Year anniversary of Ear magazine Benefit Concert flyer (1) 1983 Concert with Western wind and others organized by RIP Hayman, April 8, 1983 at St. Bartholomew's Church. Sponsored by New Wilderness foundation. 2901

Other Stages Magazine 1983 Tom O'Horgan CM A light Opera story 2952

Stormfugle (Seagull) 1983 A printed art piece by Logos Duo for multimedia performance for Alison Knowles printed in Belgium 2968

The Light Opera, LaMama Annex. Poster 1983 Large poster, Music Conceived and Composed by CM 2990

The First NY Art Parade 1983 Guide to the First NY Art Parade Madison Avenue from 104th Street to 72nd Street September 27th, 1983 CM is thanked as a volunteer/advisor 3025

WKCR Press Release 1983 Press release for 1983 WKCR-FM. 12-Hour Radio festival honoring CM's composition and music on Feb 8. 1983 in celebration of CM's 41st birthday. 3040

Walkathon: A Walk for Survival 1983 Stop the Cruise and Pershing

II Missiles October 1, 1983 In which CM and the Grand Conch Chorus Performed 3078

New Wilderness Summer Solstice 1983 1983 Poster 3086

Inroads Multimedia Art Center Schedule 1983 presents its Performance Art Series 1983 In which CM, Butch Morris and Armand Schwener performed a concert of freely invented music language 3093

Benefit Concert for EAR Magazine 1983 in celebration of 10 years of publication April 8th 1983 St. Bartholomew's Church 3102

WMUH 91.7 Summer 83 Program Guide 1983 Featuring column about Sound Poetry 3127

Richard Wagner in Zurich and Richard Wagner's Buddha-Projekt "Die Sieger" 1983. 3196

Not Suitable for Framing: Arrangements for Sound and Structure 1983 Short biographies and example installations from Norman Andersen, Max Eastley, Don Jean-Louis, Peter Sepp and Associates, Peter Vogel, Doug Beck, and Steve Higgins. Published out of the Art Gallery at Harbourfront, 235 Queen's Quay W. Toronto February 11 through March 13. 3288

Invitation to Improvise at the 1983 International Radio Solstice Event 1983 -Letter from Peter Sepp of C.A.T. Gallery to Participate in Radiio Solstice-Proposal for spectator-activated sound sculpture-Press-Drawings-Plans 3289

Poster: Link Arms Against Arms 1983 A Candlelight Vigil in NYC, October 21 Poster 3366

Trax Anthems 2 1983 a zine. A compilation dedicated to anthems, each participant being asked to perform an alternative version of its own real or imaginary national anthem. 3369

Poster/Tracklist for WKCR CM Festival 1983 and other plans for CM Festival 3378

Posters/Programs for Kaleidoscope '83 City Celebration Events 1983 Events concept by Marilyn Wood-City In Celebration, presents A Celebration of Kansas City's Historic Union Station - Grand Finale of City in Celebration Week-Beach Ball presenting Calgary City Ballet, Edmonton Musical Theatre Scoiety, Cecil George Steel Band, Jeffrey Jenkins, Lee and Sandy Paley, program director: Grainne Holman -New Reflections: an Urban Fantasy, a vivid spectacle of light, sound, and dance-A Night with the Classics a Celebration of Artists 3387

Ear Benefit Concert 1983 Program 3418

Music for Trumpets and Trees 1983 Message from Dick to Carol Tuynman about T&T not being a submission to Ear Magazine, but written for CM to be performed on his land in Vermont. 3478

Dick Higgins Letters to CM 1983 Letter about donations to the Archive and Plans for funding from The John W. and Clara C. Higgins Foundation. Sent from Barrytown, NY 3480

Letter from Dick Higgins to Paco Underhill 1983 NWF Board meeting for Ear Magazine. Dick will be in Europe. 3503

Lyrics by Armand Schwerner 1983 Lyrics include, insult before gift-giving, her elegy, in the telling, my brother. 3588

Alvin Curran, New Solo and Environmental Works Music for, A Way A Lone, and Riverrun. 1983 Also a note to CM and a Letter about the state of the music business in '83. Signed. 3590

Link Arms against Arms Poster 1983 Poster for a Demonstration and candlelight vigil in NYC. List of sponsors. 3609

Daniel Spoerri postcard for show 1983 Show at Galerie Marika Malacorda, Geneve Galerie Renee Ziegler, Zurich 3618

Alison Knowles postcard for show opening " Loose Pages" 1983 Knowles and Coco Gordon Feb 14 Thru March 6 at Artworks 537 Broadway 3619

Music in the key of J 1983 Video: one of a series of cable tv live streamed performances, Manhattan Cable channel J 3623

Ear Magazine originals proofs Vol.6 #2 1983 Article and original artwork. Higgins piece has been moved to book #7. 3643

Windband Music Folder, Riding upon the wind, George's Delight, Resting Upon Emptiness, Principles for playing Corals and Other Music, Music for Windband. 1983 Other Media 3654

Extra Posters and Flyers 1983 Multiple Extras in individual envelopes all in one box: 12th Inter. Sound Poetry Fest.1980 Benefit for Ear Magazine 1983 Wind Band Museum Mile 1981 Summer Alleluia 1981 Summer Solstice Celebration 1981 Great Wind Event Posters 1982 Ear Magazine Radio 1984 Summer Solstice, Posters Riverside Park 1980 Summer solstice Lincoln Ctr. Posters1981 Summer Solstice Music And Light Posters 1978 Collaborations with J. Rothenberg and CM Programs 1987 Cross Rhythms Concert Posters 1977 Wave Music Posters Sept. 1977 Wave Music Posters June 1977 Wave Music info letter June 1977 Birth Celebration Ear Mag. Posters, April 1977 Beneath the Turtles Shell poster 1976 Spencer Holst & Tui St. George Tucker Poster Nov. 1976 Summer Solstice Poster June 1976 New Wilderness Events Posters April 1976 New Wilderness presents Frederick Marantz Posters March 1976 New Wilderness New & Old Explorations Posters 1976 New Wilderness 22nd event Poems songs and Transformations Feb. 1976 New Wilderness The Body is a Bell Posters 1975 New Wilderness The Grand reunion Posters June 1975 New Wilderness 20th Event Posters May 7 1975 New Wilderness 19th Event Posters April 1975 New Wilderness Fish, Frog, Violin and Hymn Posters Feb. 1975 A Gathering of Healers Posters Feb, 1975 Avery Jimerson, Seneca Singer Flyers Sept.New Wilderness Band Riff Off Posters Oct 1975 NWF Ritual Drama & Poetry Workshop Flyers 3670

Dick Higgins letter 1983 A letter from Dick Higgins to CM about Eric Andersen a Fluxus member from Copenhagen would like to visit, could

CM find some good gigs for him. 3685

Eric Andersen Letter To CM 1983 Eric announcing his upcoming trip to NYC and a draft of a concept show at Jean Dupuy's Gallery. Eric will be staying at Alisons loft on Spring St. Return letter from CM also. 3781

Maestoso, Non Troppo Alvin Curran 1983 Two copies of the score and a 5" reel with an excerpt at 7.5 ips from Alvin with a note to CM from Alvin Curran Musiche via Giovanni Vestri 8 00151 Roma, Italia 3819

Donna Henes Poster Rough for Vernal Equinox Celebration 1983 Also a Press release by CM. Also Dressing our wounds in warm clothes piece 3822

Music in the Key of J 1983 Four Copies of (4) spreadsheet notes on Scene, Time, Event for the presentation of the piece.Oc Orch., Horz. Vertical Band, R.I.P. Hayman, Steve McCaffery, Alison Knowles. Conch Chorus. 3834

Letter from Stefani Starin and program from Music for Flute, Voice, and Homemade Instruments. 1983 CM performs Cloud Song, Julie Kabat performs. 3853

Letter from Malcolm Goldstein to CM 1983 Malcolm is in Europe and has sent CM his latest Folkways Record "The Seasons of Vermont" for a review in Ear Magazine. 3862

Postcard from Armand Schwerner 6-29-1983. 3866

Bobby Buecker (two pieces of correspondence) 1983 Notes to CM 3875

First NY Art Parade Newspaper. Lower Manhattan Cultural Council 1983 A newspaper format promotional piece with art from many different groups and artists 3877

Ear for Ear, A John Cage musical piece that was used as an Ear magazine Cover. This is a smaller clean copy. 1983 Antiphonies, (widely separated single voices, one visible, the others not all the tones for a single letter are to be sung without vibrato, one breath. p-pp. 3939

The Summer Solstice Vocabulary Gatha, by Jackson Mac Low 1983 from Ear Magazine RIP collection. 3950

Benefit Concert for EAR. 1983 Tenth year anniversary. Fri April 8 at St. Bartholomew's Church, sponsored by New Wilderness Foundation. Concert program. 3958

New Wilderness Horspiel 1983 Notes on a proposal for the German Market 3975

CM Festival 1983 3 studio Track lists for the 8 tapes. Engineer: John Guth, Assistant: Connie Kieltyka. Producer: CM 4005

The Collected Poems of Rose Drachler 1983 Assembling Press 4039

Short R, Charles Doria 1983 A small pamphlet published by Assembling Press 4172

Transformational Unit, A small pamphlet by bpNichol 1983 #233 of limited edition, signed to CM 4175

Poetry, The Ecology of the Soul, Joel Openheimer 1983 Talks and selected Poems 4239

Benefit Concert for Earworks Small ear posters B&W (9) 1983 small version of Ear Poster 4265

Peter Van Riper Scores 1983 Two pieces: Lotus Pod Shaker piece and Seeing score. Both in original envelope with instructions. 4300

A Show of Arms 1983 For the new Music America Festival. Piece by CM, RIP Hayman and Carol Tuynman 4340

Bruno Laverdiere Clay Horns 1983 A Quote from Bruno for the production of Clay Horns for a Horn Orchestra, Several photos of Bruno's work and a photo of Bruno. 4345

100 Artists 100 Postcards 1983 An arts exercise project instructions are in a letter. CMs composite artwork in multiple stages. 4347

Grand Harp Event Postcard (about 25) 1983 Giant Black Postcard with gold ink overprint Music for 30 Harps by John Cage, Wendy Chambers & CM 4352

Audio Child Newsletter 1983 The Gerlovins, CM and Carol Tuynman with letter from the Gerlovins 4361

Wave VII Production notes 1983 Includes Harpists names and numbers. Letter from Wendy Chambers, costs and connections. 4380

Art Parade 1983. 4419

Bread & Puppet Volunteers Flyer (3) B & P Museum Booklet (1) 1983 An early flyer from NY days Museum book is illustrated by Max Schumann. 4487

Benefit Concert for Ear Magazine Poster (40) 1983 Screen print color blend poster for event at St. Bartholomew's Church. 4489

Wave VII Grand Harp Event Flyers 1983 Pluck by Wendy Chambers A postcard from Heaven, John Cage, Wave VII, CM 4491

Appearances at Spring St. Pier, Flyer 1983 Artwork By Annoymous Artists Alliance Also found in Master Graphics 4494

Beethoven Crosstunes by Tom Johnson 1983 Pub 218 Press 4501

Dror Feiler Letter to CM 1983 Letter about possibility of getting gigs in the US. Swedish Group 4532

Bread & Puppet Theater Washer Woman Nativity, Flyer Press Release from George Ashley, Photocopy Of Washer Women Storybook for Washerwoman Nativity 1983. 4569

Tunnel Hum Bonnie Barnett Folder, Flyer, 1983 Vocal Resonance and Vocal Multiphonics, Resume, Press and related material 4580

Tunnel Hum Bonnie Barnett Project Folder 1983 Vocal Resonance and Vocal Multiphonics B&W photos. Project outline for funding. 4581

Quarter Note Bridge, Clochard 1983 11X14" film positives of the George Washington Bridge. This is an art piece that might have been used in Ear magazine. As a bridge lets us transport from one place to another, music serves a similar role, transporting the soul, spirit and body to distant spaces and states. 4585

Letter and Boxing Stamps from Carlo Pittore 1983. 4603

Letter from Wendy Chambers to Carol Tuynman about 83 Solstice 1983 Info on Wendy Projects 4613

Festival of Latino poetry flyer 1983 Jerry and Diane Rothenberg letter on the back. Note to CM about Zapeda 4659

Daisy Dopps Vermont, Elka Schumann Drawings by Peter Schumann 1983 Orleans Historical Society some water damage 4738

Contemporary Swedish Prose, Ingemar Algulin 1983 Signed By Heidi 4771

Gerardo Delgado 1983 Pinturas 1979-1983. 4805

Prose For Dancing, Spencer Holst 1983 Signed CM's Copy From Spencer Holst Collection of very short prose pieces 4818

The Development of Sound Poetry 1961-83 Paula Claire 1983 An Illustrated Lecture Texas Tech University #12. 4819

A Bean Concordance, Alison Knowles 1983 Printed Editions, Barrytown NY Volume 1. 4822

Sounds of the River Naranjana, Armand Schwerner 1983 The Tablets I-XXIV. 4830

Once: A Lullaby, bp Nichol 1983 Illustrations by Ed Roach Black Moss Press Windsor, ONT. 4869

Singing the Stars, MacLennan 1983 Coach House Press, Toronto. Signed to CM 4873

Jord Vaxling, Heidi von Born 1983 Signed to CM 4876

Untold Angels, Tony Green gee. 1983 Signed to CM 4893

Translations, Experiments in Reading, Don Wellman editor 1983 O.ARS 3 Cambridge MA 4900

Victor Pokaler, F.P. Jac 1983 signed to CM/Cafe Victors Forlag Eks-Skolens Forlag Aps 4910

Translations: Experiments in Reading 1983 O.ARS 4. 4914

Facial Index 1983 West Coast Print Center 4922

Contemplacion, Gregorio Fonten Correa 1983 Libros de la Elipse 4962

The Maximus Poems, Charles Olson 1983 University of California Press 4999

A Bean Concordance, Alison Knowles 1983 signed to CM 5001

Strategies, Kimberly Lyons 1983 Prospect Books 5018

Contact sheets and negatives of Bread & Puppet and Peter Schuman, CM and others 1983 Photographed by Lona Foote 5073

Program for EAR Benefit Concert and an Advertising piece for the 1988 New Music Annual 1983 Event held at St. Bartholomew's Church NY Cover Photo by Lona Foote 5074

Miro Lithographs Joan Miro 1983 Dover Publications 5102

Cahier de Musique 1983. 5126

Electric Life Phonograph Record Budget 1983. 5267

Dr. Know Live, Henry Korn booklet Philip Know 1983 Booklet with story and two Graphic promos. Jacki Apple, Thirteen Flags over Utah 5275

Summer Solstice 83/84 Four panel Graphic 1983 Scan is in Master Graphics 5322

Peter Muller Bio Music for unborn Children 1983 Berkeley Arts, Charles Amirkhanian signed note 5327

Early Solstice Planning and Auditions Letter from Carol E. Tuynman 1983 NPR Joyce Jacobs 5467

Turn Up for New Music on Your Radio, WKCR 89.9 FM 1983 Schedule for Dec. 12-16 Brooke Wentz, Host Subotnick, Buckner, Velez, Lockwood, Rathe, Guth. 5526

Samizdat (self published) Poster 1983 Poster for installation of the self published book of Soviet Artists: Explosion 1984. Curated by Rimma and Valery Gerlovin. Feb. 15th-March 20th at Anderson Gallery Performance Feb. 15 Music by Carol Tuynman and CM. 5530

A Paper on The Importance of Sound and Music 1983 possibly by Dr. C. Muses 5541

Bread & Puppet Domestic Resurrection Circus Poster 1983 Aug. 13th Glover VT Damage needs restoration 5553

Graphic of sound in the inner Ear 1983 Yoshi Wada 5574

NEO-Music Newsletter 1983 Letters criticizing the established music producers for not letting the new underground players in. 5604

Proposal for Funding Satellite Program 1983 NPR 5657

Distant Signals 1984. 133

DIstant Signals 1984 safety 1119

Radio Konsert: Danmarks Radio 3.18.1984 Nikolajkirk, Copenhagen ARs Nova 1145

Wave Music VII: 30 Harps 9.22.1984. 1159

Solstice event broadcast 1984 Live events in NY clubs with national and international telephone connection to poets was organized for live world broadcast on radio from Record Plant Studios, NYC; to Sweden, Brazil, Greenland, and Denmark. 1302

Wave Music VII: 30 Harps 1984 Thirty harpists sit in a figure-8 formation, wearing headphones over which they hear a cue track and drums via local FM link. The music traces through its spatial organization the the motion of sound waves. This is followed by lively dance music in the form of an additive canon. 1357

A Cleansing Ritual 1984 This staged ritual collides a Jewish sabbath ceremony with a Christian sabbath ceremony. A minion of basses in skullcaps and prayer shawls, each has their bass attached by an extra metal "string" to a tub of water. A choir in robes processes in and out. 1480

CM and Barbara Held 1984 Músicas Colectivas personales. 1533

1984 Poetry Project New Years Benefit 1984 Jan 1st at St. Mark's Church NYC. Poster designed by Louise Hamlin. 1540

Explosion at Penn Station 7-1-84 1984 Original Artwork for the poster, and a press release. Original performance notes and ideas. An Event commisioned by Mary Luft & Joseph Celli to kickoff New Music America. A procession of conch horns, ocarinas, and three bass saxophones, each on its own float, is pulled by dancers. They make their way from 7th Avenue to the tracks on 8th Avenue. All become silent every time the station announcer "all-aboard Simmons" calls the trains, including a fictitiuos one. 1545

Far Out at Sea (Text by H.C. Anderson, P. Borum) 1984 Original Score, Notes & Script This choral opera is based on the H.C. Anderson's classic, "The Little Mermaid."Danish poet Poul Borum's wrote the libretto and lyrics, in English, on commission by the Danish vocal ensemble, Ars Nova. The end of the original story was changed by Borum from "She'll suffer in purgatory less if you children act good," to Wittgenstein's "Eternity belongs to those who live in the pr Sound processing and sampling are used to create the aging of the characters' voices over time, an under water sequence, and an atmosphere of obsessiveness. The world premier at Nikolajkirk, Copenhagen was recorded and broadcast by Danish Radio. It included solo dance choreographed and performed by Nanna Nillson. 1598

Laceclock 1984 unrealized work by Moniek Darge and CM notes and correspondence: series of images - suture, flower market sound of hand lace making - clicking of "bobbins" 1688

Nanna's Machine Dance 1984 A short film conceived directed and scored by CM, on the theme of performance ritual. Swedish dancer Nanna Nilson enters her mirrored Copenhagen studio, straps herself to her homemade exercise machine, works out, and exits. Commissioned by Bellevue Studio, Copenhagen and premiered on Danish TV. 1822

Denmark Concert 1984 Original pencil score, Notes, Variations on a Danish Hymn Genesis Song, The heart of leadership, Psalm 23. 1828

A Car is Driven*Beatty admits his Guilt 1984 Original music and Production Notes Two found texts from the NY Times are interwoven as the text for a song for one singer (any range) with one percussion and two melody instruments. One story tells of how an automoblile crashed through the window of a restaurant and was found where a table used to stand. The other is the description by a convicted politician about how easy it is to lie,"just relax". 1916

Music for Homemade instruments  Statue of Liberty 1984 Original music and notes 1917

New Wilderness Letter 12/Wch Way 5 1984 Two Boxes of books 1923

Explosion at Penn Station 1 July 1984 Original performance notes and ideas. An Event commisioned by Mary Luft & Joseph Celli to kickoff

New Music America. A procession of conch horns, ocarinas, and three bass saxophones, each on its own float, is pulled by dancers. They make their way from 7th Avenue to the tracks on 8th Avenue. All become silent every time the station announcer "all-aboard Simmons" calls the trains, including a fictitious one. 1928

Far Out at Sea (Text by H.C. Anderson, P. Borum) 1984 Seven More Copies (as above) 1945

Mac Moon Songs 21 June 1984 Poems by Paul Borum for CM to set to music 1971

IBM Thermotronic 1 1984 9-30-84. 2230

Information Withheld 1984 Juan Downey, color video, 28:06, stereo, CM on screen 2250

Poetry reading Log, Dick Higgins some recent snowflakes and other things 1984 1977 Date of Creation Milwaukee WI. Published by Printed Editions W. Glover VT. 2448

Timeless Light Newspaper 1984 Issue from January Avant garde magazine with submissions from Peter Frank and other artists and writers. 2508

12th Annual Summer Solstice Celebration Postcard 1984 About 100 Also one on Poster shelf 2533

Photo of CM and John Cage 1984 8x10 Photo of CM and John Cage 2579

Collective Farm Wonderkids Collective Farm #4 1984 A unique handmade bool of Artwork, Famous artworks influensed by childrens artare completed by children of contemporary artists Augustin Dupuy, Valeriy Gerlovin, Rimma Gerlovina, editors 2627

1984. 2639

City Wave/Fools fest 1984 Cross Reference Box 39 and Box 51. There are many pieces and scores in both boxes 2664

Ten Events for Media by CM 1984 Basic thoughts on Events and media A manuscript to be Filed with The Writers Guild of America. 2690

John Cage Postcard & Photo with CM 1984 Article and original artwork. Higgins piece has been moved to book #7. 2748

KONGO 1984 Large Poster Kunst Musik Forbrug 2774

Niagara-Erie Writers NEWSLETTER Vol.6 April 1984 Vol. 6 May 1984 1984 Kemp and CM at Peopleart. May issues has comments on Penny and CM performance. 2843

Bread & Puppet early Posters 1984 Insurrection Oratorio, Josephine the singer and The Door. 2844

Bread & Puppet program 1984 Our Domestic resurrection Circus 1984 Glover VT Some Recipes and Schemes for Circus Music letter from CM about improving the overall presentation of the band. 2864

Western Wind Papers 1984 License Agreement,Rehearsal Schedule, interview CM, expenses for Light Opera, one sheet for Light Opera. 2867

Laceclock 1984 Ideas and Notes for a film 2917

New Music America 1984 Bios 1984. 2920

Maritime Rites by Alvin Curran 1984 Printed booklet of a series of environmental sound works that take place on over or near bodies of water. Illustrations, scores and graphics. With a note from Alvin to CM. 2955

Memorial For Merle Lieb Steir at Saint Mark's Church in the Bowery 1984 Program for the Memorial for Merle Lieb Steir at Saint Marks Church in the Bowery at which CM played Horn Music for Merle. 3012

Mbira and Matepe 1984 Kavin Volans Scores For two harpsichords and rattles 3063

A Call for Bread and Puppet Volunteers for the Summer Solstice Celebration 1984 Flyer Reading "Bread and Puppet needs volunteers for: American midsummer Sermon for the 12th annual summer solstice celebration in Central Park East Meadow off Fifth Ave. entrances at 97th and 99th streets 3106

Music for Homemade Instruments 1984 Music for Homemade Instruments at La MaMa's La Gallaria October 29 CM and Carol Tuynman premiere "Statue of Liberty" 3114

Commusication Kommunikatie (2) 1984 Bulletin for Commusication Kommuzakatie New Music December Featuring mixed-media page on CM's work 3116

Ze'eva Cohen and Dancers Dance Series 1984 Ze'eva Cohen and Dancers Dance Series December 11th. The Ym-Ywha of the Metropolitan New Jersey. A region of the United Jewish Centers of MetroWest Music for Shifting Ground by CM 3125

KOPN 89.5 fm Radio Guide 1984 Volume 11 No. 3 June KOPN Radio Guide featuring posting of the Summer Soltice event inside 3126

10 Events for Media: A Media Event Film 1984 10 Events for Media: A Media Event Film Presented by CM 3224

Score for "Hefty, Hefty... Wimpy, Wimpy." 1984. 3293

Central Park, Map and Guide 1984 Illustrated Brochure to Central Park 3307

Solar Plexus Maungawhau 1984 Two page newspaper spread. Text by Phil Dadson and Dave Simmons. Pictures by Elizabeth Leyland 1984. 3335

Correspondence between Carol E. Tuynman and Dick Higgins 1984 concerning award towards Paul Berard 3363

The 12th Annual New Wilderness Summer Solstice Celebration 1984 Schedule of Events 3388

Bread and Puppet seeks Volunteers for Summer Solstice 1984 Poster: Bread and Puppet needs Volunteers for American Midsummer Sermon for the 12th Annual Summer Solstice Celebration in Central Park 3389

Political Theater Addresses Issues by Chris Braithwaite 1984 featured in the Chronicle, August 15. 3392

Poster: Join Pauline Oliveros in Performance of her work "The Grand Buddha Marching Band" 1984 presented by NWF on 12th Annual Solstice Celebration 3431

Laitman, J. T. (1984). The Anatomy of Human Speech. Natural History, 93(8), 20-27. 3464

Dr. Kalanath Jha Letters from Bhagalpur University, India 1984 Correspondence between Dr. Jha and Dick Higgins and CM about the Dr.'s trip to the US to record his works for New Wilderness. 3589

Malcolm Goldstein Letter 1984 A letter to CM hoping he is well, and inviting him to a presentation of Philip Corners work in NY on Tues Dec. 11. 3595

Juan Downey Show postcard 1984 Juan Downey show of video Tapes in Holland, Brussels, Paris, NY, Junio Chile. 3616

Memorial flyer for Merle L. Steir 1936-1984 1984 Held at St. Mark's Church. CM to start the program note from Danielle. 3691

Fylkingen Experimental Music of Sten Hanson & CM 1984 Veterans Marathon NY/Stockholm 3695

Original Art Mechanical for An International Survey of recent Painting and Sculpture 1984 Museum of Modern Art NY 3703

Art Life One Year Performance poster 1984 An Exhibit at 111 Hudson St. NYC 10013. A show by Elaine Summers Experimental InterMedia Foundation. with (Monique Darge)?? 3717

Music for Homemade Instruments at La Mamas La Galleria 1984 A hand done small poster for this performance. CM and Carol Tuynman present the premiere of Statue of Liberty. Oct. 29 at 262 The Bowery 3737

For Ear Magazine 1984 A short piece about Nature, Celebration and Healing and some early thoughts of CM on ambience and sound atmosphere. 3774

Franklin Furnace Grants poster 1984 Contact Ann Rosenthal, Publicist. An annocement that they have been selected one of 13 finalists for a national endowment for the arts award. This is a hand Painted poster by Artist G. Berkowitz. 3810

John Cage Graphic Postcard Music for Piano 4-19 1953 from series 66 1984 A Dear CM postcard from Don 3816

New Music America program and Letter from Mary Luft and Joseph Celli, and review from the Village Voice. 1984 The letter thanks CM for his generous assistance and participation in the New Music Festival. 3849

Alan Hovaness interviewed by CM (transcription). 1984 Composer to Composer 3909

Hi DE, BP Nichol 1984 200 copies 24th and final of the grønkintermediate series 4044

The Little Mermaid, H.C. Andersen Den Lille Havrue 1984 Signed by P. Kirkeby to CM 4136

60 Clarinets Photo from Battery Park performance. 1984 Copy Neg from Trasparency, work order from Alchemy Color.(1) 8x10 B&W glossy photo. 4210

French Sonnets, Jackson Mac Low 1984 Signed to CM & Svetlana 4261

DMT, Danish Music Newsletter #2 1984 Continuous Free Chanting Article by CM Pg.82 4262

10 Events for Media & A Media Event Film (2) 1984 Presented by CM, Other Media Explanation of Events and the importance of Media Coverage 4310

Far Out At Sea Press Kit 1984 Promo Package for CM's U.S, Premier. Performed by Danish Vocal ensemble Ars Nova. WHNC NY. Produced by Bent Eric Rasmussen. 4344

10 Events for Media & Event Projects 1984 Master sheets for Events, Promotion, Budgets etc. Also Ten Events for Media & a media event film papers 4351

Citywave Press 1984 Back Stage article CM Makes Massive Music. Letter from Monica Lichtenfeld, Koln, W, Germany 4370

Letter to Jack Hubler about Beale St. project, Research material about Memphis by Mary Nell Hawk. 1984 Beale St., WC Handy, Memphis Blues, Folkways article A Portrait of a People 4371

Grand Harp Event Postcard (about 25) 1984 Giant Black Postcard with gold ink overprint Music for 30 Harps by John Cage, Wendy Chambers & CM 4390

Wave 7: 30 HARPS Notes for Press and promotion. 1984 Commissioned by and dedicated to Wendy Chambers for World Premiere at the Cathedral of St. John the Divine on the autumn equinox Sept. 22, 1984. 4416

Ear Magazine Biographies 1984 Jackson Mac Low, Eleanor Hovda, Michael Peppe, Thomas Albert, Gordon Monahan, Jocy De Oliveira, David Yoken, Zygmunt Krauze, Beth Anderson. 4417

Keith Haring Secret Pastures Postcard (4) 1984 Next Wave Festival BAM Opera House Nov. 15 & 16. 4488

200 copies 24th and final of the grønkintermeddiate series 1984 A letter explaining the cancellation of the Essen Festival project till next year. To CM, David Mosconi, Alvin Curran, Paul Panhuysen, Douglas Quin, W.D.& U Trustedt. 4524

Running 1984 A City Wave Song, Includes studio recording notes. 4540

Bread & Puppet Touring ScheduleTraveling Circus Diagonal Man Flyers 8x10 Glossy of lg. Mother Earth 1984 Also B&P statement about politics and Central America issues. Green Mt. Trading Post with Aug. 1984 Cover. The Chronicle Aug. 15, 1984 Article Valley News Photocopy of anti Nuke parade in Hanover, NH 4570

Craft International Newspaper Sari Dienes article "In Celebration of Change 1984 by Karen Chambers 4573

Summer Solstice Poetry Reading Log 1984 4582

WBAI NY, Solstice Issue 1984 Forth Annual Solstice Cover Illustration by Virginia Kaycoff NWF article by Margot Adler 4625

Note from Jackson Mac Low to CM. 1984 Dada Works with Jerry Rothenberg Love verses from Soviet Sources, begun about 4-14-77 Second note to Jerry from Jackson about Soviet Love Poems. 4656

Fairbanks Alaska Event Letter, Louis O. Nelson 1984 Mr. & Mrs. Gus Jurgeleit 4693

Sketch for 30 Trumpets, Wendy Chambers 1984 A small Musical notation 4707

Digtsamling, Morti Vizki 1984 Printed in Denmark, Signed for CM 4745

Magam, Robert Browning 1984 Music of the Islamic world. Signed to CM 4828

Echoes of the ancient skies, Dr. E.C. Krupp 1984 signed to CM, Meridian 4911

Tradfesten, Heidi von Born 1984 signed to CM, Forfatter Forlaget 4958

Sensations, Barbara Rosenthal 1984 signed to CM, Visual Studies Workshop Press 4986

CityWave Silkscreen Prints of Event Timing (2) 1984 A Graphic Art piece by CM created for the Citywave Festival Copenhagen Printed by Francesco Conz (One of these is on the stairway wall at 1961 Roaring Brook Road, the Vermont residence of CM. 5070

New Music America, Real Art Ways of Hartford 1984 catalog and program 5133

Radio Solstice 1984 FOLIO (20) 1984 Guide for Listening to non commercial Radio 4th International Radio Solstice Cover 5245

Electric Life Scores 1984 Contains Farmer, Grandpa, Little Girl with Letter of Ownership and Rights. 5298

Center for Celebration Files 1984 List of Board Members, Incorporation Papers, Jan. 28th 1983 Meeting Notes, Bank Info. Budget, Members, Projects. etc. Village Halloween Parade. 5364

The Sun Buffalos Entertainment Weekly 1984 Good Example of Music Scene from 1984. Boy George Shenandoah, Arlo, Bromberg. 10,000 Maniacs, Marvin Gaye Dies. 5366

Niagara- Erie Writers Newsletter Vol.6 #9 1984 May 5435

12th Annual New Wilderness Solstice Celebration Post Card by Marilyn Wood 1984 Join Us, Listen on June 21st, 12-1PM on WKCR 89.9 FM 5447

The New Oakland Skyline Newsletter & Workshops 1984 Grassroots Community Arts 5479

Mark Laiosa Letter for Help from CM 1984 Plan for performance 5496

Bread & Puppet Circus Poster 1984 Damaged. Restoration Needed ? 5552

The Territory of Art Poster 1984 Museum of Contemporary Art, Los Angeles List of Programs, Oldenberg Photos of Glen Velez and female? 5567

Dobro, Conch: Porter/CM 1985. 86

Dobro only: Porter/CM 1985. 87

Banjo: Porter/CM 1985. 92

Banjo v.2: Porter/CM 1985. 93

Perfume Vocalise 1985. 135

Shawmut Piano #2 1985. 137

CM & Burt Porter 1985 Indoors 605

AT&T network Systems 1985 ** 0) Open Mix- raise drum, 1) Open mix- keeper, 2) Close w/string tag 3) Close w/o string tag 4) String Tag alone 5) Time segement 6) Team Segment 7) Customer Segment 14) Scenes 2-4- NG **DAT IS DAMAGED 644

Sporanox and Floxil 1985 and Floxil 658

Metropolis Copenhagen 1985 718

Metropolis Copenhagen: A Sound Journey 1985 A personal sound portrait of the city using location sounds and original music. The piece borrows the finale of "Copenhagen Waves." 1003

Blue Glass Series - virtual windows SKYSONG 1985 series of art works with gold calligraphy on blue glass: drinking glasses, vases, water pitchersvirtual windows - 2 in cma, 2 in VT - blue plexiglass framed in light colored wood, they have four legs which attach to a surface to allow light from the rear. Text: Skysong 1093

David Garland 1985. 1108

CMA Demo Reel 5.85 1985. 1142

Copenhagen running -instrumental 1985 Song by CM performed by Bob Kinkel in NYC. 1156

Metropolis Copenhagen: A Sound Journey 1985 A personal sound portrait of the city using location sounds and original music. The piece borrows the finale of "Copenhagen Waves." 1235

Solstice '85 event broadcast 1985 Public event in Central Park from dawn to darkness. [more, as per other Solstice descriptions?] 1291

The Birth of the War God 1985. 1351

Pillowcase with hand stitched music notation 1985 Created for an event at WDR, it is part of a collection of artworks by sound artists 1400

Staten Island Reservoir Inauguration 1985 Sound effects were created for the opening of the big water valve at a new park and reservoir in Staten Island. 1430

Philip Corner Notes 1985 Copies of notes including Gamelan

pieces,Together bells, Om, Om towards pure color (vowels). 1556

Copenhagen Waves - Citywave FOOLS FESTIVAL V 1985 2,000 performers from all areas of Danish music life were led by radio as they gave five concerts in five outskirt arenas in Copenhagem. These concerts were followed by the gathering of processions, flotillas, and bicycle groups at the finale at Nyhavn. The Fool, played by Morti Viski, ran through city streets and arrived for the finale, making a grand entrance to join the gathered forces. The Fool was raised by a cherry picker to the top of the Charlottenborg Building. Accompanied by all the musicans and singers, the Fool sang CITYWAVE and disappeared into the sky. A helicopter -- cancelled in the live event -- was to have carried him off the harbor, still singing CITYWAVE. 1593

Metropolis Copenhagen 1985 A personal sound portrait of the city using location sounds and original music. The piece borrows the finale of "Copenhagen Waves." 1597

When the Clouds Shall Break 1985 Original handwritten music 1606

Poul's Song 1985 Original Music and production notes 1612

WINS Sounder 1985 Small piece of handwritten music. 1655

Copenhagen Waves - Citywave FOOLS FESTIVAL V 1985 Copenhagen 1657

Celebration of the Line 1985 Original music, written for NEWBAND, Dean Drummond, Stephanie Starin. 1915

Water and Light A cleansing Ritual for Sabbath Evening 1985 Original Music and Notes. UCSD Brtra, Turetsly, {hoyos NY Becky Cohen, Feb. 1926

1985 Cleo Awards Opening 1985. 2001

Citywave Mandoline 1985 music by CM, words by Paul Borum 2095

Summer Solstice '85 NWF event broadcast 1985 10 mins tape 203a 2227

Karin Bacon 'Events' demo 1985 Thanksgiving/Starrett/Elephants/Buildings/Castle day/Great egg 9/20/85 24:00 mins 2231

CityWave Kopenhagen in NY 1985 CM at Emily Harvey Gal. Jan 14 '86. 2241

CLIO Awards opening 85 1985 7/10/85. 2246

Frito Lay 1985 'Sneak thief' pecd5013 :30 'Sneak thief' pe cd5025 :15 'Sneak thief' pecd5030 :10 5/22/85. 2254

Distant signals 1985 film transfer master j#110576 14 85. 2300

Nanna's Machine dance 1985 #4. 2316

Nanna's Machine dance 1985 Music film by CM 2318

Most recent works 1985 Clio WINS radio Hefty TMTV Aug. 1985. 2331

Music showreel 1985 17 titles 2332

CMA demo reel 1985. 2334

CMA demo reel 1985 New master! 8 13 85. 2351

Naming Event, Rothenberg 1985 Notes for naming event game. 2440

Watercolor 1985 A 20"x 24" watercolor by Ken Friedman 2501

The First Reader CM's Bracelet (for two readers) 1985 CMs Copy from Spencer Holst. Original manuscript 81/2" x 11" 2503

Sun Times 1985 Sun Times a Special publication of Ear Magazine Issue for Solstice Celebration June 21, 1985. Program Notes, Solstice radio, Bread and puppet, over 200 in box. 2507

Primal Plok Poster 1985. 2523

Meredith Monk 1985 Meredith Monk at Carnegie Hall Concert poster 2570

Electronic Music in Sweden 1985 A small book Edited by Olle Olson Signed 2610

Greek Songbook 1985 Signed 2613

Bird Song 1985 From City Wave 2641

Fools Fest Program 1985. 2644

Garden of Harps 1985 postcards, review, press for event at Museum of Modern Art NYC. Music for 15 Harps by John Cage, Wendy Chambers CM and R.I.P. Hayman Photo by Lana Foute 2785

Winter Solstice Celebration Poster 1985 7:30 AM at Cathedral of St. John The Divine, Dec, 21. 2811

AD Suite 1985 A group of commercial pieces for copyright (Spring is here) 2829

Fools 5 posters (4) 1985 Citiwave is in Fools 5. 2861

CM's Bracelet, Spencer Holst 1985 A 14 pg manuscript on Green Paper 2927

CM Sign 1985 Vanavond in 't stuc om 22u 2948

Stichting Logos NYC 1985 solstice/score gent belfort 2953

Sun Radiants & Shadow Program 1985 12th annual Summer Solstice Festival, Central Park, NY 2960

The Westsider "In Touch with the Solstice" 1985 "In Touch with the Soltice" by Lionelle Hamanaka About the Solstice celebration in Denmark. Three publicity shots included in the folder. 3010

Electric Hum by Starry Krueger 1985 OTHER MEDIA, NY and Stockholm Description/Composition of Electric Hum 3035

Correspondence with Dick Higgins 1985 Letters from Dick Higgins to Carol Tuynman concerning outstanding debts for Dr. Jha's visit to NY. 3107

What's Cooking 1985 University of California, San Diego February 14-17, Center for Music Experiment 3115

Listening Room Cassette Notes 1985. 3210

Sunday 2 1985 The Entertainment Company Group with Bobbie Lazar and Jane Teller present Sunday 2 the Continuing Saga or Music, Poetry, etc. 3212

Japanese Ghosts and Demons: Art of the Supernatural 1985 by Stephen Addiss Spencer Museum of Art, University of Kansas 3327

Alenikoff Tee-shirt designs for New Wilderness 1985 and ordering information 3334

Newspaper spread about 1985 International Radio Solstice. Copy of newspaper page 3339

High Energy at High Noon 1985 Poster: 12th Annual New Wilderness Summer Solstice Celebration Designed and Directed by Marilyn Wood Produced by New Wilderness Foundation 3383

Time Reading with Regina Vater 1985 New Wilderness Summer Solstice Celebration Artistic Director: Marilyn Wood 3390

"Fifth International Radio Solstice WKCR-89.9FM Joins the Network of the Sun," in a June Issue of Sun Times (special issue of Ear Magazine) 1985. 3433

Corporate Image TV Campaign 1985 Shooting Script Energy to Serve/Energy to Care Volunteerism 3440

Letter to Ear Readers from Carol E. Tuynman 1985 inviting readers to the 12th Annual Solstice Celebration, notifying of a reader questionnaire, and lobbying for pledges. 3465

Listen! Post Card (20 1985 Postcard for Listening Room at New Wilderness 355 Spring St. NY, Room 208. 3494

Lace Clock and Series II Pages 1985 Letter from Moniek Darge to CM about an idea for a film project they should do together. She has called out film shots and basic timing. Series II project for slides and solo voice. Notes for creation of project about the Shield Shrimps of central Australia. 3508

Pneumaphones and Mythology by Moniek Darge 1985 Logos Project about the movement of Air, air sound, Wind sound. 9 pages on transparent paper. 3562

Message from Dick Higgins 1985 A note about distributor for Audiographics cassettes. And for CM to make an offer on 40 acres of Sugarbush. 3582

Message from Dick Higgins 1985 A note of Warning about the intuition piece. 3583

Mes Petites Amaureuses by Pierre Berthet 1985 A musical score with actions, with letter from Pierre, and a postcard. 3587

Stichting LOGOS, letters 1985 Letters to CM from Moniek Darge. 3593

Glen Velez Promo Glossy 1985 Copyright by Layne Redmond 3605

A Performance Art Workshop invitation 1985 Self mailer Flyer from Arleen Schloss 3608

Vocal Works Folder, Breath Canon, Song of Deborah, Voice Dance, 3 Passes, Meditation on a Persian Theme, Night Sky Song, Dawn Song Lullaby, Sun Chant, Three personal Chants, When the Clouds Shall Break,

Poul's Song, Sky Song. 1985 An envelope with Vocal Works. Other Media 3652

Copenhagen Waves Graphic Score 1985 Copy of Citywave original score with actions June 8. 3663

Dick Higgins letter 1985 A letter from Dick Higgins to CM about Nannucci and Higgins studio time to prepare Requiem for Wagner the Criminal Mayor and Bodies Electric. 3684

Dick Higgins letter 1985 A letter from Dick Higgins to CM about payment on the Vermont Sugarbush property. 3686

When the Clouds Shall Break 1985 Other Media, Stockholm 3751

CM Press and promotion 1985 Music on the CM: The jingles keep on Coming CM Associates Sounds it's Own Horn 1988

Pomposello & CM Make Tracks for NBC Later with Bob Costas 1988 Hefty declares war on "wimpy" Bags 1985 CM scores MTV Zombie spot CM scores for Bennihanna and McKinney and Silver 1988 CM Associates scores for Aller Act 1988 CM scores spots from Gas to Beds 1985 CM makes Massive Music 1983 Solstice on Ice Great Harp Event CM & John Cage 1984 Music: Garden of harps at the Modern Museum 1985 3794

Citywaves Bicycles 1985 Timed performance sheets of actions for the event. 3797

Invitation to New Years Day Party from Armand Schwerner 1985 Hand Made Card on Black Paper with Silver Ink for party at 15 W 12th St. 1G 3855

UKIYOE Handkerchief 1985 A beautiful Japanese printed handkerchief. 3861

Ancient NY Mosaics at Emily Harvey Gallery, Flyers(8) 1985 A video tape by Valery Gerlovin with Music by CM 537 B'Way 2nd floor NY 3929

Dharma Music Festival Programs 1985 Ten different Programs for 1985 performances. Sponsored by The Samaya Foundation. 3959

A performance for 30 People and one dress, Eric Andersen 1985 Two 5x7 performance photos for RIP Hayman 3960

Postcards to CM from RIP in Tibet 1985. 4023

Gert Mortensen 1985 Percussion Flyer, A repertoire on the Back 4159

William Britt Poster (5) 1985 Sandals poster 4182

The New Look, Mills College Music News. 1985 Look is a publication of the Mills College Center for Contemporary Music articles and reviews by Phil Harmonic. 4211

Fools Organization Citiwave/Morti Vizki 1985 Correspondence and Royalty on cassettes. Letters. 4219

A Classical Symphony in 4 movements 4 bp Nichol 1985 Oct. 30 by CM for bpNichol on the event of his uberraschung Festschrift 4335

Wave Music VI 1985 40 Horns Original notes and performance facts and budget. 4341

Samples of Arctic Music 1985 A list of Arctic music with artists names 4354

Letter from CM to John Rockwell, music critic NY Times. Letter from CM to Bjarna Thanning about Kobenhavns Internat'l Festival 1985. 4355

How to use Radio Programing in other fields. Bent Eric Rasmussen 1985 How to make extended use of music and theme programs. A paper 4374

Summer Solstice Festival 1985 Marilyn Wood, Central Park June 21, 1985. 4376

Stockholm & Citywave Materials 1985 Includes Maps, Business Cards, Notes, Photos & City Wave CM's Workbook and Notes. Ars Nova, Dansk Radio, Bo Holton. Per Erik Wing Radio Denmark. 4389

City Waves/Other Media 1985 A letter from Claes Cornelius from Mega records Copenhagen concerning funding for the video Production. Also a telex about shipment of the 2' master of Citywave. 4410

Danish Radio Chamber Orch. series 1985. 4434

FLUXUS Mailing List 1985 SOME MOLD 4443

Fusion 1985 Tom Tits 4444

Music that Crossed the Ocean 1985 Folder Proposals and correspondence 4457

Shaman's Toolbox 1985 Proposals and letters 4464

Solstice 1985 Folder 4469

Grand Buddha Marching Band Poster 1985 Pauline Oliveros call for musicians for Central Park Solstice Celebration 4505

12th Annual Solstice 1985, Marilyn Wood 1985 Master folder of Art, Programs and press. Regina Graphic, Bread and Puppet Graphic, Sun Fun, Run for the Sun 4506

Artist Bio Sheets for promotional or press (24 copies)Anna Halprin, Marilyn Wood, Phyllis Yampolsky, Elsie Bernhardt, Wendy Chambers, Susan Keiser, Evelyn Roth, Pauline Oliveros, Caroline Simonds, Bread & Puppet Theater, 1985 Anna Halprin, Marilyn Wood, Phyllis Yampolsky, Elsie Bernhardt,Wendy Chambers, Susan Keiser, Evelyn Roth, Pauline Oliveros, Caroline Simonds, Bread & Puppet Theater, And Solar Diptych for 15 Dancers and 30 Trumpets. 4509

Lynn Wilson's notes to NWF 1985 Thank you Letter for including her work in the anniversary issue of Ear Magazine. 4528

Summernight in Copenhagen, CM Borum 1985 Lyrics Citylight, City Air Alone with Crowding Life Everywhere. 4539

Bread & Puppet Washer Woman Calendar 1985 Printed at Troll Press St. Johnsbury VT 4571

Polyphonix festival letters 1985 A letter from Bernard Heidsieck to CM, would he be in Europe for that date. A letter from Paris, on Polyphonix letterhead from TJ 4601

Two Letters from Francesco Conz 1985 Knud Pedersen reference

4604

1985 Solstice Folder NWF 1985 Press materials, Contacts, Band Members, Grand Buddha Marching Band list, Gloria Mc Lean & Life dance press Marilyn Wood, Anita Halprin, Solaris 4631

Time Reading, Regina Vater 1985 A poster type art piece about placing an egg white in water overnight and taking a reading the next day to see your future. Produced for the 1985 Solstice, Marilyn Wood, Artistic Director 4644

Pauline Oliveros, The Grand Buddha Marching Band 1985 Invitation to Participate, A description of the Event for Central Parks east meadow New Wilderness Event 4645

East West Fusion Theater Promo Materials 1985 Sent to New Wilderness by Teviot Fairservis Pourchet, Artistic Director Sharon CT 06069. 4655

Making Sense of Animal Sounds, article from Science news Letter to CM from Kirk Nurock 1985 KoKo article and cross species mentioned. 4694

One Second Before Sunrise, Horizon Communications 1985 Proposal and info packet, Dick Higgins sister is Elizabeth Null. 4702

DOC(K)S No. 71 1985 An Italian Publication of New Art and Photography 4758

Schirner Files 1985 Letter of Introduction, Faxes 4851

Rough Ride, David Tremlett 1985 Works made in Africa, Australia, Mexico Limited Edition Signed To CM From Carol Signed by David inside Back 4871

Lettrism And Hypergraphics, Jean Paul Curtay 1985 The Unknown Avant Garde 1945-1985. 4895

Oriental Tales, Marguerite Yourcenar 1985 Collins publisher FSG 4921

Jodiske eventyr OG historier, Judith Winther 1985 Cafe Victor 4927

1. Acustica International 1985, Komponisten Als Hörspielmacher 1985 Westdeutscher Rundfunk Köln 4957

Dada in Zurich, Arche 1985 Kunsthaus 5035

Mina första kärlekar, Ivan Klima 1985 Brombergs 5047

Waiting for the Dawn, Mircea Eliade 1985 University Press of Colorado, signed to CM 5087

CM Epic Songs of War and Peace, Poster (5) 1985 Sat. Oct. 12 Music in a Great Space with The Western Wind Vocal Ensemble A Dramatic musical healing event 5144

Valery Gerlovin and Rimma Gerlovina Exhibit 1985 April 19 thru May 17th at Emily Harvey Gallery A folded creative mailer. 5162

Carlo Pittore Envelope w/Stickers 1985 Bern Porter Commemorative Stamp 5223

Printed Editions Special Editions Catalog, Higgins, Knowles 1985

Signed John Cage and Alison Knowles 5262

Fools Fest 5 Brochure 1985 Copenhagen International Theater Festival 8 30-85. 5357

Ancient NY Mosaics, The Gerlovins 1985 CM Wave Music V from Other Wave Music 1982

Other Media ASCAP 1985 A single page of information Made possible by The Mattress Factory, Pittsburg, PA and Grants from Warner Amex Community Programing Trust, Pittsburg Foundation, Pennsylvania Council on the Arts. Howard Hines Endowment. 5359

Music in a Great Space Fall 1985 CM w/Western Wind listed for Oct. 12 Performance 5401

Village Voice Centerfold Copy New Wilderness 1985 East Meadow 99th + 5th Ave. The same announcement appeared in the Chinese Newspaper and The NY Times. A copy of each. 5482

.......... 1985. 5493

One Year Performance, Tehching Hsieh 1985 Letter to CM, Deciding not to do the performance, List of people who offered to hold the Torch. 5494

Daniele Lombardi, Intoduction letter Program 1985 Florence 5495

Public Radio New Sounds Source List 1985 WNYC 5501

Marriage Invitation to Robert & Kala's Annual Wedding and Festival of the Arts, 1985 Taft Point, Goldsboro, ME. A Creative Folded Invitation 5508

International Radio Solstice Newspaper article Artists on the Air June 22 1985 Campus Radio will be broadcasting the event live as happening in NYC, Manhattan Island the Medieval city of Ghent in Belgium and Auckland City in the South Pacific. 5538

Artifacts of Exploration Photos by Olivia Parker 1985 Six Pages of Parkers photos 5539

Center for Celebration Large Art, invitation art 1985. 5547

William Britt Poster (Sandals) 1985 On the Concourse May 20-24 1985 Empire State Plaza, Albany NY 5548

HEFTY HEFTY Wimpy, Wimpy 1985 Vocal Cues for Commercial by CM 5579

Letter from Morten B. Poulsen/Mort Vizki 1985 Non Contractual letter of intent to CM from Morti in Denmark 5583

Oracle Oracle letter to CM from Jeanette Ingberman 1985 From Exit Art Projects,List of Artists to Perform, CM, Henes, Velez, Knowles, Moorman and others 5584

Fanfare in the Air, Karen Bacon 1985 Notes and Billing, Contracts 5589

Lucinda Childs Solos,1985 Presented By Dancing in the Kitchen, Music by Philip Glass performed by George Andoniadis 5594

Notes on European Music Tradition 1985 Hand written notes #1-14

Pages 10-12 missing 5601

CM Itinerary, Copenhagen Oct. 3-14 1985. 5605

Housework, An Asylum 1985 Rose and Jacob Draculer, Greetings A story of Freedom 5610

Movement and Sound Workshop Simone Forti and Peter Van Riper 1985 At The Creative Music Studio, Woodstock NY Aug. 4 thru 9 Flyer for Registration 5611

Solstice 11983 and 1985 misc. papers and notes 1985. 5615

Variations on the Danish Hymn MORGAN 1985 Morgan, Silent Echos, Whisper Echos, Geometric Echos, Drones and Chosen Point Echos, Augmentations, Tempo Layers, Xchorus in 3 parts,Tempos given by external input, Splicing, Free Improvisation. 5621

Collaborations An Independent Project by Andrew Veljkovic 1985 Invatation to 10 day Arts program and party Alternative Museum Shalom Gorewitz, Edmond Chibeau 5626

The Women of MTV, Bruce Pileto 1985 The Founding women of MTV and how they got there. Also Top 40 Chart for March 5628

The Night of the Music, also 1986 info 1985 A Program conceived and produced by Andrea Andermann RADA film Service. History of the Production and the Players 5629

Village Voice review of New Wilderness Celebration By Linda Sanders 1985 Central Parks East Meadow 5631

First ACUSTICA INTERNATIONAL Sept. 27 thru Oct. 1, 1985. Cologne, Germany. Brochure, Composers as Horspiel Makers. Multimedia performers gather to present in the WDR concert halls. John Cage, Malcolm Goldstein, Alison Knowles, CM and others. 5636

Little Red Liklihooh Poster(3) 1985 January 21, St. Marks Church with Cheri Fein, Michael Andre, CM 2561

Grape Nuts Pres. 1986 “Iko” Remix + Harpsi.+Tpt. 144

99ˇ Deal TV & Radio 1986. 352

CMA Commercials reel 4 1986 Ford demo 86 Diet Coke Boat, Diet Coke, Whale, Nabisco, Serious Choclate, French’s, Frisky 1098

Dave Taylor: Ascending Music version 1, 2 10.20.1986. 1117

CMA Demo Reel 5.28.1986. 1140

Noyes & Laybourne: Clifford Sing Along CMA Scoring Reel Jan. 20, 1986 Scholastic Films, Children can sing along with everyone’s favorite large dog, on a total of 17 songs. 1164

Universitas - Leuvan, Belgium 1986 An event utilizing the faculty, students, carillons, and campus of the old Catholic Belgian university in Leuven, Belgium. The event is interupted by a gang of motorcycle riders and culminates with a tableau of Van Eyk’s “Sacr Content: National anthems, song: momentary music (text: Poul Borum), debate on ethics in Flemish played on outdoor video monitors. Envelope contains Map, Production Notes, posters, etc. 1391

Citywave Copenhagen Score print on canvas 1986 Large Edizone Conz print on Canvas 1401

Walls 1986. 1436

Blast Monthly Vol.1 # 6 (8) 1986 Small Magazine by Collaborative Projects 1486

Terezka, a new show 1986 A poster for performance by Margo Lee Sherman. At The New Theater 64 East 4th St. NY Signed by Margo 1496

CM En Tom Pomposello 1986 Metropole Cafe benefit April 24. 1532

The Great Ape Activity Tape 1986 Tape prepares parents or other childcare providers for the next unexpected snow storm or rainy day when the kids complain in endless chorus that they are bored. In this tape, the lovable Great Green Ape and other activity experts demonstrate 15 activities aimed to inspire. Read more: http://www.answers.com/topic/the-great-ape-activity-tape#ixzz29AmZ4D7V 1578

Solstice '86 event broadcast 1986 Live performance at Central Park, NYC, by CM with Don Cherry and his sons, Glen Velez, Tom Pomposello, the Loisaida Samba School, and The Quando Chorus, directed by Michael Schenker. The live radio broadcast was hosted by Andy Caploe and Abby Lincoln from WNYC FM. Included in the transmission were signals from Kansas City, Mo. and a South Pole research station. 1591

Fanfare in the Air 1986 Musicians on the superstructure of the Municipal Building, introduced by Mayor Ed Koch, played the Fanfare for the inauguration of new radio stations at WNYC, municipal radio. Half a block away the loud speakers on the Tweed Courthouse echoed the sound from the band and the Emulators played looped samples of the announcer's and the Mayor's voice: "Hi, I'm Ed Koc...Ed Koc...Koc...get a pencil." The hand-operated delay between the two sound systems washed waves of sound over Chambers Street. On the radio, the live event played as a wild music/sound poem. 1603

Memories of Preparations for Holy Week in Seville 1986 The Image Dusky March night. Chill. Breath stream joins fog. Struggling to learnto negotiate corners, a group of young men bear the platform that will hold the holy statue later on that holy week. The platform is filled withheavy bags. The Performance, 20 minutes. 1. PRELUDE OF ECHOS: each harpsichord is sitting in its own location in the hall. 2. PROCESSIONS: the six harpsichords are born on the shoulders of the bearers. The harpsichordists are carried also, sometimes playing and sometimes separated from their keyboards. Each group has a lamp to light the music - and a lamp to light the way. The floating instruments arrive on the stage. [need help to see this one] 3. THE WAVE OF THE HAND: the six harpsichords play in ensemble, wave musicwith waves of the sound and waves of the hand. --note: the harpsichordists and the bearers are in costumes of painted material. The fabric and paints are chosen for their potential for lighting effects. The costumes include gloves which are fingerless in the case ofthe harsichordists. The ambience is the sense of signalling while in passage - musical, physical, and personal. 1608

Belgium Event 1986. 1618

Dream Event 2 1986 Fusion Arts collaboration with Shalom Neuman. Many artists participated in this twelve-hour long gathering on NY's Lower East Side. 1619

Time/Life: "Healthy Home Cooking" and "The Vietnam Experience" 1986 Light scoring for two television ads; one selling a cookbook, the other a series chronicling the Vietnam War. 1622

Works For Flute, Viola and Harp 1986. 1663

Celebration of the Line 1986 Sculptor Ken Hiratsuka's one line maze in adhesive tape begins at the outer edge of the performance space and spirals into the center. A harp is placed at the beginning and end points. After the overture, the harpist takes up the adhesive tape, moving along the line to the center, where the finale is played. 1800

Soul To Soul 1986 Collage song in which the chorus "soul to soul" -- a bite out of the South African national anthem -- returns after phrases of bites of anthems for many political hotties, including Libya, Poland, USSR, Brazil, and the USA. 1811

Tompkins Square Park Event 1986 Music and Notes for performance 1927

Running Piece (Copenhagen, Helsingborg) 1986 Helsingborg - Helsingør - a the path of a running marathon is analysed for sonic opportunites, a percussionist marathon runner is trained to cause a series of sound events along this path including a finale. The premier was named, "Running in Springtime City". An instrumental track was written by CM and performed by Bob Kinkel in NY. 2036

Tokyo Music TV; TM TV 1986 2 versions of advertisement for Tokyo Music Television, Inc. Animated. Title on description: TM TV blitz. 2071

Venice Biennale 07-09/1986 Hands across Amerca SSTV Packaged death (Contra aid news item) SSTV The negotiators NO SOUND 2182

1986 Solstice Jam DIGITAL 2197

EAR w Missile 1986 V 1 multiples 5 20 86V 2 5 27 86. 2205

Citrus Hill plu Calcium 1986 digital safety (1630?)9.23.86. 2226

Juan Downey 'JS Bach' 1986 Video. Bach 300 color 28 mins, stereo, NVidTSC 2242

No Se No Sculpture Garden News 1986 Sculpture Inside out Sept. 6 thru Oct 4, 86 42 Irving St. NY 2452

Poster and Program for Musik und Sprache 1986 Poster for Musik Und Sprache Feb. 27- Mar. 9 Program also here. 2536

Poster for CM 1986 Vrijdag 25 April In De Zwarte Zaal 2542

Sari Dienes Retrospective By Thorpe Intermedia gallery 1986 A photo book of her life and work 2616

Polyphonix 10 Program 1986 Program and schedule of performances in Paris CM, Jerome Tom Johnson, Dick Higgins one original and one copy 2626

Hefty Elephant 1986 Parts and Scores for 15. 2640

Freely Invented Poster (2) 1986 Music/Language performance at Inroads 150 Mercer St. NY May 2 & 3 with Armand Schwerner, Butch Morris, CM. 2750

Need Money, for 75th Birthday for Bern Porter 1986 Two flyers and envelope for contributions for Art projects. w/Stickers. Also for Carlo Pittore. Stamps of Roland Legiardi-Laura. 2825

Bicycles to Dreamland Poster 1986 B&W Poster NWF, Fusion Arts & Experimental Intermedia Foundation with Logos Duo, Godfried-Willemraes & Moniek Darge, CM and Shalom perform Dream Event II, at 57 Stanton St. NY. 2941

Fusion Event Poster 1986 40 Rivington St. July 25, 1986 Many artists 2951

CM and Tom Pomposello 1986 Metropole Cafe Donderdag 24 April, Brussels, Belgium 2954

Dreamsound Pillow notes by RIP Hayman 1986 A small 16 page booklet on dreaming and sleep. 2980

Breath River Route 1986 A performing installation space by Malcolm Goldstein and Alison Knowles at the Emily Harvey Gallery 537 Broadway. 2988

Bicycles to Dreamland 1986 Bicycles to Dreamland presented by New Wilderness Foundation, Fusion Arts, Experimental Intermedia Foundation October 25th Supported by Meet the Composer Logo Duo & Dream Event In program: "Gloria McLean, Margalit Lubling, CM, Shalom and Eve Teitelbaum, perform with sculpture." "Organization Design by CM, Shalom Neuman, and Eve Teitelbaum" 3013

Blast 1986 Blast (Zine) October, 1986 A Monthly Publication of Collaborative Projects Cultural Council Foundation Management and Resources for the Arts 3058

Saint George and the Dragon poster 1986 Saint George and the Dragon by Luca Pizzorno at Prixunic Gallery Gala Notte, Demo Moe plays 3303

Art work by Laurie Edmonds 1986 "Mirror," 3304

logos-blad 1986 logos-bladtijdschrift van stichting logosintelling van openbaar nutkongostraat 359000 gentbelgium April Article about CM inside 3354

Yellow Springs Review, the Letter of the Yellow Springs Institute for Contemporary Studies and the Arts Fall 1986 Volume 3, Number 1 Richard Schechner and Pauline Oliveros featured inside 3356

Letter from Rene Bloch about Solstice Celebration 1986. 3382

Blast: Monthly Publication of Collaborative Projects 1986 Cultural Council Foundation 3386

Zounds presents Z-2 1986 5-22-86, at Cuando Community College with Tracie Lozano, Kathleen Nester, Elizabeth Panzer, Tina Pelikan. Playing works by Cage, CM and others. 3489

Gematria 308, Jerry Rothenberg Some numbers for you CM 1986 18 pages of numbers 3491

AUTO AUTHOR, Inter-Media by Moniek Darge 1986 LOGOS EDition D1986/2421/2 6 pages, Printed on transparent paper 3561

WARART MYTH by Moniek Darge 1986 17 Pages on Transparent paper LOGOs Edition D1986/2421/3 Belgium 3563

Bell Poems by Moniek Darge 1986 5 pages on Transparent paper LOGOS edition D1986/2421/5kongostraat 35 b-9000 gentbelgium-tel.091/23.80.89. 3564

A 2 Z IN LETTER by Arleen Schloss 1986 A single page letter piece 3565

Out of the Question by S. Random at Galleria Dell'occhio 1986 Poster for event with a letter on the back About Bern Porter 75th birthday Tribute from Carlo Pittore. 3572

Conch Tales poems by Gerd Stern 1986 Poems by Gerd Stern drawings by David Weinrib screened by Sheila Marbain of Maurel Studios. A signed edition of 50 copies & 10 Artists proofs. Signed to CM Happy Birthday. 3634

Conch Chorus Activities Letter 1986 schedule for activities 3644

Trio for Flute Viola and Harp, Celebration of the Line 1986 Other Media 3662

Melvin Charney and Krzysztof Wodiczko Small Folio of Projection Demos 1986 Laser Copier color sheets examples of their work in Projections and lighting public spaces. 3821

Program for Feb. 1986, and performance schedule for March Radio show. Schedule for performance and installations in Berlin. CM midnight Chant March 1 CM, Jean Dupuy, Tom Johnson and others featured 3851

1986. 3864

Representative Works 1938-1985 Jackson Mac Low 1986 Signed to CM and his long friendship 4034

Some Scapes bp Nichol 1986. 4045

The Map Catalog, Joel Makower 1986. 4090

Visible Language XX Vol.1 1986 Guest Editor Dick Higgins, Foreward by Dick Higgins Special Issue Pattern Poetry: a Symposium 4187

Dream Event, Oct 25 1986 1986 Audio Documentation of the Dream Event, Two Audio Cassettes and handwritten Notes 4321

Radio Art, Alvin Curran, Cora, Willem deRidder 1986 Walkman Belin 1986 at the Daad Galerie 4323

Hercules on the Lotus 1986 MOLD 4450

Simma World Press Inst. 1986 Summer Photos 4465

Solstice 1986 Folder 4470

Meet the Composer Folder, Forms, Notes, Contracts 1986. 4583

Letter to CM from Alison Knowles 1986 She resigns from New Wilderness and closes Printed Editions Press. 4602

Beth Anderson Promo Package 1986 Jeffrey James Arts Consulting, Several pieces, Swales & Angels 4667

Read the Way He Writes: A Festschrift for bp Nichol 1986 Ontario Arts Council. Also a letter inside from Paul Dutton to CM 4740

Homo Futurus, Barbara Rosenthal 1986 Signed for CM 2018. 4750

Rothenberg Writings 1986 Typed Poems and other short pieces by Jerome Rothenberg. Drafts 4774

Walls Script and letters, Wagner Rasmussen 1986 Agreement with Bellevue Teatret, Denmark 4795

Sari Dienes Retrospective Booklet 1986 Retrospective was presented at Thorpe Intermedia Gallery Oct. 12 thru Nov. 30. 4797

In Love with the Gratuitous: Armand Schwerner, Sherman Paul 1986. 4824

64 Poems, Brondum 1986 signed to CM 4889

Additional, 1986 signed to CM,Tryckt hos vänersborgs offset AB, Vanersborg 4944

Gold in the Morning. Alfredo Jaar 1986 signed 4993

New York Dada, Edited by Rudolf E. Kuenzli 1986 Willis Locker & Owens 5036

Musk un sprache 1986 CM P.174, Akademie der Kunste 5039

Hugo Ball, Leben und Werk 1986 Publica 5041

Confronting Stravinsky edited by Jann Pasler 1986 signed to CM, University of California Press 5045

International blues calendar 1986 calendar 5116

Letter to CM, Bernard Heidsieck 1986. 5120

Breath River Route, Malcolm Goldstein & Alison Knowles 1986 A performing installation Space 5241

Burt Porter Manuscripts 1986 Feeling like an Asshole, The Ballad singer 5252

Sari Dienes: New Work postcard promo 1986 Promo for show at A>I>R> Gallery 66 Crosby St. NY 5280

Artspeak A Gallery Review 1986. 5411

Gilbert Heiso Graphic Postcard (6) 1986 Printed by Conrad Gleber Printing Co. 5422

Letters and drawings to CM from LanaIntern Jelly Network. 1986 Graphic piece, and Illustrated letters from Rome 5510

Ear Memo from Ivy F. Winick, Advertising Mgr. 1986 Ear is looking for Ad accounts promo letter 5576

Glen Velez solo 1987. 88

Jello 1987 cm, music only 257

Jello 1987 Reed Hayes, music only 259

Jello 1987 CRM, music only 260
Jello 3 spots tight 1987 3 spots together 261
Jello 1987 CM, music only 262
Jello 1987 Reed Hayes, music only 263
Jello 1987 CRM, music only 264
Ellen Burstyn 1987. 392
Webster 1987. 393
Star Man 1987. 394
Sidekicks 1987. 395
Moonlighting 1987. 396
Life with Lucy 1987. 397
Colby's 1987. 398
Dynasty 1987. 399
Perfect Strangers 1987. 400
Sledge Hammer 1987. 401
MacGyver 1987. 403
Head of the Class 1987. 404
Spencer for Hire 1987. 405
Heart of the City 1987. 406
Jack and Mike 1987. 407
Growing Pains 1987. 408
MacGyver 1987 Re EQ'd for CMA reel, 6/13/89. 409
Heart of the City 1987 Re EQ'd for CMA reel, 6/13/89. 410
Colby's 1987 Re EQ'd for CMA reel, 6/13/89. 411
Jack & Mike 1987 Re EQ'd for CMA reel, 6/13/89, TL 412
30 Something 1987 HL 414
Slap Maxwell 1987 415
Dolly 1987. 416
Once a Hero 1987. 417
I Married Dora 1987. 418
Hooperman 1987. 419
Full House 1987. 420
Techno Country Pop (Buck James) 1987 TL 421
Full Sing 1987 HTL 422
Full Sing, more vocal 1987 HTL 423
Excedrin IB 1987 pain FX - spoken "IB" 564
Excedrin IB 1987 pain FX - spoken "IB" 565
First Eastern Bank - demo 1987 demo - track plus sung tag 566
demo 1987 demo - piano track plus sung tag 567
Frito Lay Chips 1987. 568
Beyond Night & Day 1987 16track 15ips 1/2" recorded in Sweden for sound track 1116
B.S. Bates M&M's :30 8.19.87 1987. 1146
Winter Bells -- Celebrating the Winter Solstice - event broadcast

1987 A procession of bell players, conch players, a large bass drum, and stilt walkers, move to the celebration site, where they perform. At noon everyone ceases and listens to the bells of NY ring from all directions in a pre-arranged chorus. [was this realized? if so, it should have a year, specific site, and be in past tense] 1258

Solstice '87 event broadcast 1987 Public event in City Hall Park and Tompkins Square Park, NYC, with media connections to Lapland, South Pole Station, and Rome, Italy. The cast included E. Koch, J.Rothenberg, J. Cage, J. Sanborn, P. Glass, M. Fenly, L. Redgrave. The event was broadcast internationally on TV and radio. Fusion artist Shalom designed and organized the "World," a sculpture/performance site. 1280

Sound drawers 1987. 1403

Sound Reliquaries 1987 The sound reliquaries are individual single and double sound memory types built in to jewelry or other boxes with one or two compartments. The owner places a sound via a small microphone into the 10 - 20 second digital recorplaces for posterity. 1405

Wave Music VIII: 6 Harpsichords 1987 Six harpsichords in the dark are activated by light cues from six dancers, building to continuous sound and light. The second movement is a rapid moto perpetuo exploring polytonality in scales. Amplification is gradually added as the sound thickens. 1413

Kaddish for the Homeless (with by John Kalish) 1987 A rich-voiced radio announcer (Steve Post) introduces this montage of interviews with public figures and homeless individuals. Sound effects and music form the score. 1458

Hiroshima 1987 This is a variation on "Emergency" and the "Triangulation Event." Many vehicles carrying ringing bells travel from their homes -- perhaps days away -- to arrive at a common place in Hiroshima at the same time. There they perform together. They fall silent. Later they depart playing simultaneously, or alternatively, one-by-one. 1524

Solstice 87 Program (2) 1987 A City in Celebration. June 21 program of activities and performances around NYC. First copy just for viewing 1548

Sunset Chant By Tibetan Monks for World Peace 1987 CM will join in for a special finale. Presented by Richard Gere and Tibet House in association with the New Wilderness Foundation and NY Parks & Recreation. Battery Park, NY at sunset. The orange of the robes, the Staten Island ferry and the sunset merged. 1555

Fusion Arts & Plexus Party 1987 A poster for a party Jan. 17, 1987 at 57 Stanton St. NYC special thanks to Downtown Magazine 1559

Columnar Number Languages (Ratios): Counting the Temperature 1987 This piece was composed after many years of being stimulated by composer Tom Johnson's visit and discussions about whther I would ever compose a new number music work. The ratios expressed in lists can be decoded aurally, as music. The 5:9 ratio (offset by 32) of Celcius-Fahrenheit convertions is the ratio used: 0, 32; 5, 41; 10, 50; etc. 1580

Beyond Night and Day 1987 Directed by Paul Anders Simma, this is the first feature film in the Sami language. The score and song in Sami include sampled arctic sounds; notably that of the arctic grouse, or ptarmagan. The score was recorded and produced in Stockholm. [mention English subtitles with price, length, etc.] 1604

Mermaid Parade 1987. 1616

Hercules on the Lotus 1987 Printed song sheet 1617

Boarshead Ham 1987 This score uses sampled cello and chorus in a silly scenario of avoiding the quick switch of the ham in the deli counter. 1633

Tales from the Darkside: The Geezenstacks 1987 Number 312. 1640

Between Night and Day 1987. 1646

2M4U: M&M's International 1987 words and music. M&M's International. Music and lyrics added to preexisting lyrics. 1669

Tales From The Darkside: Spirit Photographer 1987 Episode title. 1670

PSE&G 12-10-1987 1987 PI Films Gas Image, 01-87 Electric Image PSEG 02-87 Community Image PSEG 03-87 :30. 1991

WNYC Solstice Logo Art event broadcast 1987 Logo art used on WNYC 2018

Solstice '87 event broadcast 1987. 2170

Solstice '87 event broadcast 1987. 2171

WINS Radio 1987. 2181

The Cinchels 1987 MBCS_0143 :30 MBCS-0144 :15 Jan 9, 1987. 2184

M&M Mars Snickers bar 1987 MZSN0960; 30 'More to satisfy/price'MZSN0962; 30 'More to satisfy/non-price'1986. 2207

IBM 1984 TV spots 1987 Costs/Doors/Programs/Portable/Problem fighting/Dealer/PC family/Ass. series 2208

Summer Solstice tape 26 #203 event broadcast 1987 Performance Bread & Puppets 2215

Summer Solstice tape 22 #203 event broadcast 1987 Pandemonium & fireflies, Balloons, Ladgi cmara Ken Sculptor 2216

Summer Solstice tape 25 #203 event broadcast 1987 Congo dancers Wendy Chambers Grand buddha Kerchak 2217

Summer Solstice tape 15 #203 event broadcast 1987 The sculpture Assorted Kiels 2218

Summer Solstice tape 14 #203 event broadcast 1987 Gamelan/Flute?/Skip//DAncer/Sun Pata 2219

Summer Solstice tape 18 #203 event broadcast 1987 Trumpet Fanfare Dance Balloons 2223

Summer Solstice tape 29 #203 event broadcast 1987 Brazilian Parade 2224

Summer Solstice tape 28 #203 event broadcast 1987 Muscum del Barria:Balloons Wendy Chambers trumpetsGamelan/Kids w/music James Oliver Dancers in red 2225

Ann Magnuson Vandemonium 1987 Filmscore Joshua Selman 2234

Summer Solstice tape 28 #203 event broadcast 1987 Bread & Puppet theater Brazil parade 2237

Lappland footage 1987 non broadcast dub fr Swedish TV 1 Nils Somby 2 Simma 2238

Summer Solstice tape 24 #203 event broadcast 1987 Tetjak Bread & Puppet theater 1 2239

Summer Solstice tape 20 #203 event broadcast 1987 Story telling/ Drums/Dancers/Caroline/Simonds/the Sculpture/ Animals tales theater KIDS 2247

Summer Solstice tape 21 #203 event broadcast 1987 assorted 2248

Summer Solstice tape 16 #203 event broadcast 1987 Sunpath, kids, ice sculpture, dance, gamelan, City of NY 2249

Time flies Rolodex 1987 It's here someplace t-630--1-120 1/29/87. 2253

Summer Solstice tape 23 #203 1987 Haircut/Balinese cost./sunpath dnc/Wendy Chambers dnc/circle music proc./Gr Buddha marching/Ketjak-balinese dance 2256

Solstice TV presentation 1987 video. 2267

Tales from the darkside #220 1987 Distant signals 2268

Solstice '87 event broadcast 1987. 2275

Tales from the Darkside #312 1987 Geezinstacks :22 3/12/87. 2281

Tales from the Darkside #? 1987 Spirit photographer:22 3/12/87. 2282

Solstice '87 event broadcast 1987. 2283

Wollman Rink Solstice Winter Bells event broadcast 1987 12/30/88. 2284

Solstice '87 1987. 2289

Solstice '87-The day the Sun... 1987. 2290

Solstice '87-The day the Sun... 1987. 2292

Solstice '87-Broadcast 1987 edited tape/first 20 minsbroadcast 2293

Solstice '87-Broadcast 1987 edited master dub f review 2294

Solstice '87-Broadcast 1987 edited tape broadcast 2295

Solstice '87-The day the Sun... 1987 2297

Solstice ? 1987 ??? not quite edited 2307

Fusion Event '87 1987 dub fr VHS 2315

Solstice '87-The day the Sun... 1987. 2317

Digital CMA master 1987 different titles compiled 2323

Beyond Night and Day 1987 NTSC master 2324

Beyond Night and Day 1987 NTSC master 2325

CMA reel '87 #1 1987 audio tr2. 2345

4/4 Demo reel 1987. 2346

CMA demo reel '87 1987 M&M's, MTV "World prem Video 'PSE&G, MTV Pavarotti AT&T Telcom 2354

MTV "Pavarotti" 1987 FRED ALLEN MTV "Pavarotti" MTV "Pavarotti" 8011 (:30) 2424

Roger Ely, Dreams, Fantasies & Recollections 1987. 2442

Summer Solstice Posters Original art for 87 & 89 1987 Poster Art from Solstice 87. 2472

The Number Six 1987 Performance notes and score with letter from Tom Johnson with copies of number Music Part 1and Number Music part 2. Also an exerpt from the "Podewil" program. Also DAT (Phill Nibloch) 2-7-94 and flyer from Podewil, Berlin Tom Johnson on the Cover. 2504

Harpsichord Mania Poster (5) 1987 A surround sound environment for six amplified Harpsichords and 20 playback tapes Music By John Cage, Lejaren Hiller, Wendy Chambers, CM. One poster is autographed by performers. (damaged) 2565

WIENERLIEDER, Sten Hanson (3) copies 1987 Published by Other Media 2583

ES IT GENUG, Sten Hanson (2) copies 1987 Published by Other Media 2585

Number Music and Expanded forms of Number music 1987 Two Printed copies 2637

Soul To Soul 1987 By CM and the Natives 2643

A Peal in Air 1987 Collected poems volume 3 Phenomenon Press, Toronto, Canada 1978, 52 pages of graphic poems by Bob Cobbing Signed to CM 2646

Performances and Oil Paintings by Maggie Eins (Slides) 1987 Page of slides of Oil Paintings and Costume designs 2765

1987 Solstice Artwork. 1987 Original Artwork for 1987 & 1989 Solstice event. Paste-up and copies 2805

WNYC Report and Press w/Solstice 87 Script (8) 1987 Press Kit and Highlights from Last sixty Years 2824

3 Songs in numbers (from Heavyweight Sound Fight). 1987. 2828

Solstice 87 Program (10) 1987. 2848

Neighbor Note Study 1987 Note Study by CM, realization by T. Reid 2873

Sten Hanson Extrasensory Conceptions II (10) for soprano and chamber ensemble 1987 A musical piece by Sten Hanson created during a workshop with Harpins Kraftin Fylkinham, Stockholm in 1973. Harpins Kraft also performed it in the ISCM World Music Days in the same year and recorded it on Caprice Cap 1970 published by Other Media 2889

Sten Hanson WIENERLIEDER (5) mit texte von Gerhard Ruhm und Ernst Jandl 1987 A musical piece by Sten Hanson published by Other Media 2891

The Rivington School, No SE No 1987. 2946

Fusion Arts & Plexus Party 1987 57 Stanton St. Many Performers 2949

Invitation to the Nordic Conference in Expressive Arts 1987 Call for proposals to the 1987 Nordic Conference in Expressive Arts "The Creative Process and Mental Health" "The State of the Arts in Education" Inside invitation to CM to contribute to conference from Phillip Speiser Director of Scandanavian Institute for Expressive Arts 3011

Spiderwoman Theater Inc. Press Kit 1987 Descriptions and press about Spiderwoman Theater, Inc. by Lisa Mayo 3033

The Second Coming Exhibit 1987 Postcard advertising: The Second Coming Exhibit Hiro Cafe, Party for Downtown Magazine & Artist Reception Sunday, January 11th, 1987 produced by Fusion Arts 3060

Video & Muziek 1987 Poster from Video and Muziek gallery'vub trioflaan teogang 6 1050 Brussel 3070

Treviso Protagonista 1987 September 1987 edition of Treviso Protagonista 3088

Logos Files 1987 Files and Press on Logos, Universiteit Brussel 3090

Photograph of Dick Higgins 1987 Photograph of Dick Higgins 3149

Christmas Cards 1987 Holiday Greeting Cards from CM Associates 3179

BACA Downtown Presents Shelley Hirsch, Lauri Nagel, David Simmons: Voice, Dance, Instruments 1987 BACA Downtown Presents Shelley Hirsch, Lauri Nagel, David Simmons: Voice, Dance, Instruments 3305

Program for Hörspiele Im Westdeutschen Rundfunk 1987 Book with information on Programs for Horspiele Im West Duetschen Rundfunk Programs for John Cage events inside 3308

Mr. Sexy Atomic Hot List 1987 List of Events from Mr. Sexy Atomic Hot List of the Magic Orbit from Outer Space Inc. 3338

CM Spirit Voices - No Se No Equinox 1987 Poster for CM the Rivington School Spirit Voices - 3340

Revised Schedule for the Summer Solstice Festival, 1987 1987 Fanny Schoening: Paper Landskab 3362

Article about Spring Equinox, Summer Solstice, and "Spirit Voices" 1987. 3364

Correspondence with Sheldon Cohen 1987. 3384

Postcards to NWF 1987 Postcards to New Wilderness: -Art by Ferret Studios and -Mail-Art Networking for a Peace International lobbying for ideas about MAIL ART under the themes paradox and way of light. 3385

Correspondence with Renee Rockoff/KIVA Foundation for Art 1987 about a Performance for NY's Hungry and Homeless 3397

Harmonic Convergence: Riding the Wavelength of Planetary Synchronization 1987 Planet Art Event 3398

Visual Sound Forum 1987 Box with "Menu" and other information

3448

The Second Coming Exhibit, Mailer 1987 Party for Downtown Magazine at Hiro Cafe 112 First Ave, CM and Mark Sloan provide Music artists listed on card. 3495

Conch Music 1987 5 copies of music and four copies of Sets for sundown. An event designed by CM and Spontaneously realized by the performers. 3664

Solstice 87 Artwork 1987 B&W Illustration of the Sun with a radio and TV high above the city. Illustration by Laurie Edmonds 3715

Cold Sun Standing Still Winter Solstice Poem for CM 1987 A 3 page poem for the Winter Solstice 12-21-87 Unknown Author. 3716

Laurie Edmonds Drawings 1987 An envelope to CM with 13 small sketches by Laurie Edmonds 210 E. 21st St. 3726

Letter from Logos Foundation to CM about his itinerary for Nov. in Belgium. 1987 Belgium, Moniek, Simma 3740

Solstice 88 A Celebration of Light 1987 Production Notes and Schedule for Solstice 88. Concept ideas. Paul Anders Simma, Stella Olson, Tom Pomposello 3741

Hymn Transformations 1987 A year of daily Variations for Bugle Calls and Other Music Other media, Stockholm 3752

Sunday First Spring Sunset 1987 A concept Poem where each word is in its own box. 3773

International Jelly Roll Network 1987 The aim of the network is to establish a direct contact between artists in first person, a direct connection between artists and promoters.(with illustration) 3778

Summer Solstice 1987 Press Release by Marie Leone and Judith L. Weiss 1987 WNYC's Radio Broadcast, Press Release and some production notes 3791

4th of July to Geoffrey Hendricks 1987 Number Piece by CM 3796

Gianfranco Salvatore Letter 1987 Letter to Tell CM that he is sending a copy of his production of Anadyomene by Roberto Laneri. 3803

Postcard from Gilbert Hsiao Show 1987 A signed postcard graphic 3815

Rivington School NO SEE NO Poster 1987 Schedule for Jan-April Events CM on Mar 17-31. 3817

Radium Records Catalog (in English) A catalog to introduce their new music to the USA 1987 Radium 226.05 Records Sodra Allegatan 3, S-41301 Goteborg, Sweden 3874

A Car is Driven-Beatty Admits his Guilt 1987 For Tom Buckner and Friends, Music by CM. A small musical piece based on a News story. Other Media 3918

Asia Society Presents Tibetan Singing Bowl Ensemble (4) 1987 Concerts for Peace Japan 1987. 3954

Raphael Mostel, composer/Director Concerts for peace. with the

Tibetan Singing bowl ensemble 1987 An 8 1/2 X 11 single page printed concert promo. 3965

Ken Hiratsuka letter to CM 1987 The letter tells of his trip around Australia and stone projects he did along the way. He would like to get back to NY and do some projects with CM. 3998

Open Letter 6th Series No.9 Steve McCaffery 1987. 4036

Solstice Westar graphic (3) 1987 Radio station links graphic for solstice 1987 Toronto 4192

Pincher Creek Film Society Invitation Photos 1987 Photo of CM and Chief of Blood Tribe at Pincher Creek Invitation, Thank You letter, Press Conference Notes. Indian Summer, World Festival of Aboriginal Motion Pictures 4218

Indian Summer Film & Video Directory Indian Summer, World Festival of Aboriginal Motion Pictures 1987 This could be from the first festival, as the other program says 1988 Indian Summer, World Festival of Aboriginal Motion Pictures 4251

Letter from Arsenije Jovanovic to CM 1987 A letter about a possible collaboration for radio Belgrade, 4315

Diet Coke "Machine" 1987 Score for diet Coke spot 4403

Solstice 1987 Bad Mold 4466

Solstice 87 1987 Folder 4471

New Wilderness Foundation Performance space sketch and Plans. 1987 Sketch Ideas for a Performance space with sound and electrical ideas 4508

Skater On Fire Press Release 1987 Returns to Central Park Wollman Rink Central Park Part of Solstice 1987 Robert Steinar skater Performance designed by fire sculptor Paolo Buggiani CM from NWF 4541

Summer Solstice 1987 Program Downtown Newspaper 1987 Spring Fertilazation Art Founders Welcome by CM. CM on Page 25A (trumpet) 4547

The Cutting Edge Show (2) 1987 Created by Baird Jones at the Paterson Museum Oct. 4-Nov.-4 1987 Announcement and Curators Statement List of Artists 4607

Experimental Intermedia Flyer 1987 For shows at EIF and the Clocktower Niblock 4608

DADA Performance, Edited Mel Gordon 1987. 4743

Extrasensory Conceptions II, Sten Hanson (3) 1987 For Soprano and Chamber ensemble Published by Other Media 4794

Sten Hanson, WIENERLIEDER 1987 Other Media 4809

Extrasensory Conceptions II, Sten Hanson 1987 For Soprano and Chamber ensemble, Published by Other Media 4812

Robert Adrian X, 1987 Gallery Grita insam Signed to CM 4826

Drottningholms Slottsteater, Program 1987 Proprius books & music 4975

The Music Men, Margaret Hindle Hazen and Robert M. Hazen 1987 Smithsonian 4977

Pattern Poetry Guide to an unknown literature, Dick Higgins 1987 State University of NY Press 5000

Chanson Dada, Tristan Tzara 1987 Coach House/Underwhich 5034

The Collected Poems of Charles Olson, George F. Butterick 1987 University of California Press 5095

Music by Tom Johnson, Counting Duets 1987 A Five page w/cover counting Music Folder by Two-Eighteen Press Village Station NY. Cover is in poor shape but music is fine 5147

Mandolin Bros. Catalog 1987 Staten Island Since 1971. 5197

Article on Chanting from the Encyclopedia of Religion, Mircea Eliade 1987 M 5283

Small Badge for Solstice 87 1987 A production of the New Wilderness Foundation. Badge is enclosed in a small envelope marked: Telephone booth number 755 by Reverend Pedro (an art Piece) 5383

Videografie, Event Dates 1987 Nam June Paik, Philip Glass, Peter Greenaway, Holger Czukay, John Cage, CM 5403

Gematria Performance Instructions 1987 A Score by CM 5408

Murri Image Brisbane Queensland Indigenous Media Assn. Info 1987 With a list of Australian Media Organizations and Community Video, Film Service 5417

UTE Indian Tribe Audio Visual Promo Piece 1987 Equipment list, Facilities, Staff and Archive. 5421

Black Horse Society Proposal, List of Members 1987 Programs for 1987, Budget for 1988. 5434

New Wilderness Foundation International Summer Solstice Celebration Program (4)Italy 1987 Radiouno, Audio Box, Gran Vocio 5466

Concert Program High Tech Jazz 1987 Teatro in Trastevere April 87 Roberto Ottaviano, John Surman, Mark Ducert Trio, Umberto Fiorentino 5481

Winter Bells, Script and budget, Program notes 1987. 5620

Solstice 87 Planning letters between Chase Morrison (BBC) and CM 1987. 5634

SOLSTICE MASTER SCRIPT 1987 Do not Send out, Copy if Needed 5647

99˘ Deal TV & Radio w/o Tom's Line 1988. 353

Senses 1988 TL, revised copy 357

Menu 1988 TL, revised copy 359

Sticks and Stones 1988 no leader 360

Sticks and Stones 1988 no leader 361

Sticks and Stones 1988 no leader 362

A Penny Saved 1988 HL 370

Common Sense 1988 TL 371

Chinese Gangs 1988 374
Chinese Gangs 1988 375
Alleract-Rough Mix w/o Ancr. 1988 HL 381
Alleract-Rough Mix w/ Ancr. 1988 TL 382
Certain Kind of Hero, v.1 1988 HTL 429
Certain Kind of Hero, v.2 1988 HTL 430
Certain Kind of Hero, v.1 inst. mix 1988 HTL 431
Certain Kind of Hero, v.2 inst. mix 1988 HTL 432
Conches w/ tag 1988 HTL 436
Conches w/o tag 1988 HTL 437
Rhythm & Bass w/ tag 1988 HTL 438
Rhythm & Bass w/o tag 1988 HTL 439
Perc. w/o tag 1988 HTL 440
Sampler 1988 HTL 441
Howard Bank, etc. 1988. 520
Howard Bank 1988. 521
Howard Bank 1988. 522
Howard Bank 1988. 523
Howard Bank 1988. 525
Howard Bank 1988. 526
Howard Bank 1988 old time car effect with horn; drive away 527
Howard Bank 1988 old time car effect: motor choking 528
Howard Bank 1988 old time car effect: engine banging/wheezing 529
Howard Bank 1988 smack 530
Howard Bank 1988 playing card effects, riffles, dealing 531
Howard Bank 1988 car sequence 532
Howard Bank 1988 metal bang - distant 533
Howard Bank 1988 work sounds 534
Howard Bank 1988 creeks - house/wood 536
Howard Bank 1988 creeks - house/wood 537
Howard Bank 1988 car spot: full mix - stop rhythm ending 538
Howard Bank 1988 house spot: full mix 539
Party 1988 Fellini band demo (party) 540
Movers 1988 country fiddle/gtr (synth) demo 541
Party 1988 Fellini band revised demo (party) 542
Movers 1988 country fiddle/gtr "movers" (synth) demosession - live musicians only 543
Movers 1988 country fiddle/gtr "movers" (synth) demosession - live musicians only mix with voice 544
Movers 1988 country fiddle/gtr "movers" (synth) demosession - live musicians only mix without voice; add tag 545
Party 1988 final mix 547
Movers 1988 mix - not final 548
Movers 1988 final mix 549

Voices 1988 1. Performance 2. Concert (w/CM voices) Horspiel-CM Performance + Concert 574

The Lund Experience 1988. 717

The Lund Experience - based on Montgolfier Musique w 1988 This event celebrates the Montgolfier brothers, 18th century French founders of hot air ballooning. A horse and brass band show, accompanied by taped music, play the overture to the rising of four balloons with sound systems and musicians. A conductor in top hat rises on a mechanical ladder and conducts the launch. An equestrian solos and then leads an exit parade of the band. Location: Lund Sweden. 919

Arctic Yukon: Fish & WIldlife 1988. 1099

McCaffrey McCall: Mercedes Benz 1 1988 5.1.84 3.9.88. 1109

McCaffrey McCall: Mercedes Benz 2300 VW Coupe 1988 5.1.84 3.9.88. 1110

The Devil's Chauffeur, The Tell Tale Heart 1988 9.28.88. 1118

Locomotiv Koncrete 3.29.88 1988. 1123

LU COOKIES: LUNATICS - music 1988. 1139

SY'PHONY 4.4.88 1988. 1154

CMA Commercial Demo 1988. 1194

Solstice '88 event broadcast 1988 Celebration at Riverside Park, NYC, with a street procession to Cathedral of St. John the Divine, public square dance and art show, candlelight procession, dark performance, and midnight flash from cathedral tower. Included in a National Public Radio broadcast of West Deutsche Rundfunk (Hoerspiel) artists radio works. 1269

Montgolfier Musique (with Sten Hanson) 1988 T(as above) 1336

CM's Vivaldi's "Spring" (from "Four Seasons") 1988 The phrases of Vivaldi's "Spring" are separated by abrupt systematic pauses filled with percussion, solo violin improv, and fighting kite sounds. This re-composition was created for the New Wilderness, NYC Dept. of Parks Spring Equinox event, "March March," in Central Park, NYC (March 22). "CM's Vivaldi's 'Spring'" is also conceived as equestian music. The arrangement is for wind ensemble/marching band. 1347

Concerts by Composers: Program No. 09 - works by Larry Kucharz, CM, Takehisa Kosugi 1988. 1375

Five Minutes for Armand Schwerner 1988 This is a script for the minute by minute activity over 5 minutes. 1396

S'phony or CM's Farewell Symphony 1988 In this parable of modern times, the computers graduallyassist and then take over an orchestra, driving them off the stage. This spin on the Haydn "Farewell" Symphony is about thepermanent vacation orchestras are beginning in the late 20th century. The computers are visably mounted on mechanized stands, in front of the orchestra. They very statically play the "continuo part" (traditional keyboard support) in the first movement, then the continuo with percussion in the second, and then in the third, replace the orchestra person-by-person as the musicians exit. The conductor leaves. Alone on stage, the computers play and dance mechanically in a short gloating epilogue. 1435

Khurbn (Text by Jerome Rothenberg) 1988 Poet Jerome Rothenberg reads his Khurbn (Holocaust) poems. Synthesized lines telegraph in mono tone the voice rhythms with bass notes marking the phrases. Pocket trumpet, sampled crowd sounds and sampled strings accompany the reading. In the performance version of Khurbn, the poetry and instrumental playing are live with pre-recorded synth/sampler sound-track. 1469

Improvised Music 1988 A German Booklet of Musicians and Concerts in Berlin 1494

Swedish Bullseye for CM, Dick Higgins 1988 A song for CM to stay home more. 1503

Jaime de Angulo The music of the Indians of Northern California Edited by Peter Garland 1988 A book with a note inside from Peter to CM. 1507

Berlin Wall Project Proposal 1988 Proposal for sculpture and art project from Franc Palaia. Included are drawings and photo. 1572

Gematria Poems (Text by Jerome Rothenberg) 1988 This piece uses the numbers from which each gematria poem is derived to generate musical phrases, instrumental and vocal. The numbers are translated into altered Morse code. A dot is du. Zero is dah In this scheme,1-5-0 becomes <du<dudududu<dah, where < is a slight pause. 1584

Voices document 1988 A Hoerspiel (radio play) commissioned by Westdeutschen Rundfunk, Cologne, Germany, Klaus Schoening, producer. Broadcast date: February 14. CM writes, "A picture of my own history and influences, from the churches and synagogues of my childhood, the work with American Indian music, the work with healing both in the hospital and in ritual, my own personal shamanistic adventures, animal communication and environmental compositions, conch orchestra, works with machine language and communication technology, and live sound processing. 'Voices' is a bit like Woody Allen's 'Zelig,' in that my own voice emerges chameleon-like from the influences, hopefully to find its authentic forms. At time of production, my wife and I were expecting a child. The impending arrival shaped the ending of 'Voices' where a baby's cry emerges from a simultaneous montage of all the voices in the piece. 'Voices' brings together this new family member with ancestors, my father, grandfather and grandmother."I dedicate Voices to Stephanie Rose Morrow, born May 1989. 1621

Winter Bells II-- Celebrating the Winter Solstice event broadcast 1988 A gnomon sculpture by Bill Duesing was set out on the ice in Wollman Skating Rink, Central Park. It marked the path of the sun on the horizon on this Winter Solstice. Ice skaters performed with transducers on their skates' blades. The signal went by FM radio signal to mix with a soundtrack created from animal sounds, bells, Central African horn music, and 12 live trombones, symbolizing the months of the year. Church bells rang throughout New York City. Many bell players rang their bells, while children danced on the sides of the rink. Radio stations played Morrow's one minute composition of bells and birds and Frank Simms sang an original Morrow song, "Winter Bells." 1625

Chopin Variations - Did George Sand Kill Chopin. Chopin Cello, 1988. 1649

Lully Variations 1988 midi sequenced work for use in Nam Jun Paik's vidoe installation atthe Palis de Versailles, France. Drum machine + Orchestral samples. 1650

Court TV - Music Compilation (Dub) 1988. 1651

Whale Music from the Sky 1988 Electro-acoustic music for event: Montgolfier Music. Event co-created by Sten Hanson. Summer in Lund, Sweden 1654

COCA COLA USA 11-14-88 1988 LINTAS: NY Diet Coke KODC-9428 :45 "Boat w/short copy Rev. 1 1975 Oh YEA Budget Gourmet 2-23-1988 All American Gourmet Co. DI IORIO WERGELES Budget Gourmet Dinner BGTD-3219 :30 OH YEA $2.19 Master 1981

Snake Charmer HEFTY 12-9-1988 Wells Rich & Greene Inc. Mobil/ Hefty Trash Bags MBCS 0243 "Snake Charmer"(:30) 45518. 1982

MTV " TV Lovers" 6-16-88 1988 FRED ALLEN MTV- TV- Lovees MTV TV- Lovers 8011 (:30). 1983

Snake Charmer HEFTY 12-9-1988 Wells Rich & Greene Inc. Mobil/ Hefty Trash Bags MBCS 0255 "Snake Charmer" (:15) 45518. 1985

24 Hr. Rock & Roll 1-28-1988 The Ink Tank MTV 24 Hr.Rock&Roll (Doris) :10 Rock News (Max) :1024 Hour Music News (SAM) :10. 1986

Carolina Light & Power 8-31-1988 McKinney & Silver Multidub 2 Spots A Penny Saved CPLC 8841 :30 Common Sense CPLC 8842 :30. 1987

Oh YEA Budget Gourmet 2-23-1988 All American Gourmet Co. Diorio Wergeles Budget Gourmet Dinner BGTD-3219 :30 OH YEA $2.19 Master 1981

Boars Head Ham 1-11-1988 Altschiller-Reitzfeld QBDN-2563 "Ask for it" :30 1990 M&M Candy "Movies" 1-20-1988 Dalton Fenske Movies -Recommended Generic :30 305635. 1993

NCNB National Bank 6-17-1988 McKINNEY & SILVER "Error free Checking" NCNC-8840 24 Hr. Machine :30 1994 CM Associates DEMO REEL 1-30-1988 1988 EE Master 1999 CM Associates DEMO REEL Protection Master 1988 Protection Master Length 5:38 1993. 2002

Spring Mysteries 1988 Idea notes for a performance piece and installation. References to 1. video documenting: Spirit Voices performance at No Se No sculpture garden, NYC 19872. CM event/arrangement of

Vivaldi's SPRING (Four Seasons) 2037

Whirligig, Mac Wellman 6-26-1988 1988 Script, production and 2038

Farewell Symphony (Sy'phony) 1988 studio demo of composition for orchestra and live synth performance. 2228

Sharacu 1988 w/layback final stereo audio on trx 1&212 14 88. 2271

NWF Solstice 1988 9 19 88. 2272

Solstice '88 1988 dub dub fr VHS tape #1 2285

Solstice '88 1988 dub dub fr VHS tape #3 2286

Solstice '88 ? 1988 ??? 2287

Solstice '88 1988 dub dub fr VHS tape #2. 2291

Wollman Rink Solstice Winter Bells 1988 12 30 88. 2298

Voices 1988. 2309

CMA Demo reel 1988. 2313

CMA scoring reel 1988 4 19 88. 2314

Voices 1988 digital audio 2320

Scoring reel 1988 4 19 88. 2335

CMA demo reel '88 1988 10 spots 2360

Solstice Poster 1988 Graphic poster of CM Illustration 2454

Ballongkonsert Montgolfier 1988 Poster for Ballongkonsert at Lunds Universitet 2457

24" large CM Face Mask 1988 A poster board Illustration Mask made to be worn. Artwork by Laurie Edmond signed to CM 2487

Music of the World Summer Solstice festival 1988 Music of North and South India with Parween Sultana, Mohammad Dilshad Kahn, Shankar, Hariprasad Chaurasia, Zakir Hussain at the Town Hall NYC 2488

Exemplum Avaltes 1988 A Graphic piece by Ken Friedman for Emily Harvey in the early 80's completed by Ken 2493

Indian Summer Poster 1988 World festival of Aboriginal Motion Pictures 2514

Fluxlux Oct. 16 1988 1988 A memorial ceremony for Robert Watts with a list of all in attendence and a great list of Fluxus members. 2621

Performing Language conference and festival April 15-16 1988 New Arts and Verbal performances CM gives an evening performance 2622

Yay Vol. 1, Issue 1 1988 An Arts publication from NYC 2628

Art and Revolution Catalog Russian and Soviet Art 1910- 1932 1988 Catalog from show at Ausstellung im Österreichischen Museum für angewandte Kunst 2687

Solstice '88 Production 1988 Production Notes, Logistics, Communications, Publicity Winter Solstice 87 early notes. 2688

Officina d'architettura Audiobox 1988 A creative printed piece from the Audiobox people 2689

CMs Chatter Issues 1,2,3, 1988 From NY each with three pages 2695

bp Nichol Poster 1988 Quote from Zygal In Memoriam: bp Nichol 30 Sept. 1944-Sept. 25, 1988 poster by Slug Press Vancover BC. 2697

Sy'phony third Movement Finale 1.2 1988 Musical score, manuscript with production notes, orchestra stage setup. 2827

Sten Hanson Hallo Piano Hallow Room (8) 1988 A musical piece by Sten Hanson commissioned by New Music concerts Toronto and first published by them in 1973 by pianist Monaka Gaylord, published by Other Media 2888

Sten Hanson Es IST GENUG. for Organ (10) 1988 A musical piece by Sten Hanson published by Other Media 2890

White Man Sleeps by Kevin Volaus 1988 A musical piece for two Harpsichord, viola da gamba and percussion 2904

Article about CM in BRUTUS magazine 1988 Article is under the NY Money section 2974

READING In celebration of the New Year and Gertrude Stein's birthday. Presented by Alison Knowles, Anna Lockwood and Jean Rigg with the help of the Participation projects Foundation. 1988 Description of floor plan, exhibits, and purpose of Denmark's Rock Museum 3048

Indian Summer 1988 The Second Annual Indian Summer World Festial of Aboriginal Motion Pictures Theme: Achievement Contains descriptions, proposals, and budgets for films included in the festival. 3072

Postcard: Kirsten Monique 1988 Norwegian Postcard from Kristen Monique following a lecture CM gave 3143

Performance Language Conference and Festival 1988 Featuring CM in the Evening performances 3156

Program from The Mahabharata 1988 A play by Jean-Claude Carriere Adapted into English and directed by Peter Brook At The CIty of Zurich and the Union Bank of Switzerland with Centre International De Creations Theatrales and the Royal Shakespeare Theater 3170

Public Illuminations Magazine Editions from 1988 to 1994. 3178

Rites of Solstice: Dancing, Poetry, and Immersion 1988 by Gregory Jaynes in "The NY Times" Article about the 1988 Summer Solstice Event 3181

Other Media Catalogue, Compositions Chronological List 1988 Chronological List of Compositions Under Other Media Productions Ranging from 1961 to 1988. 3218

Letter from Skip Blumberg 1988 to Laurie Anderson, David Byrne, Alvin Curran, Peter Gordon, Chris Janney, Richard Lerman, CM, Liz Phillips, Nigel Redden, David Van Tieghem about a VHS on New Music America (1980). 3306

Jean Cocteau and His World 1988 by Arthur King Peters The Vendome Press, NY and Paris 3320

"Can Archetypes be Heard" by Gianfranco Salvatore 1988 Essay 3445

Artwork to CM from Joakim 1988. 3449

The Making of Americans, Postcard (2) 1988 Reading in celebration of the New Year and Gertrude Stein's birthday. Presented by Alison

Knowles, Anna Lockwood and Jean Rigg with the help of the Participation projects Foundation. 3488

ISHI Time Changing Spaces Malcolm Goldstein 1988 Notes for Production at Whitney Museum at the Equitable Center Includes 2 Glossy Promo 8x10's. 3579

Sy'phony second movement Finale 1.2 Movement Finale 1.2, Second Movement, Forth Movement. 1988 Musical score, manuscript with production notes, orchestra stage setup. 3651

Solstice '88 Newspapers (8) 1988 Solstice 4 page flyer Graphic poster of CM Illustration inside spread. Presented by New Wilderness Foundation. 3713

Lenin, DaDa and Jung 1988 An Event for Zurich, Concept by CM, Collaborators from many professions who were influencedby the social, artistic and spritual issues ignited by Lenin, DaDa and Jung. Letters, Notes and TV draft in this portfolio. 3756

To Dick and Achilleus 1988 A possible Poul Borum piece from a performance at the Royal Museum of Fine arts in Copenhagen. 3863

Keynote Magazine for the musical Arts Jan. 1988 Polands Master Composer at 75, Witold Lutoslawski 1987 by Raphael Mostel. Also an article by Mostel in NY Times Art & Leisure. 3952

Oltre il Silenzio Magazine #0 (Beyond Silence) 1988 An international Bulletin to explore new aspects of Music and Art.Higgins, Maciunas, Cage, Curran, Miti, Chiari, Young. Back cover features John Cage photo 3953

Eight Performance Photos from Roskilde, three other city shots. 1988 5 x7 B&W photos of Eric Andersen, The Last Request, Bob Watts, Feed the Chior, Ben Pattersons Lick Piece, Geoffrey Hendricks at the Roskilde inlet, Ben Vautier, in bed Town square for a week, Phil Corner, Bob Watts, Eric Andersen, Studio Chior, Alison Knowles performance 3964

Solstice 1988 tickets or handouts 2" x 3" logos about 10. 3980

2nd Annual Indian Summer Program 1988 Workshop with Paul Anders Simma and CM Sept. 22. Pg. 6 Program has a list of over 50 film entries from around the world. Festival held at Pincher Creek, Alberta, Canada. 3984

A Pioneer in Multimedia CM 1988 Article about CM. Also a promo piece called CM, Executive Producer, Composer and Sound Designer. 3986

Ear Music News Program 1988 Thursday February 25th The Michael Todd Room at the Palladium Laurie Anderson and Philip Glass Co. Chairman A list of Party for EAR comittee 4000

CMs Chatter #1, 2, 3 1988. 4008

Flux Lux 1988 The Last Event of Robert Watts, Sunday Oct. 16 1988 Also a 4 pg paper KAO (HOM)Mage to Robert Watts which is full of

Fluxus Friends photos. 4012

David Mahler's Head Theatre 1988 A curious printed piece funded by Washington State arts commision and the Rockefeller foundation. 4028

The Sophist, Charles Bernstein 1988 Signed to CM and Lana 4056

Anne Poul, Geert Michael, Eric Andersen 1988 A small Gold foil cover book by Eric Andersen. Signed to CM Oct 23. 4147

Freibord #64, Francesco Conz 1988 Photos and Illustrations by Fluxus Crew 4152

Flux Lux The Last event of Robert Watts 1988 A schedule of events for the Memorial ceremony of Robert Watts with a list of performers and exhibitions 4166

The White Horse Butcher, Bread & Puppet 1988 A second edition of a Peter Schumann story. Signed to CM 4179

Telluride Institute Composer to Composer Poster 1988 Program Creators, Charles Amirkhanian, John Lifton, Advisory Board John Cage 4185

Northern Native Broadcasting Directory 1988 First of it's kind within Inuit communities Alaska, Greenland, Canada. A napkin with producers phone #'s inside cover. 4190

Freibord #64 1988 Early FLUXUS History and photos 4245

Program for Noh and Jiutamai Play 1988 CM attended this play in Japan. He writes "It was extraordinary especially when the Conch Horns Sounded and Dogs barked" ghosts were present. 4287

Maggie ENS 35mm Transparencies 1988 A page of slides of Maggie in various poses with her artwork 4395

Paul Anders Simma 1988 A brief Bio for film work, a rough draft probably written by CM. 4413

Balloon Festival 1988 8/27/88 Lund Sweden, presentation portfolio, project notes, Stellan Olson 4423

Roskilde Installation 1988 Slides 4461

Solstice 88 1988 Folder 4472

New Ears, Tompkins Square Arts Festival 1988 Event Posters (2) June 13th - 19th, with performance listings 4485

Sari Dienes Postcards and Calling Card (12) 1988 Business Card for Sari, Artist, Poet, Printmaker 340 Gatehill Rd Stony Point, NY 10980. Postcards are art pieces from 40- 90's. 4490

Winter Bells to Ring in Central Park, Promo Flyer 1988 A collaboration between composer CM and NWF and NYC Parks and Recreation 4520

Derviche/Le Robert, Bernard Heidsieck 1988 Editeurs Evidence, Signed to CM 4715

No Art, Boris Lurie, Seymour Krim 1988 Hundertmark, Berlin-Koln Pin Ups, Excretment Protest, Jew Art 4768

Hallo Piano-Hallo Room, Sten Hanson (7) 1988 Other Media 4807

Sten Hanson, ES IST GENUG for Organ 1988 Other Media 4808

The Foundation for Shamanic Studies Vol. 1 #1 Newsletter 1988 Dana Robinson 4817

Sounding the Full Circle, Malcolm Goldstein 1988 Signed to CM 4827

Mittringer Drawings and Sculptures 1988 Signed 4883

A Tribute bp 1988 Tribute Program for Harbourfront Friday December 2. 4890

Dikter, Margaret Atwood 1988 Prisma, Stockholm Heidi von Born Signed 4903

Midnight on your left, John Godfrey 1988 The Figures 4925

The Healing Forces of Music, Randall McClellan, phd 1988 signed, Amity House 4978

Zdravstvena Knjizica 1988 Galerija Studentskog Centra 5014

Self Portrait, Man Ray 1988 A New York Graphic Society book 5051

Sten Hanson, composer, poet, eventmaker & sonosopher 1988 Other Media NY 5055

Polyphonix 13 Listing of Artists with side comments and a letter to CM on the back 1988 Jean Jacques Lebel, Robert Filliou, Bernard Heidsieck, Paris 5152

Folder of Press Releases for CM Productions. 1988 Train to Plane, Hefty, MTV and other trade magazine releases. Article on Computer Music Production, Phil Kapp. 5196

A Ceremony in Rhyme For CM and Lana, Jackson Mac Low 1988 3 Songs for the Mystic Animals 5216

A Phoneme Dance For CM and Svetlana, Jackson Mac Low 1988 For Performance especially by Anne Tardos and the Composer 5217

Mirror, Lens and Memory, Bill Barrette 1988 Show Catalog for Lafayette College, Williams Center for the Arts 5248

Mary Rowell Press Kit, 1988 Bios, Photos and festival info. 5251

A 35mm slide of Barbra Yoshida's Sculpture piece. 1988 Sculpture shown at Arleen's Love letters Show. Sent to CM by request. 5343

Montgolfier Music Event Checklist 1988. 5356

The Party for EAR invitation w/reply mailer 1988 Feb. 25 at the Micheal Tood Room of the Palladium Co-chaired Laurie Anderson and Philip Glass. List of supporters. 5369

Invitation to Dick Higgins 50th Birthday 1988 Party at Emily Harvey Gallery 537 Bway 5380

Fashion Moda, Spring Mysteries Show 1988 A Sculpture and Sound Installation by Maggie Ens and CM April 9. 5381

Robert Black, Double Bass Event Poster w/Press Release. 1988 Saturday Jan. 30, Composers Resources Presents 5384

Ecology?Art?Fusion 1988 A paper by CM 5393

Europe, France & Bahia 1988 An Extensive Art Exhibition w/over 200 works in a wide range of media. To be held at the Museum of Image and Sound in Sao Paulo Brazi An overview of the Event Plan. 5407

Solstice 1988 Posters Design and billing. Rough ideas for Artwork 5415

Stitching Logos foundation Letter 1988 Conferming Moniek Darge And Gotfried's partisapation in the Harbour Event. 5419

First Day Issue Stamp from Alison Knowles U.S. Desert Plants 1988 122 Spring St. NY 5424

Winter Bells Solstice event at Wollman Memorial Skating Rink 1988 Schedule of Events and Players Musicians, Skaters and singers. A New Wilderness Event 5427

John Ditsky Review of CM's Birth of the War God. 1988 Western Wind, Rothenberg, Laurel CD. 5428

Press Release and performance info for SOUL 1988 Bjarne v.H.H.Solberg and CM 5430

Audio Montage for LU COOKIES, Script 1988. 5431

Mexico City Blues Flyer 1988 by Jack Kerovac. A reading with Live Music Ginsberg Savage, Brodey and 20+ others Plus surprise Guests CM Cyro Batista and a host of others Dec. 4th at The Knitting Factory. Vincent Katz 5432

State University of NY at Binghamton 1988 List of Hosts for Partici-pents in the Performing Language Conference Rothenberg, Mac Low and Schwerner. 5436

NY Folklore Newsletter Vol.9 #4 Flyer for Living on the Bay 1988 Long Island's Maritime Folk Arts Spring Meeting May 6, 1989. 5441

Extended Play, Emily Harvey Gallery Show 1988 A show Announce-ment in the shape of a Record Label. Names of artists include Jean Dupuy, R.I.P. Hayman, Nam June Paik, Lou Reed, Fedo Ertl. Curated by Ursula Block & Christian Marclay 5445

Spring Mysteries, Fashion Moda Post Card A sculpture/ Sound Installation by Maggie Ens & CM 1988 Fashion Moda, 2803 3rd Ave, NY. 5449

Greeting Card from Mitsuru Ikeda 1988 Color Illustration of Japa-nese Immortals and Dragon 5457

Letter from ? Rock Sculpture 1988 mention of Tokyo summer Sol-stice collaboration. Mention of Town of Shimodate, Japan 5512

Fluxus Poster, Yoko Ono 1988 Fluxus Exhibition at Museum of Mod-ern Art, 11 West St, NY One Woman Show of Yoko Ono Nov. thru March 5522

1988 Solstice Mechanicals for Poster 1988 three boards 5548

Summer Solstice Line-up of Artists in NY 1988 At the Ear Inn, Village Gate, 337 E. 8th St., NoSeNo, WBAI-FM Located in this Folder is Busi-ness Card For Alan Ginsberg. 5585

Flyer for Bortom Dag och Natt by Paul Anders Simma 1988 Music by

CM 5618

Hero, Jingle with song sheet 1988 Correspondence and ideas on saving Lives. Cancer education 5638

Fashion Moda Poster 1988 B&W Poster ? 2552

KR Roasters '60 "Vaguely fam.' Kenny Rogers 1989 fake kenny + chicken choir 286

KR Roasters '30 "Fear of frying' ' Kenny Rogers 1989 fake kenny + chicken choir 287

KR Roasters '30 "travel' ' Kenny Rogers 1989 fake kenny + chicken choir 288

Juan Downey 'Indian' 1989 annc edited 290

Juan Downey 'Indian' 1989 annc edited 294

Unique NY 1989. 298

In my NY 1989 Full mix 299

KR Roasters 'builder 'Kenny Rogers 1989 full mix w kr vo 301

KR Roasters 'builder 'Kenny Rogers 1989 full mix w kr vo 303

KR Roasters Music 1 'Kenny Rogers 1989 music only 304

KR Roasters Music 2 'Kenny Rogers 1989 music only + piano 305

Unique NY 1989 plback mix w music and choir -full version 306

Unique NY 1989 plback mix w music and choir -donut version 307

Unique NY final 1989 music only 308

Purdue 'more meat' 1989 ruff mix w video layback. very noisy! 309

Purdue 'more meat' 1989 Music only 310

Arby's-Mix 2 1989 ea. title HTML 350

Arby's-Mix w/more melody 1989 ea. title HTML 351

Words and Pictures, music low 1989 no leader 363

Words and Pictures, music high 1989 no leader 364

Words and Pictures 1989 no leader 365

Words and Pictures 1989 no leader 366

Child Abuse (Ad Council) 1989 HTL Words & Pictures full mix 367

Child Abuse (Ad Council) 1989 TL Words & Pictures inst. mix 368

w/effects 1989 TL 372

w/o effects 1989 TL 373

Freckles piano, no v/o 1989. 383

Blue-Jean Lady guitar, no v/o 1989. 384

They Said vibes, no v/o 1989. 385

Freckles piano, v/o 1989. 386

Blue-Jean Lady guitar, v/o 1989. 387

They Said vibes, v/o 1989. 388

Christmas Fire w/o vocal 1989 REMIXED 5/2/90 HTL 389

Christmas Fire w/ vocal 1989 REMIXED 5/2/90 HTL 390

elements: train, "help", bear, outs 1989. 425

Grizzlies 1989 HTL 426

Train 1989 HTL 427

Grizzlies, less SFX 1989 HTL 428

Harps w/ tag 1989 HTL 433

Harps w/o tag 1989 HTL 434

Chopin/CM Prelude 2 1989 dub from 1/4" mix master collaboration with Paik 489

Chopin/CM Prelude 6 1989 dub from 1/4" mix master collaboration with Paik 490

Emergency 1989 7" reel 573

Arctic sounds 1989 1 cd taken from cassette 1 cassette (master) 886

Solstice 89 Radio Special 1989 Solstice 89 Radio Special 1106

Telephone Interviews for Arctic 1989. 1111

Carol Geddes YUKON 1989 11.7.89. 1115

NPR: Interview w Paul Anders Simma 1.23.89 1989 Song Number One: CM Vocal 1.3.89. 1127

CMA Commercial #1 1989 Arbys AT&T Benihana Child Abuse CP & L BF Goodrich Chinese Gangs Clerasil Alleract Debeers 1148

CMA Commercial #2 1989 ABC 1987 promos Franks Place 1149

CMA Commercial #3 1989 Bell Atlantic American Cancer Society Eclipse 1150

KNR: Arctic: Evening First Day 1989. 1151

Japan demo 1/2 1989 11.89. 1155

Paul Anders Simma: Phone Interview 9.18.89 1989 regarding Greenland trip 1165

Commercial Projects: Arby's to ABC TV 1989 DAT 247 Part 1 1187

Commercial Projects: Bell Atlantic and More 1989 DAT 247 part 2. 1188

Jerry Rothenberg 1989 transfer from two reels reading, with and without musical accompaniment 1279

Stephanie Rose's Toy Piano Power 1989. 1365

My Daughter is an Erinofille 1989. 1392

Louie Milan reconstruction for Miralda 1989. 1416

News Releases CM NWF 1989 Press releases for Solstice on Ice, Beyond Night and Day, Singing Bicycles to Dreamland, Here Comes the Sun, City Wave Copenhagen comes to NY. 1519

Confusion News 1989 A conceptual art piece. The undisciplined Interdisciplinary Irregular Fusion Art Newspaper. Artwork by Shalom, with an article by CM, Ecology?Art? Fusion. 1547

Solstice '89 event broadcast 1989 Live performance at Battery Park, NYC, by CM with Don Cherry, Sun Ra and his band, the boat horns of NY harbor, and the Loisaida Samba School. Pre Produced radio hosted by Ray Gallon and CM from WNYC FM broadcast excerpts from the past 16 years of Morrow's Solstice events. 1626

Tibetan Monks at Sunset in NY - poster 1989 The organizers of the world tour of eight monks from Drepung-Loseling Monastery in India asked CM to design a unique presentation. The mountain dwellers performed beside the harbor waters at Battery Park, NYC, at sunset, the Statue of Liberty on the horizon. The harbor boat horns echoed the monks' horns. The monks' yellow robes matched the ferry boats' yellow hulls, which were bathed in sunset colors. A cross-cultural trio of Brazilian drum, cello, and cornet joined the monks who played conch shell trumpets. (May 19) 1627

Nimis 1989 Music for film by Swedish director Stellan Olsson 1641

Mitchum "24 Hour TV" :15 1989. 1686

Solstice 1989 6-20-89 event broadcast. All notes and correspondence for the production, performers, bands,etc. Many early copier photos of CM. Where are the original negs to print better copies? 1965

Pentax IQ Zoom 9-26-89. 1989

The Bloom Agency QPCQ 9013 "Eye"(:30) QPCQ 9015 "Eye" (:15) QPCQ 9023 "Eye European") (:30) 56026. 1979

American Fare 1-16-89 1989 DI IORIO WERGELES American Fare Presentation Reel: General Spot Bed & Bath, Horticulture, Bakery, Prices, Toys, Apparel, Produce, Grocery Prices, Fresh Fish 1984

Puppy Love AT&T 11-03-1989 1989 Brand Choice AXAT 4916

Puppy Love :30 Closed caption Duel Mode 1988 AT&T Cordless 5000 11-6-1989 N.W. AYER Consumer Products Cordless 5000 series AXAT4959 :30 Closed captioned Duel Mode 1996

Lenin, Dada & Jung Pinkus-Genossenschaft: Katalgue 93. 1989 Antiquariat Pinkus,Froschaugasse 7, 8001 ZurichSozialismus, Politik Wirtschafts -und Sozialwissenschaften. CM met Pinkus through Paul Gredinger, Zurich as part of LENIN DADA & JUNG event development 2048

Information Withheld - Juan Downey 1989 5 12 1989, j#7957. 2154

Arby's 1989 1 not another burger; 302 cheeseburger; 30. 2210

Resale Legend 1989 music + vo layb on ch18 samples 2276

Size/Video voice (CM interview) 1989. 2278

Ode to Spike Jones 1989 master 2279

AT&T 'Puppy love' 1989 w music mix 5 12 89. 2280

Sun Ra & Don Cherry 1989 VH1 interview & performance tape 1. 2305

Sun Ra & Don Cherry #2 1989 VH1 interview & performance tape 1. 2312

Animation Pres reel 1989 Master 5/89. 2330

Animation Pres reel 1989 5 30 89. 2336

Animation Pres reel 1989 5 30 89. 2338

The Cinchels/MobilOil Hefty Bags 1989 1x:30 3x:15 versions 3/15/90. 2347

Fudge tastics 1989 gfbm-9968 :15 'Upside down'2/16/89. 2348

CMA demo reel 1989. 2349

CMA demo reel 1989 115D 5-'89. 2350

Ecofest Flyer (2) 1989 A celebration of rare and endangered species. At Riverside Park Sept 10,1989. 2478

EGALITE, Sten Hanson (3) Copies 1989 Commandee par GMEB, Bourges pour Synthese 89 Published by Other Media 2582

The Beckett Festival of Radio Plays Press Kit 1989 A collection of radio plays by Author Samuel Beckett press kit from NPR with a letter to CM to write a review. 2649

Rothenberg and CM Performance notes 1989 Various production notes for shows and performances, including budgets and extras. Simone Forti, Ken Jacobs, Henry Sapoznik. Early letters and notes on The Temple. Living Theater Handbill 2667

CM Press releases and various news articles Clove Lakes Park Festival, CM and Armand Schwerner 1989 Photos in he Staten Island Advance 2668

Voicing Voices Original Artwork 1989 Ink and graphite on Paper 2 sheets 11 x 8 1/2. 2775

16th Annual Village Halloween Parade Call for volunteers Flyer (6) 1989 Theme of Parade Endangered Species/Rainforest 2859

Letter to CM from Francesco Conz 1989 Francesco Conz explaining to CM that he should combine his music with artwork, as there is less artwork available. Francesco tells CM he needs an agent. May 5. 2969

ArsNova 1989 Publication about Danish singing group 3043

Sound Track 1989 Ear article on "Sound Track" a soundscape project by the LOGOS foundation organized by the New Wilderness Foundation. By Van Godfried-Willen Raes and Moniek Darge. Also included: Letter from Moniek 3065

Asian Society Pow-Wow 1989 Tapes 3080

Letter to New Wilderness from Tom Johnson 1989 Attempt to get a copy of his tape, "Secret Songs." 3131

Sy'phony, or CM's Farewell Sy'phony 1989 by CM 3141

The Number Six by CM and Tom Johnson 1989 Correspondence between CM and Tom Johnson and Score 3144

Film Music Project, Soundexpedition 1989 -Edition of Film music Project. -Artwork by Musshall-Soundexpedition: for the regeneration of industrially devastated areas 3146

Collection of CM Sound Art 1989 Program from Vox Populi Some compositions 3193

Logos Posters 1989 Soundtrack Klankspoorlogos-duo with Moneik Darge and Godfried Willem Raes and Stichting logos organigram 3337

Notes on Some Contributions of the Legend of the European Vampire Toward the Understanding of Certain Persistent Fantasy Organizations Found in Clinical Work 1989 by Richard M. Gottlieb, M.D. 3342

"Voice of the Voiceless," words by Ella Wheeler Wilcox, music by Barbara Trinkaus, Arranged by Rich Siegel 1989, NSMA Publishing//Siegal

Publishing ASCAP National Society of Musicians for Animals 3353

High Performance 1989 High Performance: a Quarterly Magazine for the New Arts Audience Fall 3394

Montgolfier Music Wind Event 1989 produced by New Wilderness Description 3412

Performance Instructions for A Gong Perplex by CM 1989 Hand drawn/written by CM Other Media Productions, Stockholm/NY 3456

Drawings of the Sun's location during Solstice and Equinox 1989. 3460

Special Edition for Hypermetropes, Postcard Jean Dupuy 1989 Opening of show at Emily Harvey Gallery Tuesday May 16. 3487

For Matsui San 1989 CM Graphic, Today I Play Horigai to Baby in Belly Also Birth Announcement for Stephanie Rose Geller Morrow 3493

Wedding Invitation & program for R.I.P. Hayman & Barbra Anne Pollitt June 22, 1989 At St. Luke in the Fields 487 Hudson St. at Grove St. 3507

Press release for Beyond Night & Day film by Paul Anders Simma 1989 Press release from New Wilderness Foundation for Simma film to be shown on WNYC, Window of the World television. 3639

Dick Higgins Letter to Klaus Schoning 1989 Letter about Dicks performance at the Whitney. (Three Double Helixes). 3761

Letter from Dick Higgins to CM 1989 Follow up letter to CM about the Whitney presentation of Three Double Helixes live horspielproject. 3762

Emergency (2 copies) and notes 1989 A 12 minute sound event composition. Musicians perform from vehicles. 3802

bp Nichol memorial Celebration 1989 May 31, 1989 UCSD Program for Memorial Readers, Including Jerome Rothenberg, Steve McCaffery etc. Audio setting by CM. 3806

Solstice 1989 Informational piece from New Wilderness Foundation. Produced by Ray Gallon in Lower Manhattan, Sun Ra, Don Cherry, Max Roach. 3916

Hot Air Balloon papers Donna Roseman 1989 Letters from Donna to CM, and from Airship Advertising Co. 3917

The Daily Planet, Flyer for City of NY Parks and recreation(2) 1989 Single sheet Parks Celebrate Spring vernal equinox. Joseph Curran Commissioner. Celebration was organized by CM, Founder of the New Wilderness Organization. 3947

Music Program Zero: A continuing experiment in holistic musical development. 1989 at Bard College Annandale on Hudson 3957

New Music America 1989, Village Voice Insert (2) A festival Guide insert from Village Voice. WNYC Sponsor Many concerts around the City including The Kitchen And the Knitting Factory, Village Gate. 3972

Writings & Drawings, CM 1989 A collection of thoughts, sound and text pieces from 1977-1993 Other Media NY and Stockholm. An introduction by Charles Bernstein. This is a copier copy. Includes 19 pieces. 3983

Charles Bernstein on CM 1989 A narrative history of CM's life and work to 1989. Could have been a CMA promotional piece. 3989

SWAMI, The state of Washington as a Musical instrument by Stuart Dempster 1989 In honor of Washington's centennial in 1989. 4002

Interview with Sydney Alonzo, Chairman of the board of New England Digital 1989 A three page transcript about digital sound. 4003

A Victorian Scrapbook, Cynthia Hart, John Grossman and Percilla A. Dunhill 1989. 4120

Juan Downey, Of Dream into Study 1989 Santiago, Chile 4122

Shadow Architecture at the Crossroads Annual 19X Paul Zelevansky 1989 Signed to CM 4141

Putting the Land on the Map, Curated by Wystan Curnow 1989 Art & Cartography in New Zealand Since 1840. 4142

The Same Boat, The Passion of Chico Mendes, Verse by Burt Porter 1989 A Bread & Puppet Publication signed by Burt to CM 4177

Brooklyn Academy of Music Festival poster 1989 Oct. 3 thru Dec. 3rd Line up 4181

Absolut Vodka Poster proof 1989 From Ear Magazine Warhol- Rev. 3 estate of Andy Warhol Water damage from CM flood 4183

Back in the USA, Wystan Curnow 1989 Black Light Press Poems 1980-82. 4188

19th Inter. Festival og Experimental Music 1989 Synthese, Bourges 4189

1989 Margaret Mead Film Festival newspaper flyer 1989 At American Museum of Natural History. Program lineup 4194

Yoshi Wada Postcard "The Appointed Cloud" Interference section 1989 Sent to RIP Hayman for a show at Emily Harvey Gallery NY 4225

SingOut Vol 34 #4 1989 Folk Song Magazine Fall 4249

Reflections, The End of Nature 1989 Photocopied article by Bill McKibben 4308

Hudson River Solstice Paddle 1989 Hanson & CM 4453

Solstice NW Summer 1989 Folder 4468

Solstice 89 1989 Folder 4473

Swatch Watch 1989 Nam Jun Paik project. CM arranged and programmed theme from Haydn Clock symphony accelerating 4475

A counting Piece by CM 1989 Counting Piece based on Celsius to Fahrenheit 4534

Ear Magazine color ad proofs 1989 Proofs for Ear Inn, Bombay Gin, Absolut 4591

Reasearch lists of competition in Ads and jingle market TV, Film and Tape Directory 1989 Sample industry Ads from John Clapps 4636

Of Dream Into Study, Juan Downey 1989 Also 2 Programs from the

Whitney Museum of American Art From May 3, 1994 Juan Downey (1940-1993). 4739

Poems Spring '89, Burt Porter 1989 A signed Copy 4792

Still Performances, Rimma Gerlovina, Valeriy Gerlovin 1989 From a show at the Anderson Gallery and MIT Visual Arts Center. Lots of Photos 4823

Bill Barrette, at fiction/non fiction 1989 Gallery booklet 4836

Women & Performance, Dept. of Performance Studies 1989 A Journal of Feminist Theory 4845

O.ARS 6/7 Voicing, Oppenheimer, CM, McCaffery and others 1989. 4847

Beltrametti, Blaine, Koller, Raworth, 1989 Coyote's Journal, Gang of Four 4859

Four Lorca Suites, Federico Garcia Lorca 1989 signed to CM, Editorial Ariel 4952

Isole Sonanti, Gianfranco Salvatore 1989 ismez il ventaglio 4982

O.ARS Voicing 1989 Don Wellman 4994

Of dream into study, Juan Downey (2) 1989 editorial Lord Cochrane 4998

Speak to me, Tala Till Mig 1989 signed to CM, The Spirit That Moves Us Press 5016

Khurbn & other poems, Jerome Rothenberg 1989 signed to CM, A New Directions book 5028

TDR 1989 MIT Press CM interviews 5038

Rouge, Vert & Noir, Olivier Cadiot- Bruno Carbonnet 1989 Block, signed to CM 5084

Katalog 391 1989 widerspruch? Zurich? 5104

Still Performances, Rimma And Valeriy Gerlovina, 1989 Celebrating the hundred and fifty first anniversary of photography Show at List Visual arts center, Cambridge Ma. Sept 5 thru Oct. 8. 5166

Sunset Chant By Tibetan Monks (6) 1989 Promo Flyer 5177

Downtown Paper w/Solstice 89 cover 1989 Downtown Mag. 5178

Hefty Hefty Hefty, Wimpy Wimpy Wimpy An Interview with CM by Rebecca Schneider 1989. 5237

Creativity Magazine, CM article 1989 Weird Time CM article, Jingles Career, Hefty Hefty Hefty. 5269

Lenin, Dada, and Jung T.V. Draft 1989 2 Page outline of TV script. Letter to Consul Dag Sebastian Ahlender, Nov. 18,1996. 5285

Dick Higgins Letter to CM 1989 Letter concerning Francesco's debts to Dick. Also mentions 1961/2/3 piece. Verona 5379

Eggs on end by Donna Henes. Postcard Invitation 1989 Donna Henes Vernal Equinox March 20 Standing on Ceremony, World Trade Center Plaza 5382

Stone Press Weekly 1989 An Art Card weekly Graphics conceptual

Art Piece, Postcards 5391

Tantrum 1989 A Digital Sampling keyboard piece for four hands 5404

Solstice 89 Poster (10) 1989 Poster with Sun Ra and Don Cherry hand lettered. 5416

15th Global Documentary Festival invitation and poster, 1989 Joseph Papp Presents 5420

Indian Summer, World Festival of Aboriginal Motion Pictures 1989 Announcement and Brochure for Pincher Creek International outdoor Museum of Sculpture. 5433

Brooklyn Academy of Music Poster 1989 Including New Music America 10th Anniversary 1979-1989. 5546

Composer to Composer Poster 1989 August 18-20 Telluride Colorado Joan LaBarbara, Annea Lockwood, John Cage Tom Johnson, Anthony Davis and others 5566

Cool Cape May sheet music Victorian Waltz sheet music Signed by Dalors Love 1989. 5600

International Electroacoustic Music Competition 2e magisterium Bourges 1989 Catalog info and Winners info. 5623

Promo stuff presentation New Wilderness Foundation. Balloon Fest Event and budget. Solstice on Ice. Article by Gregory Janes. Conch Shell Tribute, (Dunlap) Ad Worlds Music man. CM Scores spots. 1989 Promo articles in a binder 5681

Knitting Factory Calendar Poster Nov. Dec. ? 1989 Fuck Con Edison 5555

CMA Demo: Logo 1990. 79

Logo alt 1990. 81

Logo alt #2 1990. 82

Grape Nuts "Iko" 1990 comes before #15 non numbered ID 94

"People are Counting on You" RM 1990. 105

"People are Counting on You" RM` 1990. 106

Interlude, compress+EQ 1990. 107

Interlude, compress+EQ 1990 no ANNC 108

Global View 1990. 109

RSB RH/CM vers. 1990 RH/CRM Demo 145

CM Demo 1990. 146

Nose 1990. 148

Remix 1990. 156

Robitussin Fred ref 1990 music, sfx and VO 165

Grape Nuts Iko 1990 full mix w voc 189

Brawny 1990 mono w VO 209

De Beers 1990 demo 212

De Beers 1990 demo 214

Spiral sound A 1990 Spiral sound down 292

Spiral sound B 1990 Spiral sound slow 293

Arctic WDR 1990 starts w rain 312

Arctic WDR 1990 breaking ice 314

Arctic WDR 1990 whole tape 1 proj 315

Arctic WDR 1990 snowmobile 316

Oyster Dreams ORF 1990 starts w bird 317

Oyster Dreams ORF 1990 breaking ice 318

Oyster Dreams ORF 1990 rubbing clothes 319

Oyster Dreams ORF 1990 slaps 320

Oyster Dreams ORF 1990 birds again 321

Oyster Dreams ORF 1990 ORF version 322

The First... 1990 AT&T TV commercial score 354

Puppy Love 1990 no TL, AT&T TV commercial score 355

Puppy Love 1990 no HTL, AT&T TV commercial score 356

Paik - Lully - CM reconstruction 1990 Commissioned for Versailles Video Wall 500

Excedrin IB 1990 pain FX 556

Excedrin IB 1990 pain FX - analog 559

Excedrin IB 1990 pain FX - cuckoo 560

Excedrin IB 1990 pain FX - vocal "IB" 562

Dogs 1 1990 CD Master Clone Tone@ :10 Program 2:00-38:48 with Start ID's 575

DOGS 7-90 1990. 576

Shanty Choir Vlissingen 1990 Scheldeloodsenboor C.p.IC.p. III - for Borderline 577

Arcticfx 1990 from the YLE sound library. Swapped by CM for recordings of conch shell horn 578

Asa Simma & Norman Charles 1990 ritual songs, etc. Sami and Native American 634

Asa Simma & Norman Charles 2 1990 1 (917) 842-1642. 636

CM New Music Sampler: Song of the Ptarmigan + VO 1990 Arctic Song with VO voice - Asa Simma-CM voice and lyrics of Asa Simma Charles 696

CM New Music Sampler: Farewell Sy'phony 1990 mvt 2 (exc) 698

Paik-Lully-CM reconstruction 1990 Commissioned for Versailles Video wall stop rhyms designed to echo through the palace 700

Dick project 1990. 777

Higgins 1990 to be identified 884

Dogs 1 1990 CD Master Clone Tone@ :10 Program 2:00-38:48 with Start ID's 932

DOGS 7-90 1990. 950

If you ever meet a Dinosaur - Camilla During Dadson 1990 1. Wrinkly Fingers 2. In the Band 3. Autumn Leaves 4. In my Garden 5. Clap,Clap 6. You'll never Guess 7. Insect Dance 8. Who's That? 9. Flying 10. Rosie

11.Get Out 12. We can hear you 13. Let's make noises 14. My Place 15. Can you eat your Teddy Bear 16. You can Jump 17. What Can you do? 18. Jake the Snake 19. Summer Lullaby 20. If you ever meet a dinosaur 952

AUDI Demo 1990 DAT is damaged 961

Hymn to the Great Spiral (Part III) 1990. 989

John Cage - James Joyce, Marcel Duchamp, Erik Satie: An Alphabet 1990 CD 1, English. CD 2, German. Performance of play by John Cage. "James Joyce, Marcel Duchamp, Erik Satie: An Alphabet". WDR Sound Festival, "2nd Acustica Internaional", 1990. CM voice of Henrik Ibsen. 1036

CMA Commercials reel 5 1990 Hefty Compilation 1100

CMA Commercials reel 6 1990 Hefty Compilation 1102

CMA Commercials reel 7 1990 Hefty Compilation 1103

CMA Commercials reel 8 1990 Hefty Compilation 1104

CMA Commercials reel 9 1990 Hefty Compilation 1105

Stephanie Rose 1990 Stephanie Rose11.28.90. 1107

EHCKTER INUGHUIT Reel 1 1990 reindeer sounds 1128

EHCKTER INUGHUIT Reel 2 1990 reindeer sounds 1129

Greenland radio Show excerpts 2.28.90 1990. 1130

Arctic - rough mix 1990. 1131

Reindeer Sounds 1 1990. 1132

Reindeer Sounds 2 1990. 1133

Arctic 1990. 1160

Oyster Dreams 1990. 1163

Arctic - reel 1 2.14.90 1990. 1166

Commercials Presentation 1990. 1183

Duet for Two Towns 1990 Event scenario on one page. Location: Helsinborg and Helsingør Features frogmen.I propose a celebration that will cross from light to darkness from just before sunset, through sunset and into night, that includes actions on both shores and on the water. This giant stage is large enough that everyone should feel in the event, rather than as spectators. The scenario is to be written after a site survey and determination of what are the possibilities for participants and budget; A moment by moment action plan, fully directed. The lights will create an atmosphere of signalling, in which many little mini-dramas and presentations will take place. Through the use of radio, people can be guided through the event, and brought into the changing scenario. 1395

Star Bangled Banner, Moving My Vowels, Systematic Shifts in the Service of Patriotism 1990 Applying transparent rules for substituting vowels for each other, CM produces a series of variations on the U.S. National anthem. 1421

Hymn to the Great Spiral - the Event 1990 Performance in the underground cathedral in Matera, Italy. 1422

Union Square Farmers' Market Event 1990. 1429

WDR Booklet (2) 1990 A German Radio Stations musicians magazine with a story on CM. 1495

WDR Booklet 1990 WDR German Radio Booklet of Musicians and mini bio's 1498

Composer to Composer Poster 1990 Gathering of Musicians in Telluride, Colorado July 13-15 1990. 1515

Composer to Composer Poster 1990 July 13-15 1990 Telluride, Colorado, Concert poster 1564

Hymn to the Great Spiral - the CD 1990 This12-part ritualistic suite was inspired by the Italian musicologist Gianfranco Salvatore. It explores the idea of "spiral" as a sound archetype, an audio icon. The overall sequence is invocation, journeying into and onto the spiral, reaching the still point in the center, rising up and out (prompted by memories of the world on the surface). A short coda reflects on the journey. The music is a combination of computer generated variations on sound samples and live performances: vocals, programs, and horns. The players were Morrow, along with vocals and Africa violin: Moniek Darge; The LaScala Opera String Quartet; soprano sax: David Liebman; frame drums: Glen Velez; banjo: Burt Porter; whirling instruments: Walter Maioli. 1620

Voices -- Live Performance 1990 The 1988 radio work "Voices" is cut to 30 minutes. The parts where CM's solo voice appeared in the radio work are opened for live performance. A video of CM family in the 50s accompanies the performance, concluding with Lana and Stephanie Rose Morrow 1623

Arctic 1990 Sound study of the arctic. A 45-minute minute version was created for Westdeutschen Rundfunk, and a 30-minute version for ORF, Vienna. 1624

Oyster Dreams, Oyster Steps 1990 Audio elements from CM's Arctic sound works form a ground for improvised reactions to arctic images: voice; water in pots and ladels; rocks and shells; microphones rubbed on skin; clothing such as hats, scarves, shirts, pants. The dance score version is 73 minutes long. Commissioned by Nana Nilsson New Now Dancers, Copenhagen, Denmark. A 30-minute version was performed at Experimental Intermedia Foundation, NYC, April 20. 1628

The Image of "O" and the Image of "S" and "Ch" 1990 Two three-minute loops installed in the works of fusion artist Shalom. The two virtual tracks were created from the same program at two different tempos on Performer software, mixed to Digital Audio Tape, and dubbed to cassette loops. 1629

Not with Me 1990 Music for stage play by Croatian playwright/director 1648

The Creation and Development 1990 Performance work with sound track for festival in Zagreb 1653

Hymn to the Great Spiral 1990 Event research notes, letters, maps and brochures, some water damage. Two Envelopes 1936

Ear Magazine of new Music - as delivered from Pauline Oliveros archive 1990 Ear Catalog (16) copies Feb. 1990 (1) issueNov/Dec 1980 (77) issues Nov 1978 (1) issue Nov/Dec 1985 (37)issues May/June 1978 (1) issue w/record insert April/May 1981 (8) issues Summer 1976 (1) issue Oct/Nov 1981 (6) issues Nov/Dec./Jan 1982-3 (1) issue July/Aug 1984 (21)issue March 1984 (1) issue June/July Aug 1983(14) issues Sept/Oct 1983 (1) issue Feb/March 1981 (1) issue Feb/Mar/April 1983 (1) issue June/July 1980 (2) issues April/May 1979 (2) issues Dec/Jan 1978-79 (14) issues 1937

1990 IMCT-9566 Corporate - 60 sec. 1973

Polly-O 5-10-1990 1990 Kraft General Foods for Young and RubicamKRGP 9181 No Hands/New :15 1976 Polly-O Grated 5-9-1990 1990 Young & RubicamKRGP 9203 "No Hands/New Rev./CC" (:30) Closed Captions 1980

GF/Fudgetastics 5-9-1990 1990 Young & Rubicam GFBM-9992 :15 Upside Down New Music DMCC 1992

Carolina Power & Light 3-15-1990 1990 Mckinney & SilverCPLC 9002 :30 "6% Energy Loans" CPLC 9003 :30 "EZ $64" CPLC 9004-L :30 "Heat Pump" REV. 1997

Hymn to the Great Spiral; Parts I, II, III 1990 (see above) 2072

Hymn to the Great Spiral: Parts I, II 1990 (see above) 2076

Tihana Herceg 1990 Collection 2109

Hard Times and Culture, Juan Downey, Cm score 1990 07/90 Vienna fin de siecle CM - "sweetens" Schonberg - Verklaerte NachtStrauss walt = Blue Danube scoring 2156

Hard Times and Culture, Juan Downey, CM score part 1 1990 07/90 Vienna fin de siecle CM - "sweetens" Schonberg - Verklaerte Nacht-Strauss walt = Blue Danube scoring 2157

Robitussin 'Pharmacy' 1990 2 versions, 10/1/90. 2165

Majorca-Fantsuw, Paik, Cm score 1990, 4'52, stereo 2172

The Cinchels/MobilOil Hefty Bags 1990 MBCS_0143 :30 MBCS-0144 :15 Jan 29, 1987. 2206

Hefty Steel Sack :30 1990 Steel sach ;30. 2212

Hefty Cinch Sack :30 1990 Lawn & Leaf ;15. 2221

Rie Koko/Moving Mountain Prod. 1990 (212) 475-6165. 2270

Det ar val ingen konst 1990 Stellan Olsson show for Swedish TV with CM score 2308

Siberian dance performance 1990 Asian soc. tape #2 - NY meeting of American Indian Community House and traveling company from Siberia c/o Smithsonian Folklife, organized by CM with Asia House and AICH directors. A happy meal and sharing of stories. 2326

Siberian dance performance 1990 Asian soc. tape #1 (as above) 2327

Global view 1990 tr2>TC 7/31/90dub j#14151. 2328

Japan Presentation 1990 Master Color corrected tr1 audio tr2 TC 2329

McKinney & Silver demo 1990 20 year demo 2357

McKinney & Silver 1990 Carolina Power & Light 3 spots :30. 2358

Voices 1990. 2458

Voices - WDR Program Guide (2) 1990 Pg. 58 CM Listing for Oct. 3, airing of Voices 2459

Performance at Gent/ Belgium Photos 1990 Photos 10 8x 10" and 5 5x7" with 5 Transparencies. copyright by Ansgar Maria Van Treeck. 2572

A Poem in Yellow after Tristan Tzara 1990 Signed for Lana for her Birthday with Love, Jerome Rothenberg 2605

A Program from Tokyo 1990. 2612

An Important article on Sound Poetry 1990 Extensive article on sound art with many CM contemporaries mentioned. 2620

The Fluxus Performance Workbook by Ken Friedman 1990 A Fluxus Happenings Workbook with suggestions for Fluxus happenings. Many artists represented. 2709

An Amulet For A Bad Number 1990 For A.S. 4-16-90 A sound Poem for Armand Schwerner. 2753

State Museum of Pennsylvania 1990 Gallery preparation and Demolition. Maps and Site plans along with notes and equipment lists. 2766

Stichting LOGOS 1990 Concert July 1, 1990 with CM. Voor een plechtige tetraëder-wijding 2767

Control, Chaos, Calamity or Complacency, Rubin Gorewitz 1990 Writings of Rubin Gorewitz, also A Judicial Restructuring. 2830

5 Minutes for Armand Schwerner 1990 Thirteen page score, Five chapters about the time interval 12:00-12:05. 2834

Skrumpen 1990 A Book by Gunnar Wille with a promotional color print. 2841

Sari Dienes Retrospective 1950-1970 1990 Retrospective Flyer for Gallery J&J Donguy, Paris also three Sari Business Cards from Stoney Point NY 2866

Confusion News 1990 Special Edition #1 Artist Proof Artwork is Headline by Shalom 1989. 2871

Events Poster from Balboa Lecture Series Moscow 1990 Moscow Spring 1990 Copley Auditorium. CM Performance. 2945

Back Stage, CM interview 1990 CM "The jingles keep on Coming" Article on CM in Backstage Magazine. 2972

Kugla Press material and Posters 1990 Kugla are one of the only independent performance groups in Yugoslavia. Mixing rock music with strange costumes and bizarre movement, they represent the outer limits of contemporary Yugoslavian art. 2978

Kugla large poster 1990. 2979

Kugla dossier Zeinimuro (9) 1990 An early press kit from Kugla with performance notes and contract. Several small promo pieces and a few 8x10 glossies, Lana Frkovic, Damir Bartol. 2982

Kugla Poster 1990 An early poster from Gallery at Student Center Zagreb. 2983

A Duet for Two Towns 1990 The New Wilderness Foundation, Inc. Description of "A Duet for Two Towns" 3009

Fluxus Street Fair 1990 First draft by Hannah Higgins Various images and text related to Fluxus Street Fair 3026

Nomads 1990 Application for Eurimages support for producing a documentary film "Nomads" by Paul-Anders Simma Synopsis of "Nomads" 3027

Dream Songs and Conch Music 1990 Posters (2) CM performs At the San Diego Museum of Art February 8th 3029

Eric Andersen 1990 Two pieces of writing/press on Erik Andersen, Dick Higgins mentioned 3064

Audio Box 1990 Audio Box Resegone Internazionale Di Sperimentazione Sonora October 1990 3082

Ellsworth Kelly's Early work by John Coppola 1990 with edits 3100

Three Double Helixes That Aren't for Sale by Dick Higgins 1990 a musical horspiel for one actor 3150

2nd Acustica International Sound Art Festival 1990 Featuring CM "Voices" Life performance with CM, video, and tape. Bill Fontana, Sorrel Hays, Phil Corner, Malcolm Goldstein, Jackson Mac Low, Gerhard Ruhm, Dick Higgins, Jerome Rothenberg. Festival had two parts Performances and a show at the Whitney Museum. 3151

Whirligig 1990 The Cooper Square Theater Presents the shaliko Company's production of Whirligig by Mac Wellman Music by CM 3152

Learning Alliance April-August and Ecology, Art, Fusion 1990 Options for Education and Action Featuring brief on Art and Ecology: Painting the World Green Also included: Ecology?Art?Fusion by CM and an explanation of Art and Ecology 3155

Three Hats 1990 Copy-edited manuscript for play with three hats, each representing different components of CM's career. 3160

Experimental Intermedia 1990 April 1990A personally controlled computer music series 224 Centre Street at Grand NY Featuring CM: Recent midi controlled stuff for performance and installations 3161

New American Film and Video Series 1990 Whitney Museum of American Arts New American FIlm and Video Series American Fluxus Art on WDR Featuring Bean Sequence, 1982, by Allison Knowles 3163

Sound Art Festival, Acoustica International II, Goethe House NY 1990 Program from Sound Art Festival Featuring Dick Higgins, Jackson Mac Low, CM, Jerome Rothenberg, performance at intermission CM performs "Voices", CM is also the line producer of the Festival for WDR.

3168

Music Today '90 1990 Saison Group Presents Music Today '90 Small publication 3173

Vox Populi 1990 Poster for Vox Populi 1990

Paleis Voor Schone Kunsten, Brussel Featuring CM 3184

Proposal for Acustica International Competition 1990 for Invisible Art #735 by CM Associates 3187

Biography of Annea Lockwood 1990 3216

Archive Newsletter 1990 Sponsored by the UCSD Library featuring poetry by: Mikhail Iossel, Harold Jaffe, Barbara Einzig, David Guss, Jackson Mac Low, Sherley Anne Williams. Publicizes readings at the Price Center Gallery B with afore- mentioned poets. 3312

Correspondence about "The Tribune" in the Sound Art Festival 1990 Concerning the production of Mauricio Kagel's "The Tribune" at the Whitney Museum of American Art in the 1990 Sound Art Festival from Everett Frost to Paula Breckenridge and CM. 3345

Correspondence about Sorrel Hays "Sound Shadows" 1990 Sound Art Festival 3346

Correspondence concerning Alison Knowles "Setsubun, Day of Change" for 1990 Sound Art Festival 1990. 3347

Sound Art Festival Announcement 1990 2nd Acustica International Announcement Draft 3348

Correspondence concerning Jackson Mac Low's "Woerter nd Ender aus Goethe" in the Sound Art Festival 1990. 3349

Earthly Freight by Lindsay Knowlton 1990 a collection of Poems 3393

The Zuerich Event: Lenin, Dada and Jung 1990 Performance gathering between three worlds 3414

Audio Box 90 1990 Audio Box 90 RAI: Radio Televisione Italiana Radio Uno 5 degree Rassegne Internationale Rassegna Stampa Materials 3450

Three Double Helixes that Aren't for Sale 1990 A musical horspiel for one actor 3470

Happenings & Fluxus 1990 Charles Dreyfuss. Water damaged flyer for promotion of Fluxus Catalog. Good for Names 3496

Bread & Puppet Domestic Resurrection Circus Poster (Linen) 1990 A Large Two color screen print on cloth. A second smaller poster on paper is in the same sleeve. 3632

Experimental Intermedia performance schedule 1990 Schedule for April 1990 A personally controlled computer music series.CM w/recent midi controled stuff for performance installations. 3690

Hymn to the Great Spiral 1990 Presented in Matera, Italy Sunday Oct. 7 and Mon Oct. 8th File contains Photos and letters, program drafts and ideas. Concert was recorded live for WDR in Germany 3730

Three double Helixes that arn't for sale Dick Higgins 1990 A Letter from Dick to Paula Breckenridge at the Equitable Center Whitney Museum of American Art. Concering his performance. Includes a note to CM about the Prop List. 3735

SHALOM Bio, Exhibitions, Collections, Writings, Teaching lists 1990 Prague, 3754

CM Assoc. Business, General Ledger Jan.1 /Dec 31, 1990 and Purchase Journal, Employee Summary, Income Statement 3755

Message from Dick Higgins 1990 Message to CM from Dick in Barrytown 3758

Paul Devereux Summer Solstice Color Photo 1990 Castle Ring Stone Circle Photo, Lake District England. Summer Solstice 3843

Oh the Places You'll Go. 1990 Dr. Seuss 3907

Backstage Shoot Magazine Music on the CM Nov. 16, 1990 An article about CM's productions in NY studio. Pg. 60 Scans can be found in Master Graphics. 3908

Elinor Coleman Dance Ensembles Summer Dance Celebration Program 1990 Danse Mirage presents, All Dancers and musicians are listed with Bios, Sponsors, Patrons and Friends. 3933

Sexy Music 1990 A short piece for Ear Magazine 1-13-1990 by CM. A second paragraph by Dan Erkilla 3938

Ear Magazine Ad, in New Music America, Montreal Festival Program 1990 3943

The Politics of Poetic Form, Charles Bernstein, Editor 1990 4057

Fluxus S.P. Q.R. Maggio -giugno 1990 Galleria F. Borghese, Roma Polaroid Photo and business card from Eugina Botti in front of book 4095

TDR The Drama Review MIT Press 1990 NY University/Tisch School of the Arts. Making Waves an interview with CM by Jerome Rothenberg 4100

Winter on the Finish Taiga, Hannu Hautala 1990 Otava Publishers Kaleva 1990 Signed 4123

Eyeline Magazine #13 1990 Spring/Summer 1990 Australian Magazine with articles on Fluxus, Paik and Conz. 4163

The Knitting Factory Poster 1990 Entertainment lineup for July & Aug. 4180

CM, Japanese Press 1990 Press 4283

WDR, Alphabet Performance 1990 Production notes for production WNYC and Whitney Museum. Also 1981 solstice 4342

Various Events Proposals and papers. 1990 A folder of Events planning: Barcelona Event, Zoo Music, Telephone Performance, New Music America, Equestrian Music I & II, Stockholm Snabb,and Music, Call of Order by RIP Hayman.Wave Music I &II, 3000 Bugles, Balloon Piece. 4348

Acoustical Research Event 1990 Flyer for Event with Wendy Chambers and CM cleaner copy is in Master Graphics 4397

Also 2 Programs for 2nd Acustica International 1990 and a program from 1996. 4388

Dick Higgins Message To CM 1990 Message states Dick did not know he was to be Bucky Fuller in John Cage's Production EIN Alphabet. 4394

2nd Acustica Festival 1990 Program 4397

Flyer for International Conference on Celebration 1990 Marilyn Wood Director, A notice about Hotel & Meeting rooms. Mention of a Meet the Composer grant. Mention of 12 Kennedy Ctr. festivals in the spring. 4408

Jeffery Isaac Brochure 1990 A panorama brochure of the Isaac piece "Brazzano Superiore, 1989-1990. 4414

Border Line 1990 Ideas for Whitney, Site survey. Pre production notes, WPRO letter, Commentary on trip. 4425

Dick Higgins Memo To Goethe House Peter C. Seel 1990 Message about rehearsal time 4498

Space Moose, synopsis, Noel Frankel 1990 for an original screenplay by Noel Frankel 4517

Touch Screen and Pedestal Design for "Gearing Up" 1990. 4526

Ten B&W photos of I Wayan Sadra and other musicians. 1990 Sadra, Tenney, Anderson, Oliveros, Reynolds, Photos by John Fago. Crafting the Artistic Freedom Manifesto. 4589

Spencer Holst Manuscript, Something to Read to Someone 1990 Note to CM on top of page. 4596

Love of Life Orchestra Poster 1990 Directed by Peter Gordon Dance at The Franklin St. Arts Center Other side is poster The Flying Hearts and a Monthly Schedule 4612

Old VHS and 3/4 inch lists 1990 Boxes 1-13 Lists of VHS and 3/4 inch tapes. 4652

Derek Bailey & Company Bio Company Records Catalog 1990. 4661

Notes for the Sun Book 1990 Ideas and notes for a book on the Sun 4678

Sound Installation CM, Denmark, Poster 1990 Institute for the Blind 4699

Spel Van Spiegelssonnetten In Beweging Jan H. Spiegels 1990 Poeziecentrum Gent Signed with Adress for Jan 4721

CM Faxes 1990 Joel Stuart, Kine Aune, Monique Jensen, Rothenberg, Oda, Marit Moen, Bent Eric Rasmussen 4775

The Lorca Variations I-VIII, Jerome Rothenberg 1990 Zasterle Press 4779

The Bomb, Makoto Oda 1990 signed to CM, Kodansha 4912

Freaks: We Who are Not as Others by Daniel P. Mannix 1990 Pocket Books 4988

1990. 4989

Week van de hedendaagse muziek 1990 Koninklijk Muziekconservatorium 5042

The New York Trilogy, Paul Auster 1990 A Penguin Book 5048

TDR The Drama Review MIT Press 1990 NY University/Tisch School of the Arts. Making Waves an interview with CM by Jerome Rothenberg 5063

Sound art photos 1990. 5110

Moving my Vowels, CM 1990 sound piece with lyrics (copy) 5122

Sound art festival, Second Aucustica International, Dick Higgins 1990 rehearsal schedule 5127

Sound art festival, Second Acustica International, Dick Higgins 1990 rehearsal schedule 5128

Niugini Spirit, Tan Kwan Liang 1990 Photographs, Watercolors and Pencil and Ink Art of Papua New Guinea 5208

Gianfranco Salvatore, Sergio Messina, Short Bio's 1990 5215

A Door Eye On - CM 1990 In the Hallway outside the Empty Flat 5220

Oda Makoto 3 Articles 1990 Pacifism or War-ism (Japans Direction in the 21st Century. Stomping on Aboji. A Voice in the Dark by Christopher Stephens 5244

Events and Productions Booklet (2) 1990 CM Associates Promo piece Events 5295

Church World Service 1990. 5309

Toyohiro Okazaki 1990 Booklet of Japan Arts and Musicians in Japanese. 5354

Artist and Poet Postcards 1990 A small group of Postcards by Friends Not travel postcards, but artistic statements. Examples Carol Barge, Rothenberg, Toby Olson, Peter Wild. 5371

Deep Listening Catalog from The Oliveros Foundation 1990 156 Hunter St. Kingston NY 12401. 5373

Gift Notebook to CM with 1 page message Japan? 1990. 5388

SYNAPSE VIDEO CENTER, brochure and Poster 1990 1103 College Place, Syracuse, NY 5390

Great Doodles From CM 1990. 5425

Big Blue Dot, Promo and Illustration 1990 Samples of their creative work. 5440

Death of the Avant Garde 1990 A Call for Resurrection. A essay on Art by CM 5443

A Ten Minute Film Idea 1990. 5456

For Me and for my Gods, Zbigniew Karkowski & Ulf Bilting (2) 1990 Swedish Musicians, Sound Artists Promo piece University of Gothenburg Gunner Sjostrom, Professor 5471

Niugini Spirit: Tan Kwan Liang 1990. 5473

Bill Art by And or Or and A social-cultural Art Event 1990 Art Assault of the Massachusetts College of Art and Charlotte Moorman will realize.

5525

Composer to Composer 1990 July 13-15 Telluride Colorado Adams, Allen, Laurie Anderson, Pauline Oliveros, James Tenney 5565

Ragged Valley, Yoshiko Chuma, Poster 1990 Also Camptown play on same poster The Performing Garage 33 Wooster Street notes to CM on back. 5593

A Duet for Two Towns, CM 1990 A performance Piece Raising Hell at the Crossing Diagram of the production 5595

George Johnston, Tlingit Photographer Carol Resume 1990 Press, Filmaker Carol Geddes one Photo B&W Film Grant Info Native American Film & Video Festival 1997 Brochure 5596

A Pioneer in Multimedia Press, (2) copies 1990 An overview of services, press article. 5598

Events and Productions by CM Sales Piece 1990 Spiral Bound Events Photos Promo piece 5599

Notes to Klaus Schoening about Michael Mazzola's notes on Lighting 1990 Performance of Penny Kemp & CM (workshop) and letter from Higgins. 5642

ACUSTICA 2 rehearsal Schedule 1990 Program Listing April 27 -29 NY, WDR Schoening, Whitney Museum John Hanhardt 5648

CM Associates Christmas Card to Clients 1990 611 Broadway Suite 817 NYC 5656 Warren Miller Publications Summary 1990 from Warren C. Miller 220 E. Reading Way Winter Park, FL 32789. 3763

CLE new 1991 tr1 prg tr2 tc music only 4

CLE theme 1991 tr1 prg tr2 tc music only alt vers/less ritm 5

Soundbites final/no music 1991 tr1 prg tr2 tc full mix/no music 6

Judge O'Connor on CTV 1991 tr1+2 prg VO only 7

Court TV 1991. 8

In practice ancc 1991 tr1+2 prgVO only 9

Soundbites mix/no music 1991 tr1tc tr2 prg full mix/no music 10

In practice promo 1991 tr1 clr tr2 prg full mix 11

CTV Promo 7/1... 1991 tr1 clr tr2 prg full mix 12

CTV prime time 1991 tr1+2 prgf ull mix 13

When mixing DAT kept running filling tape w garbage till end!!! 1991 When mixing DAT kept running filling tape w garbage till end!!! 15

Kenny Rogers 1991 vo only. Builder 16

Kenny Rogers 1991 tag vo only. Carles Mills 17

Kenny Rogers 1991 tag vo only. Carles Mills 18

Kenny Rogers 1991 tag vo only. Carles Mills 19

Kenny Rogers 1991 VO tag, tag vo only. Carles Mills 20

Kenny Rogers 1991 Kenny Rogers Roasters VO, Full mix.Easy music 21

Kenny Rogers 1991 Music only 22

Kenny Rogers 1991 Roasters revd, Full mix stereo. Music as 8 but faster 23

Kenny Rogers 1991 Roasters revd, Music only. stereo. Music as 8 but faster 24

Wonder Cereal 1 cmor v 1991 music only 26

Wonder Cereal 2 reed v 1991 music only 27

Wonder Cereal 3 mills v 1991 music only 28

Wonder Cereal 3 reed v2 1991 music only 29

Wonder Cereal 1991 music only 30

Kenny Rogers 1991 Roasters rev1, full mix/builder 31

Kenny Rogers 1991 Roasters rev1, music only 32

Kenny Rogers 1991 Roasters rev1, music only 33

Kenny Rogers 1991 Roasters rev1, music only 34

Wonder final 1991 full mix 35

Wonder final 1991 full mix 37

Wonder final 1991 music only 38

CTV Docket :15 1991 music only stereo 39

Kenny Rogers 1991 Roasters rev1.2, full mix/brass added/travel 40

Kenny Rogers 1991 Roasters rev1.2, full mix/brass added/singer 41

Kenny Rogers 1991 full mix/brass added/builder, Roasters rev1.2 42

Purdue 'More meat' 1991 full mix/no gliss 43

Purdue 'More meat' 1991 full mix/with gliss 44

Kenny Rogers 1991 full mix/brass added/travel, Roasters rev1.2. 45

Kenny Rogers 1991 full mix/brass added/sing /tag tightened, Roasters rev1.2. 46

Kenny Rogers 1991 full mix/brass added/builder/tag tightened, Roasters rev1.2. 48

Arthricare 1991 music choir only 49

Arthricare 1991 music choir only no tag choir 50

Arthricare 1991 music choir only/edited 51

Nikon Jazz 1991 music choir only/edited 52

Nikon Jazz 1991 music choir only/edited/tr2 tc/tr1 prg 53

Wonder full 1991 full mix/stereo 54

Wonder full 1991 full mix/no VO/ stereo 55

Wonder 1991 music mix/no vocals/no VO/ stereo 56

Bad Houdini 1991 full mix 57

CTV :05 accent 1991 one piece just before id44!!/ After 'wonder' garbage 59

Wonder 1991 full mix/stereo 60

Miami Subs: radio commercial 1991 Miami Subs radio commercial. Multiple studio takes: v/o, instrumental, full mix. Tagline by CM. 61

Bahamas 1991 full mix till comm 62

Annea Lockwood 1991 Annea Lockwood, live performance at end (46:00) good applause and concert hall ambience 63

Best of the worst - Wee Twee 1991 Wee Twee recorded in studio during shoot. 64

Best of the worst - Wee Twee 'Live' 1991 Wee Twee recorded in Life cafe during shoot. 65

Robitussin 'Doctors bag' 1991 CM, Mendelssohn & Hays version/ music 66

Kenny Rogers 1991 tightened tag/builder, Roasters rev tag 67

Kenny Rogers 1991 tightened tag/travel, Roasters rev tag 68

New York & Company 1991 demo version 70

Le Petomane 1991 Strauss 71

Misc. Projects DAT 231 1991 72

Spiral part1 1991 master mix 73

Spiral part2 1991 master mix 74

ORF 'Arctic' part 1 1991 master mix part A 75

ORF 'Arctic' part 2 1991 master mix 76

ORF 'Arctic' all 1991 master mix 77

Macy's P.O.P. 1991 J. Dildine Live notes: See take sheet Sound Report Q3 pages 78

Brazil (1920's version) 1991. 100

Global View 2 1991. 110

Global View 3 1991. 111

Global View 4 1991. 112

Global View 5 1991. 115

CM "Gabriel" Presentation 1991. 116

Propa PH 1991 CM/Reed vox. 117

RM/Babi vox. 1991. 118

Propa PH 1991 RM/Reed vox. 119

Propa Ph 1991 RM/Sarah vox./Reed v/o 120

Propa PH 1991 RM remix (Baby vox.) 121

Propa PH 1991 CM remix w/sfx DROPS OUT!!!/ no VO-ANNC 122

Propa PH 1991 CM remix/ stronger vox 123

music + sfx 1991. 126

music + sfx 1991. 127

music + sfx 1991. 128

music + sfx/ FINAL 1991 track is damaged 129

music only 1991 track is damaged 130

music only 1991. 131

mus only 1991. 132

NY Rap 1991. 139

NY Rap, v.2 1991. 140

Strauss + Strings (mark up·waltz reconstruction 1991. 141

Strauss + Strings + Guns reconstruction 1991. 142

Schoenberg + Strings reconstruction 1991. 143

Macy's POP foley 1991 sfx location recording. refer to take sheet for contents. DAt #1 of 1. 160

Hard Times and Culture 1991 Includes reconstructed Schoenberg, Strauss 173
Propa PH 1991 remix, music only 223
'Business as usual' 1991 dialog only 226
Tokyo Hotel Northern Telecom 1991 dialog only 227
Prof. Scaros Northern Telecom 1991 dialog only 228
Tokyo Hotel Northern Telecom 1991 demo full mix 229
Prof. Scaros Northern Telecom 1991 demo full mix 230
Prof. Scaros Northern Telecom 1991 demo full mix 231
'Business as usual' 1991 demo full mix 232
De Beers 1991 Final r>TC , l< Programme 233
'Business as usual' 1991 final full mix 234
Tokyo Hotel 1991 final full mix 235
Prof. Scaros 1991 final full mix 237
Tavist D 1991 music only 238
Tavist D 1991 w scratch VO 239
Tavist D 1991 music only final 240
Envision 1991 cymbal roll swells (x) 241
Envision 1991 cymbal roll swells (x) 242
Envision 1991 cymbal roll swells (x) 243
Clearblue :30 v1 1991 v1. 244
Clearblue :15 v1 1991 v1. 245
Clearblue :30 1991 v2. 253
Clearblue :15 1991 v2. 254
Clearblue :30 1991 v1. 255
Clearblue :15 1991 v1. 256
Dr Scholl 1991 :30 music only 265
Dr Scholl 1991 :30 music only w FX 266
Dr Scholl 1991 :30 full mix 267
Dr Scholl 1991 :15. 268
Dr Scholl 1991 :15 full mix 270
Reynolds Wrap :Dog 1991 music 271
Clearblue 1991 full mix v1 272
Clearblue 1991 full mix v2 273
Clearblue 1991 full mix v3 keeper 274
Clearblue 1991 music only v3
***last few tracks are damaged 275
Macy POP 1991 < TC >prg 289
Swissair SFX 1991 airport control tower amb 323
Swissair SFX countdown 1991 NASA control capcom 325
Swissair SFX launch 1991 rocket launch sfx 326
Swissair SFX launch 1991 kinkel countdown 327
Swissair VO 1991 ANNC(scratch) 328
Swissair VO 1991 ANNC(real) TAG 329

Swissair VO Skilift 1991 ANNC(real) TAG 330
Swissair VO Skilift 1991 ANNC(real) 331
Swissair VO Linata 1991 Fullmix 332
Swissair 'Launch' 1991 Fullmix Spaceship 333
Swissair 'Seasoned travelers' 1991 Fullmix 334
Swissair VO Alpine Exp 1991 fullmix 337
Swissair "Liberty bell' 1991 fullmix 338
Swissair "Silenzio' 1991 fullmix 339
Swissair "Eur, non comp" 1991 DNU vo only C Mills 340
Swissair "Eur, non comp" 1991 DNU vo only C Mills 341
Swissair "Eur, non comp" 1991 DNU vo only C Mills rev 4 342
A Man without a world 1991 *Backup* Edited version 344
Warren Smith 1991. 345
Clear blue Clara 1991 v1 tv 30 l > prgr > TC 442
Clear blue Clara Alt 1991 v2 tv 30 l > prgr > TC 443
Clear blue Clara Alt 15 1991 v3 tv 15 l > prgr > TC 444
Ultra Goodsense & Mixes 1991 Ultra Goodsense v/o and mixes 495
Oktober 1991 Scheirmonnihoog, boat Shipyard Birds Vissinger 579
CM Chant/You are the One 1991. 582
CTV Narrations 1991. 583
Man without a World 1991 L)music R) smpte reels 1-4. 585
A Man without a World- Data Backup 1991 Data backup- For Soundtools 586
A Man without a World 1991 - DAT 1 Reel 1, TK 1,2. 587
A Man without a World 1991 - DAT 2 Reel 1, Tk 3 Reel 2 TK 1,2. 588
A Man without a World 1991 - DAT 3 reel 2, tk 3 reel 2 letter scene incomplete reel 2 letter scene complete 589
A Man without a World 1991 - DAT4 1. Reel 3, tk 1, 2. False Start, 3. Reel 3, insert from Start, 4. Hava Nagila inserts, 5. Reel 4 full take, 6. Mr. Death Pops, 7. Love Theme ending, 8. Insert reel 3 fronts 9-10 inserts from reel 3. 590
Sandals 1991. 616
Hitachi 1991. 729
CM Chant/You are the One 1991. 920
Voices 1991 1. Performance 2. Concert (w/CM voice)Horspiel-CM Performance + Concert** 931
A Man without a World 1991 - DAT 3 reel 2, tk 3 reel 2 letter scene incomplete reel 2 letter scene complete 939
A Man without a World 1991 - DAT 2 Reel 1, Tk 3 Reel 2 TK 1,2. 941
A Man without a World 1991 1. Reel 3, tk 1, 2. False Start, 3. Reel 3, insert from Start, 4. Hava Nagila inserts, 5. Reel 4 full take, 6. Mr. Death Pops, 7. Love Theme ending, 8. Insert reel 3 fronts 9-10 inserts from reel 3** **recording divided in half and copied to 2 CDs 942
A Man without a World 1991 1. Reel 3, tk 1, 2. False Start, 3. Reel 3,

insert from Start, 4. Hava Nagila inserts, 5. Reel 4 full take, 6. Mr. Death Pops, 7. Love Theme ending, 8. Insert reel 3 fronts 9-10 inserts from reel 3** **recording divided in half and copied to 2 CDs 943

A Man without a World 1991 Reel 1, TK 1,2. 944

Shanty Choir Vlissingen 1991 Scheldeloodsenboor C.p.I C.p. III. 948

Shanty Choir Vlissingen 1991 Scheldeloodsenboor C.p.I C.p. III. 949

Oktober 1991 1991 Scheirmonnihoog, boat Shipyard Birds Vissinger 951

Arctic II: Ice & Bears 1991 This soundscape is a story told in arctic sounds--the sounds of weather and nature. The bear, a significant power animal around the northern polar regions, is a totem of the sound artist. 977

Arctic II: Ice & Bears 1991 (as above) 978

CMA Jingles 1991 Misc. tv/radio commercials and projects. Part 1 of DAT 234. 1022

CMA Demo: Jingles 1991. 1023

CM New Music Sampler(44.1 Sample Rate)

1991 New music sampler, CM. Radio, TV commercial, art music, poetry, etc. 44.1 Sample Rate, shorter track versions 1033

SwissAir 1991 SwissAir commercials, sound effects, voice over, various mixes and samples. Voice over C. Mills? 1038

Miami Subs: radio commercial 1991 Miami Subs radio commercial. Multiple studio takes: v/o, instrumental, full mix. Tagline by CM. 1066

A Man without a world: Part I and II 1991 *Backup* Edited version. Original DAT divided into 2 cds. Part I and II of IV. 1067

A Man without a world: Part III and IV 1991 *Backup* Edited version. Original DAT divided into 2 cds. Part III and IV. 1069

CMA Misc. Commercials 1991 Nikon, Robitussin, PSE&G gas, Wok-a-Bowl, NY & Company, Chopsticks, Kenny Rogers Roasters 1071

CMA Misc. Commercials 1991 Nikon, Robitussin, PSE&G gas, Wok-a-Bowl, NY & Company, Chopsticks, Kenny Rogers Roasters 1072

Ultra Goodsense & Mixes 1991 Ultra Goodsense v/o and mixes 1073

Best of the worst - Wee Twee 'Live' 1991 Wee Twee recorded in Life cafe during shoot. CM and other performers. 1082

Wonder cereal, CM V/O 1991 multiple takes 1083

Unidentified sfx 1991. 1084

Misc. Projects: Kenny Rogers to Wonder Cereal 1991 Kenny Rogers Roasters, Wonder Cereal, Nikon, CTV, Purdue. Various mixes and takes 1085

Nikon 1991 9.4.91. 1120

Arctic ORF 1991. 1161

Arctic - outtakes 1991 Benihana Taviste Debeers 1.21.91. 1162

Spiral Mother: Moniek Darge 1991. 1167

Annea Lockwood 1991 at end (46:00) good applause and concert hall ambience 1172

Court TV 1991 tv commercial: voice overs, sound bites, various mixes 1181

Kenny Rogers - Dub Master 1991 3 X 60". 1255

Kenny Rogers - 2 - Raw V/O 1991 3 X 60". 1257

Kenny Rogers - 2 1991 Voice Over, Kenny Rogers Roasters 1262

Kenny Rogers - Edit 1991 Voice Over, Kenny Rogers Roasters 1263

New York & Company 1991 New York & Company logo music, Leonard Lopate's radio show various mixes 1273

C. Mills Voice Over 1991. 1277

Misc. Projects from DAT 231 1991 all tracks from DAT except 40-42 (Spiral) 1288

Heartbeat Machine - and the beat goes on 1991. 1404

Sami Reunion Festival 1991. 1439

John Cage, Barbara Fahrner, Philip Gallo, Daniel Klem 1991 Copies of pages from limited edition poetry piece. Granary Books, 1991. 1512

Manhattan Profile/CM 1991 A profile of CM in NY Newsday September 20. 1528

Urban Harvest festival 1991 Festival presented by New Wilderness Foundation. In association with NY Parks and Recreation. 1529-1531

Paul's Story -- A Sami in New York 1991 Documentary film about Paul Anders Simma, Sami filmmaker and former reindeer herder. The film looks at Paul during a visit to NY in the scorching summer of 1988. CM produced the film and the soundtrack. Stella Varvaris shot and edited the video. "Paul's Story" premiered in the 1989 Margaret Meade Film Festival at the American Museum of Natural History, NYC. A ten minute short version of "Paul's Story" accompanied the WNYC-TV broadcast of Simma's feature length film "Beyond Night and Day," which CM scored. 1605

A Man without a World 1991 Total accompaniment to "silent" film by Elinor Antin. Co-created by Lee Erwin 1642

The Dogs 1991. 1647

The Day 1991 The length of a performance is decided by performers. This is "a day" with the 12 or 24 continuous divisions. Further conditions: the date of the day and the location on Earth (or anywhere) provide data for music interpretation of the passage of light and darkness, the temperature, the tempo of activity during the day. 1677

Sky Song - virtual windows 1991 series of four blue plexiglass "virtual windows" with gold calligraphy + wooden frame with legs for mounting on wall. Intended for rear lighting. Size: h x w x legs. 1684

NBC Later show theme 1991 No Sleep Productions NBC Later-Opening 9100 id#12309 Vt 42. 1995

Bahamas Ministry of Tourism 12-19-1991 Promotional Film Length 4:08. 1998

USA Network 'New Season 91/92 1991 Kinkel 2114
Synchronic logo sound 1991. 2115
USA sales promo 91/92 1991. 2116
USA Sales 91/92 ruff cut 1991. 2117
Filmus demo reel 1991. 2118
Wonder Cereal 1991 AFX-913 tr2 TC, Viz code 2119
Purdue "More meat" 1991. 2120
CTV 1991 TC tr2 & Viz code drama ruff edit 2121
CTV Only One 1991 2 versions 1 w middle logo1 no middle logo 2123
Purdue "More meat" 1991. 2124
AT&T/Telcom Geneva Pres. 1991. 2125
Ralston Purina "Atomic Wonder" 1991 AFX 914. 2126
Purdue "More meat" 1991 avid conform tr2 TC & vis TC 2127
Purdue "More meat" 1991 avid conform tr2 TC & vis TC strategic YPJC 9523. 2128
CTV "In practice" 1991 adress tr only# 720528. 2129
USA TV sales work copy 1991. 2130
TAPE #30 1991 Red ball of sunset over NY skyline yellow and skyline 2131
Alan Boeding "Sculpture Perf." 1991 Demo reel? 2132
Mark Pellington reel 1991 Scratch open/Graphics reel 2134
Nikon 1991 tc tr 2. 2135
CTV March test 1991 hour 3. 2136
Urban Jungle 1991 show #109 w latin Alliance 2137
NY, New Wave at PS1 1991 Music by DNA 2138
Rice Chex "Unemployed" 1991 code# rpax1303. 2139
Karin Bacon 'Events' - presentation 1991 composite video tape 2140
East Coast Stunt Kite Champ. 1991. 2141
Un asgn # 1991. 2142
CMA Scoring reel 1991 edited master 2143
Diet Coke 1991 KODC-9428 :45. 2145
Animation Pres reel 1991. 2146
Juan Downey 'JS Bach' 1991 color 28 mins, stereo, NTSC 2147
Paul's Story 1991 A Sami in NY 2148
CMA demo reel 'Most recent work' 1991 August 1985.1) Clio opener 2)WINS radio 3) Hefty 4) MTV 2149
Brawny 'Empty' 1991 Empty, Empty alttc on ch2 & visual 2150
NBC 'Later opening' 1991 1/26/89. 2151
What's Vietnam 1991 TL-860-1-120. 2152
CMA pres reel 1991 1; Diet Coke/M%M Int./Hefty/MTV 'Pavarotti/ Train 2 Plane/Un Nat./Solt 87/ MTV id's/Boar's head/Mercedes Benz 2153
CMA presentation reel 1991 Diet Coke/Gillete Bosworht./Hefty/Bud-

get Gourmet/MTV 'Lovers'Am. Affair (2x)/M&M Movie/Diet Coke'Boat'/ Merc B engineers 2158

TNT Special Animation pres 1991. 2159

CBS 'This morning' 1991 Krulwich/Beer 2160

CMA animation presentation reel 1991 Solst 87 opening/Carrier Melt'/MTV3 heads/AT&T Telcom 4th seg/MTV 24hr rock news/Nickelodeon/MTV Pavar./MTV W prem vid./Budget Gourmet 2161

Earth works/Caskets - Shalom 1991 1)Dance video 2) Shalom 'Fusion Caskets 2162

Beauty of Diamonds 1991 vis&audio TC 2163

Lupo the Butcher 1991. 2164

Cucchi Dolphin music 1991 Pres reel 10-a 2167

New Music America #1 - The Kitchen NYC 1991. 2168

Missing Time Capsule 1991 2/3/89. 2169

AT&T Telcom 1991 Imero Fiorentino 2173

Summer Solstice tape 27 #203 event broadcast 1991 Finale 8/9 21 June 2174

Summer Solstice tape 19 #203 event broadcast 1991 Balloon sculpture 2175

Phill Niblock 'Slide piece' 1991 no audio/ dub fr 3/4 transfer 2176

3M Cut Computer Graphics 1991. 2178

Frank's Place - tv spot 1991. 2179

Circle of Fires ch3 1991. 2180

Johnny Thunders 'Live Real' 1991 Inner Tube Video 2183

WINS Radio 1991. 2185

The Laughing Alligator - Juan Downey video 1991 30 mins, color Audio ch 1&2. 2186

NickNite Id's 1991 44 id's 4 2 87. 2189

Intune WNYC 1991 Davesit 2190

Intune WNYC 1991 Yesterday Today 2191

MTV M Three head Animation 1991 July 11, '85. 2192

Hefty 'Family' 1991 Steel sach ;30 Cinch sack ;30. 2193

MTV M Three heads 1991 ;15. 2194

Time flies Rolodex 1991 7 spots Rolodex phone control 2198

Waiting records 1991 DDTS 4063;30 Waiting records' new rev. DDTS 4065;30 Waiting records' non-new rev. 2201

IBM 'The Game' 1991 isg workstation imdo 0316' The Game' ;30 DBM Logo only 2202

GTE/Sylvania 1991 1) whistle 2) No whistle rough mix, 2/12/91. 2203

GTE/Sylvania 1991 Spotlight Package Fashion lamp 2204

Boar's' Head Provisions 1991 Ask for it ;30. 2209

MTV M Three head Animation 1991 July 11, '85. 2213

MTV TV id's 1991 Rock news 24 hr rock news @ :10. 2214

MTV Spot demo reel 1991 MTI spot 2079r 11:16 6/25/85 dub w regen addtr TC & stereo J#11185. 2236

AT&T Geneva 1991 All animation to date ruff cut w unmixed music 2251

CTV Credibility/Old as America' 1991 mixed master 6/25/91. 2257

CTV Soundbites :30 theatrical 1991 w vis TC&ch2 TC 6/21/91. 2258

CTV see comm 1991 Handcuffs :05 Soundbites a :30 stock Soundbites :30 theatrical 2259

CTV For CM 1991 CMs tape 2260

CTV see comm 1991 In court today final no music Trial story final no music Top o t hour paintbox end 2261

CTV see comm 1991 Handcuffs v A Objection v B Conference at bench versions 1-3 Soundbites w LOGO 2262

CTV see comm 1991 Top of the hour :30. 2263

CTV see comm 1991 Soundbites A :30 dub w add tr TC 2264

CTV see comm 1991 Objection B :30 Conf at bench Vers A-C Soundbites (no logo) :30 In court no titles In court titles only In court today :30 In court today alt :30 Handcuffs v B :15. 2265

New Culture quartet 1991 The ship of fools TV version 2269

Robitussin 'Pharmacy' 1991 raaa 0929 ch2 tc 2273

Paul's story: A Sami in NY 1991. 2274

Solstice ? 1991 To be identified 2296

Paul's Story 1991 first cut 2304

Personal Chants 1991 transfer from 2 track master 2321

MTV 'TV Lovers' 1991 final mix on ch1 tc>tr2. 2356

Soundbites fmix 1991 tr1 prgtr2 tc full mix music less/amb more 2361

In Court today v1 1991 tc on ch2. 2362

In Court today v2 1991 tc on ch2 less percussion 2363

Trialstory v1 1991 tc on ch2. 2364

Trialstory v2 1991 tc on ch2 less melody 2365

Sting (theme) 1991 prg on tr1 2367

Sting 5" w VO 1991 vo:This is CTV prg on tr1 2368

Sting 5" alt VO 1991 vo:This is theCTV network prg on tr1. 2369

Sting 5" alt VO only 1991 vo:This is the CTV network prg on tr1 2370

Sting 3" 1991 prg on tr1tc on tr2. 2371

Sting 3" w VO 1991 prg on tr1vo: This is CTV 2372

Top of the Hour 1 1991 prg on tr1tc on tr2 vo: This is CTV 2373

Top of the Hour 2(edit) 1991 prg on tr1tc on tr. 2374

Handcuffs 'b' (music) 1991 prg on tr1tc on tr2. 2375

Handcuffs 'b' (music+sfx) 1991 prg on tr1tc on tr2. 2376

Newsbreak full 1991 prg on tr1tc on tr2. 2378

Newsbreak 8" 1991 prg on tr1tc on tr2. 2379

Soundbites (music) 1991 prg on tr1tr2. clr 2380

Soundbites (annc only) 1991 vo only on tr1tr2 clr 2381
Sting (trumpet) 05" 1991 vo only on tr1tr2 clr music w gavel 2382
Sting (trumpet) 05" 1991 vo only on tr1tr2 clr music w gavel 2383
Sting (trumpet) 03" 1991 vo only on tr1tr2 clr music no gavel 2384
Sting (trumpet) 03" 1991 vo only on tr1tr2 clr music w gavel 2385
Sting (trumpet) 03" 1991 vo only on tr1tr2 clr Music no gavel 2386
Objection (b) :10 1991 prg on tr1tr2 =TC Music/VO judge 2387
Objection (b) :10 1991 prg on tr1tr2 =TC Music only 2389
America 1991 prg on tr1+2 (stereo) Music only 2390
Credibility 1991 prg on tr1+2 (stereo) Music only 2391
Important trials 1991 prg on tr1+2 (stereo) Music only 2392
Be there live 1991 prg on tr1+2 (stereo) music only 2393
Handcuffs :5 1991 prg on tr1+2 stereo music only 2394
Handcuffs :15 1991 prg on tr1+2 stereo music only 2395
Conference at bench 1991 prg on tr1+2 stereo music only 2396
Soundbites 'theatrical' 1991 prg on tr1+2 stereo music only 2397
Trailstory 'columns' 1991 prg on tr1+2 stereo music only 2398
In practice :30 1991 prg on tr1+2 stereo music only 2400
In practice :30 1991 tr1 prgtr2 TC music only 2401
Important trails :25 1991 tr1 prgtr2 TC full mix tag:real life drama of justice 2402
Be there live 1991 tr1 prgtr2 TC full mix tag:real life drama of justice 2403
Credibility 1991 tr1 prgtr2 TC full mix tag:real life drama of justice 2404
Old as America 1991 tr1 prgtr2 TC full mix tag:real life drama of justice 2405
Soundbites VO 1991 tr1 vo tr2 TC vo only 2406
be there live ?? DNU!! 1991 tr1 prgtr2 TC drop out!!!!! DNU 2407
Objection w gavel 1991 tr1 prgtr2 TC 2408
Objection/gavel only 1991 tr1 prgtr2 clr 2409
Soundbites v/o only 1991 tr1 prgtr2 clr 2411
In practice opener 1991 tr1 prgtr2 tc music only 2412
Old as America 2 1991 tr1 prgtr2 tc music only revised w new tag full mix 2413
Credibility 2 1991 tr1 prgtr2 tc revised w new tag full mix 2414
Be there live 2 1991 tr1 prgtr2 tc revised w new tag full mix 2415
Important trails 2 1991 tr1 prgtr2 tc revised w new tag 'important trails'full mix 2416
Important trails 2 1991 tr1 prgtr2 tc revised w new tag 'Be there live'full mix 2417
Real life 1991 tr1 prgtr2 tc revised full mix 2418
Soundbites fmix 1991 tr1 prgtr2 tc full mix 2419
Soundbites fmix 1991 tr1 prgtr2 tc full mix 2420

Cage, Fahrner, Granary Books 1991 John Cage, Writer and Composer Barbara Fahrner, Painter and designer, Phillip Gallo, Printer & Typographer. Daniel Klem, Bookbinder. Signed copy. 2462

New Music America Poster 1991 Walker Art Center Minneapolis June 7-15. CM performs Sunrise Celebration June 11, 6:00 AM 2464

Old Black Joe Poster by Camille Billops 1991 A large graphic Signed poster to CM, by Camille 2546

LA DESTRUCTION DE VOTRE CODE GENETIQUE PAR DROGUES TOXINES ET IRRADIATION 1991 Published by Other Media Stockholm 2586

Nightwoods III (2) copies 1991 For three Clarinets and a Tape Published by Edition Suecia, Stockholm 2589

The Lorca Variations ( XV1) Jerome Rothenberg 1991 Water jets 2609

Sari Dienes 1950- 1970 1991 A book of her works and Memories from artist friends. Rip Hayman, John Cage, Charlotte Moorman, Nam June Paik. 2615

RUNA Magazine 1991 Beowolf Review on pg. 27 Benjamin Bagby 2623

Memories Dreams and Reflections Shalom-art works CM -sound art (100) 1991 A celebration of the autumn equinox and harvest at Emil Leonard Gallery Ltd. 9-21-91. About 100 Postcard invitations. 2721

Recycle Art Posters, Garbage, Trash, Junk (24) 1991 Three posters from the urban Harvest festival. Junk, Garbage and Trash. About 8 of Each. Presented by New Wilderness Foundation. 2801

International Conference on Celebration 1991 Held in Santa Fe New Mexico 2821

Holy Wars, Papo Colo 1991 Poster for exhibit at The Cultural Space 336 Canal St. NY A space to do artwork without cultural, bureaucratic interference in complete democratic freedom. Papo Colo is co-founder of Exit Art. 2902

Ideas for Whitney Museum 1991 Ideas for Whitney Museum Borderline draft description The Eyes Have It: An Arctic Year Measurings: Sound Clock, Sound Compass, Reading the World 3076

Silent Echoes 1991 Program and Poster from "Silent Echoes" Presented by Hayti Heritage Center (St. Joseph's Historic Foundation) and the Duke University Institute of the ArtsIn Cooperation with the National Perofrmance Network Thurs and Fri. November 14 and 15 1991 Music by Warren Smith and CM. 3145

Southeastern Center for Contemporary Art 1991 Published Quarterly Fall Volume One Number One 3147

Frances E.J. The Kelp Installation 1991 Booklet Downey Museum of Art Downy, California 1991 And a postcard advertising Frances E.J. Early Paintings 3162

Sari Dienes 1991 Book about Sari Dienes, Information about the

A.I.R. Gallery Exhibition, acceptance and agreement with CMA to participate in media being made about her life. 3190

Collaboration between Shalom and CM 1991 File for Emil Leonard Gallery Celebrating the Autumn Equinox 1991, "The Urban Harvest Recycled-Art" Parade culminating the Emil Leonard, multiple copies of postcard advertising the event with Shalom's art picture 3192

Western Wind, "The Fire Song" 1991 Letter from the Western Wind Vocal Ensemble seeking authorization for their use of CM's "The Fire Song" in a commercially released recording, "The Passover Story." 3203

REWE 1991 Postcard/invitation to "REWE" 1991

An installation by Juan Downy, NY 3204

The Connecticut Sidewalk Symphony 1991 The Farmington Valley Symphony Orchestra The Greater Hartford Convention and Visitors Bureau The Hartford Advocate and the Hartford Downtown Council present The Connecticut Sidewalk Symphony at the Bushnell Memorial Hall 3221

Poem, "Moon Rises, Sky Sets" and chart about Jerome Rothenberg 1991 Poetry with drawing, "Moon Rises/Sun Rises" Created in July 1991 in NYC at the Palmer House 3310

Postcard: Agnieszka Waligorska - Pekka Siren, Alak - Son of the First She- Shaman 1991 Postcard: Agnieszka Waligorska - Pekka Siren, Alak - Son of the First She- Shaman. 3422

Fluxus Concert by George Maciunas 1991. 3598

Man Without a World, CM & Lee Irwin 1991 Other media A score for the film Man without a World. 3661

Music that Crossed the Ocean 1991 Draft of a project for Discussion By Potential Partners. How did certian styles and forms of Music, born in Diverse locations around the world, cross the oceans and become international? 3790

Letter from Bernard Heidsieck 1991 Bernard has just been awarded the National prize for Poetry, and is inviting CM to a Feast. Also a mention of The Swedish Cultural Center as being a good place for a presentation. 3825

Jack Ox Color Gallery Promo 1991 Gallery show of works from Symphony #8 By Anton Bruckner, at Meyers and Bloom Gallery 2112 Broadway 3837

Shalom Neuman and CM Harvest Event 1991 Schedule for event at the Emil Leonard Gallery 138 Wooster St. NY. Event included Burt Porter and Indian performers, Joe Cross and Donna Couteau with poets reading Harvest poetry. 3871

Solstice TV Presentation 1991. 3889

Mind Game for Lana (for a circle of Friends) 1991 A parlour type game by RIP Hayman for Lana's Birthday 3942

Benefit Concert for Ear Magazine at Town Hall 1991 Kazoo Poster 3971

Music that Crossed the Ocean 1991 Project Folder for a 13 part Radio or TV series. Draft for potential partners. 3982

Ear Magazine Benefit concert Ad 1991 Tues. May 21 1991 at Town Hall Featured guests The Kazue Sawai Koto Ensemble and The Les Miserables Brass Band. 3997

As good as Gold Billy Apple 1991 Wellington city Art Gallery 4058

Pleasures and Dangers, Clark & Curnow 1991 Artists of the 90's 4087

Under the influence of Fluxus brochure 1991 A promo brochure for an exhibition of 43 large scale prints by 21 artists associated with the international Fluxus activities. 4164

Bible, Schumann 1000 copies by Troll Press St. Johnsbury Vt. 1991 A Bread & Puppet Book 4178

Bern Porter Interview by Margaret Dunbar 1991 Paperback book 4221

Environmental Arts Retreat, Aug. 11, 1991 Aspen/Snowmass Arts Council registration Form 4322

L'Arte dell' Ascolto 1991 held in Rimini 3-8 September 1991. Curated by Roberto Paci Dalo in collaborazione con RAIRadiouno/Audiobox. CM speaks or performs. 4406

Urban Harvest Flyer 1991 Parade and Street Fair at Emil Leonard Gallery, sponsored by New Wilderness Foundation 4481

Nanna Nanna Nilson resume and photos from Dizzy Duck 1991 Photos by Peter Lind 4502

Urban Harvest Festival Review in Back Page Shoot Magazine CM and Shalom 1991 CM and Shalom interview about trash and music 4537

DTW News in Review Vol.26 #2 1991 Paul Zaloom article 4551

International Conference on Celebration 1991 Program, maps and agenda 4776

Joy Praise, Jerome Rothenberg 1991 New Direction Publishing Co. Signed To CM Ta'wil Books & Documents, Encinitas, CA 4783

Après LE JEU DU Silence !0 Poems, Jerome Rothenberg 1991 CIPM 4787

Charles Doria, The Toy Palace 1991 Signed to CM Designed by Bryan McHugh, Drawings by Mirko Gabler 4806

Tales from the American Frontier, Richard Erdoes 1991. 4857

Honeymoon Project, Antoni Miralda 1991 Holly Solomon Gallery Foss Printing 4868

The Unreason, Schumann 1991 1000 copies by Troll Press St. Johnsbury, VT 4886

Hungerbarnet, Heidi Von Born 1991 signed to CM, Pan 4943

The Drama Review, John Gronbeck-Tedesco 1991 University of Kansas 4960

Turbulence, Pierre Joris 1991 St. Lazaire Press 5011

en bok om ake holm, Av Stellan Olsson 1991 signed to CM, Wiken 5026

Archive newsletter 1991 Archive for NY Poetry 5054

Sozialismus Arbeiterbewegung 1991 A catalog of socialist materials 5064

International Conference on Celebration Folder 1991 May First 1991 Santa Fe, New Mexico. Various pieces from the conference flyers, Letters, Program etc. 5175

Vorticosa Productions Catalog, Gianfranco SalvatoreItalian Producer, Pop & Jazz & Avant Garde. 1991 CM, Hymn to the Great Spiral Nueva Records CM page 1. 5225

Urban Harvest Celebration, Sept 5th 1991 List of Events and Performers 5334

The Urban Harvest Info Flyer 1991 Presented by New Wilderness Foundation 5365

TDR Cover scan, CM 1991 Published by MIT Press 5399

Proposal for a Seminar in Performance For Ensembles 1991 A Draft of the Concept of Late 20th Century performance for the Traditional musical ensembles by CM 5446

Letter to CM from Wolfgang Somary Eight poems & letter from CM to Bern Porter 1991. 5485

Heart Machine, CM 1991 Plans and ideas for the Heart Machine and sound drawers. Copier Photos 5488

Mills College invitation for CM to apply for teaching position. 1991 Mills College, Dept of Music Michelle Fillion, head 5531

Composer to Composer Poster 1991 July 11-14 Telluride Colorado Amirkahn and John Lifton 5564

Letter from LOGOS Foundation 1991 Concerning the Time Festival. Moniek Darge 5573

Alarms and Excursions CM, Scott Westerfield also Making Waves an interview with CM, Jerome Rothenberg 1991 Copier pages of both interviews. 5613

Letter from Yuki Watanabe to CM 1991 Thanking CM for help with the Japanese Band 3429

Cop Rock Demo 1992 RH version -mus.+sfx 95

Cop Rock Demo 1992 RH -mus. only 96

Cop Rock Demo 1992 RH -mus.+sfx.+v/o 97

Cop Rock Demo 1992

RM -mus. only 98

Cop Rock Demo 1992 Track is slightly damaged RM -mus. only 99

RH Fanfare, filtered 1992. 101

RH Fanfare, unfiltered 1992 track is damaged 103

Cymbal roll 1992 part of Tulip Paint; multiple takes (check several IDs) 149

RM "Hallmark" remix 1992. 155
Panthene 1992 **some tracks are damaged 157
Child Abuse 1992. 159
Dr Scholl demo 1 1992. 161
Dr Scholl demo 2 1992. 162
Dr Scholl 1992 w VO 163
Dr Scholl 1992 music only 164
Robitussin CMA ref 1992 music, sfx and VO 166
Robitussin CMA ref 1992 music only 167
Spiral Excerpt 1992 whistle sfx 168
Spiral Excerpt 1992 whistle sfx 170
Spiral Excerpt 1992 whistle sfx 171
Italian Shoes 1992 demo mix 172
Envision 1992 voc+music 174
R.Meitin Rh sample 1992 not important 175
McKinney demo 1992 Intro and cue 176
Swipes 1992 music mix 177
Swipes 1992 music mix 178
McKinney slow & fast 1992. 179
Clio Awards Music 1992. 181
McKinney slower 1992 slower tempo alt rh sounds 182
Synchronal 1992. 183
Synchronal 1992. 184
Dr Scholl demo 1992 music 185
Dr Scholl + brass 1992 +Brass 186
Dr Scholl 1992 + harmonica 187
Polar Vision demo 1992. 188
Volvo Presentation 1992. 190
Volvo Presentation 1992 w crm vo 192
Volvo Presentation 1992. 193
Volvo Presentation 1992. 194
Volvo Presentation 1992. 195
Volvo Presentation 1992. 196
Volvo Presentation 1992. 197
Volvo Presentation 1992. 198
Volvo Presentation 1992. 199
Volvo Presentation 1992. 200
Volvo Presentation 1992. 201
Volvo Presentation 1992 w C Mills vo/ drops out 203
Volvo Presentation 1992 w C Mills vo 204
Volvo Presentation 1992 music only 205
Hefty 'Plates' 1992 full mix 206
Polarvision 1992 mono 207
Polarvision 1992 split: music - SFX 208

Brawny 1992 music only 210
Brawny 1992 music only 211
Tavist D 1992 music demo 215
Polar Vision 1992 full mix mono 216
Polar Vision 1992 full mix mono w xtra Yoik 217
Polar Vision 1992 mon mix extra sfx 218
Polar Vision 1992 split 219
NY State Lotto 1992 l > mix r < TC 220
NY State Lotto 1992 l > mix w ANNC r < TC 221
NY State Lotto 1992 l > mix w ANNC r < TC 222
Frances E.J : Kelp loops 1992. 246
Frances E.J : Kelp loops 1992. 248
Sea Lion SFX 1992 som seals squawkin' 249
Seagull SFX 1992 som gulls squawkin' 250
Animal SFX 1992 som birds squawkin' 251
Sea Lion SFX 1992 seals squawkin' sampled and proc'd 252
Envision A 55+5 1992 Full mix 276
Diet Coke 'Ballpark' 1992 presentation 277
Envision B 55+5 1992 Full mix 278
Arthricare 60 1992 voc mix + annc 279
Arthricare 60 1992 no annc 281
Arthricare 30 1992 no annc 282
Ise Farms 'Chicken Ch.' 1992 full mix 283
Ise Farms 'Hometown, 1992 full mix 284
Ise Farms 'Long March' 1992 full mix 285
Macy POP v2 1992 < TC >prg 295
Macy POP final 1992 < TC >prg 300
Misc. Projects: Diet Coke to Court TV 1992 Diet Coke, News 4 'pet-food', In the Mix, Ninkasi, TBS, CTV, Cable TV, Envision, Mitsubishi. 311
Swissair "Alp exp, revd" 1992 DNU vo only C Mills+CM 343
Promise 1992. 349
NWU 1992. 445
World Business - demo 1992 with cm scratch vocal 448
Business Report -demo 1992 with cm scratch vocal 449
Dies Irae - basic 1992 basic solo vocal track for multitrack delays 450
Dies Irae 1992 multiple vocal 451
Dies Irae 1992 mix of solo part with multiple voices 452
Bissiger Hund - demo 1992 with cm scratch vocal -2 takes; second is better 18:50 - track only - no vocal2130 - track no drums (only perc) 453
World Business - final 1992 2400 with cm scratch vocal -454
Bissiger Hund 1992 full drums no vocal 455
Bissiger Hund - tk 2 1992 see ID 8 456
Bissiger Hund 1992 without vocal 457
Bissiger Hund 1992 without vocal and drums see ID 8 notes 459

World Business 1992 cm scratch vocal - full mix 460

World Business 1992 track - full mix with effects - no vocal 461

World Business 1992 track - full mix with effects - no drums- no vocal 462

Business Report 1992 with CM scratch vocal 463

Business Report 1992 track full mix - no vocal 464

Business Report 1992 track mix - no drums- no vocal 465

LIKE A RIVER 1992 7" REMIX -- ERIC BAMEY Eric Calvi & Bob Kinkel 466

TIME BOMB 1992 House mix - Quarter kick, 8ths & 16ths, c-o-c hat pattern, This one is slightly techno Eric Calvi & Bob Kinkel 467

TIME BOMB 1992 12" dance mix mix Eric Calvi & Bob Kinkel 468

Nights at the Circus 1992 Erica Wexler aka Luna song. Produced by Bob Kinkel. 470

Alternative Music 1992. 471

Bees for Juan 1992. 506

CMA Radio Reel 1992 CMA

Swissair Fares to Washington DC 518

Swissair: Time & Motion Exh. 1992. 571

Swissair: Back to Basics 1992. 572

Swissair #2 1992 1. Court Tv, 2. Lilac Time, 3-5. NBC, 6. Tom, 7. Gunshot 15. Swissair Comm. #2, 16 Swissair comm. #1 581

Polar Vision 1992 I. Polarvision Classwork. 1) mouth 2)shout 3) verb flute, bells, gtr. 4) strings in minor,fluteII. Samples for Mettin Pr es. 1) Fire 2) mummerslaniz 3) Horse suite 4) Winter Bells 584

Spencer Holst #1 1992 "CM's Bracelet" tk 1&2 "Immortality circa 1954" "The Adventure of the Giant Rat of Sumatra" "The Mona Lisa meets Budha" "The Getaway Car" 594

Spencer Holst #2 1992 12/10/92 stories 1-712/14 stories 8-9. 595

Spencer Holst #3 1992 12/14/92 Stories 9-1512/15 Story 16 (start) 596

Spencer Holst #4 1992 12/15/92 Stories 16 (cont'd) -2612/16 27-29 (some of DAT damaged) 597

Spencer Holst #5 1992 12/16/92 Stories 29 (contin'd) -51 ( no #45) 598

Spencer Holst #6 1992 12/16/92 Stories 51 (contin'd) - 61. 599

Spencer Holst #7 1992 12/17/92 Stories 61 (contin'd) - 64 ch.3. 600

Spencer Holst #8 1992 12/17/92 Story 64 ch.3 - End 601

Spencer Holst #9 1992 12/18/92 Finish Story #64. 603

Spencer Holst #10 1992. 604

IBM 1992. 608

Native American tracks compilation 1992 I. 609

Swissair Voice Auditions 1992. 610

Radio Master 1992 start of DAT is slightly damaged 611

Swissair 92 1992 Also recording on September 3, 1992 Has original written notes and times from recording with DAT. 617

Swissair Radio client cassettes master 1992 1.ECO :60 2. 747 :60 3. MD-11 :60. 653

Swissair #1 mixes 1992 1) MD-11 mix 2) 747 7-8)ECO 9) 747 rev110-12) MD-11 rev. 1-3. 654

Swissair inflight 1992. 670

The Book of Hours of Catherine of Cleves 1992 mixed master with Nature and 747

Spencer Holst #1 1992 "CM's Bracelet" tk 1&2 "Immortality circa 1954" "The Adventure of the Giant Rat of Sumatra" "The Mona Lisa meets Budha" "The Getaway Car" 911

Spencer Holst #2 1992 12/10/92 stories 1-712/14 stories 8-9** **recording divided in half and copied to 2 CDs. 912

Swissair Auditor 1992 "DR16 Samp" 914

Spencer Holst #5 1992 12/16/92 Stories 29 (contin'd) -51 ( no #45)** **Length of recording divided in half and copied to 2 CDs. 915

Spencer Holst #5 1992 12/16/92 Stories 29 (contin'd) -51 ( no #45)** **Length of recording divided in half and copied to 2 CDs. 916

Spencer Holst #6 1992 12/16/92 Stories 51 (contin'd) - 61** **Length of recording divided in half and copied to 2 CDs. 917

Spencer Holst #6 1992 12/16/92 Stories 51 (contin'd) - 61** **Length of recording divided in half and copied to 2 CDs. 918

Spencer Holst #3 1992 12/14/92 Stories 9-1512/15 Story 16 (start)** **recording divided in half and copied to 2 CDs. 921

Spencer Holst #3 1992 12/14/92 Stories 9-1512/15 Story 16 (start)** **recording divided in half and copied to 2 CDs. 922

Spencer Holst #7 1992 12/17/92 Stories 61 (contin'd) - 64 ch.3** **recording divided in half and copied to 2 CDs. 925

Spencer Holst #7 1992 12/17/92 Stories 61 (contin'd) - 64 ch.3** **recording divided in half and copied to 2 CDs. 926

Spencer Holst #8 1992 12/17/92 Story 64 ch.3 - End** **recording divided in half and copied to 2 CDs. 927

Spencer Holst #8 1992 12/17/92 Story 64 ch.3 - End** **recording divided in half and copied to 2 CDs. 928

Spencer Holst #9 1992 12/18/92 Finish Story #64** **recording divided in half and copied to 2 CDs. 929

Spencer Holst #9 1992 12/18/92 Finish Story #64** **recording divided in half and copied to 2 CDs. 930

Spencer Holst #2 1992 12/10/92 stories 1-712/14 stories 8-9** **recording divided in half and copied to 2 CDs. 933

Swissair #2 1992 1. Court Tv, 2. Lilac Time, 3-5. NBC, 6. Tom, 7. Gunshot 15. Swissair Comm. #2, 16 Swissair comm. #1 934

Spencer Holst #4 1992 12/15/92 Stories 16 (cont'd) -2612/16 27-

29** **recording divided in half and copied to 2 CDs. 936

Spencer Holst #4 1992 12/15/92 Stories 16 (cont'd) -2612/16 27-29** **recording divided in half and copied to 2 CDs. 937

Misc. Commercial Projects 1992 48 sample rate, from DAT 236. Multiple projects for radio, video, demo: Kenny Rogers Roasters; Envision; Arthricare; Ise Farms; Macy; Unique NY. Original recordings done in 1991 and 1992. 1039

India (Spiral/Juan Downey) 1992 Recording from DAT 236, sample rate 44.1, burned to CD. Juan Downey reciting poems, "Indian." Spiral, instrumental music. 1040

Misc. Projects: Diet Coke to Court TV 1992 Diet Coke, News 4 'pet-food', In the Mix, Ninkasi, TBS, CTV, Cable TV, Envision, Mitsubishi. 1070

Not With Us 1992 Kugla Theater Ensemble. Some damage at beginning and end of track 4. 1086

Not With Us 1992 Kugla Theater Ensemble. Some damage at beginning and end of track 4. 1087

Rainforest, sfx only 1992 safety 12.14.92 1121

Promise 1992. 1182

Mercedes Benz - Demo 1992 Mercedes Benz spots, various mixes End of DAT, sample 44.1: Stephanie Morrow 1184

Mercedes Benz - Demo 1992 29 tracks Part 1 of DAT--second part is recording of Stephanie Morrow, which has been transferred to another CD. 1185

Stephanie CM 1992 End of DAT 246, sample rate 44.1, transferred to CD. Stephanie CM singing Twinkle Twinkle Little Star, etc. 1186

J.D. Parran and Tani Tabbal Session 1992 Knitting Factory, Brad Jones bass recorded on 8/25 and 8/26/92. 1261

J.D. Parran, Shirley LeFlore and Tani Tabbal 1992 Knitting Factory 1268

Angie Singing 1992. 1293

Mozart Reconstruction. Sonata no.11 A K331 1992 Mozart composition 1783. 1352

Citywave Hartford 1992 Version of Wave Music II. Musicians play in location around the city, strolling, eventually gathering for a finale at the Concert Hall. 1638

Music for Lidia 1992 Printed song sheet 1914

The Book of Hours of Catherine of Cleves 1992 The Book of Hours. Produced by Han Reiziger. A celebration of miniature images created by the Flemish Master of Cleves, circa 1540. Following the natural illuminations sound design adorns the music, and the celebration begins and ends with church bells. CM's music is late 20th century conceptual spin on period's style. Performance commissioned 2083

3D show opening Graphics artwork by Bob Blansky 1992 Storyboard for intro opening Graphics. 2541

Zwei Geistliche Lieder (2) copies 1992 I'm So Holy 2590

Hommage to John Cage 1992 At The Center Georges Pompidou 2602

Mediamatic vol 6 #4 Oor =Ear 1992 Magazine of articles and reviews from music and the world. Amsterdam 2617

Flucht, punkte, Linien, raume. 1992 Felsentheater Kreuzbergl Unikum Laborem Exercens 2772

Sari Dienes File 1992 memorial Celebration, Retrospective Catalog, postcards. Two more postcards added, Sari Survives Irene, Sari Dienes New Work Multimedia. 2798

HEAR Ear Ink Rent Party Poster 1992 Rent Party for Hear & Ear 2833

Bill Bissett Drawings 1992 A folio of marker Drawings, along with three promotional photos of Bill and his art. 2838

Invitation to Private Memorial for Charlotte Moorman 1992 Saturday February,15 1992 at Whitney Museum of American Art 2870

Encounters with John Cage by Rip Hayman 1992 A four page article by Rip Hayman written at Quaker Farm, Pomona NY 2921

Sound is Health by Rip Hayman 1992 R.I.P. Hayman Composer a single sheet about research into sound and Health. from Pomona NY. 2922

Letter from CM To Sten 1992 A five page letter 2924

Man Without A World, sound cues 1992 Basic Themes for Improvisational Accompaniment and Music Cue for the SIlent Movie. "Man Without a World." by Lee Erwin and CM. 1992 from Other Media 3037

Damir Bartol 1992 Press about Damir Bartol from Grupa Kugla 1992 CM is mentioned in article 3071

VR News 1992 Various Editions of Virtual Reality Newsletter from 1992 to 1993. 3084

Draft for the Proposed NY - Japan Festival 1992 Draft for the Proposed NY - Japan Festival 1993 Date 1992 Knowledge Recovery Foundation 3089

Sick Science Syndrome: Differential Diagnosis, a letter to Medical Students 1992 By CM 3202

Vernal Equinox Celebration 1992 Festival of Light and Volunteer Head Quarters DedicationEvent Flyer Featuring CM's "Mauro" and The Grand Conch Chorus of the New Wilderness Foundation 3207

Soundings on Moral Traditions and Performance 1992 Jerome Rothenberg Reading Poets House, A Poetry Library and Resource Center Introduced by Armand Schwerner 3209

Haiga: A little farfetched and hard to believe A complete surrogate biography of Larry Wendt 1992 And Henri Chopin and Sound Poetry by Larry Wendt 3225

A Card Game for Sari 1992 By CM, 1992. 3309

Rites of Spring: Procession to Save Our Gardens Poster 1992 At the

Alternative Museum Scan of Poster Backed up on drive 3371

Correspondence with Hiromu Ikeda 1992 about the Chikurin shoja Band concerts at Carnegie Hall 3401

Poster: Flucht: Punkte, Linien, Raume 1992 Laborem Exercens Grupa Kugla, Felsentheater Kreauzbergl 3415

Rare Cage: Essential Music 1992 Evening of celebration of John Cage's 80th Birthday Invitation 3423

Postcard from Henning Christiansen to CM 1992 Emily Harvey 3426

Starving Artists' Banquet 1992 organized by Paul and Melissa Eilia at Wunderbar Club and Restaurant 3428

Radio City Music Hall Sunday Shows Concepts/Plans 1992 3437

Rubbed Stones: Poems from 1960-1992 1992 by Rochelle Owens Signed to CM from Rochelle 3469

Poets House Jerome Rothenberg Soundings on Oral Traditions and performance 1992 A performance by Rothenberg, CM, Stephanie Heyl with an introduction by Armand Schwerner. March 23, 1992. 3566

Health to Listening, Peter Van Riper 1992 Signed Graphic on Foil based stock of an Ear. foam core mounted. From the Ear Inn Jan. 7 at 3 PM 3585

Non sequitur Booklet 1992 Experimental music sound and Language. A catalog of Books and Recordings. 3650

Letter from CM to Zygmunt with a copy of The Motorcycle Clock, for Poland 1992 Motorcycle Clock 3764

List Stories #1,2,3,4 & FOR ARMAND 1992 Short Stories by CM written in April & May. 3766

Paik Bibliography and Book Release Announcement 1992 Nam June Paik Book Release 256 Pg. 21X 27cm An edition of 500 By Lebeer Hossman Editeurs 3768

Mapplethorpe Sculpture Donation 1992 A Letter from Michael Andre for Robert Buecker asking CM if he can find a buyer for a Maplethorpe Sculpture which was donated to the SOHO Baroque Opera. There are also papers from the appraiser Frances Redell White and photo copies of other Maplethorpe works 3770

Balloon Event 1992 B&W photocopies of photos from the Balloon Event. 3771

Dreamspeakers '92 1992 Flyer for The First Peoples world film Celebration. Also a poster for the event. Sponsored by The Aboriginal Film Makers Association of Alberta. A paper explaining their mission. 3779

Grand Sonata For Jaun 1992 Other Media NY & Stockholm 3785

Cage Musicircus 1992 A four hour celebration of the life of John Milton Cage Jr. Sept. 5 1912 --Aug. 12, 1992 Note on the bottom of performers Stephanie Rose, CM, crying and being asked to leave the hall. 3799

CM notes and numbers on turning fifty. 1992 A letter or essay on childhood memories of his Grandmother and the Museum. 3826

Production Notes from a Volvo Ad. 1992 Musical notations from a recording session for Volvo 3977

Grand Sonata for Juan 1992 Other Media, NY & Stockholm. Salvaged from the Flood Boxes, I don't know if there is another copy elsewhere. 3993

The Great Things about NY 1992 A research Paper for Berti, 3 pages 4004

Knitting Music, Dorf 1992 A five year history of the Knitting Factory 4246

John Cage Death Notice in NY Times Aug 15, 1992. 4392

After John, Sten Hanson 1992 A Sten Hanson Poem 4398

Arctic II 1992 Contacts, contracts, studio cue sheets, WDR letters, booklet on N. Norway, Arctic Rim, project notes 4420

IBM L.A. Event 1992 Hanson & CM 4454

1992 Cable Building Suite # 817 Plans Proposed Music Agreement By Robert Freedman for CMA 1992 renewal lease for 817 and executed release from Park Center Associates form former. 4518

John Cage Newspaper article Turning 80 1992 Birthday Celebration 4706

The Fast, Hannah Weiner 1992 United Artists Books 4727

Film at Wit's End. Stan Brakhage 1992 Documentext McPherson & Company 4769

Culture Wars, Richard Bolton 1992 Documents from the recent Controversies in The Arts 4789

MusikTexte #46-47 John Cage 1992 Memorial Issue for Cage with Homage to John Cage pieces from other musicians. 4790

New Music America 1992 Edited by Iris Books Rip Hayman pg. 7, Glen Velez pg. 43 Pauline Oliveros Pg. 65. 4816

Alison Knowles, show catalog 1992 Galerie Schuppenhauer. Koln Jan-Feb 1992 signed to CM 4839

Pomes all sizes, Kerouac 1992 City Lights Books 4949

Frog Peak anthology, Carter Scholz 1992 Frog Peak music 4963

Tom Johnson Folder 1992 A Letter to CM about #6 piece. Music for two pieces, a review by Robert Maycock in London. A complete score for LeChoeur, and a listing of his recordings and radio pieces and Theater works. 5150

Flux Flag Postcard from Budapesti Oszi Festival 1992. 5264

Wizard and Bear 1992 Plot for a Play Draft rev.1 page 4. 5312

3M Jazz Music Sheets 1992. 5320

Postcard Folder of Chinatown San Francisco 1992 Several fold out Postcards, To CM from Sabina 5345

Grand Sonata for JUAN 1992 Other Media NY and Stockholm 5358

Art Piece by the Gerlovin's 1992 Little flipbook, handmade 5378

Music Box Letter from RIP Hayman 1992 Music Boxes for Milano,

Drawings from RIP of Music Chamber for Francesco Conz. Early surround sound plans. Letter from Francesco about his possible move to Milano. 5483

.......... 1992 Dance Music Video 5492

Construal Of Musical Process Architecture, Dennis Bathory-Kitsz 1992 A paper produced as a supplement to the Newsletter of the Consortium of Vermont Composers. 5521

Sound Art Foundation Poster 1992 Down Town Ensemble at Rene Weller Concert Hall Poster with Yoko Ono, Pauline Oliveros, Jackson Mac Low, Daniel Goode also, Andrew Bolotowsky, William Hellermann, Gabriela Klassen. 5524

I was Thinking Notes to CM from Rip Hayman 1992 Brainstorms from Hayman about a CD- based Game Concept 5608

RIP Hayman letter to Francesco Conz Proposal for a Show 1992 Three Music Chambers for CM, Hayman, Hansen for Show in Milano 5617

World Music Catalog, Recordings/Videos/Books 1992 By Original Music Tivoli NY 5622

Script for Comstock Bacon and Roaring Brook Maple Video 1992 Storyboard copier papers, Originals were lost in the CM Cellar Flood. 5633

The Book of Hours of Catherine of Cleves, Draft 1992 Draft for Discussion 5652

CM “Country” 1993. 150

CM “Country”, mus. only 1993. 151

RM “Hallmark” 1993. 152

RM “Hallmark” mus. only 1993. 153

RM “Hallmark” 1993. 154

Grape Nuts “Iko” 1993 Fullmix 297

Molson Demo 1993 Notes on DAT: “Molson ‘93”; “AT&T Network Systems ‘94”. 492

Euroturner 1993. 493

Swissair Spots 1993. 494

Chants dub 1/93 1993. 497

SwissAir 1993. 499

PAIK ITALIAN TV SPOT 1993. 501

PAIK: Alt. Italian shoes 1993. 503

PAIK Italian wet 1993. 504

PAIK Italian Flam Mix 1993. 505

RHO - full mix 1993. 507

RHO - Cello 120 1993. 508

RHO - Bees 1993. 509

RHO - Cello 48 1993. 510

RHO - flute 1993. 511

RHO - hum 1993. 512

I Love NY 1993. 514

I Love NY 1993. 515

Swiss Air w/ Hank Stohl 1993 ID 29 @ 48 kHz 6/2/93 Swiss Air walking mix 516

Gone Fishin' #1 1993. 517

Back to Bedrock/Boomerang 1993. 519

Talking Horns - final mix 1993 Talking Horns: elements and mix. tracks written on Audio Services Corporation track list, 3/31/93. 570

EUROTURNER 1993 Theme music for Euroturner network. Boston media agency client 618

Readings of Spencer Holst Stories #1 1993 First half of live recording of reading of Spencer Holst stories at Open Center, NYC. Participants: George Quasha, Francine Prose, Susan Brownmiller, Jackson Maclow, Anne Tardos & Spencer Holst, Karen Swensen 619

Readings of Spencer Holst Stories #2 1993 Second half of live recording of reading of Spencer Holst stories at Open Center, NYC participants: George Quasha, Tuli Kupferberg, Hugh Seidman, Armand Schwerner, Allen Planz, Taylor Mead, Robert Kelly 620

Computer Learning Center 1993 CLC versions 1-4. 621

Swissair-93 1993. 622

Samples Ice Cube, Crystal Light 1993 samples for commercials Crystal Light, ESPN, Sport Tag 623

Ethan Allen 1993 Ethan Allen mixes Sound effects 625

Ethan Allen Sisters 1993 Ethan Allen Sisters Full (Voices) 626

Ethan Allen 1993 Feb. 10. 1994 3 spots. Sisters Full, split tracks 627

The Rose of Tralee/CM Orchestral Samples 1993. 628

Fogelsymfonin 1993 Nils-aslak Valkeapää 629

Copernicus 1993. 630

Janssen - tracks 1993 1. Music Mix, 2. Drums only 3-7 strings/pain 8.Vilp music demo -11Line graphup, 13-19. Reschart, 21-27. Unreschart,29. Relief Ball, 31 Activity whole, 33. Snippet, 35. pain, 37. Molecules, 39. Fizzing only 41. pre-cam, 43. NG 637

ADHOC #2 1993 1. Debit Chinese, 2. Debit Hebrew, 3. Debit Japanese, 4. Debit French-start 639

ADHOC #3 1993 1-2 Debit French cont'd, 3. Debit Italian 4. Debit Filipino 5. Debit Hebrew, 6. NG, 7. Debit Korea 640

ADHOC #4 1993 1. Spanish-throway remake, 2. French rev., 3. Spanish rev, 4. English rev. 641

AD HOC-Dutch 1993. 642

AUDI Demo 1993 DAT is damaged 643

RHO - demo not used/LANDING & all that jazz. 1993 voice of Charles Mills reading about magnetism's small plane landing from archive Japanese train 677

RHO - demo not used/LANDING & all that jazz.. 1993 voice of Charles Mills reading about magnetism's small plane landing from archive Japanese train 701

UntraGoodSense 1993 editor Doug Jines Ultra GoodSense, marble sound effects tracks written on Audio Services Corporation track list, 3/31/93. 706

Asa & Norman 1993 Asa Simma Charles, Norman Charles 945

Asa & Norman 2 1993 Asa Simma Charles, Norman Charles 947

AT&T network Systems 1990 1993 ** 0) Open Mix- raise drum, 1) Open mix- keeper, 2) Close w/ string tag 3) Close w/o string tag 4) String Tag alone 5) Time segement 6) Team Segment 7) Customer Segment 14) Scenes 2-4- NG **DAT IS DAMAGED, Partially copied 962

Talking Horns 1993 A Tale Wagged Without Words from the Epics of the Horn People's Wars. An animation without a picture, this grand episode, told in sound and music, begins with the characteristic Bassetto's phrases story telling. From the Bassetto's phrases appear the scheming devils on the beach. They abduct TCreated, composed and directed by CM at CMA-Cable Bldg. Studios, NY. Guest Bassetto: J.D. Parran Additional Sound Design by Janet Lund. 1028

I Love NY 1993. 1041

I Love NY 1993. 1042

Davvi Suvva 1993 6-27-1993 This event was produced by CM's friend Asa Simma and her Sami associates on top of a mountian near Karusuando, SE. It was a gathering of circumpolar artists and peoples. CM was a friend of the festival, helping to handle bookings and predroduction. Stephanie and Lana Morrow traveled with CM. The mosquitos were fierce. Most memorable was the opening and closing act by a Maori princess. She chanted to the forces of the universe asking their favor for the gathering. The sky clear. It began to rain almost immediately. 2051

Heartbeat Machine - Roskilde and Tom Tit's 1993. 2428

Rip Hayman Encounters with John Cage & On the Way & LASP 1993 Three articles by Rip Hayman Encounters with John Cage, On The Way, and LASP, which is Live Acoustic Social Phenomenae for the University College conference March 1994. 2481

Rolywholyover by John Cage Project Description 1993 A circus for Museum, one of the last compositions before his death, within the galleries 200 works by 50 artists. 2601

Fashion MODA MOAA Closing Party poster (10) 1993 CM presents live Telephone duets also appearing Liz & Val, Franz Vila 2782

Operation Orfeo by Hotel Pro Forma 1993 Performance by Hotel Pro Forma, Concept by Kirsten Dehlholm, Music by John Cage and Bo Holten 2865

Ray Gallon Curriculum Vitae and Representative Productions 1993. 3005

Karin Bacon Events Inc. Promotional Catalogue 1993 Compilation of articles and services regarding Karin Bacon Events, Inc. 3022

The Sound Clock 1993 by CM Composition 3036

Letter regarding "Arcticum: The Meeting of the Tradition and the Present" 1993 Letter to Steen Cold from Markka Valkonen of Finnish Fund for Art Exchange October 19 1993 Description of Arcticum Naky, Helsinki Frame: Finnish Fund for Art Exchange 3108

Experimental Intermedia Twenty-Fifth Anniversary 1993 Publication describing Experimental Intermedia 1993 List of Artists who've been presented 3167

Hej Tatta Gorem 1993 Internationell Text-Ljud Festival 6-8 Mai 1993/ pa Fylkingen 3172

Fourteen Stations 1993 Signed Poster from Fourteen Stations 1993 A suite of charcoal drawings by Arie Galles and gematria poems by Jerome Rothenberg 3185

Hefty/Wimpy Contracts 1993 Agreements, correspondence, and contracts with Warner Bros. involved in including "Hefty, Hefty... Wimpy, Wimpy" in "Demolition Man." 3186

Garfunkel Demo Songs 1993 Music and Lyrics for Songs to Appear on "Garfunkel Songs" a Demo "Rock My Soul," "Not Much," "Take Me Away," "Rocking Through Time," "I's a Long Long Way," "Coyote is an Anarchist," "If you don't get lost," "Roll the Dice," "Wondrous Earth" "Little Girl from Sarajevo," "All I Ever Needed" 3189

Spencer Holst/CM's Bracelet Audiograph 1993 File Concerning CM's Bracelet: Spencer Holst reads Spencer Holst 3191

Correspondence between Dick Higgins and CM 1993 December, 1993. 3411

Invitation to Phill Niblock's 60th Birthday 1993 with a concert at the Catharina church in Eindhoven 3416

The NY Film Festival's "Video Visions" Presents a Memorial Tribute to Julie Downey 1993 Postcard to CM: The NY Film Festival's "Video Visions" Presents a Memorial Tribute to Julie Downey "The Laughing Alligator" (1976) "Information Witheld" (1981) "Hard Times and Culture" (1990) 3424

Peter Moore Memorial Service 1993 Postcard Judson Memorial Church 3427

Letter to CM from Sonja Nyegaard 1993 thanking him for his teaching at the Danish writer school and asking to receive some work of his. 3452

A Private Bio CM 1993 CM writes his memories ups and downs. 3784

International Text-Ljud Festival 1993 6-8 Maj 1993 Fylkingen 3788

Juan Downey Postcard and Gallery Invitation for Chile 1993 Juan Downey Instalaciones, Dibujos y Videos 3846

Roskilde Festival Program (2) 1993 Theme Program, CM gives a gentle Lullaby at closing. (Backpage) 3941

Interpretations: Annea Lockwood and Mary Jane Leach 1993 April 14th at St. Peters Church NYC. 3956

Schule für Dichtung in Wien 1993 April and July Performance Program, With performances by Anne Tardos and Jackson Mac Low and others. Pg. 11 & 13. 3999

Who's Who in Space, Michael Cassutt 1993. 4107

Tele Skulptur 1993. 4112

Africa Africa, 1993 Photographers from 19 Countries document 42 African countries Images of Africa 4133

Acid, Vincent Katz 1993 Signed Booklet, Color Cover Edition of 200, 26 w/color cover 4150

Living on the Earth, Bill Dusing 1993 Signed To CM & Family 4260

Circle Letter from Moniek of LOGOS 1993. 4280

International Text-Ljud Festival. Postcard Promo Piece 1993 CM, Jerome Rothenberg, Sten Hanson and others sound poetry festival 4325

Masks Their roles in various Cultures Filmstrip and Study Guide. Faces of Culture (masks from the Hood Museum of Art 1991-1993 exhibit Brochure, 1993 Photocopies of Masks from CM research. Cassette Tape Audio track for Filmstrip. 4373

Aarhus Festival Folder 9/2/1993 List of possible bands, budgets, letters from booking agents, Contact numbers 4418

California 1993. 4427

Citywave 1993 MOLD Replace 4428

New Music America 1993 Snow White 4458

Roskilde Festival Material 1993 Festival information Brochure, 3 Rock Museum Postcards, Roskilde Motor Hotel Graphic Placemats, cities Dance Piece Budget, Electronic Cafe Budget, and KIT Dancin Cities Program Budget. Trevor Davies Letter, Dennis Moore Letter. other 1996 travel and misc. 4595

Reflections, Alvin Lucier 1993 MusikTexte 4788

Jack OX 1993 Exhibition Booklet from Galerie Schuppenhauer, Koln 4801

Understanding Hypermedia, Cotton, Oliver 1993. 4858

River Styx #38, Lee Fournier editor 1993 Book of Poetry, Fiction and essay 4877

The things that meant so much, Eleanor Sutton 1993 Center for the Improvement of Education, School of Education Queens College of the City University of NY 4928

The Little Magazine 1993 Judith E. Johnson 5010

Literally Speaking (3) 1993 Borgströms Tryckeri 5046

The Zebra Storyteller, Spencer Holst 1993 Station Hill 5049

Davi Suvva 1993 Indigenous Peoples Festival 1993 Signed program booklet Nils-Aslak Valkeapaa, Buffy Sainte Marie, Mari Boine, Pauline Motzfelt, Wimme, Saari Ja Radio Rinne 5059

Dick Higgins postcard 1993 to CM 5112

Book of Hours Fax 1993 Peter de Groot from CM 5268

PreFace, Rimma Gerlovina and Valeriy Gerlovin 1993 Promo Piece for Steinbaum Krauss Gallery. Feb. Fold out 5 Panel with 4 photos of their graphic faces 5278

1993 Jobs List 1993 List of commercial jobs 5311

Carnival 93 Trinidad & Tobago Promo Materials 1993 Production Info and Contracts 5397

Furnitures Magazine Issue #12 1993 Mark Nowak note to CM. The Magazine of Ideophonics 5409

Whitney Museum of American Art, Upcoming Exhibitions 1993 News letter type Exhibition Dates. One show being In the Sprit of Fluxus, July 16-October 3, 1993 Cage, Oldenberg, Ono, and Nam June Paik. 5444

33333 1993 25th Anniversary, 07700208 Founded 1968 Third Annual festival. Performing Artists listed 5490

World Music Institute & Thomas Buckner present Interpretations, The Downtown Ensemble 1993 Barbara Benary, Program and CM notes in the border 5499

Njinga The Queen King 1993 The Story of Queen Nzingha of Angola Benefit for Madres 10th Anniversary Composed by Pauline Oliveros 5519

Yoshiaki Ochi performance at the Annex Theater. Presented by Lamama ETC. VISUAL SONIC 1993 Poster and bio. 5682

Chikurin Hoja Band Letter 1993 A thank you letter and invitation to their Carnegie Hall Concert. To CM President of The New Wilderness Foundation from Hiromu Ikeda Chairman of executive Board Niigata Sogo Gakuin, Niigata City, Japan 3769

Touch the Earth A 1994 Side A final mix 346

Touch the Earth B 1994 Side B final mix 348

Touch the Earth 1994 Indian vocal outtakes 561

Touch the Earth 1994 Indian vocal outtakes 563

New York & Co. 1min 1994. 592

New York & Co. :20 1994. 593

Swissair Auditor 1994 "DR16 Samp" 631

Hotel Pro Forma/Snow White Voices 1994 1-6 Girls- Spieglein.7-8 Joan Spieglein 647

Polar Vision 1994 Verses 1-9. 648

Snow White/music, elements 1994 1-7 CM Humming 8-9 Prod. version of verse 2. 649

Snow-Instrumental 1994. 650

Snow White-Spieglein 1994 Original Master Verses- 1-9, 11 takes. 9' each 651

Pictures of Snow White 1994 Scene Music: Hunters, Dwarf Dance,

Bees 1, Dwarf Dance 2, Bees 2, Dwarf Dance 3, Mozart Transportation, Bees 3, Procession, Bees 4. 652

Saturday Hours 1994. 655

Dog Spot; Jurney NBC 1994 Dog Spot Journey NBC believe Plex "Oil of Olay" sample. 659

Roy Rogers Demos 1994. 660

Nestle Sample 1994 Stephanie Morrow, Plexvoice sound effects 661

Nestle Crunch Samples 1994 1) Plex & CM 2) Stef 3) Samba 662

Nestles 1994. 663

Viacom 1994. 664

White House Music 1994. 665

Waldbaums 1994 Version 1 Driving:a) w/copy & beatables b) Music & beatables c) music only Version 2 Jazzy:a) w/ copy & beatables b) music and beatables c) music only 666

Catherine- Worktape. Book of Hours 1994. 667

Catherine- Worktape. Book of Hours 1994. 671

Jerry Rothenberg, Crystal light, Blueberry Morning Cereal 1994 1- "Hell of Smoke ,- Jerry Rothenberg 2-Crystal Light demo- gtr 3- CL demo- marimba? Blueberry morning take 1,2,4. 672

Roy Rogers Samples 1994. 673

Hours of Mary 1994. 674

Judith Malina - poetry reading 1994 poetry 675

Karen Svenson 1994 poetry 676

Rothenberg: Hell of Smoke 1994 1- "Hell of Smoke" - Jerry Rothenberg 2-Crystal Light demo- gtr 3- CL demo- marimba ? Blueberry morning take 1,2,4. 678

CM New Music Sampler: Paik-Lully-CM (exc.) 1994 Commissioned for Versailles Video wall 693

CM New Music Sampler: Wanderers Nachtlied 1994 Performers: Yuval & Kathy Waldman 694

CM New Music Sampler: Eclipse 1994. 695

Snow White Spieglein 1994 Verse 1-9 Joan 719

Sarah 1994. 799

Snow White Spieglein 1994 Verse 1-9 Joan** **recording divided and copied onto 2 CDs 964

Snow White Spieglein 1994 Verse 1-9 Joan** **recording divided and copied onto 2 CDs 965

Snow White/ music, elements 1994 1-7 CM Humming 8-9 Prod. version of verse 2. 966

Hotel Pro Forma/Snow White Voices 1994 1-6 Girls- Spieglein. 7-8 Joan Spieglein 967

Pictures of Snow White 1994 Scene Music: Hunters, Dwarf Dance, Bees 1, Dwarf Dance 2, Bees 2, Dwarf Dance 3, Mozart Transportation, Bees 3, Procession, Bees 4. 970

Snow White-Spieglein 1994 Original Master Verses- 1-9, 11 takes. 9' each** **recording divided in half and copied to 2 CDs 971

Snow White-Spieglein 1994 Original Master Verses- 1-9, 11 takes. 9' each** **recording divided in half and copied to 2 CDs 972

Touch the Earth 1994. 985

CM Harp Piece Rehearsal 1994 Wave Music: 30 Harps 9.30.84. 1157

Touch the Earth 1994 Part 1, final mix Part 2, final mix 1175

Nestle Crunchy Samples 1994. 1193

Barcelona International Frum (RAA planning) 1994. 1440

Barcelona International Forum - consultant 1994. 1443

Rhymes of the Magical World/Burt Porter 1994 Box of limited edition signed by Burt Copies 1-100. 1924

Onamatapoea, Spanish blue, Stef, Waltzerama Sort of, Bent n'Gootit 1994 Onamatapoea Trk 1 0-549 Spanish Blue 551-1046 Stef 1050-1644 Waltzerama 1648-2036 Sort of 2040-2735 Bent'n Gootit Tk 1 2740 +3/250 15ips Dolby SR 2008

Skittering, Weehawken Waltz, Extra Light AcGtr, London, Gus and Iggy 1994 Skittering Tk 1 0-405, Skittering Tk2 407-752, Skittering Tk, 755-1230, Weehawken Waltz w/Gtr 1233-1958, Extra Light, Ac Gtr 2000-2509, London is the Capital of London 2515-2912, Gus and Iggy Tk 1 2915-3300, +3/250 15ips Dolby SR 2012 Blues 1 1994 Blues 1 +3/250 15ips Dolby SR. 2014

Norflex BID, 3M Pharmaceuticals 1994 3M Pharmaceuticals presents a collection of original jazz recordings. Composed and arranged by CM. Performed by various artists. 2098

Child abuse 1994 Sticks and stones 2339

Roskilde Festival File 1994 Letters, notes and correspondence and production notes, also brochure overview of previous years bands and attendance records. 2758

Artwork by Jeff Isaacs 1994 Two small paintings on masonite given to CM. 2900

Meredith Monk Volcano Songs 1994 Program from Meredith Monk Volcano songs. Held in Performance Space 122. "Non-linear in structure, it explores questions of aging, mortality, and transformation through layered images of death and rebith woven together by music, movement, costume, light, video, and object." 3046

Burt Porter Writings 1994 Preface written by Burt Porter, 1994, Glover, VT. Burt Porter poems on attached floppy disc. 3182

Rhymes of the Magical World 1994 Rhymes of the Magical World by Burt Porter poetry manuscript. Other Media Books 3198

"Soundworks" in three volumes: "Place," "Drawings," "Inscription." by Max Neuhaus. 1994 Neuhouse, Max. "Soundworks Volumes I, II, and III." Cantz 3255

Pointe-A-Calliere 1994 Textes de Francois Magendie Entrevue Georges Adamczyk et Dan Hanganu 3269

"Something in the Air: Music Outside the Concert Hall." 1994 Notes and drafts for lecture 3279

A Pocketful of Buddhist Statues Vol. I 1994 Jumonji Bishin Sinchosha 3D Stereo Museum 3313

Music from the Center of the Earth 1994 Two Proposals by Alvin Curran "The Magnetic Garden" "The Listening Well" 3409

93 Olives 1994 A limited edition piece by J. Isaac from the Dimensione Grafica Spello 3584

Armand Schwerner The Aquarium Fancier 1994 A ten page Story in the original envelope 3734

Notes for Tom Johnson's May Berlin performance for The Number 6 1994. 3912

Roskilde Festival '94 '95 Folder of letters and notes 1994 Festival 95 was the 25th year of Roskilde. Leif Skov asked CM to put together a Charity World TV Broadcast on the subject of Children. Since the festival began it has donated over 9 million to international humanity projects. Complete 3936

Pulse of the Planet, Jim Metzner 1994 Extraordinary Sounds from the Natural World 4119

Fluxus is Here Flyer for Santa Barbara Museum of Art 1994 Brochure of Events and performances of Fluxus in California. Also a postcard mailer. 4216

Do not go Gently 1994 Burt Porter Concept 4435

The Book of Hours of Catherine of Cleves 1994 score and libretto by CM 4753

Barbara Rosenthal, Retrospective 1994 A small folder signed. 23 pages of her past work. 450 Broadway Gallery, NYC 4754

Joel Fisher Sitting on the Gate 1994 William Paterson College 4849

Fuglen Der lander, Poul Borum 1994 signed to CM, Gyldendal 4931

Fylingen, NY Musik & Intermediakonst1994 Utgiven Pa Fylkingen Forlag 5052

Om Sommaren, Jan Olsheden Stellan Olsson 1994 signed to CM. Bra Brocker 5053

Auditory Scene Analysis, Albert S. Bregman 1994 The Perceptual Organization of Music, MIT Press 5077

Frog Peak Music Complete Catalog 1994 12 Shaw St. Behind the Green 3 Blocks, Lebanon, NH 5183

CM Sy'phony 1994 with Notes and ICMC submission form 5263

Rhymes of the Magical World, Burt Porter 1994 Other Media Books NY and Barton VT. Includes Letter from Richard Wilber and a signed promo letter. 5370

When Consonance Is Not Enough, Elide M. Solomon Ph.D 1994 Synopsis of a Doctoral Dissertation, Dissonant Music in Psychotherapy.

Aaron Copland Competition 5540

Shofar: Interpretations Concert program Notes, Alvin Curran 1994 5641

CM New Music Sampler(full list of tracks) 1995 New music sampler, CM 496

AT&T/Garfunkel 1995. 498

1st Fidelity 1995. 612

Duracell 1995. 614

Music for Lydia 1995. 615

Waldbaums-Beatable/Unbeatable 1995 1. Long Island Expressway 2. Fathers Day 3. Motor Vehicle 4. Strawberry 656

CM Session DAT 2 1995. 682

Khurbn/Hiroshima (Rothenberg) 1995 poetry and reading by Jerome Rothenberg and Makota Oda 704

Magnetism 1995 voice of Charles Mills reading text from University Physics. + small plane landing sequence, Sound Ideasmaster vo recording, Mix at approx 1:15:00-1:29:00. 710

Phill Niblock Interview 1995. 733

CMA Backup-3/95 1995. 758

Reed Numbers 1995. 808

Polar Vision 1995 I. Polarvision Classwork. 1) mouth 2)shout 3) verb flute, bells, gtr. 4) strings in minor, flute II. Samples for Mettin Pres. 1) Fire 2) mummerslaniz 3) Horse suite 4) Winter Bells 938

Blueberry Morning 1995. 953

Janssen 1995 1. Music Mix 2. Drums only 3-7 strings/pain 8.Vilp music demo -11Line graphup, 13-19. Reschart, 21-27. Unreschart,29. Relief Ball, 31 Activity whole, 33. Snipet, 35. pain, 37. Molecules, 39. Fizzing only 41. pre-cam, 43. NGDAT IS DAMAGED, ONLY PARTIALLY COPIED 960

Saturday Hours 1995. 973

Sporanox and Floxil 1995 and Floxil 976

Scrutiny in the Great Round 1995 DVD 1009

SwissAir 1995. 1037

A Sound Reliquary 1995 A small box in one or more sections, each fitted with a microphone, audio memory, amplifier and loudspeaker. When the drawer or lid is opened, a stored audio message is triggered. The message may be a one shot or a repeating loop. The messages are individual recordings. The 1998 version built in NY for Philip Corner and Phoebe Neville is a double drawer jewel box. One drawer is to contain a message from Philip to Phoebe and the other a message from Phoebe to Philip. Those messages can always be updated. The box contains the last message from each to the other. 1171

Mitsubishi Expo/LRV 1995. 1173

Mitsubishi Expo/LRV 1995. 1174

Scrutiny 2 - Audio Mixes 1995 by CM. See file on Mac. 1232

Scrutiny - w/CM Vocals Mixes 1995. 1233

Scrutiny Music Register 1995 Scrutiny cues complete 1243

Scrutiny - Tape 1 1995 1995/22. 1250

Scrutiny - 6/27 1995 1995/15. 1251

Scrutiny Audio Mixes 1995 1995/14. 1253

Town: The Crosstown Ensemble - Tribeca Hall 1995 recorded by Ben Manley 1260

Bruce Gremo (B) - Flutes and Electronics 1995. 1265

Town: The Crosstown Ensemble - Tribeca Hall 1995 recorded by Ben Manley 1266

Bruce Gremo (A) - Flute and Electronics 1995 C.O. Production Master 1271

Cantate of Fire: Back up 1995 1995-41. 1274

Plex 1995. 1275

BK - Cues For Game 1995 1995-28. 1276

AT&T Elements 2 1995 1995-40. 1278

Koaler Demos 1995 1995-44. 1281

AT & T Guitar 1995 1995-30 1-29, 28 bells 1282

AT & T - Burt Porter 1995 1995-13. 1283

AT & T - Mixes 1995 1995-12. 1284

AT&T - Elements 1995 1995-11. 1285

AT & T - Sound FX 1995 1995-11. 1286

ODA #1 1995 1995, Original Master 3. 1301

ODA - TV Day 1995. 1303

Charles Amirkhanian (words for Steve Hanson) 1995 tribute by CM. 1304

Alvin Curran - Spork Forms 1995 "totally", etc. 1305

Kerouac: The Beat Generation 1995 1995/10. 1308

Circumpolar Arctic Spring - radio 1995 Safety clone 1309

Vincent Katz reading O'Hara 1995. 1310

Marilys Downey, Kennedy Space Center vox sample 1995. 1312

Circumpolar; Polar Effects 1995. 1314

Khurbn - Hiroshima - The Bomb 1995 Jerome Rothenberg and Makoto Oda: demo tracks for Oda 1315

Oda, Jerome Rothenberg reading 1995 Oda - Hiroshima, Jerome Rothenberg 1995-5. 1316

Henrik Termalsen - Concert 1995. 1317

Wildlife Conservation Society - Bronx Zoo Music 1995 1995/16. 1319

Circumpolar Arctic Spring 1995 Production Master 1320

Sprok Forms - Dodge, et al. 1995 1995-32 Charles Dodge 1321

Sprok Forms - Two Words from Logos 1995 -39 Two Words for CM from Logos 1327

Kickboxing - World's Deadliest Man 1995 Original Track: World's

Deadliest Man 1328

Polar Presentation 1995 English - Swedish - Danish 1330

Circumpolar - Music Contributions 1-7 1995 Music contributions 1-7. 1331

Kennedy Space Center - Blue Tour Bus Audio - Jim Lovell v/o 1995 Jim Lovell voice over, Blue Tour Bus Audio, Kennedy Space Center 1332

Kennedy Space Center - Blue Tour Bus Audio - Jim Lovell raw v/o 1995 Jim Lovell voice over, Blue Tour Bus Audio, Kennedy Space Center 1333

Kennedy Space Center - Red Tour Audio 1995 Red Tour Audio, Kennedy Space Center 1334

Kennedy Space Center Visitor Center Blue Tour - Final Cut 1995 Blue Tour Audio Final Cut, Kennedy Space Center 1337

Kennedy Space Center Blue Tour - Final Cut 1995 Blue Tour Audio Final Cut, Kennedy Space Center 1338

Kennedy Space Center Blue Tour - Kim Jenkins 1995 voice over, Kimberly Jenkins, Blue Tour, Kennedy Space Center 1339

Kennedy Space Center Red Tour - Al Straner 1995 voice over, Al, Red Tour, Kennedy Space Center 1340

Kennedy Space Center Blue Tour - Kim Jenkins 1995 NEW READING - voice over, Kimberly Jenkins, Blue Tour, Kennedy Space Center 1341

Kennedy Space Center - Red Tour Bus Audio - Sally Ride 1995 TAPE 1 - Sally Ride voice over, Red Tour Bus Audio, Kennedy Space Center 1342

Phill Niblock - Reed Numbers 1995 1995-34. 1343

Kennedy Space Center - Red Tour Bus Audio - Sally Ride 1995 TAPE 2 (same as Tape 1) - Sally Ride voice over, Red Tour Bus Audio, Kennedy Space Center 1344

Kennedy Space Center - Red Tour Audio - Jim Lovell 1995 Jim Lovell voice over, Red Tour, Kennedy Space Center 1345

Bellevue 1995 I created passive sculptural sound works, such as "Bellevue" and "Listening Glasses" which capture ambient sound for the listener who interacts with the sculpture. The show in EXIT ART, NY in January - April 2000 included these and other works co-created by Joe John which required the visitors to place themselves into middle of the sound, a them that would later blossom into 3D sound projects like the Sound cube. 1407

Listening Glasses 1995 I created passive sculptural sound works, such as "Bellevue" and "Listening Glasses" which capture ambient sound for the listener who interacts with the sculpture. The show in EXIT ART, NY in January - April 2000 included these and other works co-created by Joe John which required the visitors to place themselves into middle of the sound, a them that would later blossom into 3d sound projects like the Sound cube. 1408

Resonant tube, starlight, listeners lay-on trolly 1995 I created passive sculptural sound works, such as "Bellevue" and "Listening Glasses" which capture ambient sound for the listener who interacts with the sculpture. The show in EXIT ART, NY in January - April 2000 included these and other works co-created by Joe John which required the visitors to place themselves into middle of the sound, a them that would later blossom into 3d sound projects like the Sound cube. 1409

French's Mustard 1995 DKFM-9005 "PICNIC" DKFM-9015 "LUNCH PARTY" DKFM-9025 "PARTY" :15. 1974

A Dog's Life 1995 dogs 2073

Scrutiny in the Great Round 1995 Interactive art by Tennessee Rice Dixon and Jim Gasperini. Music and sounds by CM. For Windows and Macintosh. 2093

Scrutiny in the Great Round 1995 Printout, 50 pages. Preexisting material: the book of the same title, some artwork, photos and footage. Interactive art by Tennessee Rice Dixon and Jim Gasperini. Music and sounds by CM. For Windows and Macintosh. 2094

Music for Scrutiny in the Great Round 1995 Interactive art by Tennessee Rice Dixon and Jim Gasperini. Music and sounds by CM. 2099

Scrutiny in the Great Round 1995 Projector Scrutiny Associates 270 Riverside Drive 12A NY 10025. 2106

Scrutiny in the Great Round 1995 CD Rom. Interactive art by Tennessee Rice Dixon & Jim Gasperini music and sounds by CM Interactive computer artist book. 2107

Visions: Museums Demo 1995. 2113

French's Mustard 1995 Picnic Lunch box party all :30. 2359

CM Color Photo 1995 Promo Portrait by Howard Weinberg about 8"x 12". 2455

Khurbn - Hiroshima - The Bomb 1995 Jerome Rothenberg and Makoto Oda: demo tracks for Oda 2665

Khurbn - Hiroshima - The Bomb 1995 Letters, Notes, Press, and production notes for performance. Jerome Rothenberg and Makoto Oda: Oda nava's original drawings and letter. Oda's letters to CM. "This is Japan" story by Oda Makoto. Also a mimio copy of four 2666

Circumpolar Arctic Spring Map Graphic 1995 The Map of Radio stations broadcasting the Circumpolar event. 2938

Juan Downey, Instalaciones, Dibujos Y Videos 1995 Juan Downey Instalaciones, The Juan Downey Foundation, inc.

Museo Nacional de Bellas Artes Santiago de Chile 2993

Intra Venus by Hannah Wilke 1995. Published in conjuction with exhibition of the same name. Ronald Feldman Fine Arts, NY Sent to CM 3003

The Roskilde Festival World TV Special: A Time to Share 1995 Explanation of Roskilde Festival Broadcast and Brochure of the Broadcast 3157

Tribute to Charlotte Moorman 1995 at Holly Soloman Gallery Postcards advertising "Topless Cellist" Charlotte Moorman, Howard Weinberg and Nam June Paik Distributed by Electronic Arts Intermix Interview about her arrest 3180

A Jack Kerouac Romnibus CD-ROM 1995 Teacher's Tips by Penguin Electronics 3200

Raffael Rheinsberg 1995 Der Krieslauf der Dinge Tingenes kredslob The Cycle of Things 3315

Photoglyphs 1995 Rimma Gerlovina and Valeriy Gerlovin Curated and Organized by Mark Sloan New Orleans Museum of Art 3322

Fanny Schoening: Papirlandskaber 1995 Collage Skulptur Lydobjekt Video Essays of Marianne Bech OG Petra Meyer/Museet for Samtidskunst Soskilde Danmark 3361

Letter to CM and Jana announcing the death of Jean 1995 from Richard 3365

The Fourth Annual NY Video Festival 1995 Invitation Walter Reade Theater at Lincoln Center 3441

Art from Tablet XXVI by Armand Schwerner given to CM on his birthday 1995. 3442

The Ice Frontier, Simma Files 1995 An Original script by Paul Anders Simma. Also project Kaamos pre production material and other Lapland papers and contracts. Floppy disk of Simma graphics and Bowler Hat logo. 3629

Scrutiny in the Great Round Postcard 1995 Post Card for the Publication Party At Here 145 Ave. of the Americas. An interactive Artwork by Jim Casperini, Tennessee Rice Dixon and CM. 3742

Fax Message from Paul Anders Simma 1995 Message to CM about Paul buying a Fostex DAT in US. 3767

Letter from Charles Amirkhanian 1995 Sten Hanson, Djerassi Program, Woodside CA. 3830

Jean Erdoes Obituary sent from her home in Santa Fe, New Mexico 1995 Supporters of the Native American movement Jean and Richard Erdoes. 3876

Child Song World wide campaign 1995. 3945

Ear Magazine interview Transcripts 1995 Three interviews for Ear Mark Schubin, Anderson, Music chief of Danish Radio, and Sven Ake Lindstrom, International Affairs of Swedish Radio 4001

Poems For the Millenium. Volume 1, Jerome Rothenberg and Pierre Joris 1995 University of California Press 4074

Poems For the Millenium. Volume 2, Jerome Rothenberg and Pierre Joris 1995 University of California Press 4075

FLUXUS: una storia veneta 1995 booklet 4096

Oyvind Fahlstrom, The Installations 1995 Signed. Sharon Avery 4099

Paperland Skaber, Fanny Schoening 1995 Signed, Roskilde Danmark 4154

New Years Card from Peter & Elka Schumann 1995 Woodcut Graphic Original greeting card from Peter & Elka at Bread & Puppet 4193

Borderline - Map 1995 An art piece by CM for VPRO Radio, Hilversum, Han Reisiger, producer 4402

Heartbeat Machine 1995. 4447

Metropolis Atlantis, CM 1995 Submission to Acustica International Competion in the long form Category, journey to Atlantis from Burmuda shore. 4647

Virginia Fagini, Gallery Show book 1995 Signed to CM 4841

FYLKINGEN, Sten Hanson & CM 1995 Program for Gallery Show and live performance. 4842

Geoffrey Hendricks, Show brochure 1995 Sky notes. Show at Emily Harvey Gallery. A conceptual piece with performance notes. 4843

Shalom and CM, Emil Leonard Gallery NYC 1995 Collaborative and Individual works, Also Neo Nuky, Madonna with sound, Toxic Paradise w/sound Dioramas, Blue Glass Calligraphies 4844

Oyvind Fahlstrom, Die Installationen 1995 Nordstern Kunstversicherung 4973

The Collected Poems of Frank O'Hara edited by Donald Allen 1995 California 4984

Sextus Propertius, Vincent Katz 1995 signed to CM, Sun & Moon classics 5012

Sextux Propertius translated by Vincent Katz 1995 Sun & Moon Press 5024

Letters to Roskilde promoters concerning Child Song 1995 Contacts: Mark Tomisawa, Mark Offitzer, and Leif Skov, Letters sent by Sabina. 5344

Metropolis Atlantis Drawings and Currents of Life Art pieces 1995 CM Doodles 5376

Public Illumination Picture Gallery 1995 A small booklet (PIP) A show of the works of five emerging and distinctive Artists Michael Chandler, E.L. Baum, Jeffrey Isaac, Jan Luss, Donna Page 5534

A Speech by Nikolai Lenin Photo Flyer 1995 A musical composition by Bob Dombrowski 5592

CM DAT 1 1996. 681

3 City Dance Music 1996 master recornding of music from workshopin 1996, Copenhagen 689

3 City Dance Video 1996 video of performance in Japan by Akeno 1/2. 690

3 City Dance Video 1996 video of performance in Japan by Akeno 2/2. 692

Paris Elegies - Rothenberg 1996 reading and poetry of Jerome Rothenberg 703

Earth Pledge Music 1996. 705

Mar 18 96-5 1996. 722

May 21 Audio B 1996. 723

OCT SET 4 1996. 726

OCT SET 7 1996. 727

MAR 18 96-4 1996. 728

OCT SET 2 1996. 737

MAY SET 6 1996. 738

OCT SET 1 1996. 750

OCT SET 3 1996. 751

3 City Dance Music 1996 master recornding of music from workshopin 1996, Copenhagen 759

3 City Dance Music- Denmark recording 1996 master recording of music from workshopin 1996, Copenhagen 760

MAR 18 96-2 1996. 761

BUEI-ENTRANCE 1996. 767

MAR 18 96-3 1996. 772

Homer MMA safety 1996. 782

Kennedy Space Center V/O SESSION 1996 german blue 6-12. 789

Kennedy Space Center v/o session 1996 German Red 1-7. 792

MARCH 18 96-1 1996. 807

Clue "Reenactment" 1996 Clue board game, Parker Brothers re-enactment :30 voice over 822

Kennedy Space Center - JAP/PROT-bermuda 2 1996. 836

bermuda location 1996 old number 6971. 837

Kennedy Space Center: German and french voice samples 1996 voice samples german and french 838

Kennedy Space Center session 1996 French - Blue 14. 840

Kennedy Space Center session 1996 FRENCH RED (TO END) FRENCH BLUE 841

Kennedy Space Center session 1996 FRENCH RED 1-10. 842

Kennedy Space Center - German Blue 1-5 * 1996 GERMAN BLUE 1-5 German language audio tour* DAT IS DAMAGED - unable to copy it to hardrive (JG 8/14/03) 843

Kennedy Space Center 1996 GERMAN BLUE 12-19. 844

Metropolis Atlantis 1996 also on Dats: D 95985 C, D, E, F. 845

Metropolis Atlantis 1996 RECUT VERSION - cut out verbal content of section 3. 847

BUEI-Flashcard master 1996 1. beak, 2. dolphin, 3 humpbackm 4 industry5. minke, 6. shrimpm 7. sperm, 8. blue 849

3 City Dance Music 1996 Loops for Denmark 982

Kennedy Space Center session - French Blue 1996 French - Blue 1198

3 City Dance - Denmark Recording 1996. 1295

Metropolis Atlantis - First Movement 1996 sub mix 1296

Metropolis Atlantis - Final 1996 C. CM/WDR 1297

Metropolis Atlantis - Mut. 3 Edit 1996 Sub mix 1298

Metropolis Atlantis - Sounds 1996. 1299

Metropolis Atlantis - PTI Mix 1 1996 sub mix 1300

Metropolis Atlantis 1996 sub mix 1318

Roundtable - S.R. Stockholm 1996. 1326

History of the Jews loop 1996 D96005-C/hayeem, Jews 1377

68 Ways to make Big Puppets 1996 Bread & Puppet Press A booklet by Sara Peattie & puppeteers Cooperative Published by Troll Press in 1979. 1492

Jack Ox 1996 A book of her work and a Bio and list of shows and installations. a piece of original art is stuck to pg. 43. 1553

Jack Ox Photo of her installation 1996. 1554

Kennedy Space Center 1996 Original score and cues 1787

The Book as a Spiritual Instrument 1996 Soft cover book by Jerome Rothenberg 1938

Voodah, Cellophane 1996 1. Voodah Tk1 0-534 2.Voodah Trk2 540-1145 3.CellophaneTrk 1 Fade edit piece 1905-20434. Cellophane Trk 2 2045-2833. 2005

Doggie, Aberdeen,Tune for Juan 1996 1. Doggie 0-938 2. Aberdeen 940-1422 3.Tune for Juan Trk 1. 1425 -2203 4. Juan edit piece 1 2214-22305 Juan 2 2238-2253 bad fade 6. Juan 3 2300-2312 click 7. Juan 4 2320-2332 best 8. Juan 5 2337-2348 from tk 2 9. Tune for Juan Tk 2 2351-31 +3/250 15 isp Dolby SR 2006

Weehawken Waltz, Ma Mambo, 4 by 6, Onomatopoeia 1996 Weehawken Waltz Tk 1 0-618 Weehawken Waltz Tk2 620-1320 Ma'Mambo 1323-1809 4 by 6 1812-2222 Onamatopoea Tk 2 2225. 2007

Bent n' Gootit, C.C. Rider, Amazing Grace, Auld lang Syne 1996 Bent n'Gootit Tk 2 0-404 Bent n'Gootit Tk 3 406-858 C.C. Rider Tk 2 1333-1706 C.C. Rider Tk3 1709-2136 Amazing Grace Tk 2 2139-2943 vso+ Amazing Grace Tk 2 2444-2742 vox up after solo vso+Auld Lang Syne 2743 * Amazing Grace 6+7 mixed w/ varispeed - 1.02(slower) on studer+3/250 15ips Dolby SR 2009

Billy Boy, Train>Plane, Extra Light,Clog Dance 1996 Billy Boy Tk1 0-246 Billy Boy Tk 2 303-536 Train>Plane Tk 1 540-906 Train>Plane Tk 2 908-1207 Extra Light 1209-2039 Clog Dance 2042-2748 Clog Dance alt intro 2751-2808 +3/250 15ips Dolby SR 2010

Gus and Iggy, Greensleeves, Goldy Minus, Saints go Marching 1996 Gus and Iggy Tk2 0-347 Greensleeves 350-1218 Goldy Minus 1220-2113 Saints go Marching 2115-2840 +3/25 15ips DolbySR 2013

Greensleeves, Goldy Minus 1996 Greensleeves Tks 1+2 Goldy Minus Tks 13-24 Pad /tones @ Head 2015

Blues 1, When the Saints 1996 Blues 1 Tracks 1-12 When the Saints Tracks 13-24 24/Split 30isp 2016

Goldy Minus(second Half) 1996 Goldy Minus second Half 13-24. 2017

CM Jazz: A Jazz Suite 1996 A jazz suite 2096

Banjo - Black Banjo Songsters in Appalachia 1996 Project box with media to be inventories 2421

Ex Africa Walter Verdin, Frank Michiels, 1996 A musical exploration of african art and music on Videos 2629

The Shape of Sound Program (22) 1996 A month long presentation of performances and installations at The First World 548 Broadway, NYC 2786

Future Lab International, Notes and papers 1996 Eco-cube, Club of Budapest, prof. Rudiger Lutz, Heiner Benking, German National Research Center 2854

Makoto Oda1996 A copy of his Book, A letter from him at the Nara Hotel to CM. A paper by him: Contemporary Japan through disasters and sufferings. Also an art show promo for his wife's work (Masuhr) and a small booklet of tradition Japan brush work probably by Masuhr. Also a small art show catalog and a Newspaper article by Makoto, Citizens legislation is needed to save Democracy. 2930

LOGOS poster 1996 CM performs at Logos in Ghent, Belgium 2943

Danny Hobart presents The Things 1996 Postcard advertising June 29th 601 W. 29 th St. URL Launch Party www.thing.net/thingnyc 3059

4th Forum for International Co-financing of Documentaries Participants and Program December 1996 in Paradiso, Amsterdam 3077

Some Hanging Pieces: No. 10 Object Mandala 1996 Poster Emily Harvey Gallery 1996 Signed 3183

The Old Stone House Museum by the Orleans County Historical Society 1996 Descriptions of historic Brownington, VT building and exhibition spaces/pieces in the Old Stone House Museum. 3234

A book of Kinsey's Locomotive Postcards 1996 Released by Whatcom Museum of History and Art 3272

Joachim Bandau 1996 Works of Joachim Bandau Museum Ludwig KolnJudisches Museum im Stadtmuseum Berlin Martin Gropiu Bau 3314

"A Pioneer in Multimedia" 1996 from International Musician, May, 1996 About CM 3410

Postcards from Copenhagen 1996 Reading:"New works are part of the culture," "New trends will become part of culture," "World cultures take part in Culture," "Green initiatives are part of the culture." 3434

Copenhagen: the Cultural Capital of Europe 1996 Brochure and Publication 3439

Notice for CM concert with Stichting Logos 1996 CM performs Greeting Song 3443

Avant Garde ARAMA 3 1996 Performance Music, Dance, Film, Poetry at 122 Community Ctr. 3570

CM JAZZ 1996 A Jazz Suite composed and arranged by CM. 3743

Jack Ox, Flyer for NEUE Galerie show and Galerie Chobot postcard.

1996 Also Galerie Chobot announcement Postcard also 1996. 3835

Litany for the Animals Music by Mihoko Suzuki 1996 Staged by Jill Wooley Costumes by Yahya Tarzi, other performers listed. 3858

Robert Lax, Eugen Gomringer Editions Francesco Conz brochure 1996 Brochure for a show at Trinity House Gallery, De Montfort University Leicester Oct. 31-30 Nov. 3870

Fourteen Stations Drawings, Arie A. Galles 1996 From a Show at Bergen Museum of Art & Science, Paramus NJ. This must be the show program. 3995

The Shape of Sound (7) 1996 A flyer for a month long Presentation of performances and installations. At Exit Art 548 Broadway NY. CM does a workshop for a week. 4016

The Musical Timespace, Eric Christensen 1996. 4104

The Book as a Spiritual Instrument, Rothenberg, Guss promotional brochure (9) 1996 Based on New Wilderness Letter No. 11. 4174

Legende II (2) 1996 Museet For SAMTIDSKUNST ROSKILDE 4259

Copenhagen: European Capital of Culture 1996 Report on Arts and Culture 4266

Stichting LOGOS Concert 1996 CM performs CM, Video Phill Niblock 4399

A Birthday letter to CM from Moniek 1996. 4400

Charles Robbin Mills 1996 A Celebration of his life Oct. 27, 1942 - Feb. 10 at St. Matthews Lutheran Church 4401

Baltic Festival 1996 8/27/88 Lund Sweden, presentation portfolio, project notes, Stellan Olson 4424

CMA Job#5 1996 Copenhagen, Tokyo, NY 4431

Crow Dog Story 1996 Articles 4432

Dancing Cities 1996 Artist Releases 4433

Honeymoon Miralda 1996. 4452

Party in the Hood 1996 Heartbeat Machine, Corpus Songrum 4459

Three Cities Dance 1996 Folder 4479

Ars Nova Press sheet 1996 Danish Vocal Group fully sponsored by Private sponsors and Foundations 4523

Wolf Rodosky a celebration of his life. Invitation to the party 1996 Party in Paris. CM was not able to attend. 4530

Notes From Circumpolar Event 1996 Names and Notes 4542

Lease of 2095 B'way Office 504 1996 Lease to CMA for commercial office space #96-98. 4553

Larry Austin Interpretations 1996 Larry Austins 66th Birthday celebration at Merkin Concert Hall Ives Universe Symphony World Premiere 4618

Listen to the Beat Technical Drawings 1996 Also Display Grouping Plan View 4635

The Book, Spritual Instrument Promo Flyer, order Form Rothenberg

Oxygen - Wallpaper That Moves 2001 Mono Copy Oxygen Animation and Design Team Wallpaper That Moves, CD Rom 994

The Sound Designer's Diary: "In Search of the Perfect Whistle" 2001 In search of the perfect whistle 1000

Sounds and Signals - Smithsonian Tour 2001 Sounds and Signals, Smithsonian Tour from DV 1004

Sounds and Signals - Smithsonian Tour 2001 1 of 2 Mini DV. "camera original" Sounds and Signals, NMNH, Paleontology Hall 1005

Sounds and Signals - Smithsonian Tour 2001 2 of 2 Mini DV. "camera original" Sounds and Signals, NMNH, Paleontology Hall 1006

Bill Bissett - Lunaria 2001. 1007

Feather 2001 Composed and produced by CM in the CMA sound studio, NYC. 1015

DMCD - SIIAS Powerpoint 2001 Powerpoint - PC/Mac 1019

ESB 2001 1 new English audio tour Recording DAT, Joe Serola ProTools back up 1029

ESB Tour: Demo Movie 2001 "Old Version" 1030

ESB: Audio Demo 2001 audio demo: Tony, CM, Sirola 1031

ESB Demo 4 2001 New edited movies + Premiere Project ESB casting session, "Candice" 7/13/01. 1043

ESB Demo 1 2001 Pro Tools sessions, Audio Files 1/2. 1044

ESB NY Skyride Promo 2001. 1045

ESB Audio Tour: English, Japanese, Spanish 2001 ESB Audio Tour, MP3 Files - V 1.0 . Ruest, EngEnglish, Japanese, Spanish 1047

ESB Audio Tour: English, Spanish, Japanese 2001 SD II files. V. 1.0 650 Meg. Ruest. English, Japanese, Spanish 1048

ESB Demo 2 2001 Audio File :Empire Audio Guide". ESB Movie. Appleworks, Pro Tools and QuickTime sessions. 1049

ESB Demo 3 2001. 1050

ESB Italian 2001 1 Italian audio tour recording DAT (Pro Tools backup) 1051

ESB Serola (2 of 2) 2001 Joe Serola recording, DAT 2 of 2 (Pro Tools backup) 1052

ESB Serola Tape 1 2001 Joe Serola recording, (Pro Tools backup) 1053

ESB German 2001 German audio tour recording (Pro Tools backup) 1054

ESB Joe Serola 2001 Joe Serola recording, (Pro Tools backup) 1055

ESB Joe Serola (1 of 2) 2001 Joe Serola recording, (1 of 2) (Pro Tools backup) 1056

ESB French (tape 2) 2001 1 French audio tour recording DAT (Pro Tools backup) 1058

ESB French (tape 1) 2001 1 French audio tour recording (Pro Tools backup) 1059

ESB Audio Tour demo (1 of 2) CM voice 2001 CM, voice, 3/5/01. Auditions 1/2, 3/8/01. 1060

ESB demo Auditions 2001 Auditions, 3/12-13/01. 1061

ESB Audio Tour demo (2 of 2) 2001 Auditions 2/2. 1062

ESB Joe Serola tape 2 2001 Joe Serola recording, tape 2 (Pro Tools backup) 1063

CMA - Aspen - Lecture, Ambience, Music Mix 2001 June 2001 lecture/ambience/music mix 1192

A Future Harvest - 1 WDR 2001 ProTools Sessions Audio Files 1 Fade Files 1216

A Future Harvest - 2 WDR 2001 ProTools Sessions Audio Files 2 1217

A Future Harvest - 3 WDR 2001 ProTools Sessions Audio Files 3 1218

A Future Harvest - 4 WDR 2001 ProTools Sessions Audio Files 4 1219

A Future Harvest - 5 WDR 2001 mix EQ (compressed mix) 1220

A Future Harvest - Finalizer 2001 mixes, finalizer. ProTool session 1221

A Future Harvest - sfx from Cinema Sound 2001 hauling in fishing nets - winches 2x possible work song tractor and thresher (?) 1223

Gunnar Wille - Voices for the Eternal 2001 Voices for the Eternal - Univers - and couch. mix 1226

Gunnar Wille - Voices for the Eternal 2001 Session 16/1-01. Film School 1228

CMA Presentation: Sound Lecture ASPEN 2001 5 MGB. Low res 1238

CMA Presentation: Sound Lecture ASPEN 2001 16 MGB. High res 1239

Wind Song 2001. 1241

CM Sound Lecture 2001. 1244

Meditations in An Emergency - tape 1 2001. 1246

Meditations in An Emergency - tape 2 2001. 1248

O'Hara Performance: Meditations in An Emergency 2001 Knitting Factory 1249

ESB - Empire State Building 2001 video 1 of 2. 1346

ESB - Empire State Building 2001 video 2 of 2. 1348

ESB - Empire State Building - Copy 2001 video 1 of 2.1349

ESB - Empire State Building - Copy 2001 video 2 of 2.1350

A Future Harvest - Vocalise remaster for TOOT! 2001 Jay Messina remastered for 1449

Cello Rock Poster 2001 Elias Kahila Cello, Concert Poster 1565

Excerpts/ESB 2001 Master 2054

Meditations in An Emergency - Frank O'Hara 2001 Performance of

Frank O'Hara's poetry, Knitting Factory 2062

Sound Poems 2001. 2069

Meditations in An Emergency 2001. 2078

A Future Harvest 2001 voice-Pan Morigan; percussion- Glen Velez; fiddle and banjo-Burt Porter; conch horn-CM. sound designer, engineer-Hugues de la Plaza. produced by Klaus Schoening 2079

Aspen 2001. 2087

Sten Hanson My Galloping Heart (2) 2001 Sten's dedication to chief physician Inger Axelsson and her staff at SOS hospital Stockholm. 2780

Tom Johnson Letter to CM and return letter from CM 2001 Paris, Galileo instrument, Ginsberg, Kerouac, Paleo Clock 2880

John Cage Birthday tribute invitation 2001 9th annual John Cage birthday reading. Sept. 5th at St. Marks Church Also John Cage biography Danspace project 2881

Dmitry Bulatov, NCCA International Anthology of Sound poetry 2001 Overview of 4 CD collection Russian anthology. CM gives a review statement. 2884

CM Company Promotional Folder (Sales Kit) 2001 Transforming observation into experience, with sound. CM promo with bios of current employees. 2886

Empire State Building File 2001 ESB files: first Notes & Research, Marketing Ideas, Job Descriptions. 2913

Struggle Through by Jackson Mac Low 2001 poems Gifted to CM on his birthday in 2002. 2999

Frame News 2/2001 2001 "Fluxus and its Influence" on page 6. 3007

That Dada Strain and Other Works Music and Poetry Reading 2001 Poetry Reading: CM, Jerome Rothenberg at Kulturfoereningen RODA KVARN 3197

"Filtrering: Elektronisk Musik Fra Tonegeneratorer til Samplere 1898-2001" by 2001 Moos, Henriette, and Henrik Marstal. Høst & Søn, 2001. 3248

"Tom Tits Extra Tricks: 60 New Experiments to do on your Own." Klas Fresk, and Lasse Lavemark. 2001. 3258

"Tom Tits Experiments: Testar Manniskor kroppen" by Ulla Fresk, Klas Fresk. 2001 Signed to CM from Ulla Fresk 3263

"The Suitcase: A Study of Memory and Reality. A collaboration." By Bob Dombrowski, Mary Petruska, Dorah Rosen, Laura Winton, Richard Hobbs. 2001. d/p productions, NY 3265

Layout of Studio B 2001 Drawing of bird's-eye layout of Studio B space. 3286

Season program for Studio Akustische Kunst 2001 Program for February 2001 at Studio Akustische Kunst, Das Kultur Ereignis 3377

"Fixture on the Block May Face an Upstart Neighbor" 2001 from the NY Times, Sunday December 30 Featuring Richard Hayman, and the Ear

Inn 3403

Gunnar Wille Biography and Productions 2001 A folio of Wille information With Bio, Filmography, Books, productions a Color photo and B&W photo. Also Contains a 3 1/2 "Floppy disk of works. 3776

Empire State Building Marketing & Budgets Binder 2001. 3897

ESB specs & Tour Binder 2001. 3898

Empire State Building 2002 MP3 Player Reports 2001. 3900

Empire State Building DVD printing Graphics original 2001. 3901

Tony's NY Stories DVD printing, Graphics original 2001. 3902

Empire State Building Tour Guide Questionnaires 2001. 3903

Empire State Building of DIGI 2001. 3904

Legal Documents for DNPS for Kennedy Spaceport 2001. 3905

Mary Seelhorst Harry's Story VHS and Scripts 2001. 3906

Gerd Stern, An Oral History 2001 Introduction by Ivan Majdrakoff Interviews By Victoria Morris Byerly in 1996 Signed to CM Beat scene Artist San Fracisco and Beyond 4092

One, Charles Doria 2001. 4101

Linguae, Charles Doria 2001. 4102

On Jack Smith's Flaming Creatures 2001 By J. Hoberman on the films of Jack Smith 4230

A Future Harvest (a sound Parable Draft Overview 2001 Composed and Produced by CM in the CMA sound Studio Velez, Porter, CM, ? Produced by Klaus Schoening for WDR, Cologne, Germany 4701

Birgit Ramsauer, Boxed Set of Artworks 2001. 5157

Ought One Festival. Presentation Supplement 2001 Festival of Non Pop, Montpelier, Vermont. Take-away notes and articles Sponsored by Onion River Arts Council. 5190

Program for Inter. Design Conference, Aspen 2001 Overview and Schedule 5191

NY Post 200th Anniversary and Harlem Destination edition. World Trade Ctr. 911 pages 2001 with 68 page pullout of First Edition 1801. 5222

Morrow sound Relief Logo, White on White Cut out 2001 Hat Logo Office sign by Andre BIlodeau 5554

The Story of the Drivers License from Car & Driver Dec. 2001 also The X Engine 2001 Exhibit at Henry Ford Museum estate 5627

10 Storage set 2002. 828

storage set 3 2002. 829

storage set 2 2002. 830

storage set 1 2002. 831

5 storage set 2002. 832

6 storage set 2002. 833

7 storage set 2002. 834

Gunnar Roskilde Museum - listed as Copenhagen museum 2002 3 Cds Protools sessions 860

Whisper Art History - R. Filliou 2002 2 cds 887

AETNA 2002 2 cds asthma recording on 3/12/02. 888

Holman arktis 2002 1 CD PT session 892

MJM APA booth 2002 5 cds 1 backup DAT 894

Asthma 2002 4 CDs 1 DAT PT backup1 recording DAT 895

LANA nextel phone message 2002 1 CD 896

Stephanie phone concert 2002 1 CD 898

NYC ambience 2002 2002 6 DATs of location recording1 CD index 900

Spirits BCM 2002 1 CD 907

Bees Denver Planetarium 2002 1 cd (bees) 909

Bees at Diapason Sound Art Gallery 2002 a multi-channel sound installation with Live Performances through the evening CM, voice & buzz horns, Carol Weber, saw & buzzes. Bees features two rooms of multichannel sound, one surround and one 3D ambisonic. In this shamanistic event, CM performs an evocation of Bees. Human sounds become and join bee sounds. CM is a NY based sound artist whose work spans 1950's to the present. He is best known for large scale networked performances like International Solstice celebrations and city sized events with machines and 1000's of performers like Citiwave Copenhagen and since the 90's CM has focused on sound installations for museums (Smithsonian Institution, American Museum of Natural History, Brooklyn Museum of Art) and destination venues (Kennedy Space Center, Empire State Building). Bees are a recurring theme in CM's sound poetic works and environmental works. Bees suggest dualites of nature and art, danger and honey, and in this installation, performance and observation. Dedicated to Juan Downey 1094

Mexican Radio: questions, ocho por radio 2002 Mexican Radio asked sound poets to write and record their answer to: "What is Sound Poetry." and to create a specifically radio work. CM replied and also created Ocho Por Radio based on the title a work of Mexican composer Hector Revueltas. 1177

Jerome Rothenberg/Jerry's Poems 1 2002 voice edited only 1189

Oxygen - Wallpaper That Moves 2002 Pro Tools session Mix final. Movie (final movie) 1209

Chadbourne & CMA - Submarine Montage 2002. 1237

Commercial Sampler 2002. 1294

Empire State Poetry: CM & Cecilia Vicuna 2002 ESB Performance. Empire State Poetry. Video shot by Anne Mette Nielsen Audio by Morton Wille 1322

Empire State Poetry: CM & Cecilia Vicuna 2002 ESB Performance by Cecilia Vecuna and CM. Video shot by Anne Mette Nielsen. Audio by Morton Wille 1323

Empire State Poetry: CM & Cecilia Vicuna 2002 ESB Performance by Cecilia Vecuna and CM. Video shot by Anne Mette Nielsen. Audio by Morton Wille 1325

Bees Diapason Gallery CM 2002 Bees a Multi Channel sound Installation and performance with CM and Carol Weber. 1500

Annea Lockwood Sound Maps of the Danube and Donau Rivers. 2002 Annea's Budget and production schedules for Danube project. Notes from Donau project 1510

Curriculum Vitae Proton Sonic art group Agnieszka Waligorska, Pekka Siren 2002 Short Bios of Waligorska and Siren along with Performances and 1514

Janissary Music 2002 added to the odd 10 odd violists there are these percussionists of which pick any three you like for however small even one bar part timpani, triangle, piatti, grand cassa, snare drum, tamtam, campanelli, xylophone all of them good showmen as well - both violists and percussionists percunnists (i leave that for you) are a great bunch: one Hungarian lady who studies at Otaniemi, our very own, good Russian conductor (who at the moment conductsweekly at Stockholm's Opera and flies to meet us on Mondays) and a friend - professional level player for instance at his xylophone, who is not called Duracell for no nonsense (he plays the trumpet for fun and well as you once heard when you called me to a party). he on the other hand flies to perform with us, has done that for a number of years now, from Prague where he is stationed by Nokia to take care of its Central European markets. used to play in the funny band. The violists for their part are international and great beyond compare and need no further eulogy as a bunch nor separately. some of them have also knowledge of how to play and some do anyway. but as a whole and as a band they are just simply out of their way in each respect as you as a composer and trumpetist should have found out somewhere along the line. the festivities after the 80th concert of the orchestra and the 25th of mine in one of its desks and the party with the performances of orchestra's sections will take place the 4th so for once the euro and dollar meet to express the date equally (to learn euro an easy help: dollar's worth is approx 15% more than euro's yeah, easy, and then at that point I look into the past again and still think back to sf marks) and the concert trip with the funny orch's assistance to countryside to spread culture to the sticks in country's Eastern! parts will take place the 23th-24th of March yours, one of them great guys waiting for her pixie chance to have her break through by playing her vibrant free C solo in public (how come this tickles me doubbbly) for you also known as bb (in your grey area dreams also as BB) your bed and breakfast, breast and butt or board and barrel. 1679

Brooklyn Museum American Painting Galleries - sound boxes 2002 Four sound boxes lending an atmosphere to 4 rooms, boxes build by museum, one loop per room. 2425

Dawn - Empire State Building - Cecilia Vicuna RED and BLUE 2002 Empire Red is a Blues Poem recorded a year after the attack on the World Trade Centre on the observation deck of the Empire State Building. It mourns not only those who lost their lives in the bombing, but all those who would suffer from the wrath and political opportunism of the United States. The performances by the poet Cecilia Vicuna and the sound artist CM were spontaneous responses to the others performance and were captured as still images by Francesco Cincotta and recorded by CM. The photographs and the audio were later combined by Francesco to produce this slideshow. 2426

Artwork from WEI JI 2002 Large horizontal piece of Calligraphy 2512

10th Annual John Cage Birthday Event (2) 2002 A small flyer for the Cage birthday event with listings for speakers and readers 2840

Verschrottung Poster (1) des Irrationalen 2002 ein Recycling mit Schuldt & Walpole signed to CM 2846

Sonja Hindkjaer Letters and poems 2002. 2883

Hallucinating #2 by Carolee Schneemann 2002 Birthday present to CM from Carolee Schneemann Sent from the Robert B. Menchel Media Center, Syracuse, NY 3000

Jim's Greatest Hits (A Birthday Bash) 2002 Invitation October, 31 Tuva Space 3192 Adeline (near Ashby BART) Berkeley, CA. CM is invited. 3017

Colloque Fluxus 2002 Colloque FluxusFluxus, Le temps, a loeuvre at Ecole Nationale Superieure des Telecommunication Invites: Hannah B. Higgins 3018

Press and Correspondence with Makoto Oda 2002. 3066

Schuldt, Lustrufe im Garten 2002 German Anti-War Poster signed on 2002. 3085

Jean-Jacques Lebel: Works from 1960-1965 2003 The Mayor Gallery 3230

A Song of Ecstacy to Pan by Bob Dombrowski 2002 NY 3275

Mallarme, Poster Ernest Fraenkel, Schuldt 2002 signed, for CM in friendship 3615

Broll for Rie- Larry Arbanas Mini DV 2002. 3895

Early 3D sketch of a Ball of Sound Floating in Space. 2002 This early drawing shows CM's need to fill space with sound. A simple drawing but in relation to his life's work shows the inspiration for 360 musical idea. 3981

Public Relations Recommendations to increase Awareness Recognition and Respect for CM Associates 2002 A report presented by Publicis Dialog, Jan. 4 by Sheila Simon Geltzer. 3985

James Brown House Ear Inn Virons, Andrew Coe 2002 Signed to Sir CM 4084

Emily Harvey Foundation 2002 Gunnar Wille curator, Simma 4438

The Community of Museums: seeking the common good 2002 American Association of Museums 5091

Thinc Design: New Empire state building observatory tour design concept review 2002 design concept review 5130

Whispered Art History Folder 2002 A plan for Whispered Art History CD project Signed releases from Larry Miller and Alison Knowles. Voice Talent 5184

Contract with Publicis Dialog 2002 For Public Relations work with Joel Stewart Some ideas and info on promos. 5227

Public Relations Recommendations 2002 To Increase awareness, Recognition and Respect for CM Company. Presented by Publicis Dialog Jan 4, 2002. 5313

3. Book, CM and Gunnar Wille 2002 A Hand made prototype for a 3D Book, 5325

Carolee Schneemann Embodied Opening Reception Invitation 2002. 5350

Space Wreck Notes and script 2002 Phil Heckler, Sam Himmelstein, Digibid Sandy Hook CT. 5360

Kim Cascone and Michael Schumacher 2002 For Sound Instalation at Diapason Gallery with Lazer Lights. Explanation paragraph from each Artist and Bio's Studio Five, NY's only venue for Sound Art. 5362

Empire State Building Audio Guide 2002 Large Presentation piece, Planning and Drawings 5590

ADHOC #1 2003 1. Debit Box english, 2. Cyberlog english, 3. Switch eng., 4. Debit German, 5. Debit Spanish, 6. Cyberlog spanish, 7-11 Switch english-master 638

Audubon Materials 2003 PT sessions Audubon transparencies, Bird recordings, Exhibit video ( color corrected), Selurus video, Bird demo 1-19-05, Audubon DVD back-ups2-3-05, CMs Audubon tapes 1&2 mini DV, Audubon revised 3-26-07 DVD, Flamingo footage mini DV, Sample clips of birds Selurus video. Ivory Billed Woodpecker DVD, Cornell Ornithology Lab 8-04. 853

Riverama: Beachwalker 2003 1 cd + 1 backup DAT 889

Riverama: Hudson River Museum 2003 1 DAT Annea Lockwood sound piece of Hudson River1 CD interviews 904

Riverama: Hudson River Museum 2003 1 cd 908

Swissair #1 mixes 2003 1) MD-11 mix 2) 747 7-8)ECO 9) 747 rev110-12) MD-11 rev. 1-3. 940

Riverama: Insect Mix, Binaural 2003 insect mix, Hudson River Museum installation 1025

CM New Music Sampler 2003 New music sampler, CM. Radio, TV commercial, art music, poetry, etc. 1032

Hudson River Solstice Paddle 2003 Website: www.hrm.org/solstice June 21 is the summer solstice ... the weekend of the annual Clearwater

Great Hudson River Revival Music and Environmental Festival at Croton Point Park, a site on the Hudson River Watertrail Association [HRWA] trailway. To mark the date, and to bring together the river valley's cultural, environmental, governmental, and recreational organizations, we plan a day long event, starting with a launch celebration featuring music, special guests and about 50 boats at the J. F Kennedy Marina in Yonkers, continuing with a flotilla north to Croton and arrival ceremonies at the Clearwater Festival. The parade on the river will include an assortment of kayaks, canoes, and other self-powered craft with a powered craft accompaniment led by The Klang, captain RIP Hayman. CM, conch and Jew's harp; Emil Bognar-Nasdor, drum-kit 1064

Hudson River Solstice Paddle Art Gallery (website) 2003 www. CM.com/solstice. Solstice Gallery-A site dedicated to works of art that celebrate nature and time as they intersect on the Solstice. Art by: CM, Jim Gasperini, Cecilia Vicuna, Mary Ellen Morrow 1065

ESB Audio Tour 2003 MP3 files; Data CD; sound files. English, French, German, Italian, Japanese, Korean, Mandarin, Spanish 1197

Sound Cube - CM's Sounds 2003. 1204

Lost Cabaret - Logic Songs 2003 early songs/elements of project 1205

Lost Cabaret - Chorus 2003 mixes, edited & paced 1206

Lost Cabaret - Choruses 2003 mixes, edited & paced 1207

Lost Cabaret 2003 poems, elements for final project 1208

Gunnar 1 - Copenhagen Museum 2003 Pro Tools sessions 1211

Gunnar 2 - Copenhagen Museum 2003 Pro Tools sessions 1212

Gunnar 3 - Copenhagen Museum 2003 Pro Tools sessions 1214

ESB: Tony's NY Stories 2003 full audio soundtrack to Tony's NY Stories, DVD feature of Empire State Building Audio Tour, promotional 1289

Tony's NY Stories - ESB 2003 audio music (without voices) soundtrack to Tony's NY Stories, DVD feature of Empire State Building Audio Tour, promotional 1290

Archive scores Box 1 SCORES String Quartet II 1966 2 SCORES, letters, research Light Opera 1982 3 SCORE Wave VII 1984 4 SCORES Fantasy on Repeated Notes; My Soul is Longing for Peace; Winter Music; Passaic Music; Winter Music Night; Sightings; V 5 SCORES Cokboy; The Birth of the War God; Air Music; Licorice Music; Grandma Music 1972 6 SCORES Light Music; Animal Crackers; Vas You Dere, CM; A Tuba Recital; Circus; Shorter Instrumental Solos; Beethoven Les Adieux; Spirit V 7 SCORES Music For Don't Cry Child; Three Hundred Love; Yesterday's Rule; No Road; American Airline Demo; A Boy's Best Friend; Christmas Doesn't Seem like Christmas; Mar 8 old programs, International Radio Solstice, flyers and posters '81&'82 9 SCORES Violin concerto; Sonata for Violin Unaccompanied; Pars Artis; Eight Lunes; This is the Garden; Two Alleluias; Two Par 10 Misc SCORES Oriental Cookery Show; Heavy, Willowmist; My First-by Lori Hillman; Casual; A Dream within a Dream; Born to Love Alone; Bar 11 Misc SCORES Season in Sea; M'nuchah; Charred Beloved (Jerome Rothenberg Op. 2 No. 2); Havdalah Service; Organ Sonata; Or 12 SCORES, notes & ephemera 66 Songs for a Blackfoot Bundle 1971 13 Misc SCORES String quartet #3; For Cantor and 3 voices; Barey-sheet-skins & reductions; Chamber Symphonies 1 & 2 (both incomplete); Das Murraistuck (incomplete); Excursions fr 14 SCORES Sound piece for amplified piano, Tea Music,Vocal Solo, Healing Piece, City Wave Copenhagen, Three Passes, On the Beam, Rit A Tempo, Music for Windband15 Misc SCORES Sonata II for Unaccompanied Violin; Arthurst ck (incomplete); He is There; The Song of Deborah; Four for the Rascals; Bandoneon & Clarinet Duet; A Concerto for Bandoneon & or 16 Misc SCORES Old Fashioned Fantasy for piano; Sonata for piano; Concertina for bassoon, piano & small orchestra (unfinished); T 17 SCORENaomi and Ruth 1967 18 Misc SCORES Very Slow Gabrielli (1958); Sonnet-after a poem by John Keats (1961); Trio for clarinet trumpet & horn (1957); Twas Brillig (1960) 1957-1961 19 Misc SCORES Processional (1966); Dance Piece for Nancy; Sonata de Camera; Trio for flute, viola and harp; An Apology 1966 20 SCORE & copyright A Little Brigati Music 1969 21 SCOREA Little Brigati Music (continued) 1969 22 Misc SCORE Planetarium event script; Danish music; The Fly & the Donkey; Rock of Ages; S'vigon; Dick Higgins 1982; A Little W23 SCORETrumpet Concerto 1973 24 Misc SCORES Every Day A Sunday; Ice dreams; Kids; Judi; Hurry Up Sundown; Loves on trial; Please tell love for me; Ray of hope; Thr 25 SCORE Variations on America 1973 26 Misc SCORE Wir glauben all an einem Gott '70; Bach reconstruction, piano & oboe '70; Bach reconstruction, flute & guitar '70; Requiem for the victors of Kent State; T 27 SCOREGeneral William Booth Enters Heaven 1973 28 SCOREString Quartet #1 1964 29 SCOREString Quartet #1 1964 30 SCORES-Early Music 2003 List of boxes by number and scores in them 1366

Wood Viola Violin 2003. 3D sound cube installation 1372

On the Propagation of Sound 2003 Visual essay. Images with text 1398

Sound Pictures 2003 Using a radio shack talking picture frame, I created a series of recordings and graphics with Maija-Leena Remes, using our voices to perform sound texts, which were caligraphies in the frame. Interactive sond art, electronic. Personalized for each recipient. One of a kind. Recipient can erase our sound and put their own into the memory. 1406

CM Sound Cube - New Sounds NY 2003 Works by Stephen Vitiello, Miya Masaoka, Shelley Hirsch, Phill Niblock, and Pamela Z spatial compositions, with Olivia Block moving from an echoing ship's hull to a massed drone and Steve McCaffrey updating Schwitters. 1471

The Hopi Emergence 2003 A Native American Story of the Four

Worlds of the Hopi, Roy W. Dean Grants Naoko Mishima 2885

Frog Peak Music Catalogue 2003 Frog Peak Music (a composers' collective) Lebanon, NH 3002

The High Line District Map 2003 by Ingo Fast 3021

In Celebration in the Memory of Jane Baker 2003 Program for Memorial for Jane Barker, held on October 5th, at Heckscher Theater of Museo del Barrio 3042

"Norse Penny" by Edmund Carpenter 2003 The Rock Foundation NY 3237

Jean-Jacques Lebel: Works from 1960-1965 2003 The Mayor Gallery. 3239

Improvised Musical Events 2003 Explanation of Improvised Musical Events: "Requiem for the Victims of Kent State" (1970) "Swan Game" for Seeli based on C. Saint-Saens "The Swan" 3296

Certificate from Themed Entertainment Association to CM 2003 to CM Associates, Inc. signaling membership and entitling CM to all the rights and privileges thereof. "Behind the Themes" publication Letter to CM from Themed Entertainment Association 3355

Sauna as Cultural Practice: Two Art Projects and a Video 2003 by Pia Lindman and John Christ at the Massachusetts Institute of Technology, Cambridge, MA 3402

Howl Fest Postcard 2003 First Annual Festival of East Village Artswww.howlfestival.com Allen Ginsberg poetry Festival, Art in the Park, East Village Film Festival, CM Parker Jazz fest. 3506

Pins Art 2003 An Art piece by CM 3601

Spinet by Birgit Ramsauer 2003 A promotional piece for a gallery exhibit about spinet pianos w/graphics. Also contains a biography of Ramsauer, and her other publications. 3630

Card with letter from Sunny 2003 A very nice reflection 3844

2003 Three boxes of tapes 3883

Yamamoto mini DV Tapes 1-6 2003. 3884

Naoya Hatakeyama Mini DV Tapes 1-5 2003. 3885

Sound Cube Construction Video & Discussion Mini DV 2003. 3886

MED Casting Tape mini DV 2003. 3887

Michael Kenna mini DV Tapes 1-5 2003. 3894

Tony's NY Graphics and Specs Folder 2003. 3899

All Things Flow, Yumi Kori 2003 Art & Architecture, Yumi Kori 4094

Keith Godard Posters and Prints Book 2003 Signed to CM 4158

Publishing Granary's Books 2003 20 years of publishing Granary's Books. A seminar at UC San Diego Signed to CM 4231

Alison Knowles, Show at Gahlberg Gallery 2003 Part of Alison's Bean projects, piece is signed 4232

Helsinki MUU 2003. 4449

Solstice 2003 Radio WDR 4467

Publishing Granary's Books Poster 2003 A sort of Road map of their publications in many categories 4486

Lost Cabaret or Katandogastrophic Version June 17th 2003 Gerd Stern 4638

The New Empire State Observatory Tour, Poster Campaign (5) 2003 CM Company. A Spiral bound presentation for ESB project. 5168

Lost Cabaret Postcard (6) 2003 Gerd Stern, poet playwright, CM, composer. Fringe Festival NY 5200

Letter from the Oda Makoto Family to the CM Family 2003 Family News from Oda, Suse, and Nara 5258

Franklin D. Roosevelt Four Freedoms Park 2003 Advance Promo Piece and offering. 5340

Gelman Architecture plans for New Studio 2003. 5375

The Great Yellow Duck Race 2003 Plan and Ideas for an Event. An Outline-Yonkers to the Hudson River 5406

Helsinki Travel Maps and Brochures 2003 City Tourist Map Vaxjo, Events sightseeing & Tours Sunlines, Seurasaari Island guidebook, Museum Kulttuuri- kalenteri 5646

Submarine demo 2004 demo Protools session 862

New Sounds NY 2004 Master rendered versions - 8.1, 16.1 and True 3D 1452

Sound Cube at Viitasaari Time of Music Festival 2004. 1472

Sound Cube Helsinki Newspaper Article 2004. 1489

A Celebration of the life of Emily Harvey 2004 A memorial booklet on the life of Emily Harvey and her gallery in NYC, and her support of the Fluxus movement and close friends. Higgins, Corner, Williams. Also a Memorial Booklet Program organized by Geoffrey Hendricks. (2) 1501

CM Sound Cube Poster (4) 2004 Horizontal Vertical Band at MUU galleria. 1552

Daniel Libeskind Breaking Ground, Adventures in life and Architecture 2004 Dec. 3 AIA Center for Architecture NY. Invitation to CM Guest of Rick Rell. 2443

Keith Godard, This Way Posters and Prints retrospective 2004 An invitation postcard to CM signed Keith 2444

Spinet, An Experiment on Gesamtkunstwerk 2004 Program for a Concert and Panel Discussion on the Spinet. 2445

NY Sound (3) 2004 25 years beyond new Music brochure presented by Time Out and the Kitchen of upcoming performances. 2702

The Kitchen winter/Spring 2004 program 2703

KRUPS Catalog and CD 2004 The New KRUPS catalog and CD. 2976

A Consumer's Guide to Times Square Advertising 2004 Christine Hill Featured in Creative Time with Times Square Alliance Volks boutique and Creative Time 2998

Lars Noren "The Last Supper" 2004 The Consul General of Sweden

Olle Westberg and Mrs. Igner Claesson Watsberg request CM's presence at the reception for the opening of "Lars Noren "The Last Supper" at La MaMa Theater 3019

Notes and Press on Sound Cube 2004 Press on the Sound Cube sent by Isabelle Deconinck. Inside: -Drawing of Soundcube-Graph of Excitement vs. Time Press by: -AM NY -Time Out NY -Wired -The NY Times -The NY Sun -NY Press -NYFA -The New Yorker -Arts Electric -Architecture Week -Newsday-Architecture Record 3020

Talous 2004 April 15 2004. Inside, a letter from Janne L. Rodshagen to Claes and Kristina Borjesson 3028

Home Studio Diagram 2004 Drawing of Home Studio 3038

Sound Cube Information 2004 Sound Cube Files. Contains: Correspondence with Phill Niblock Patent Diagram Correspondence with Maija-Leena Remes Shenker Incorporated Sound Cube instructions Invoices and Agreements 3039

Digital Avant-Garde: Celebrating 25 Years of Ars Electronica 2004 Program On the occasion of Ars Electronica's 25th Anniversary, a series of exhibitions, screenings, and lectures will take place in NY City from May 21st to July 18th. 3276

The Sights and Sounds of Freedom 2004 Correspondence, notes, and proposal surrounding The Sights and Sounds of Freedom, an attraction at the Branson Meadows Mall, Branson, MO 3292

Cockeyed Creations 2004 Card and business cards from Cockeyed Creations, Berkeley, California 3295

Horizontal Vertical Band 2004 Timeline Muu ry, Helsinki, Finland 3297

Correspondence between CM and Barbara Benary 2004 Concerning New Wilderness Reissue 3298

Montreal Museum of Archaeology and History 2004 Fold-out Panoramic of Montreal and information on Historic sites in Montreal in a picture-stock pamphlet 3301

Architecture Week Design-In Marathon 2004 Program at the Center of Design Marathon 3341

Spinet: and Experiment on Gesamtkunstwerk 2004 Publicity: Curated by Birgit Ramsauer in collaboration with The Cooper Union 3407

Copenhagen Memorabilia 2004 With October 10th Newspaper, article on CM in culture section 2 copies 3459

Beat -LA (Beat generation Listserv) an information Flyer 2004 An online discussion forum devoted to the study of the lives and works of the writers of the beat Generation, especially Jack Kerouac, Alan Ginsberg and William Burroughs. 3505

New Sound NY Poster 2004 Presented by Time Out NY, organized by The Kitchen, & The Cooper Union 3635

Den Store Lyve Skole, Hans Prehn & Jan Christer Falk 2004 Letter to

CM inside Front Cover 4127

Notes from Horse Song Session 1976. 2004 CM notes and observations from a Recording session with Jerome Rothenberg. 4168

The Kitchen Fall 2004 program 4360

Memorial for Rubin Gorewitz invitation 2004 Held at Anita Shapolsky Gallery RSVP, Ann Gorewitz 4404

New Sound NY Poster 2004 kitchen, presented by Time Out NY 4565

Spinet, Birgit Ramsauer, CM and Others 2004 DVD, NYC at Cooper Union The Great Hall 21-22 Oct. 12 Folded Cards 6 Programs, Short Article, News Articles, Color copy of a Photo Contact sheet 5153

Lentils restrained in paper for CM, Alison Knowles 2004. 5213

Design of Bowler Hat, Thomson & Thomson 2004 Copyright Search Report 5314

The Kitchen Art Gallery Program for 3-30 thru 5-1 2004 The CM Sound Cube, Curators CM, Stephen Vitiello, Christina Yang, Michael Schumacher 5355

Albert Edelfelt Newspaper, Show History, Maps, Info of his Life. 2004 Beautiful piece on this Artist. 5516

Small Press Distribution 35th Anniversary Invitation 2004 Note inside from James Sherry to CM Special Guest authors Robert Creely, Lydia Davis, Renee Gladman. 5536

Via Duck Groucho Club Newsletter poster 2004 Soho/London 5563

Indy Canal 2005. 1356

Sound Art in Public Spaces WHITE PAPER 2005 proposing a historical and functional context for sound art in public spaces 1397

Horizontal Vertical Band at MUU Gallery Helsinki 2005 One man show at MUU Gallery, Helsinki with sound cube built by Luomas Peltola, sound drawers, posters from NWF CM archive, catalogue for browsing 1473

New music in a Great Space 2005 Concert Series at St. John the Divine NYC. From Sept. 22 thru Nov. 2. 1537

31st Annual New Year's day Marathon Reading 2005 Held at St. Marks Church Jan.1st. Several New Wilderness poets are represented 2905

Siggraph 2005 L.A. Collected business cards and a program from The World Stage Performance Gallery starring Billy Childs. There is also a flyer for the World Stage Jazz Festival tribute to Harold Land SR. Sax player. 2984

Junia Neiva Postcard 2005 Postcard of Art Show by Junia Neiva at free will Art Space NY. CM ad on back for Sound Art and new Objects 2991

Zoe's First Poem 2005 Zoe's first poem Sent to CM by Alison Knowles "Oh blood brd oh/bloo brd. yourfethrs sow bloo./soring throo thescie lic a bigbloo baloon/bloo tuffll fethers./hat are t calrs/av the ram boe./good bye bloo brd/goodnite goodnite." 2994

The Lifetime achievement honoring of Lisa Mayo 2005 Invitation honoring Lisa Mayo and Spiderwoman Theater at the Smithsonian National Museum of the American Indian, Invitation to CM 3015

Jade String Trio 2005 Programs, CD, and press 3047

Tom "Bones" Malone 2005 Signed edition of the September "International Musician" Cover Story: "Tom 'Bones' Malone Life After the Blues Brothers signed by Tom "Bones' Malone 3220

Proposed Sound Cube 2005 Concept Drawings of Proposed Sound Cube 3222

Tage Der Neuen Musik (Day of New Music) 2005 Bamberg June-July, Begegung Ost-West Plus Oberbuergermeister Herbert Lauer Veranstalter: Neue Musik in Bamberg e.V. Featuring CM performing "In life I was silent but in death I sing" 3223

Else Marie Pade: livet i et glasperlespil 2005 Pade, Else Marie, and Hans Sydow. Resonance. dk. 3230

"A Spiral Wind: Poems by Burt Porter." 2005 Signed to CM 3252

The Golandsky Institute International Piano Festival and Summer Symposium 2005 Princeton University, Princeton, New Jersey 3274

"The Presence of a Puppet," by Paul Zelevansky 2005 25-page writing on the meaning evoked by puppets in theater objects. 3277

CM/Sound Space 2005 Pamphlet from Southeastern Center for Contemporary Art from Winter, Featuring a description of CM/Sound Space, Potter Gallery, January 22-April 3 And a program for The Name Game: Allan McCollum and Mingering Mike & CM/Sound Space 3291

Eye of the Storm 2005 Explanation of 3D Sound in Eye of the Storm Attraction from 360ids Including: Proprietary Information, Illustrations, and information on the project team 3299

Correspondence with Word Art Vision 2005 with Gerd Stern of Intermedia Foundation 3408

Free Wall Art Space CM Sound Art New Objects and installation Postcard 2005 A Postcard for the Opening Reception Thursday May 12. 3801

Early Sales sheet for CMsound 3D system 2005 8.5 x 11" copier flyer for Morrosound 3D 3930

Sky High 2005 CM & Gerd Stern performance on CD. 3940

Den Vrede Dreng, Gunnar Wille 2005 Signed to CM 4085

Else Marie Pade, Livet I ET Glasperlespil 2005. 4109

Gregorio Fontaine Videos and Photos (2)CD's 2005 Chile 2005 Poems and animated videos 1 disk with Audio, ! with photos and video. 4157

Sound Art by CM 2005 May 12-26 at Free Wall Art Space 421 Broome St. NY Press Release and notes 4226

The Extended Instrument: An Investigation into Sound Art and Contemporary Music 2005 A seminar produced by the NY Council on the Arts in Collaboration with Harvestworks to Distinguish between Music and Sound Art. 4311

Fulldome Master show file IPS Standards 2005 Early standards info. 4334

CM interviewed by Joan Rothfuss about Charlotte Morman 2005 Charlotte Moorman, Yoko, Fluxus, Cage, Stockhausen 4538

Poetry Project 31st Annual New Year's day Marathon Reading Program 2005 St. Mark's Church 4654

NY Post, Alexander Hamilton special Issue 2005 This is probably where the creator of HAMILTON the play got his ideas. This piece was pre broadway play. 4668

Studio A Notebook from NYC 2005 Some notes on Audubon, also Olympics Sound Cube 5071

Ecsite, annual conference 2005 program 5136

NY Post, Alexander Hamilton Issue 2005 NY Historical Society. Is this where Meranda got his idea for the Play ? 5212

Notes on 3D sound 2005 Various promo pieces for CM Sound. Demo instructions, flyers. True 3D sonic Experiences, surround. AV introduction. 5377

Geoffrey Hendricks and Sir Rodney Newsletter #8 2005 Itinerary for Travel and events that shaped their lives in 2004. 5602

Mirrored Wing Wind Bells for Laura and Emily 2006 This commonality of spirit with what evolved as Fluxus led to a career-long association with Fluxus artists and a friendship with Emily Harvey, the gallerist who presented CM's installation based on Copenhagen Waves (1985). 1363

Horns of the Alpine Sea for Turin 2006 Winter Olympics multitrack master missed to 8.1 CMSound Cube 1370

Beowulf 2006 Co production with Jon Aaron. Recorded in Helsingborg Sweden, Stellan Olsson video, Mats Harrison DP, Christian Odiham, engineer, CM director of audio production, Maija-Leena Remes co-translator, subtitler, Rie Koko editor 1451

President's House, Philadelphia 2006 Planned the audio President's house for outdoor setting in the park on the site of the original President's House Outdoor speakers below grade were devised with rain drains. 1460

Jean-Jacques Lebel - Les Avatars de Venus 2006 40-minute morphing of Venus figures from all ages and civilizations, which have been collected by Jean-Jacques Lebel over the years. The video is part of Lebel's installation in time and space 'Reliquaire pour un culte de Venus'. 2427

Flower Music for N.J.P. Nam Jun Paik by CM 2006 Artwork on a Napkin by CM 29th Jan. 2760

Recent Images by Harold Cohen/AARON 2006 "CM, For your enjoyment (hopfully) Harold" 2996

Postcards from Italy/Charlotte Moorman Article 2006 Letter from Phil Corner (?) Italy Containing a postcard from Reggio Emilia Cathedral, Article on Charlotte Moorman, and schedule for 2005 Bowery Poetry Club DOINGS Book Party 3045

Audubon's Aviary 2006 Memorabilia from Audubon's Aviary, exhibit of 40 Original watercolors prepared by John James Audubon from 1827-1838. At NY Historical Society. Including Flyer's for Installation Professional Services Agreement 3049

Amorph!06 2006 Guide to amorph!06 exhibit. Biographical information about artists involved. MUU ry. Finland 3051

The Scenographer 2006 September edition Special Issue on Theater Volume 2 Signed to CM 3073

Letter from Peter Jagerson 2006 Regarding CM Bridge project and proposed film about time by Peter September 22. 3105

Handmade Electronic Music: The art of hardware hacking. 2006 Collins, Nicolas. Taylor & Francis. Signed "To CM: You shouldn't have to buy this. Nick. April 2006". 3241

Jean-Francois Bory, A Life Made With Words 2006 by Giorgio Dittadi Editore Francesco Conz Archive and Editions An edition of 1000 soft-cover copies, each signed and numbered by the author and accompanied by a small work 3242

Sonorites 2006 Chronique de la chose entendue 3244

"Jeg Har Hort" by Kirsten Justesen. Fama og den hellige Katrine med folge. Et udstillings katalog. Til Felix og Fabian. 2006 Signed to CM 3254

"Alive at the Village Vanguard: My Life In and Out of Jazz Time," by Lorraine Gordon and Barry Singer. 2006 Hal Leonard Corporation. 3256

"Background Noise: Perspectives on Sound Art." by Brandon LaBelle 2006 Continuum. Signed. 3257

Kirsten Justesen: Selected Works 2006. 3273

The Effect of Audio Compression techniques on binaural audio rendering by Fabien Prezat and Brian FG Katz 2006 An Audio Engineering Society Convention Paper 3282

Soundsaround by Philip Corner 2006 Some structures for artificial ambient listening. For CMs "Sound Cube" 3600

Complaints Choir of Birmingham, Helsinki, Hamburg, St. Petersburg DVD 2006. 3893

Shoveler on the Roof, selected Poems by Phyllis Rachel Larrabee 2006 Signed, L. Brown & Sons 4043

Cannon Canon Phil Corner 2006 A piece to be performed at suitable occasions 4169

Annual Fales Lecture in English and American Literature, John Hanhardtan invitation. 2006 John Hanhardt presents a lecture Off the Beaten Path, Archiving the Creative Process in the Late 20th Century 4202

Audubon's Aviary Program, CD, Exhibition Schedule, text panels, 2006 From the NY Historical Society show March 17 - May 7. 4207

Lower East Side Tenement Museum 2006 Multimedia Program for The Irish Family in America program. Proposal from CM. 4375

RHO Hotel Proforma 2006 Proposals 4460

Killing Yourself to Live, Chuck Klosterman 2006 Scribner 5081

SUOMI FEST 2006 Printed Flyer 2006 Finish and US concert with letter invitation and events Calendar 5145

Beowulf Postcard Pre Mailer for DVD (20) 2006 Benjamin Bagby 5198

xf 2006 5209

Echoes from the Mountains, Programs, Postcards & Press 2006 3-D Sound from CM Productions, Sound Cube Steve McCaffery 5219

Beowulf, Benjamin Bagby Color Promo for Lincoln Center and Laguardia Drama Theater 2006. 5236

Michael Kabotie Letter and Shows 2006 Smithsonian Research Fellowship 5323

The Cultural Olympiad Programme for Torino 2006 Italy Art- A Cinema and Sound Event 5509

Pro Football Hall of Fame SOUNDSCAPE 2007 2435

Renegades Program 25 years of performance at Exit Art 2007 1982-2007 a selection of performances from the archive. Exit Art 475 Tenth Ave. NY 2855

Once upon a time Walt Disney Invitation. 2007 The sources of inspiration for Walt Disney Studios March 8 - June 24 at Montreal Museum of Fine Arts. Lecture by Bruno Girveau. Letter from J.J. 2879

Wilma Schlizewskin in Sunnuntaisuomalainen 2007. 3014

Studio B Editing Log 2007 Studio B Editing Log January 15. 2007. 3208

Sound Business by Julian Treasure 2007 CM and the CM Sound Cube mentioned on Page 114. 3228

Sound Art: Beyond Music, Between Categories by Alan Licht 2007 Licht, Alan, Bill Fontana, Steve Roden, Jean Dubuffet, Anthony Burr, Charles Curtis, and Bernhard G‡l. Sound art: Beyond music, between categories. Rizzoli International Publications, 2007. CM mentioned on Page 117. 3229

"Sonnetailia" by Marc Nasdor 2007 Roof Books, Segue Foundation, NY. Book of poems. Signed: "For CM. A long hard time coming, but finally given birth. Marc." 3247

"Sonorites L'ecoute, et apres..." by Les Cahiers de l'Institute Musique Écologie and Champ Social Editions 2007 Hocelle Corvest, Ray Gallon, Guillaume Billaux, Antonio De Souza Dias, Robin Minard, Kaye Mortley, Jean-Marie Rapin, Anna Rispoli, Roberto Barbanti, Anne Bussard, Sylvie Guichard, Pierre Marietan, Sylvia Zambrini et Pierre 3253

"Resonanzen: Aspekte der Klangkunst." Bernd Schulz, Stadtgalerie Saarbrücken. 2007 Schulz, Bernd. "Resonanzen: Aspekte der Klangkunst." Stadtgalerie Saarbrucken. (2007) Signed to CM. 3266

Stephanie Morrow Poetry 2007 Poems: "Alone," "L'Ange de la Nuit," "Wishes Upon Threads and Seams," "Star-Spangled Eyes." 3278

Birthday Greetings to CM from ASCAP 2007 Birthday Greetings to CM from ASCAP 2007. 3436

Jackson Mac Low Memoriam CD (75) 2007 Jerome Rothenberg: Poet/Reader CM: Composer/Performer Disc is Called Awakenings for Jackson Mac Low Mastering Engineer: Jay Messina 3625

Wind Tides Sculpture, Angel Orensanz 2007 4091

Catalog L.A. Birthplace of an Art Capital 1955-1985 Catherine ©renier 2007. 4105

ESI 2007 London 4439

Fat Duck, Heston Blumenthal chef 2007 CM engaged to create sound design for an Italian seafood meal, Just two seagulls! 4441

Give me a Rock Garden by Solja Krapu 2007 A poem Signed Love from Slja to CM, 3 pages two languages 4617

Business Cards from Europe '07, 08 2007. 5306

Artists Talk on Art Program 2007 CM with Ombretta Argo, Paololluca Barbieri, Michael Schmacher, Joe Diebes. Un Silent Night 5460

Contract between VMK Academy of Music and Communication and CM 2007 5575

Storyline 2008 3 CDs + 2CDs and 2 Days for SFX 871 Listen to the River Great Lakes Children's Museum - Soundscape, Interactives 2008 3D sound experience, interactives, Traverse City, Michigan 2434

Flux Med by Robert Watts 2008 Fux Med by Robert Watts Doctor Bob at Artpool P60 Budapest, VI. Silkscreen prints from 1987 and the photos documenting Robert Watts work 2995

"Cancer Vixen" by Marisa Acocella Marchetto 2008. 3233

Arctic Hysteria: TranceState of Contemporary Finnish Art 2008 Forward by Alanna Heiss Introduction by Marko Tapio Locating Markettta Seppala and Alannna Heisss Pentti Sadeniemi, Outi uomi-Nikula, Jonni Roos, Bo Haglund Artists in the Exhibition: Markus Copper, Veli Grano, Ilkka Halso, Huutajat - Screaming Men, Pekka Jylha, Tellervo Halleinen and Oliver Kochtakipaa, Pink Twins, Annie Rapinoja, Stiina Saaristo, Jari Silomaki, Sami Sanpakkila, Mika Released by the Museum of Modern Art 3235

PAJ: A Journal of Performance and Art 2008 Featuring CM on Sound "On the propogration of sound" 3243

"Dit chemin faisant" by Pierre, Marietan. 2008 Marietan, Pierre. Dit chemin faisant: conversations, fragments-sources, geophonies. Klincksieck, 2008. Signed to CM. 3251

Democracy in America: the National Campaign 2008 Creative Time in Association wth Park Avenue Armory presents 3406

60 years Tresor 2008 An auction catalog from Bruun Rasmussen Auctioneers Copenhagen 4076

Monitoring Scenography 01, Thea Brejzek (2) Wolfgang Greisenegger, Lawrence Wallen 2008 01 Space and Power Page 62 by CM on Sound signed in front on a postcard by Thea Brejzek. Two Copies 4098

Robert Watts Flux Med 2008. 4108

Inger Hanmann Gallery Piece 2008 Color show catalog of Hanmann's work, also a single promo piece from her daugther Charlotte Hanmann with a letter on the back to CM & Maija Leena. 4160

First Rehearsal of the NY Complaints Choir Postcards (50) 2008. 5199

Saul Appelbaum studies Books 1 & 2 2008 Graphic treatments Art and architecture. Work done at Cornell. 5304

Allegro Magazine Local 802 NY, 2008 Article: Should Musicians play for free. 5410

Igore Ganikovski & Kimmo Sarje Color, Time, Place 2008 Show at Galleri Uusitalo, Helsinki with a Page of notes 5451

Mozart 3D Reconstruction. Sonata no.11 A K331 2009 Master recording on 88 key midi keyboard, recomposed in MOTU Performer by CM 1353

Mozart 3D Reconstruction. Sonata no.12 K 332 2009 Master recording on 88 key midi keyboard, recomposed in MOTU Performer by CM 1355

Royal Soundscapes - Denmark - 3D performance at castles, abbeys 2009 Multiscene history of Denmark in 3D sound. Commissioned for a tour of Danish royal and sacred sites by Copenhagen International Theatre 1423

SC Johnson Fortaleza Hall 3D Audioscape 2009 a perpetually changing sound environment themed to Brazil and driven by NOAA weather data for Racine Wisconsin - updated hourly. 1461

Listening Room project - Barton VT, Helsinki, LA, London, NY, Boston 2009. 1465

Aftertaste 3 2009 A New Agenda for the study of interiors.A seminar presented by Parsons School of Design exploring interiors, visual, sound and smell. Included in the file are a poster and catalog. 1505

Sensations: Sound Light Color (4) 2009 Spiral Bound Educational Piece A project of Steelcase and CM Productions LLC. 2439

Sensations Posters and flyers Sound, Light, Color, 2009 Display for Steelcase Co. 2815

Homo Futurus, Barbara Rosenthal 2009 Autographed book to CM with art postcards, show retrospective, and other small artwork. 2940

The Western Wind Presents Holiday Light Joyous Music for the Holidays 2009 Featuring CM's "Genesis Song" Poem: Maori, translated by Jerome Rothenberg 3158

Hotel Pro Forma: Performance Art as an Investigation of the World 2009 Publication from Hotel Pro Forma, Copenhagen, Denmark. Algebra of Place, Theremin, Operation: Orfeo, and future projects. 3287

Selected Poems 1995- 2009, Gregory Furman 2009 Signed to CM 4126

CM in Denmark 2009 Newspaper article, Press 4282

Sensations: Sound Light Color Designing the nonmaterial for well being. 2009 A presentation Spiral bound By CM Productions and Steelcase. 4511

Franklin D. Roosevelt Memorial, Kahn 2009 FDR Memorial Four freedoms Park Brochure Louis I Kahn Monument 4592

Sensations Color brochure, Other Media NYC 2009 a package of 50 Creating Environments for well being. Client Steelcase 5167

Sound Tunnel: Avant Garde Park Portrait, John Morton 2009 NY Times story Clare Weiss 5206

Sensations Color Brochure 2009 Graphic Design Billing 5477

Toot N Blink NY - closing event of Little CM Festival 2010 Joan La Barbara and Ed Herrmann are the DJs, WFMU the station. John Doswell produced the boats. Closing event of the Little Charley Fest 1359

Abulafia and the Pope - one act opera- Rothenberg Libretto 2010 Abraham Abulafia (1240Ð1291(?) 1367

Fluxus Symphony - collaboration with Sylvie Flurie 2010 All manner of foot performers and vehicles are brought together, from Flamenco dancers and motorcycles to glass stompers and industrial vehicles (garbage trucks, tankers, street cleaners) for a romp, according to a plan, in a large arena. 1381

LandSeaAir - NY - sonic history of the world 2010 Art installation. Steel Case gallery. NY 1454

Sound Journey Äänimatka - YLE Finnish Radio 2010 Radio work created for Finland public radio 1456

SI Arctic Study Center - 3D story audioscapes. Anchorage Art Museum. Anchorage AK 2010 5 stories in CMSound 3D play over 30 minutes, each a sonified story told by an elder. 1462

Little CM Festival NY - 5 days including Toot N Blink 2010 5 days of concerts including Toot N Blink - NY and Solo parades in Brooklyn 1464

Sounds for Martti Aiha Retrospective Show - Sara Hilden Museum 2010 in Tampere. Added panphonics sound panels with Mara-jaa loops - his voice w/arctic sounds - no birds 1467

Virtual Kauppatori at Habitare 2010. 1474

Audio History Library Louis M Manno Statement of purpose. 2010 A flyer asking for participation, or contribution. 2449

Poster for Club Ebony, Indianola, Miss. 2010 Poster signed to CM from Mary Shepard (Proprietor) Classic Early Blues Club 2543

Panels Art piece, McCaffrey 2010 An Art poem from Steve McCaffrey, signed art 2807

Land Sea Air, Changing climates brochure (100) 2010 In association with Steelcase. An information brochure 2816

CMsound True 3D 2010 Notes and Drawings from the Marimekko installation. 2832

Synopsis for "Space-Wreck" by G. Wille 2010 "About G. Wille." bio, comic strip Sent to CM in 2010. 3001

Concept Drawing for Museum Installation 2010. 3226

CMSound True 3D: Sound like you have not heard before 2010 Explanation for True3D 3376

Sounds of the Arctic, CM, 2010 Arctic Spring Festival Cover Photo a few stray brochures Polar partnership Arctic National Wildlife Refuge Bringing the Arctic home, time lapse dance postcard by Jody Sperling. 3798

Africa Musica, Montreal Museum of Archaeology and History 2010 CD included, Still Wrapped 4135

Helen Koster 2010 Score MOLD clean-up 4448

Toot N Blink 2010 Folder 4480

CM lecture notes on sound, source and 3D vocabulary 2010. 4533

Blue Note Primate Dance Poster 2010 In Master Graphics 4599

Concerts By Composers, Program series 2010 13 Radio Programs designed to bring the latest in new music to a national audience. WNYC Tom Johnson, Philip Corner etc. 4756

Science centers & children's museums 2010 Haley Sharpe design 5106

Blow Blow Blow Blow, Rip Hayman 2010 Song Lyrics by Hayman on the back of a flyer for a Concert by John Guth at Folk City with Jack Dryden. 5231

Studio Leo, Gunter Meier Artwork 2010 A single page of original Cartoon/Art for Christmas 5319

Lights for Paik - line of vertical lights from mountain tops to sky 2011 Spanning the horizon of mountains visible from the event site are 8 light beams, one for each decade of Nam Jun Paik's continuing life - he has passed away but is very much with us. The nature of these beams and their locations will be established by a site survey and the practical aspects of installing them. As one of Paik's soundtrack makers, it is most fitting for me to remember him with light which focuses us on the sound around us, as did he. 1364

Tweet & Toot for Jerry & Diane at 80. Collaboration with Maija-Leena Remes 2011 Improvised duet for the Jerry and Diane sitting in the front of a space: starting from their seats, two bowler hatted performers move to the opposite aisle while sending out fish ocarina trilling calls. They meet on stage. One plays conch notes to two Rothenbergs in the first row. The other trills the fish ocarina. The conch player plays jews harp articulating "Jerry Diane Jerry tidan.......achtzig!" The other rings a handheld Asian bell. 1368

Arrivals - an opening event for the Wimbledon music festival 2011 The event takes place at a location in the town center, for of Wimbledon so that audience and players can arrive by train, assemble at the train station and march to the festival site in a musical parade. The climax is a small plane flyover where the pitch of the planes sets the pitch of the finale set against drums echoing from several directions antiphonally, down the adjacent streets.? The arrivals - from the time they are headed toward Wimbledon from home - are covered in the press or on the Wimbledon media channel. Outdoors 1437

Toot! Triple CD. Collaboration with Maija-Leena Remes, Riika Haahti 2011 IX Records release. Mastering - Jay Messina. Toot N Blink Chicago, Feather, Very Slow Gabrieli, Wave Music I For 40 Cellos, Wave Music VII For 30 Harps. More music songs Book Of Hours Of Catherine Of Cleves, Breath Chant, Central Park 1850, Central Park 2007, Chorale Bounce 1, Chorale Bounce 2, Futur 1450

Guidelines for Sonic Identity 2011 CMSound True3D: Sound like you have not heard before. Explanation for True3D 1466

Marimekko 3D shops: Helsinki Berlin, Malmo, NYC 2011. 1475

Smithsonian Institution NMAAHC 2011 Engaged by Ralph Appelbaum Associates to work on the planning group from the concept through design 2436

Sonic Wind Sails 2011 Concept for Copenhagen International Festival KIT 2437

Sonic Wind Sails - Copenhagen 2011 Design build with Roskilde architect 2438

Sari Dienes Retrospective, Post Card (2) 2011 Held at the GAGA arts Center Garnerville NY April 16 Thru May 15. Destroyed by Hurricane Irene 2759

Falling Thirds w/Drum Tom Johnson 2011 Two art sound pieces by Tom Johnson 2011 & 2012. 2958

FLUXUS and the essential Questions of Life 2011 A Fluxus Event at Grey Art Gallery December 3, 2011. 2986

FLUXUS and the essential Questions of Life Program and Poster 2011. 2987

Daemon Mouse, Ink. 1993-2011, Gregory J. Furman 2011. 4115

Advertisement for Nice Magazine 2011 An Audio visual Magazine which you could play on your turntable, this is an ad announcing that issue four is ready to ship 4227

Strange Relation, Rachel Hadas 2011 signed to CM, Paul Dry Books 4964

After The Deluge: Sari Survives Irene, A postcard 2011 A Postcard invitation for an Exhibition of works of Sari upstairs at the Ear Inn, where Sari had quarters for 15 years. Some 27 pieces of art were lost when the Hudson river flooded by Hurricane Irene, the Garnerville Arts Center in Rockland County NY 5158

WAVE MUSIC Four Winds concerto grosso for four horns, soundscapes, orchestra 2012 and optional orchestra 1378

Sound Glass Space with designer Harri Koskinen. Akusmata, Helsinki 2012 Harri Koskinen's four glass works are activated as transducers in a CM True3D sound space. Four Finland soundscapes - winter-ice, lake region birds, clocks, feather slow. 1379

Book of Spells - transparent shifts in letters of names as praises 2012 systematic distribution of letters from names into patterns. Honoring the name holder. 1382

Waltz on mouth sounds 2012. 1417

Bowling in Bowlers - a sporty public performance and participation 2012 An invitation on internet radio to an artist audience to a performance by CM and learn lawn bowls produced a magical gathering at the lawn bowling area of Oakland California's great park, and a beautiful write up. Everyone received a black bowler party hat. The group unified by the hats enjoyed the games and were a visual spectacle. 1418

Arcanum 17 - 3D touring show with live Tuba and Bass performance 2012 based on the André Breton novel of the same name, was co-written by Williams and CM 1420

LandSeaAir - London - second iteration - sonic history of the world 2012. 1455

Toot! CD profile and interview YLE Finnish Radio 2012. 1457

Star Bangled Banner, Moving My Vowels, Systematic Shifts in the Service of Patriotism calmaplombprombombbalm 2012 http://www.calmaplombprombombbalm.com/Moving_My_Vowels_CM_CM.pdf Applying transparent rules for substituting vowels for each other, CM produces a series of variations on the U.S. National anthem. 1459

Nationwide Childrens Hospital 3D perpetual soundscapes Magic Forest NCH 2012 Installation of CMSound 3D in public areas of hospital. Includes sounding birdhouses with animal sounds. Columbus, OH 1463

Sound map of Helsinki - in book, on line. Collaboration with Maija-Leena Remes, Riikka Haahti 2012 Layered sound map of the city with colors for each layer and text describing the layers. In book of Helsinki Design 1468

talking talking talking whispering whispering whispering speech mine speech mime speech mime 2012 In my CHANTING, the boundary between inner and outer world is explored through voice and breath. this performance text is to be spoken, whispered and speech mimed to bring the reader across the boundaries between language as thought, as breath, as voice illuminating breath. 1579

Heartbeat Machine - Spokane 2012 Installation of the Heartbeat Machine for Spokane Science Center 2429

Spokane Appreciation of Water 2012 Exhibition space of Spokane Water Commission 2430

Museum of Jewish History and Tolerance - Shtetl soundscape 2012 Moscow Museum, Ralph Appelbaum 2431

Museum of Jewish History and Tolerance - Migrations 2012 Moscow Museum, Ralph Appelbaum 2432

Nationwide Children's Hospital 3D perpetual soundscapes Aviary NCH Columbus OH 2012 3D CMSound installation. Ralph Appelbaum. 2433

Land Sea and Air at ARUP's Phase 2 Gallery London 2012 Press release, Flyer and time line card. 2822

Poster for CM CD Release Party 2012 Poster for CM CD Release Party (2 Copies) 3023

USCO Resurrection at Anthology Film Archives 2012 Program: Multimedia Group presents six 60s works: "Verbal American Landscape," "Y," "USCO at the Church," "Ghost Rev," "No Ow Now," "From Hubbub to We Are All One." 3405

CM 3D sound poster. Cal Arts 2012 Thursday 9-12 2012 7 PM Machine Lab B214. 3706

Book No Title, August 2012-May 2015 Gregory J. Furman 2012 Signed to CM 4124

Ellis Page. UPenn broadside edition of 35 2012 limited edition graphic by CM printed by Robinson Press of the Kelly Writers House, Philadelphia, Penn. 4362

AANIVAKEA- Sound People Program from Festival in Helsinki 2012 CM performs Counting to Nine-Toadfish Language (1973) Tom Johnson also on the program 4535

Psyche And Delia a History 2012 Libretto by Gerd Stern and Edward Rosenfeld. A limited edition #11 Signed 5058

CM and Jerome Rothenberg A Retrospective Performance 2013 March 22, 2013 at the Ear Up Gallery NY Program notes and copies of Poem of Miracles, First Horse song, Ascent of Mt. Carmel 2741

The Kicthen, program for Winter 2013 season Poster by Marina Rosenfeld 2013. 2743

Photos of CM in Portland Ducks sound production 2013 Ducks production 2877 Membra Disjecta for John Cage 2013 A book about theJohn Cage Show "Wanting to say something about John"CM has a page to remember John. More than sixty other artists represented. 2973

Silence 2013 Cover reads I Taget II Taget III Taget Pamphlet from "Silence" a 2013 exhibit at the University of California Berkeley Art Museum and Pacific Film Archive co-curated by Toby Camps and Steve Seid. Inspired by John Cage. From January 30-April 28. 3041

Anna Halprin/Matrix 2013 Program from Anna Halprin's Matrix At University of California, Berkeley Art Museum and Pacific Film Archive 3061

"The Magic Flowers of Midsummer Eve" and "Fire Festivals in Other Lands" 2013 The Golden Bough: A Studyin Magic and Religion (Third Edition, Vol. 11 of 12) by James George Frazer, published 2013, first published 1890. 3462

Dick Higgins: Music for Trumpets and Trees 2013 Dedicated to CM With letter from Hannah B. Higgins 3468

Doodles from Bowling with Bowlers 2013 A lawn bowling event that took place in San Francisco. 3910

Aaron Cohen Artwork 2013 Crayon on White board Illustration of a performance group. 4018

The Listening Space Smithsonian Artic Studies Center 2013 A list of sound programs from CM LLC., with explanations and times for the Listening center. 4554

Letter to Mr. Stone From CM 2013 Posthumous letter from CM to Sten Hanson. 15 April 1936 Skålari, Klövsjö - 1 November 2013 Stockholm 5324

Headhunt Revisited 2014 Charting Cultural Change in Melanesia An Expedition and Project by Michele Westmorland and Karen Huntt sponsored by Wing Trust 3044

Phenomenal Objects 2014 Description of Jack Mankiewicz Phenomenal Objects. Interactive play objects with a universal appeal - exciting, didactical and highly aesthetical. 3052

Catalogue Presence 2014 (+Distribution) Catalogue/Ordering for cassettes 3130

2 Spontaneous Oms 2014 Directions/instructions 3455

Outburst 2014 Outburst by CM 3458

Music for Trumpets and Trees 2014 Letter from Hannah B. Higgins. We made this recording in Chicago this fall. I think Dick would have been very pleased. Contains CD dedicated to CM. 3479

MUU For Ears CD 2014 Performance Voyage 4 Tour 2014 CM Mozart Alla Turca Reconstruction Graphic flyer and one copy of CD. Nine more CD's on CD shelf 3509

Skysong Posters (20) by Geoff Hendricks 2014 Signed posters 3638

Tools a Sonographic Symphony 2014 CM Quillwork for a part of the Tools project for the Smithsonian Institutions Cooper Hewitt Museum, NY. installation. 3672

CM Milestones (paper Copy) 2014 Document Compiled By Tom Comitta 4017

Faithful Program 13-23 November 2014 2014 Program of Gallerie Mario Mazzoli Berlin CMsound Presentation. Ear Up! Gallery NYSEE Faithful II program (4) for Artists 5068

Notes on 3D Sound, CM Productions 2014 A Stack of Flyers located in Box 14 Multiples 5588

Staring Back Catalog 2015 On Picasso's Demoiselles d'Avignon, Feb. 3 thru June 21 at Fleming Museum of Art Burlington, Vt. with soundscape by Jenn Karson. A gift from Jenn, Signed, when she and Ken Mills visited the archive in Barton. 3911

Aqua project 3D ride Brazil, Sounds 2015 First experimental sounds created by Jay Walbert on a Korg Kaoss for the 3D ride in Brazil. the sounds exist in the Aqua folder on the drobo. 3927

A Celebration of Christian Wolff 2015 Oct. 22-24 2015 at Dartmouth College, Hanover NH. Piece signed to CM 4337

Imersa 2015 magazine or brochure 5139

Lincoln Castle, Magna Carta 2015 CM Sound is part of a $22 million restoration of new visitor attraction. 5180

Sound Design Session for Brazil Ride 2015 Notes and comments from first session. Original underwater sounds to follow script submitted by Jay Walbert 5299

SAT, Center for Sience and Technologies Festival Program 2015 Program for seventh edition Program Article about Monique Savoie, director and founder. Montreal, Quebec 5413

Lincoln Castle 2015 CM Press, 3d Sound, Magna Carta 5475

Buckminster Fuller Welcome Letter 2015. 5523

Moving My Vowels, The Star Spangled Banner (5) 2016 five copies of 2012 edition for the St. Johnsbury Athenaeum performance of Aug. 21, 2016. 4196

Kindred Spirits Poster 2016 St. Johnsbury Athenaeum, St. Johnsbury VT. program with Rachel & Shalom, CM other poets etc. 4197

IPS Planetarium Immersive sound article 2016 International Planetarium Society. Pg. 1+2 of Immersive sound explanation article 4206

Articles and Papers on Sound Pollution and sound Pressure 2016. 4273

Surround Sound Concert, CM, Poster 2017 Oct 3 At the Emera Astronomy Center, University of Maine, Orono 4555

Albertini 2014 The Kite 2017 CM and Jerome Rothenberg Video performance located in digital music folder and on drobo 4567

Old Town Soundscapes Portland Chinatown, Brochure 2017 Old Town History Projects and CMSound 4572

Planetarian Magazine CM is on Immersive Sound Committee 2017 4577

Resonant Spaces, Sound Art at Dartmouth Show Catalog 2017 Sept. 15- Dec. 10, 2017 At Hood Museum of Art, Dartmouth, Hanover, NH, Spencer Topal curator 4755

Songs for Schizoid Siblings, Lionel Ziprin 2017 The song cave, signed to CM 5086

Rock, Mosquito and Hummingbird, David Brooks 2017 The Trust for Governors Island NY 5093

Salome: Donna Di Valore, Adeena Karasick 2017 Università di Padova, signed to CM 5094

LA Dot Zine #1 -0 A small booklet of underground art and Photography 2017 Sandy Rodriguez, Rafael Cardenas, Tom Clancey Mecca Vazie Andrews and others Grant from City of Los Angeles Dept. of Cultural Affairs. 5277

CM Health Care Proxy 2017. 5291

CM Toot Too Graphic 2017 Back Has Poem by RIP Hayman with Illustration 5527

R41 Toot Too. Recital forty one. LP liner notes, rough draft 2018 Copy Edited by Maija Leena Remes Will be Limited edition of 500. 4611

Vermont Tech Jam, Seven Days Press 2018 #or 4 Copies of Seven Days coverage of the Burlington, Vt tech JamSound cube set up in booth. Jay Walbert and CM did the 1 Day Show. 4763

Geoffrey Hendricks 1931-2018 Celebrating the Life of Geoffrery Hendricks 2018 A printed piece for the Memorial Program 4772

Other Minds Festival 23 Program 2018 April 9-14 in San Francisco, Signed copy by Charles Amirkhanian 5065

Hear and There, Seven Days 2018 Seven Days Newspaper from Burlington, VT Article on CM and Short history of his works. 5186

R52 – Reidemeister Move – "Arcanum 17" CD & Pamphlet 2018 Recital. Published album 5661

R41 Toot Too. Recital forty one. LP 2018 Recital. Published album with booklet 5662

World Premier of Morton Feldman's Now is the Time (1965) 2018 Commissioned in 1968 by CM for his performances "What's New for Trumpet and Ensemble", Produced by Norman Seaman. Work was not performed then due to objections by Feldman's then wife that the piece was off brand for Feldman. 5663

Permanent CMSound environments. Kaiser-Permanente Medical Operations Building, Capitol Hill, Washington DC 2018 CMSound project with Kaiser-Permanente, Mid Atlantic 5664

Permanent CMSound environments. Kaiser-Permanente Medical Operations Building, Santa Monica, California 2018 CMSound project with Kaiser-Permanente, Southern California 5665

Yes and NoTations 2018 Booklet with graphics of CM pieces and diverse notation 5666

Two Cellos 2018 files mixing multiple performances of Bach gamba suite, videos of Juho Laitenin performing 5667

Tech issue of Seven Days Newspaper 2019 Event in Burlington. VT CM and Jay Walbert set up a Sound Cube in the exhibits Hall. Introduction Awesome Audio about CM Sound 5066

NY Electronic Art Festival Program (3) 2019 CM sound re-introduces the Sound Cube featuring 12 commissioned works by pioneers in electronic music. CM, Michael Schumacher see Faithful Program notes for Artists in the original production 2014 BERLIN 5067

The Brooklyn Rail Jul/Aug 2019 2019 Arts, Politics and Culture Magazine Story of Gerd Stern with Raymond Foye, Signed to CM Contains a Postcard from the NY Electronic arts Festival 2019. 5072

Music Works #134 2019 article about CM by Bart Plantenga and article on Ana Sokolovic 5111

Itinerary for Winslow Homer Project 2019 CM and Jay explore Cliff Walk, Summer home and studio space. Scope of Project Notes. Portland OR 5211

R68 Geoffrey Hendricks 2019 Recital. Published album with booklet 5668

On the Assent of the Fragile 2019 electronic montage soundwork with veery bird calls, wind. The sound of the birds flying in the week is emblematic of the soul leaving the body. The wind stops on entry to the next world and the birds are heard in that sonic space. 5669

Book of Numbers & Spells 2019 Recital: selection of writings, letter works and number works 5670

WeatherSpotSounds 2019 software driven public artwork. location sensitive. Created for Helsinki Art Museum 5671

Beethoven Amalgam 2019 mix of Grosse Fuga for string quartet and Piano Trio Op 18. A music theater event with puppets. For Peter Schumann and Bread & Puppet Theater, Glover, Vermont 5672

Serenade II for tenor voice, horn, soundscapes and string orchestra 2019 Premier at Kohta Taidehalli opening of CM: A Gathering. Published on Kohta website 5673

Transliniations, Ian Tyson 2020 Tetrad Press 4969

A Gathering. CM Art show, Finland 2020 Thumbnails of Pieces sent to Anders with measurements 5179

Noise Makes You Sick Brochure 2020. 5367

Bread & Puppet Calendar for 2020 The Diagonal Life Calendar 5591

CMLand 2020 virtual world version 1.0. Collaboration with Rond Helsinki and Stewart Bird USA 5673

R81 America Lament LP Compilation of CM compositions. 2020 Recital Editions. Boo Wa Wa Wa – 4:36 Desert Plants and Flowers – 7:54 Telephone Music – 7:02Moonwalk Interlude I – 1:18 Moonwalk Interlude II – 0:40 Sound Glass Space – 2:50 Wanderers Nachtlied – 2:38 The Goose – 7:47 America Lament – 5:57 5674

CM: A Gathering. 2020 Retrospective show of posters, media and sound installations. Kohta Taidehalli, Helsinki, Finland. 5675

Winter Solstice Celebration 2020 online streaming celebration, closing event of CM: A Gathering. Premier of Four Winds for 4 horns in diverse locations (Japan, Australia, USA, Finland) and soundscapes. Performances by host CM, Asa Simma, Phill Niblock and Philip Dadson. 5676

Race to Virtual Space. Immersivity & Inclusivity 2020 Virtual International Planetarium Society Celebration. Virtual space event online. Developed with Rond, Helsinki, Finland and CMSound. 5677

Sound & Climate Change 2020 essay with Maija-Leena Remes for Petri Kuljuntausta anthology 5678

24 Hours in 48 Minutes - comic opera with libretto in Finnish by Maija-Leena Remes. 2020 Premier at Kapsäkki Music Theater, Helsinki March 29. Sibelius 75th Anniversary prize commission from Sibelius Foundation and Finnish Society of Composers. 5679

Desert Plants: Conversations with 23 American musicians Edition 2 2021 Walter Zimmermann. Reissue of January 1, 1976 by MusikTexte, Cologne Germany. CM interview et al. 5680

Immerse with CM podcast and book 2021 Annea Lockwood, announcer. Over 50 interviews with collaborators in immersive projects. Podbean and major podcast platforms 5681

R85 Alison Knowles "Sound from the Book of Bean" LP 2021 Recital editions. CM liner notes. 5682

Ilmo Ilmaa 2021 piano trio dedicated to Ilmo Ranta 5683

iMMERSE Celebrating Michael Gerzon 2022 streaming video with interviews of Gerzon's friends and fans 5684

Rothenberg - Mottram Celebration London 2022 King's College. CM performs accompaniment. Published videos on UPenn Writers House website 5685

Sounds of the Arctic 2022 essay for Smithsonian Institution Arctic Studies Center annual newsletter. 5686

R90 CM Chanter 2022 Recital edition compilation of vocal works 1959-2022. Booklet and audio publication honoring CM's 80th birthday. 5687

Book of Breath 2022 Recital Edition. Small artist book published with numbered box series including a glass bottle with a balloon of CM's breath. 5688

Tools Notes and Releases 2022. 5513

Counting for CM (as far as Possible) Tom Johnson 2022 An Art piece for CM, Editions 75 Signed and dated by Tom Johnson 5569

Grosse Fuga with 7 Stretches 2022 Beethoven's work with 7 very slow sections. Created in Audacity. Notated in Dorico 5570

12th International Sound Poetry Festival 2022 Recital Edition R91: 4 audio cassettes, 236p book 5571

Heavyweight Sound Fight 2022 Ideal Records 229: 2 LPs & booklet 5572

One Two 2022 Organ music for Kaija Saariaho 5573

Slow Dance AI 2022 Commissioned work with Orlan's orgasmic voice for Slow Music project 5574

Chant for Alexis' Horse 2023 Solo chant: horse song. To be layered with itself out of sync 5575

Like the eye, the ear doesn't blink 2023 book with publisher Peter Mittenthal, IPI Press/goats & compasses 5576

Sun Ra interview with Charlie Morrow LP 2023 Recital R106 - co-production with CM 5577

Dick Higgins: Poems & Metapoems LP 2023 Recital R33 - 2017 co-production with CM 5578

Jackson Mac Low - Poetry & Music CD 2023 Recital R51 - 2018 co-production with CM 5579

Jean Dupuy - All of the Time LP 2023 Recital R53 0 2018 co-production with CM 5580

Rip Hayman - Dreams of India & China LP 2023 Recital R59 - 2019. 5581

Anne Tardos - Gatherings CD 2023 Recital R62 - 2019 co-production with CM 5582

Geoffrey Hendricks - Stones & Dreams LP 2023 Recital R68-2019 co-production with CM 5583

Rip Hayman - Waves: Real & Imagined LP 2013 Recital R33 - 2021. 5584

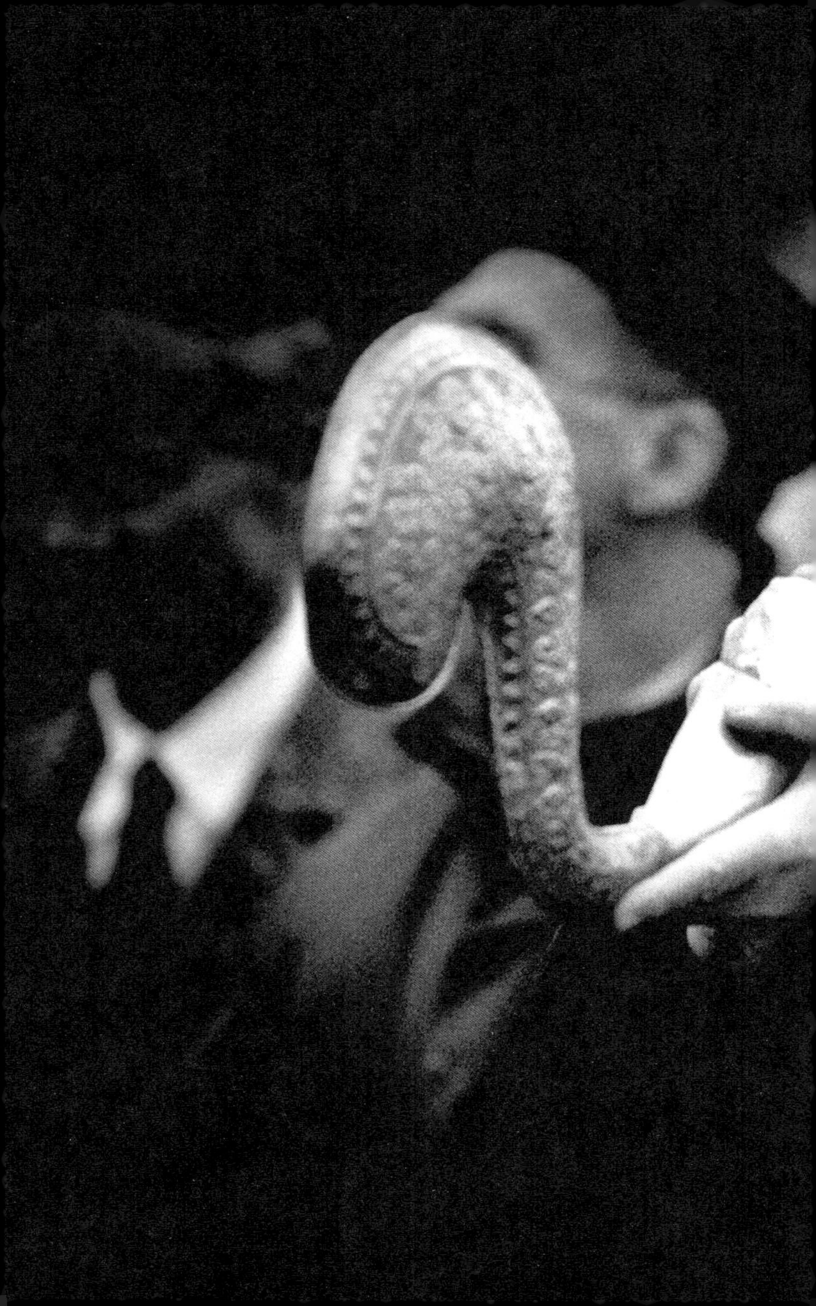

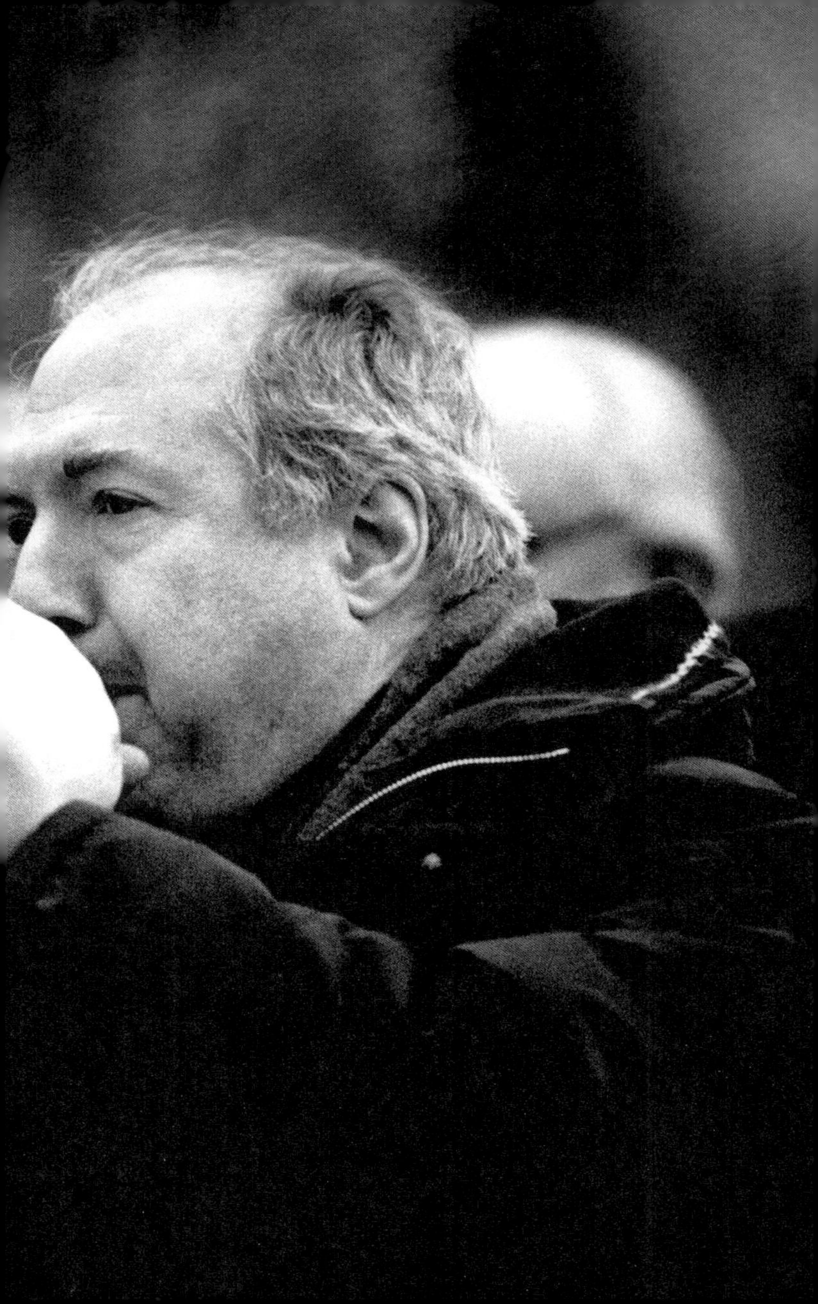

How to Read the Archive
Barton VT, 14 April 2023

Welcome to the Charlie Morrow Archive in Barton, Vermont, where there are more cows than people and more trees than cows. Some folks here are serious about fish farming.

I am a composer, producer and publisher. I am writing these words in the archive house, which is on land that I purchased from multi artist, publisher Dick Higgins, of Fluxus and Something Else Press fame.

I dedicate this book to Maija-Leena Remes, artist-curator and Jay Walbert, archivist. They created the Barton archive. Jay has meticulously cared for it.

Thanks to daughter Stephanie Morrow, brother Bob Morrow MD and co-felon Rip Hayman with whom I have long ley lines of communication and shared laughter. These ley lines provide the flow. Thanks to Jerome and Diane Rothenberg for collaboration and co-commiseration. Thanks to Sten Hanson for our remarkable co-creations and even for some disgusting moments. And to Tom Johnson, fellow number composer, for a career long conversation.

The Archive is home to my collection of thousands of analog and digital recordings, music scores, press, ephemera, correspondence, reference works used in productions, signed books and manuscripts, photos, event designs, drawings, musical instruments and more.

This catalog has assets and events in a timeline dating from before my birth in 1942 to 2023. It includes QSL cards from my childhood radio amateur activity where, as K2LIS, I first mastered joking in morse code. Recipes for my teenage conceptual works are there for cooking up new events. For example, Unknown to the Conductor, which instructs: the orchestra has planned this surprise, to be performed while playing any work of music. At a pre-arranged minute, the musicians stop to belch, cough, and scratch.

There are project documents and publicity from my life in pop music and the jingle trade, public events, digital art and virtual worlds. 5584 holdings listed, more to come.

This book, a work on paper, defying gravity and other conventions, is the fruit of collaboration with editor, book designer, publisher Peter Mittenthal. Thanks to anthropologist William Fitzhugh for introducing us. We share a love of the north, living in north Vermont, and the far north.

There is a heavy book wrapper with words lifted from my writing.

Three layers of time-based content are braided on every page of this book:- the Morrow archive catalog with four interwoven lists title, year of creation, description and catalog number. - a magenta and teal text, in large typeface, appears a word at a time on each page - a series of images of me chanting, shot by Margot Zalkind-Schurr for a 1970s poster promoting my chanting performances. She designed Personal Chants, my first audio publication. It's a cassette with a bear on the cover.

These three layers reward the reader for flipping pages and for reading in different directions. I thank Peter for his vision and execution of this book which is to be read like a spiral of text, OR like a flip book of me chanting, OR as a chronological list of works in the archive, OR...

It is a collaboration. Most of my work is collaborative. Our goal is to make seeds for others to grow new ideas.

Stefan Wolpe in our 1960s times together, inspired me with a Niels Bohr atom model and inferred how life and matter are linked through changes in energy. Somewhat earlier, I had been wound up by Wassily Kandinsky's idea of the concentric and eccentric motions of his painted forms based on locus of motion of their colors. This is a book of names, works and ideas growing from those changes.

The work path begins with my trumpet recital What's New for Trumpet 1967. It's a recital of new trumpet music which I commissioned from diverse contemporary composers and then toured. Thank you, Norman Seaman, concert producer and Ed Murray, conductor and pianist.

Next milestone is building a sound studio, which made it possible to grow technically and musically via production. The studio led to the founding of Charles Morrow Associates Inc which evolved to its present form, MorrowSound. It spawned the New Wilderness Audiographics cassette label. Thanks Dave Butler, John Guth, Terri Blaine, Connie Kieltyka, Peter Gordon, Denis Thalson, Patricia Burgess, Hugues de la Plaza. Thanks to the family at Record Plant Studio New York, Jay Messina, Roy Cicala. Thanks to WNYC, WBAI, WDR, YLE.

Parallel is the founding and development with poet Jerome Rothenberg of New Wilderness Foundation Inc based on the idea of New Wilderness, new/old explorations of sound and oral poetry. Along came voice and breath works as well as reconnecting with my prenatal sound world, the inner water world. Ear magazine and New Wilderness Letter, Solstice celebrations, broadcasts and international coproductions. Thanks Mary Nell Hawk, Mary Jane Leach, Paul Abels, Carol Tuynman, Rip Hayman.

My mom, Laura Morrow MD, deserves big thanks for support of all sorts including buying a used 4-track Ampex 1/2" tape machine so I could record Jerome Rothenberg's horse songs and start my own studio where I recorded my chants and the projects of so many collaborators.

Special thanks to Jerome Rothenberg, Philip Corner, Rip Hayman, Annea Lockwood, Alison Knowles, Dick Higgins, Richard Erdoes, Leonard and Mary Crowdog.

In this space, imagine that all the projects in the catalog and archive take place.

Fast forward to the 21st century. As jingles faded as a viable business for a sole practitioner, much as medicine has become the province of large venture capital based service providers, I developed and patented a solution for 3D sound illusion. Installations and projects followed in hospitals as well as museum, planetarium and concert venues.

Markus Levlin and Willie Fastenow are partners in the commercial exploration of my patented method for sonic immersivity for use in learning, healing and work spaces. Thanks, Brian Katz for the idea. Thanks Ilmo Martikainen and Genelec speakers, for your support.

Thanks to the International Planetarium Society.

The once analog multi-site, city-wide celebrations I did in the 20th Century are now digital and much easier technically. New solstice broadcasts resumed in 2016. Podcast iMMERSE with Charlie Morrow has over 50 discussions with co-creators of the immerse. Thanks bart plantenga, Sean McCann and Lisa Gray.

Media masters in the Archive are being licensed for reissue. Sean McCann is managing the Archive. His Recital Edition has done many new releases including The 12th International Sound Poetry Festival box set and book (2022), Morrow's LP albums Toot! Too (2018), America Lament (2020), and Chanter (2022), along with collaborative publications: The Heavyweight Sound Fight 2xLP (iDEAL Recordings) and a huge New Wilderness Audiographics wood box with eleven LPs and a newly authored book (to be published by Vinyl On Demand in 2024).

Many posters from my productions have recently been curated by Anders Kreuger of Kohta Arthall, Helsinki for the show, Charlie Morrow: A Gathering.

Systematic, scalable silliness is part of my toolkit. It is what Peter Mittenthal brings to this kinetic book. This is a book of names, works, ideas, pranks. Play, humor, trickster stuff.

Please do not forget to wash your hands before and after you play with this book.

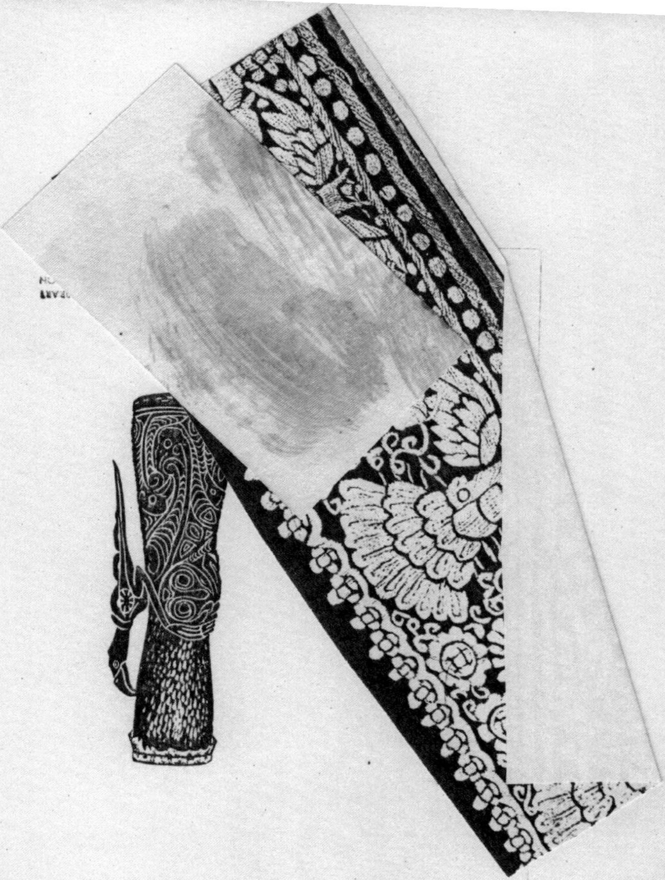

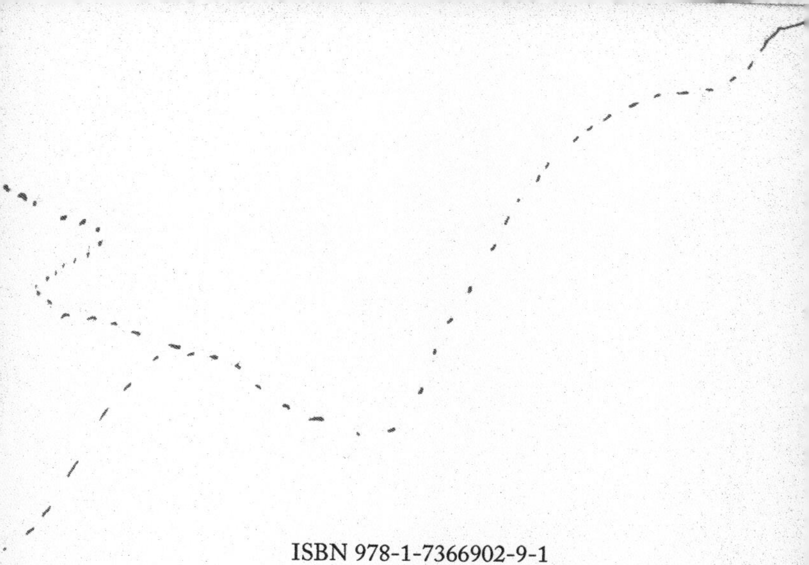

ISBN 978-1-7366902-9-1



Distributed by Casemate Publishers in the US
and Oxbow Books throughout the world.

goats & compasses
Post Office Box 10
Peacham, Vermont 05862
ipolari@gmail.com

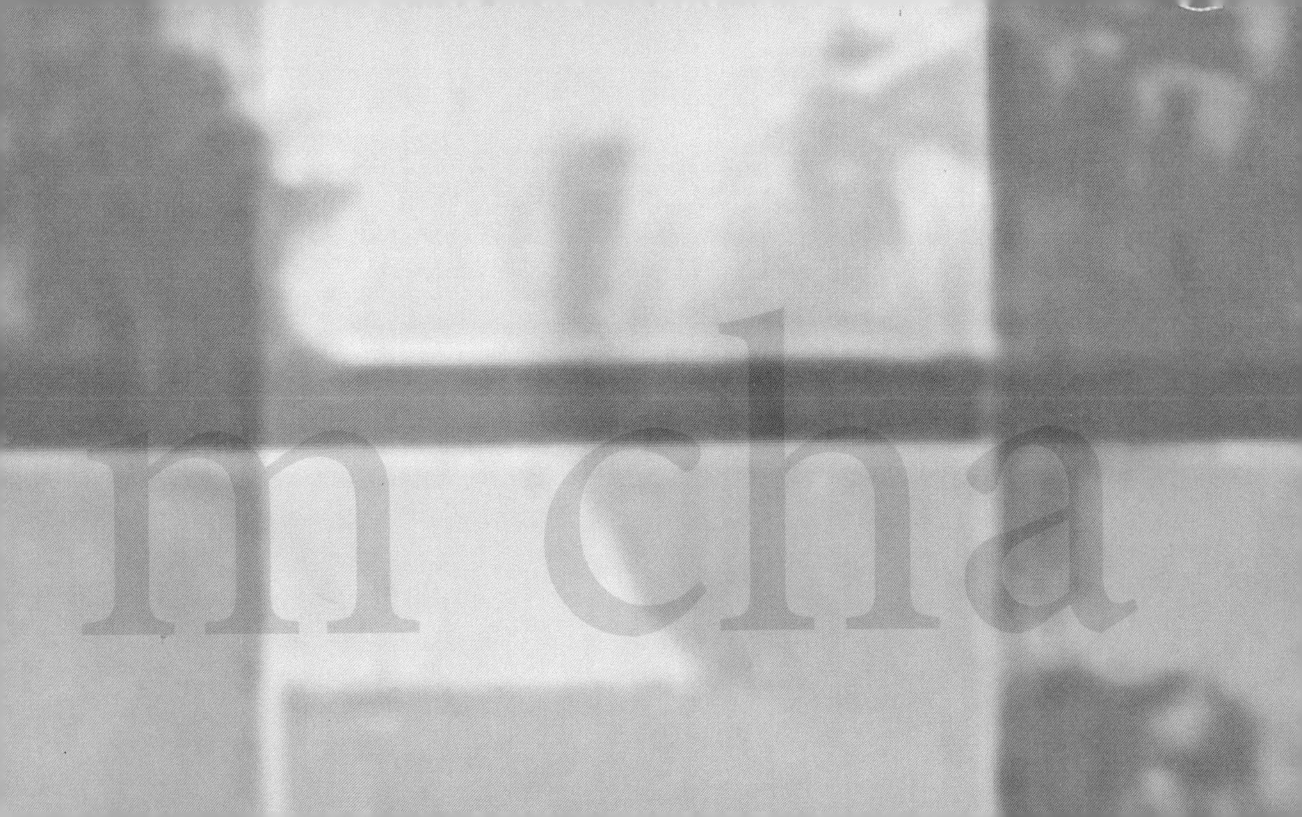
m cha

# what's new in music for trumpet & ensemble?

goats & compasses

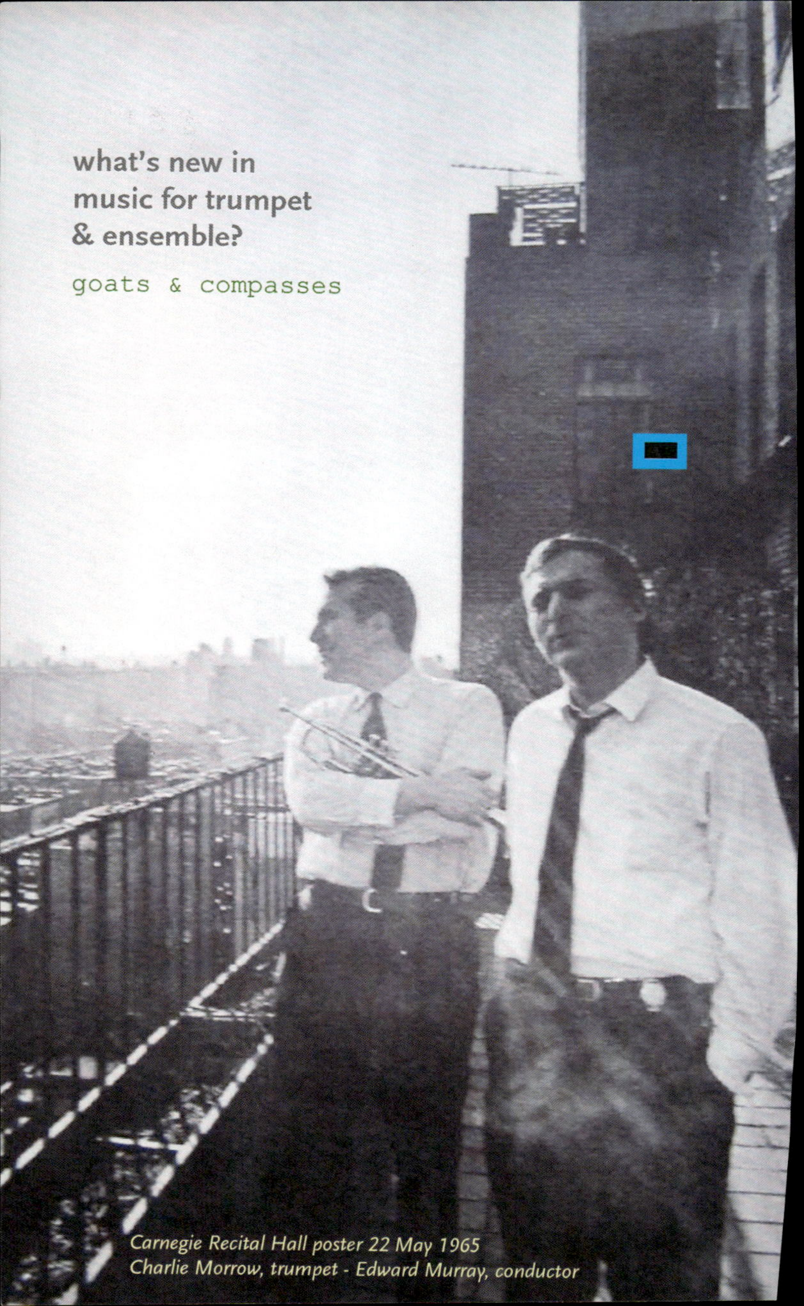

*Carnegie Recital Hall poster 22 May 1965*
*Charlie Morrow, trumpet - Edward Murray, conductor*

What they (might have) said about Charlie Morrow:

Charles Ives= Don't pay too much attention to the sounds —for if you do, you may miss the music.

Buckminster Fuller= 'Charlie' seems to be a verb.

Mozart= The music is not in the notes, but in the silence between.

Ezra Pound= If a patron buys from an artist who needs money, the patron then makes himself equal to the artist; he is building art into the world; he creates.

Buster Keaton= . . . and if there is sweeter music this side of heaven I haven't heard it.

John Cage= It is better to make a piece of music than to perform one, better to perform one than to listen to one, better to listen to one than to misuse it as a means of distraction, entertainment, or acquisition of 'culture.'

Rene Magritte= Everything that is visible hides something that is invisible.

Nicolas Slonimsky= All manifestoes are fakes.

Agatha Christie= I don't think necessity is the mother of invention. Invention, in my opinion, arises directly from idleness, possibly also from laziness —
to save oneself trouble.